Writer's International Guide to Book Editors, Publishers, and Literary Agents

Make the Whole English-Speaking Publishing World Yours

JEFF HERMAN

PRIMA PUBLISHING

I dedicate this book to the international continuum of thinkers, creators, and writers. May all the borders between us become objects of interest, not obstruction or separation.

Library of Congress Cataloging-in-Publication Data

Herman, Jeff
   Writer's international guide to book editors, publishers, and literary agents : make the whole English-speaking publishing world yours with this one-of-a-kind guide / [compiled by] Jeff Herman.
     p.   cm.
   Includes bibliographical references (p.) and index.
   ISBN 0-7615-1481-3
   1. Authorship—Marketing Directories. 2. Publishers and publishing Directories.
3. Literary agents Directories. 4. Editors Directories. I. Title.
PN161.H475   1999
070.5'2'025—dc21   99-25640
                                         CIP

99 00 01 02 DD 10 9 8 7 6 5 4 3 2 1
Printed in the United States of America

How to Order
Single copies may be ordered from Prima Publishing, P.O. Box 1260BK, Rocklin, CA 95677; telephone (916) 632-4400. Quantity discounts are also available. On your letterhead, include information concerning the intended use of the books and the number of books you wish to purchase.

Visit us online at www.primalifestyles.com

Contents

Acknowledgments

No, I didn't do it by myself. This was very much a team effort and success. It was my publisher, Ben Dominitz, and my editor, Susan Silva, who actually came up with the idea for this book. They have been supportive and exceptionally patient. Brenda Frazier, Clive Goodall, Julie DeVillers, and Greg Ionou are largely responsible for the research and composition of the publisher sections. Mandi White, Meredith Browne, and Sara Ward helped to administer every aspect of this challenging prospect.

It's rare, if ever, that I see any worthy project to completion without the participation of my brilliant wife and sidekick, Deborah Levine Herman.

Introduction

Welcome to the first edition of the *Writer's International Guide to Book Editors, Publishers, and Literary Agents*. This is the first book created for the English-speaking world that penetrates the veil surrounding the world of book publishing outside of the United States. The world is getting smaller. Much of Western Europe is now virtually unified, economically if not politically. Those depressed nations once known as the Eastern Bloc are now capitalist wanna-bes. And low-cost, real time conversations are possible between almost any two places on the globe—via print, audio, and video.

No longer will writers in the international community be left outside in the dark, trying to peek in the windows of book publishing. This unique book reveals the names of the people who stand between you and your published book. And it provides an exclusive opportunity to learn from respected editors and literary agents who tell you in their own words how you can dramatically increase the odds of becoming a successfully published author throughout the world.

The world of publishing often seems like a fraternity closed off to all but a chosen few. My hope is that this book will be your guide to a successful initiation into the elite fraternity of published authors.

This book is divided into four parts. Part One: Writer's International Directory of Book Publishers and Editors provides you with the contact names of publishing houses in the following countries where English is the official or primary language: Australia, Canada, England, Ireland, Hong Kong/China, New Zealand, Scotland, Singapore, South Africa, and Wales. You'll discover who the editors are and what they are looking for. Refer to the interview with Stuart Proffitt of Penguin Putnam UK to hear a publishing director's opinions. Read the interview with Judy Piatkus of Piatkus Books for an inside look at the world of the editor and publisher. (Note: Turnover in the publishing industry is rampant. To be on the safe side, call the publishing house to confirm the editor you have selected is still the appropriate contact.)

Part Two: Writer's International Directory of Literary Agents is the place for you to get to know some literary agents personally. A *literary agent* is the writer's business representative. Literary agents bring the writers and publishers together by pitching manuscripts and proposals and negotiating contracts. Literary agents have relationships with publishers and know the preferences of the individual editors. You'll hear from the literary agents who responded to our interview requests. You'll discover what these agents do and don't want to represent, learn where they were born and educated, find out about their career background, and see samples from their lists. Refer to the interviews with Darley Anderson, Gerald Pollinger, and Jon Thurley for an agent's views on the business.

Part Three: Insider Road Maps to Your International Success provides valuable material to increase your knowledge about the book industry. It includes essays on the state of book publishing in the United Kingdom, the insights of two UK publishers, the views of three UK agents, what sells overseas, query letters and proposals, selling rights overseas, foreign rights agreements, how you can use the Internet to your advantage, and a bibliography of useful books on international publishing.

Part Four: International and Domestic Resources gives you several listings of very valuable resources for your use in either the international or domestic book markets. It includes lists of both international and domestic World Wide Web sites, other more traditional international resources, and a listing of international book fairs.

Before you submit your work, you should be familiar with some of the terms widely used in the industry. Your first contact with an editor or agent will often be through a query letter. Many publishing houses state they do not accept unagented/unsolicited submissions. *Unagented* means that the submission was not made by a literary agent. *Unsolicited* means that no one at the publishing house asked for the submission. These submissions go right into the dreaded *slush pile,* the often enormous stack of manuscripts that may sit indefinitely, waiting for the chance of a review.

The best way to avoid the slush pile is to send a query letter. A *query letter* is a brief presentation to an agent or editor designed to sell both the writer and the book idea. It is your sales pitch. The letter should be short (less than half a page), easy to read, professional, and to the point. You might send a brief bio that highlights your writing experience and relevant professional credentials. Don't overwhelm the editor—your goal is to make him or her want to see more. Include a self-addressed stamped envelope (SASE) and remember to include the appropriate international postage.

If the editor is interested in the query letter, he or she will ask to see the complete manuscript or a book proposal. A *book proposal* is a package generally used to sell nonfiction books. Most agents and publishers prefer to see a complete manuscript for fiction. However, nonfiction books can sell based on a book proposal and sample chapters. Several books are available detailing how to write a book proposal, including *Write the Perfect Book Proposal: 10 Proposals That Sold and Why*, which I co-authored with Deborah Adams (John Wiley & Sons).

You're ready to use this book! My associates and I have made every attempt to provide you with the most up-to-date and accurate information available. To keep this book current, we will update it frequently, and I welcome your comments and suggestions for future editions. I look forward to hearing your success stories.

PART ONE

Writer's International Directory of Book Publishers and Editors

Australia

ANGLICAN PRESS AUSTRALIA

Level 2
St. Andrew's House
P.O. Box A287
Sydney South
NSW 1235
Australia
(61) 2 9283 2641
fax: (61) 2 9283 3987
publishing@aec.edu.au (e-mail)

Anglican is the publishing division of the Anglican Education Commission Diocese of Sydney. It incorporates the **Aquila Press,** which produces Christian Education Publications (CEP).

Even though CEP titles all address Christian Orthodoxy, they are broad in scope. They range from in-depth studies of Bible books and teachings and interpretative titles offering spiritual guidance to educational packages and resource materials for young people. **Connect,** an example of the latter, is a religious education curriculum committed to integrating child development and biblical knowledge. Accurate historical and cultural information is combined with a rich variety of student activities. Students have the opportunity to learn the key components and themes of the Bible and Christian beliefs. A 2-year cycle of core content encourages children to develop their understanding of the Bible and its application to their lives. Each year covers a substantial amount of both Old and New Testament.

From **Aquila**: *Know & Live: Ephesians,* by Stephen Hale (nine studies about the implications of being a Christian); *Apocalypse Now & Then: Reading Revelations Today* by Paul Barnett (According to Dr. J. I. Packer, Regent College, Vancouver: "*Revelation* is a complex piece of writing that has mystified many, and it is no small achievement to write a simple commentary on it that dispels the fog. Most useful—and highly recommended!"); *How to Really Stick at Being Christian: Youth Bible Studies from the First Letter of Peter* by Tim Hawkins; and among the bestsellers, *Remember the Lord & Practise Being Godly* by Colin Buchanan.

Query letters and SASEs should be directed to:

Pamela Webster, Sales Manager

HALE & IREMONGER PTY LIMITED

P.O. Box 205
Alexandria NSW 2015
or
19–21 Eve Street
Erskineville NSW 2043
Australia
(61) 2 9565 1955
fax: (61) 2 9550 2012
haleire@ozemail.com.au (e-mail)

Hale & Iremonger is an independent Australian publisher that has been in business more than 25 years. It has acquired a reputation for publishing quality general nonfiction that ranges over all aspects of Australian society and culture. Its subjects of interest specifically include Australian history, natural history, society and culture, biography, the arts, business, health, self-help and practical guides, and parent/teacher reference. H & I also publishes Australian contemporary poets. It has an established reputation as a publisher of specialist and sponsored histories and has won many awards for its histories and poetry titles. Finally, H & I's list features a strong stock of writer's guides that are widely used throughout Australia and New Zealand.

Among H & I's latest catalog offerings: *Finding Families: The Guide to the National Archives of Australia for Genealogists* (compiled by Margaret Chambers and published in association with the National Archives of Australia for Genealogists); *Feng Shui for Australians* by Gerry Heaton; *The Satin Bowerbird* by Jean Kent (the third collection from a prize-winning poet); *From Trench to Troopship: The Newspapers and Magazines of the AIF 1914–18* by David Kent; *Effective Ineptitude: The Secrets of Corporate Climbing* by John Smartt; *Writing for Children & Young Adults: The Business of Creativity* by Hazel Edwards and Goldie Alexander; *The Bush Alphabet* (a color-illustrated book) by Will Douglas; *Switch on Your Brain: A Guide to Better Reading, Concentration & Co-ordination* by Allan Parker and Margaret Stuart; *Founding of Australia: The Argument About Australia's Origins* (edited by Ged Martin); *Donatello in Wangaratta*, a collection of poetry by Peter Rose; and *Successful Self-Publishing: Making and Selling Your Own Book* by Sherryl Clark.

Hale & Iremonger will consider unsolicited manuscript submissions if sent as a package that includes the following: cover letter, synopsis, chapter outline, one or two sample chapters, and a self-addressed stamped envelope.

Query letters and SASEs should be directed to:

Heather Cam, Senior Editor

Bert Hingley, Publisher

Karen Morrison, General Manager/Marketing Manager

KINGSCLEAR BOOKS

Suite 3/77 Willoughby Road
Crows Nest 2065
Australia
(61) 2 9439 5093
fax: (61) 2 9439 0430
kingsclear@wr.com.au (e-mail)

Kingsclear—which also trades as Atrand Publications—is a small but successful Australian house specializing in local histories, tourism, health, and crime books. Recent offerings include: *Get Well: An A–Z of Natural Medicine* by Russell Setright (preventative medicine for everyday illnesses); *If I Eat Another Carrot I'll Go Crazy* by Dr. Ross Walker (a bestseller on heart disease prevention); *Bushwalking in Mt. Warning NSW* (120 bushwalks in North East New South Wales); *50 Crimes That Shocked Australia* by Alan Sharpe (on crimes from 1806 to the "Backpacker Murders"); *Wollongong* by Alison Gibbs and *Newcastle* by John Turner (both from the *Pictorial History* series containing early photographs and histories of Sydney suburbs and cities).

   Query letters and SASEs should be directed to:
Catherine Warne, Publisher

LOTHIAN BOOKS

11 Munro Street
Port Melbourne
Victoria 3207
Australia
(61) 3 9645 1544
fax: (61) 3 9646 4882
books@lothian.com.au (e-mail)

In 1888 John Inglis Lothian moved to Australia to become the first independent British publishers' representative in Australia and New Zealand. In the hands of his son Thomas, the business became an Australian publisher and distributor. And thus Lothian Books became part of the history of publishing in Australia. From its early beginnings in the bustling heart of Victorian Melbourne, Lothian Books published works by great Australians such as Bernard O'Dowd, Adam Lindsay Gordon, John Shaw Neilson, and Henry Lawson. From publishing 6 books in 1906 to 65 books in 1995, the story of Lothian Books has so far progressed through four generations of family. Today, Lothian books remains family owned and proudly independent. With a new company logo that symbolizes its fresh and modern style, the company is set to continue as a progressive force in publishing. Peter Lothian, the current head of the company, is dedicated to the continued expansion of Australian publishing and counts as an integral part of Lothian's strategic development, representation of major overseas publishers. Currently among Lothian's profile of overseas houses are A & C Black, Aurum Press, Barron's, Cherrytree, Constable, Creative Publishing, Dover, Exley, General Publishing Group, Kyle Cathie, Macdonald Young, Michael O'Mara, North-South, Salamander, Souvenir Press, Summersdale, Taunton Press, Walter McVitty, and Wayland. Lothian's Publishing, Sales, Marketing, and Distribution are all located at the head office in Melbourne, but the company has branch offices in Sydney and Brisbane, and agents in Adelaide, Perth, and Hobart.

On Lothian's high-profile and award-winning list of authors and illustrators are Tess Mallos, Bob Graham, Peter Gouldthorpe, Narelle Oliver, Gary Crew, John Marsden, Robert Ingpen, John Patrick, Jane Edmanson, Keith V. Smith, Allen Gilbert, John Brookes, Shirley Stackhouse, Colin Campbell, Rodger Elliot, David Jones, Judy Jacka, Dorothy Hall, Dr. Paul Galbraith, Dr. Warwick Hartin, Dr. Bob Montgomery, Dr. Laurel Morris, Deborah Brearley, William Vayda, Richard Raffan, Cheryl Maddocks, and Jean Kropper.

Lothian titles cover mainstream nonfiction, including Australiana, travel/humor, cookery and entertainment, self-help, business, health, New Age, horticulture, and woodworking, as well as fiction genres such as children's and young adult fiction.

Some of Lothian's latest: *I Left My Heart in Chinkapook and My Knickers in New York: Travel Tips and Tales* by Kerry Cue; *The Aussie Outdoor Cookbook: In Association with the Red Cross* by Peter Russell-Clarke; *Secrets of Successful Step-Families* by Sue Hart-Byers; *Team Play: Strategies for Successful People Management* by Shirley McKinnon; *Nature's Super Foods: Top 40 Medicinal Foods, Herbs, Supplements* by Nancy Beckham; *Women's Big Dreams: Life-Changing Night Experiences* by Jennie Hatherley; *Cherry Stones: A Book of Numbers* by Sally Heinrich (a children's picture book); *Australia's Southern Shores* by Harry Breidahl (with foreword by Alan Reid, President of the Gould League); *Elves & Fairies* by Ida Rentoul-Outhwaite; and *The Cannibal Virus* by Sue Robinson and illustrated by Peter Gouldthorpe.

Query letters and SASEs should be directed to:

Peter Lothian, Publisher

THE ROYAL SOCIETY OF VICTORIA

8 Latrobe Street
Melbourne
Victoria
Australia 3000
(61) 3 9663 5259
fax: (61) 3 9663 2301
rsvinc@vicnet.net.au (e-mail)

In 1854, just 3 years after the discovery of gold in the fledgling colony of Victoria, both the Philosophical Society of Victoria and the Victorian Institute for the advancement of Science were formed. The two bodies amalgamated to become The Royal Society of Victoria in 1859. From the very outset, the Society effectively established the foundations of science in the colony—stimulating, fostering, and sustaining the development of astronomy, anthropology, agriculture, the natural sciences, engineering, and meteorology. Today, in tandem with the increased dependence on scientific and technological development, the importance of the Society's work has increased.

Through its various publications and other activities, the Royal Society of Victoria brings together scientists from many disciplines, stimulates scientific discussion, and disseminates scientific and technological information to both the scientific and lay communities. The Society is the publisher of the prestigious *Proceedings of The Royal Society of Victoria*. This revered scientific journal, which the Royal Society distributes internationally, is one of the oldest scientific journals on the international scene, having been published continuously by the Society for almost 140 years.

Also from the Royal Society: *Gem Minerals of Victoria, Volcanoes in Victoria,* and *Spiders Commonly Found in Melbourne and Surrounding. . . .*

Query letters and SASEs should be directed to:

H. H. Bolotin, President

TRS LITERARY AGENCY

P.O. Box 29-023
Ngaio, Wellington
tfs@elseware.co.nz (e-mail)
Chris Else; Barbara Else, Directors

UNIVERSITY OF NEW SOUTH WALES PRESS

University of New South Wales
Sydney
NSW 2052
Australia
(61) 2 9664 0903
fax: (61) 2 9664 5420
c.perkins@unsw.edu.au (e-mail)
www.unswpress.netaus.net.au

UNSW Press is acknowledged as one of Australia's leading publishers in the areas of Australian studies and ecology; their list also includes a wide range of titles on other subjects and in other disciplines. Areas currently undergoing significant development include: Books of ideas—on society and politics, cultural studies and the arts, the environment, history and philosophy; books in the sciences, to interpret current thinking for a wider readership; General reference works in ecology and natural history, including botany and horticulture; books on New South Wales or the Sydney region; textbooks for university and TAFE students, including accountancy, business, management, psychology, horticulture, engineering, building, and health sciences, and study skills books for students. UNSW Press also publishes selected books on behalf of public and private institutions, but they do not publish fiction or poetry and unrevised dissertations.

A UNSW Press selection of new titles: *Dinosaurs of Australia and New Zealand and Other Animals of the Mesozoic* by John Long (illustrated throughout in full color; the most authoritative and up-to-date reference on the Mesozoic animals in the antipodes); *Cross Cultural Caring: A Handbook for Health Professionals* (edited by Nancy Waxler-Morrison et al; a practical handbook for those working directly with ethnic patients—nurses, social workers, physicians, dentists, and psychologists); *Death So Noble: Memory, Meaning, and the First World War* by Jonathan F. Vance (an unorthodox look at the Canadian experience of the First World War as a cultural and philosophical force, rather than as a political and military event); *Foreign Dialogues: Memories, Translations, Conversations* by Mary Zournazi (conversations with key intellectual and artistic innovators of the late twentieth century, from Australia and overseas, about the personal forces shaping their ideas and work); *Cooking with Roses* by A. Dunnage-Roy (recipes, both new and old, easy to prepare, delicious to taste, and delightful to smell; accompanied by exquisite line drawings); *Down-Under Dolphins: The Story of Hector's Dolphins* by Stephen Dawson and Elizabeth Slooten (an accessible study of Hector's dolphins—how widely they exist, where they hang out, how they communicate; illustrated with color photos and maps throughout); *The Long Dispute: Maori Land Rights and European Colonisation in Southern New Zealand* by Harry Evison (a compelling narrative in which all parties have their say—traders, sealers, whalers, missionaries, and officers, Maori chiefs, colonists, government officials, governors, judges, and academics); a revised edition of the award-winning *Te Waipounamu: The Greeenstone Island)*; *Measuring Progress: Is Life Getting Better?* (edited by Richard Eckersley, using new measures of "progress," an examination of what middle Australia thinks about the changes reshaping their lives); and *Toxic Sludge Is Good for You! Lies, Damn Lies and the Public Relations Industry* by John Stauber (an exposé of the modern propaganda industry, revealing how PR wizards concoct and spin the news, organize phoney grassroots front groups, spy on citizens, track reporters, and conspire with lobbyists and politicians to thwart democracy).

UNSW Press welcomes new authors. A detailed proposal, rather than a complete manuscript, should be submitted in the first instance. The proposal should include a one-to two-page outline and rationale; proposed length (number of words); a detailed table of contents; information on charts and illustrations (not originals); an assessment of the audience for the work; details of any similar or competitive titles, with a summary of their strengths and weaknesses; some suggestions for possible reviewers for the proposal; and a brief résumé with details of relevant background or previous publications. If available, copies of two sample chapters may be submitted with the proposal.

UNSW Press books are sold worldwide and contact with overseas publishers is augmented by UNSW Press's active participation in the annual Frankfurt Book Fair.

Query letters and SASEs should be directed to:

Robin Derricourt, Managing Director
Commissioning editor for politics, social and cultural history, and books of ideas for the Australian scene.
r.derricourt@unsw.edu.au (e-mail)

John Elliot, Publisher, Science
Strong interest in all aspects of natural history, particularly ecology, the environment, and the philosophy of science.
john.elliot@unsw.edu.au (e-mail)

Peter Browne, Publisher, Social Sciences and Humanities
Commissioning editor for social sciences, current affairs, and the humanities. Interests further include Asian studies, political biography, and media studies.
pbrowne@netspace.net.au (e-mail)

Canada

ANVIL PRESS

P.O. Box 1575, Bentall Centre
Vancouver
British Columbia V6C 2P7
Canada
(604) 876-8710
www.anvilpress.com

Anvil Press began in 1988 as the publisher for *sub-TERRAIN Magazine.* In 1991, it expanded into the book-publishing field with the mandate to discover and nurture new talent in Canada. It now publishes 4 to 5 titles a year, and sponsors the International 3-day Novel Contest every September (more information about the contest is available on their Web site: www.anvilpress.com). Although it does occasionally publish nonfiction, Anvil specializes in contemporary literary fiction, poetry and drama; it does not publish genre fiction.

Recent Anvil titles include: *Salvage King Ya!* by Mark Jarman; Dennis Bolen's *Gas Tank and Other Stories*; and Lyle Neff's book of poetry, *Ivanhoe Station.*

For fiction/nonfiction submissions, Anvil requests a brief, one-page synopsis of the entire manuscript and 20–30 pages of the manuscript itself. For poetry, 8–12 poems should be submitted. Anvil requests the entire manuscript for works of drama, unless excessively long. Anvil only publishes material by Canadian authors. Only manuscripts accompanied by a SASE will be considered.

For more information, contact:

Brian Kaufman, Managing Editor

ARSENAL PULP PRESS

103, 1014 Homer Street
Vancouver
British Columbia V6B 2W9
Canada

Arsenal Pulp Press is a book publisher based in Vancouver, Canada, with 135 titles currently in print, ranging from fiction and poetry to cultural, gender, and multicultural studies. Arsenal Pulp Press began as Pulp Press Book Publishers in 1971, founded by a collective of university students and associates disenchanted by what they perceived to be the academic literary pretensions of Canadian literature at the time. The press is now well established as a premier British Columbia publisher of provocative and stimulating books that continue to challenge the status quo.

Areas of interest: literary fiction (does not publish science fiction/fantasy, thrillers, mysteries, westerns, romances), literary and art studies, gay and lesbian interest, cultural studies, political/sociological studies, aboriginal/First Nations studies, regional studies, women's studies, irreverent cookbooks, satiric humor. At this time, Arsenal does not consider poetry manuscripts.

Arsenal titles of note: *Queer View Mirror* (edited by James C. Johnstone and Karen X. Tulchinsky); *Vancouver: Representing the Postmodern City* (edited by Paul Delany); *Archive for Our Times* by Dorothy Livesay; *American Whiskey Bar* by Michael Turner; *Whispered Art History* by Keith Wallace; *Death Writes* by Darlene Barry Quaife; *The Little Black & White Book of Film Noir* (edited by Thompson and Usukawa).

Submissions should include a covering letter, synopsis of the work, sample (do not send entire manuscript), and SASE. International submissions must enclose international reply coupons, but be aware that Pulp is not currently considering manuscripts by non-Canadian authors. Direct submissions to the editorial board by mail only; Arsenal does not respond to queries by phone, fax, or e-mail.

BEACH HOLME PUBLISHING

2026–2040 West 12th Avenue
Vancouver
British Columbia V6J 2G2
Canada
(604) 733-4868

Beach Holme Publishing, so-named in honor of the owner's house, is a small Vancouver publisher with a mandate "to promote indigenous creative writing to the wider Canadian public." Its literary roots began with its former incarnation, Press Porcepic, which published such renowned authors as Dorothy Livesay and James Reaney. **Porcepic Books** persists as an imprint of Beach Holme, and continues to build its own niche in the Canadian literary heritage with newer talents like Evelyn Lau and Jane Urquhart. Novels, plays, poetry, and short fiction are all featured under the Porcepic Books imprint. Beach Holme also publishes children's books (**Sandcastle Books**) and young adult fiction.

Titles typical of the list: *Moving Water* by Joan Skogan; *Flesh & Blood* by Michael Crummey; *The Lion of Venice* by Mark Frutkin; *I Am Not Most Places* by Richard Cumyn; *The Self-Completing Tree* by Dorothy Livesay.

Beach Holme Publishing only produces work by Canadian authors resident in Canada; foreign manuscripts will not be considered and should be directed elsewhere. Submissions should be sent to the attention of:

Joy Gugeler, Managing Editor

Teresa Bubela, Assistant to the Editor

BLIZZARD PUBLISHING

73 Furby Street
Winnipeg
Manitoba R3C ZAZ
Canada
(204) 775-2923
fax: (204) 775-2947
cfoster@blizzard.mb.ca (e-mail)
www.blizzard.mb.ca/catalog

Blizzard Publishing, located in Winnipeg, Manitoba, specializes in plays and theater studies. It was founded in 1987 and has since become Canada's leading publisher of contemporary Canadian drama with over fifty titles that include the plays of Carol Shields, Ann-Marie MacDonald, and John Murrell.

Blizzard Publishing is dedicated to publishing lesser-known playwrights through its innovative *International Readers' Theatre* series of chapbooks, which runs as a global publish-on-demand script service.

Recent Blizzard trade publications include: *Anniversary* by Carol Shields and David Williamson; *Rhubarb-o-rama! Plays and Playwrights from the Rhubarb! Festival;* and *The Short Tree and the Bird That Could Not Sing* by Dennis Foon.

Blizzard Publishing welcomes unsolicited manuscripts for its *International Readers' Theatre* series, but recommends that you include its submission form with your material. You can request the form by phone or download it from their Web page: www. blizzard.mb.ca/sub_form.gif

Direct questions and submissions to:

David Fuller, Co-ordinator, International Readers' Theatre

CORMORANT BOOKS

R. R.1
Dunvegan
Ontario K0C 1J0
Canada
(613) 527-3348

Cormorant Books publishes a small, select list of literary fiction and trade nonfiction. This small press also produces several works of fiction in translation.

Notables from the Cormorant catalog: *Lives of the Saints* by Nino Ricci; *Kitchen Music* by Charles Foran; *Frog Moon* by Lola Lemire Tostevin; *Gaff Topsails* by Patrick Kavanagh; *North of Jesus' Beans* by Bill Gaston; *Depth Rapture* by Carol Bruneau; *Drowning in Darkness* by Peter Oliva.

Recent nonfiction titles: *We Who Can Fly: Poems, Essays and Memories in Honour of Adele Wiseman* (edited by Elizabeth Greene); *A Very Large Soul: Selected Letters from Margaret Laurence to Canadian Writers* (edited by J. A. Wainwright).

Cormorant only publishes work by Canadian writers. Queries and SASEs should be directed to:

Jan Geddes, Publisher

Barbara Glen, Assistant to the Publisher

COTEAU BOOKS

401, 2206 Dewdney Avenue
Regina
Saskatchewan S4R 1H3
Canada
(306) 777-0170
fax: (306) 522-5152
cocteau@coteau.unibase.com (e-mail)
http://coteau.unibase.com

Coteau Books publishes a range of Canadian works, with a particular focus on the literary genres—novels, short fiction, poetry, drama, and juvenile fiction. Coteau presents an annual list that reflects literary quality across the country, including First Nations authors, with a focus on prairie voices of all kinds. Nonfiction work, especially memoir, is a growing interest as well.

Coteau has recently launched a new poetry series called *Open Eye,* with the intent to feature new, young poetic voices and attract a broad readership to the genre.

The Coteau list features such upcoming titles as the international short fiction anthology *Two Lands, Two Visions* (edited by Janice Kulyk Keefer and Solomea Pavlychko); Open Eye poetry title *My Flesh the Sound of Rain* by Heather MacLeod; and *The Intrepid Polly McDoodle,* the second in a juvenile novel series by Edmonton author Mary Woodbury.

Recent titles include Governor-General's Award-winner Anne Szumigalski's greatest hit *On Glassy Wings,* which received the Canadian Authors Association Poetry Prize, Barbara Nickels' first poetry book, *The Gladys Elegies,* which was awarded the Pat Lowther Memorial Prize as the best book of poetry by a woman; and the short fiction collection *In the Misleading Absence of Light* by Regina author Joanne Gerber (which has received five national and provincial awards to date).

Coteau also publishes the annual daybook *Herstory: The Canadian Women's Calendar* compiled annually by the Saskatoon Women's Calendar Collective.

Queries and SASEs should be directed to:

Nik Burton, Managing Editor (Regina)

Author's submission guidelines available upon request.

Douglas & McIntyre Publishers

2323 Quebec Street, Suite 201
Vancouver
British Columbia V5T 457
Canada
(604) 254-7191
fax: (604) 254-9099
genmail@groundwood-dm.com (e-mail)

Toronto office:
585 Bloor Street West
2nd Floor
Toronto
Ontario M6G 1K5
Canada
(416) 537-2501
fax: (416) 537-4647

(The Toronto office handles fiction and children's books; the rest of the Douglas & McIntyre list is issued from the Vancouver office.)

Douglas & McIntyre Publishers (founded in 1964) offers a publishing program with Canadian emphasis—often with a specifically British Columbian inflection. The house produces hardcover and paperback books in both fiction and nonfiction. Nonfiction areas of interest include native art, current affairs, history, travel, and nature studies. Douglas & McIntyre fiction tends toward literary works, serious popular fiction, and tales of mystery and suspense.

Nonfiction titles: *The Clouded Leopard: Travels to Landscapes of Spirit and Desire* by Wade Davis; *Bill Reid* by Doris Shadbolt; *Haida Art* by George F. MacDonald; *Cold as Charity: The Truth Behind the High Cost of Giving* by Walter Stewart; *Politically Speaking* by Judy Rebick and Kiké Roach; *HeartSmart Chinese Cooking* by Stephen Wong and The Heart & Stroke Foundation of Canada; *Working Dollars: The VanCity Savings Story* by Herschel Hardin; *Mike Harcourt: A Measure of Defiance* by Michael Harcourt with Wayne Skene; *The Immortal Beaver: The World's Greatest Bush Plane* by Mike Rossiter; *Bishop's: The Cookbook* by John Bishop; *Back to the Front: An Accidental Historian Walks the Trenches of World War I* by Stephen O'Shea.

Fiction and literary works: *Understanding Ken* by Pete McCormack; *Ingratitude* by Ying Chen; *Bachelor Brothers' Bedside Companion* by Bill Richardson (illustrated by Rose Cowles); *eye wuz here: 30 women writers under 30* (edited by Shannon Cooley); *The Lesser Blessed* by Richard Van Camp; *Let the Drums Be Your Heart: New Native Voices* (edited by Joel T. Maki); *Local Colour: Writers Discovering Canada* (edited by Carol Martin); *A Story as Sharp as a Knife: An Introduction to Classical Haida Literature* by Robert Bringhurst; *Notes from the Century Before: A Journal from British Columbia* by Edward Hoagland (illustrations by Claire Van Vliet).

The **Greystone Books** imprint offers travel guides, one-day getaways, regional histories, sports books (especially hockey), and titles on popular culture, natural history, and outdoor recreation. Representative titles from Greystone: *Beauty Queens: A Playful History* by Candace Savage; *Midlife Man: A Not-So-Threatening Guide to Health and Sex for Man at His Peak* by Art Hister, M.D.; *River of the Angry Moon: Seasons on the Bella Coola* by Mark Hume with Harvey Thommassen; *Vancouver: The Ultimate Guide* by Judi Lees and Terri Wershler; *Etched in Ice: A Tribute to Hockey's Defining Moments* by Michael McKinley; *British Columbia: A Natural History* by Richard Cannings and Sydney Cannings; *Cold War: The Amazing Canada-Soviet Hockey Series of 1972* by Roy MacSkimming; *Hockey the NHL Way: The Basics* by Sean Rossiter; *The Nature of Shorebirds: Nomads of the Wetlands* by Harry Thurston; *Orca: Visions of the Killer Whale* by Peter Knudtson; *Fishing in the West* by David Carpenter; *52 Weekend Activities Around Vancouver* by Sue Lebrecht and Judi Lees.

Douglas & McIntyre handles its own distribution, as well as purveying books from additional houses and institutions including the Canadian Museum of Civilization, the Mountaineers, the New Press, Sierra Club Books, and Thames and Hudson.

Query letters and SASEs should be directed to the **Acquisitions Editor**; correspondence will be redirected in house.

GROUNDWOOD BOOKS

585 Bloor Street West, 2nd Floor
Toronto, Ontario M6F 1K5
Canada
(416) 537-2501

Groundwood Books publishes titles for preschoolers through young adults. Ground-wood was established 20 years ago with the goal to publish the best possible Canadian children's books, emphasizing Canadian content but also worldwide distribution.

Representative titles: *So You Love to Draw: Every Kid's Guide to Becoming an Artist* by Michael Seary (illustrated by Michel Bisson); *Jade and Iron: Latin American Tales from Two Cultures* (translated by Hugh Hazelton; edited by Patricia Aldana; illustrated by Luís Garay); *A Completely Different Place* by Lars Klinting (for ages 5–7); *The Rooster's Gift* by Pam Conrad (illustrated by Eric Beddows; picture book for ages 4–8); *Steel Drums and Ice Skates* by Dirk Mclean (illustrated by Ho Che Anderson; picture book for ages 6–9); *Sarah and the People of Sand River* by W. D. Valgardson (illustrated by Ian Wallace; picture book for ages 5–9); *Enchantment in the Garden* by Shirley Hughes (ages 8 and up).

Query letters and SASEs should be directed to the **Acquisitions Editor**; correspondence will be redirected in house.

DUNDURN PRESS

8 Market Street, Suite 200
Toronto
Ontario M5E 1M6
Canada
(416) 214-5544
fax: (416) 214-5556
info@dundurn.com (e-mail)
www.dundurn.com

Dundurn Press was established 25 years ago to bring Canadian history and biography to a general readership. Its publisher, Kirk Howard, felt that there was a dearth of contemporary learning materials in the area of Canadian history and biography, and began publishing books on such overlooked topics as the multicultural dimension of the Loyalist immigration. Since its inception, Dundurn has expanded its mandate to include important works of creative nonfiction, with books on Canadian art, architecture, crafts, music, local histories, politics, current issues, and military history. Other areas of interest include mystery, native studies, women's studies, philosophy, plays, poetry, health, how-to, educational, and reference. Dundurn also seeks to publish new works of literary fiction by emerging Canadian voices.

Dundurn has also acquired **Hounslow Press**, which publishes popular nonfiction and self-help titles; **Simon & Pierre Publishing,** which specializes in books about the theatre, new fiction, and Quebecois fiction and drama in translation; and **Boardwalk Books,** a publisher of quality fiction for children and young adults.

The following titles are highlights of the Dundurn Group list: *Light for a Cold Land: Lauren Harris's Life and Work* by Peter Larisey; *Flim Flam: Canada's Greatest Frauds, Scams, and Con Artists* by Mark Bourrie; *The Actors' Survival Kit—Third Edition* by Miriam Newhouse and Peter Messaline; *The Great Canadian Trivia Book 2* by Mark Keaney and Randy Ray; *Marsh Hay* by Merrill Denison; *An Opera Sampler: Miscellaneous Essays on Opera* by Carl Morey.

Dundurn accepts unsolicited manuscripts; include a SASE, summary, and sample chapter. Manuscripts should be directed to:

Barry Jowett, Editor

FIREFLY BOOKS

3680 Victoria Park Avenue
Willowdale
Ontario M2H 3K1
Canada
(416) 499-8412
fax: (416) 499-8313
fireflybooks@global.serv.net (e-mail)

Firefly produces trade nonfiction in areas that include popular biography, popular science, lifestyles, the natural world, hobbies and crafts, gardening, food, sports, recreation, and health.

Representative of the Firefly list: *Nightwatch: A Practical Guide to Viewing the Universe* by Terence Dickinson.

Firefly Books handles its own distribution.

Firefly does not consider unsolicited manuscripts.

Lionel Koffler, President

FITZHENRY & WHITESIDE

195 Allstate Parkway
Markham
Ontario L3R 4T8
Canada
(905) 477-9700

Fitzhenry & Whiteside Ltd., founded in 1966, specializes in Canadian trade nonfiction, Canadian secondary school texts and Canadian children's books.

Query letters and SASEs should be directed to:

Sharon Fitzhenry, President

GOOSE LANE EDITIONS

469 King Street
Fredericton
New Brunswick E3B 1E5
Canada
(506) 450-4251
fax: (506) 459-4991

Goose Lane Editions is a small Canadian publishing house that specializes in literary fiction, poetry, and a select list of nonfiction titles. It does not publish commercial, genre fiction, or confessional works of any kind. Occasionally one of its books will appeal to young adults, but it does not publish books specifically for that market, nor does it publish books for children.

Recent Goose Lane titles: *Forgotten Empress* by David Zeni; *World Enough* by Lesley Choyce; *Saint John at Work and Play* by Grant Kelly and Sue McCluskey; *Phantom Islands of the Atlantic* by Donald S. Johnson; *Gifts to Last: Christmas Stories from the Maritimes and Newfoundland* (selected by Walter Learning); *Cutting the Devil's Throat* by Andrew Steeves.

As a member of the Literary Press group, Goose Lane Editions has a Canada-wide sales force serving the book trade. In addition, the company employs several regional sales representatives to non-traditional outlets such as gift stores. Academic sales are handled by Irwin Publishing and U.S. sales by Stoddart Publishing. **General Distribution Services** takes care of order fulfillment.

Goose Lane considers submissions from outside Canada only occasionally, and only when both the author and the material have significant Canadian connections and the material is of extraordinarily high interest and literary merit. Writers should submit a synopsis, outline, and sample (30–50 pages) with a SASE if in Canada; international authors should include a SAE and international reply coupons with submission. Please query by mail or phone before submitting; direct queries to:

Laurel Boone, Acquisitions Editor

GUTTER PRESS

P.O. Box 600, Station Q
Toronto
Ontario M4T 2N4
Canada
(416) 822-8708

Gutter Press, established in 1992, is a leading publisher of alternative titles. This small press ambitiously seeks to revise—or perhaps pervert—the Canadian literary canon by publishing work by challenging, emerging voices. Publisher Sam Hiyate, whose roots lie in the literary magazine *Blood + Aphorisms,* provides a home for an eclectic mix of titles which might not fit into the list at more conventional houses.

Gutter Press concentrates on fetish-riddled fiction, popular culture, belles lettres, short stories, poetry, film, anthologies, and essays. Gutter previously published *The Quarterly,* a self-proclaimed "outlaw periodical" specializing in fiction, poetry, and visual art.

Gutter titles include: *The Reluctant Pornographer* by Bruce LaBruce; *The Small Words in My Body* by Karen Connelly; *Blue Paige* by Danny Vinik; *Nerve* by Barbra Leslie; *Stories from Blood + Aphorisms*; *The Necrophiles* by Donna Lypchuk; *Dark Rides* by Derek McCormack.

All queries should be directed to:

Sam Hiyate, Publisher

Ken Sparling, Senior Fiction Editor

HARPERCOLLINS PUBLISHERS

1995 Merlchem Road
Scarborough
Ontario M1B SMG
Canada
(416) 321-2241
www.harpercollins.com/imprints/harper_canada/

HarperCollins Publishers is a general trade publisher with an emphasis on literary fiction, literary nonfiction, children's books, and trade nonfiction. HarperCollins has a mandate to be a successful, profitable general trade publisher with a strong commitment to support and nurture literary fiction and nonfiction in Canada. HarperCollins has several imprints: **HarperFlamingo**, a literary imprint; **HarperBusiness**, and **Phyllis Bruce Books**, a literary imprint concentrating on both fiction and general nonfiction. Harper-Collins produces about fifty original titles each year. HarperCollins publishes books of merit in the following areas: fiction, business, true crime, history, and politics.

Recent HarperCollins titles include: *The Red Shoes: Margaret Atwood / Starting Out* by Rosemary Sullivan; *Bulldog Spirit of the New Entrepreneur* by Ellie Rubin; and *The White Bone* by Barbara Gowdy.

HarperCollins does not accept unsolicited manuscripts and suggests that potential authors contact a literary agent.

HOUSE OF ANANSI PRESS

34 Lesmill Road
Toronto
Ontario M3B 2T6
Canada
(416) 445-3333
fax: (416) 445-5967
www.genpub.com

House of Anansi Press is a literary press, founded in 1967 by Dennis Lee and David Godfrey, with a mandate to publish innovative literary works in fiction, nonfiction, and poetry by Canadian writers. Anansi acquired a reputation early on for its editors' ability to spot talented writers who push the boundaries and challenge the expectations of the literary community. This continues to be a part of the press's mandate, while it also maintains its rich backlist and keeps important works by Canadian writers in print.

Anansi has published works by such Canadian luminaries as Northrop Frye, Margaret Atwood, Michael Ondaatje, and Dennis Lee. The house emphasizes literary fiction, trade nonfiction, poetry, politics, philosophy, social thought, literary criticism, theory, autobiography, biography, and women's studies. Anansi also publishes *Alphabet City,* an edgy annual journal of cultural theory, literature, philosophy, and architecture.

Representative of the list: *The Unconscious Civilization* by John Ralston Saul; *Body Music* by Dennis Lee; *Anchoress* by Esta Spalding; *The Elsewhere Community* by

Hugh Kenner; *Taken* by Daphne Marlatt; *The Tracey Fragments* by Maureen Medved; *Awake When All the World Is Asleep* by Shree Ghatage; *Queen Rat* by Lynn Crosbie; *Power Politics* by Margaret Atwood.

Queries should include a SASE, summary, and sample chapter. Submissions should be directed to:

Martha Sharpe, Publisher

Adrienne Leahey, Editorial Assistant

INSOMNIAC PRESS

393 Shaw Street
Toronto
Ontario M6J 2X4
Canada
(416) 536-4308
fax: (416) 588-4198
www.insomniacpress.com

Insomniac Press, established in 1992, publishes a small, eclectic list of books, most of which have an experimental bent. Though focused primarily on literary fiction, Insomniac also produces select nonfiction and popular trade titles. Poetry and graphic novels round out the catalog of this unique press.

Nonfiction areas of interest include: architecture, social commentary, political science, business, personal finance, travel and food, black studies, and pop culture. Insomniac also publishes literature of gay and lesbian interest and is celebrated for its high-caliber spoken word anthologies.

Works representative of the nonfiction list: *The Uncommon Investor* by Benjamin Gallander; *Get Stuffed Toronto* by Julie Crysler; *Black Like Who?* by Rinaldo Walcott; *Room Behavior* by Rob Kovitz.

A sample of titles from the literary line-up: *Written in the Skin* by Rob McLennan (with photographs by Jules de Niverville); *Silver* by Matthew Remski; *The Quilted Heart* by R. M. Vaughan; *Bull* by Mark Sinnett; *Guilty* by Sky Gilbert; *The Heart Is Its Own Reason* by Natalee Caple; *Carnival* edited by Peter McPhee; *Desire High Heels Red Wine* by Timothy Archer, Sky Gilbert, Sonja Mills, and Margaret Webb; *Hard Candy* by Jill Battson; *Paul's Case* by Lynn Crosbie.

Insomniac does not accept unsolicited manuscripts; send queries and SASEs to:

Michael O'Connor, Publisher

KEY PORTER BOOKS

70 The Esplanade
3rd Floor
Toronto
Ontario M5E 1R2
Canada
(416) 862-7777
fax: (416) 862-2304
www.keyporter.com

Key Porter Books Ltd. (founded in 1981) publishes a primarily nonfiction list with a Canadian twist. Key Porter produces titles in current affairs, science and health, travel, the environment, ecology, politics, sports, and a solid line of money books and entrepreneurial guides. Key Porter also issues books for children and young adults. In addition, the house offers coffee-table and gift editions, as well as fiction and literary works.

Frontlist Key Porter titles are provided full promotional support that spotlights targeted review venues, national media exposure, magazine advertising (including co-op arrangements), and foreign-rights sales. The house maintains a strong backlist, which includes literary titles published under the **Liester and Orpen, Denys** imprint.

Among Key Porter highlights: *100 Years of Figure Skating* by Steve Milton (principal photographs by Barbara McCutcheon); *Rebel Daughter: An Autobiography* by Doris Anderson; *No Fat Chicks: How Women Are Brainwashed to Hate Their Bodies and Spend Their Money* by Terry Poulton; *The Fight for Canada* by Diane Francis; *I Have Lived Here Since the World Began: An Illustrated History of Canada's Native People* by Arthur J. Ray (a joint venture with Lester Publishing); *Throw Your Heart over the Fence: The Inspiring Story of the Famous People Players* by Diane Dupuy; *What Are We Going to Do Now? Helping Your Parents in Their Senior Years* by Dr. William Molloy; *Women in the Know: How to Build a Strategy to Achieve Financial Success* by Janice Book; *Goalies: Guardians of the Net* by Daniel Daignault (photographs by Denis Brodeur).

Key Porter titles are distributed in Canada by **General Distribution Services.**

Query letters and SASEs should be directed to:

Susan Renouf, President and Editor-in-Chief

KEY PORTER KIDS

Key Porter Kids is an imprint that specializes in works for younger readers, including pop-ups, board books, storybooks, novels, and reverence works.

Introducing **Key Porter Kids Classic Horror Series:** *The Hunchback of Notre Dame* by Victor Hugo (retold by Tim Wynne-Jones; illustrated by Bill Slavin) and Bram Stoker's *Dracula*—these are the first two volumes in a new series that brings classics of the horror genre to young children (ages 8 and up). Forthcoming: Mary Shelley's *Frankenstein*.

Other titles: *The Story of Canada* by Janet Lunn and Christopher Moore (illustrated by Alan Daniel; a joint venture with Lester Publishing); *Songs for Survival: Songs and Chants from Tribal Peoples Around the World* (edited by Nikki Siegen-Smith; illustrated by Bernard Lodge); *Animal Hideaways* by Anita Ganeri (illustrations by Halli Verrinder); *Creepy Crawlies in 3-D!* by Rick and Susan Sammon (photography by David Burder).

Query letters and SASEs should be directed to:

Susan Renouf, President and Editor-in-Chief

KIDS CAN PRESS
29 Birch Avenue
Toronto
Ontario M4V1E2
Canada
(416) 925-5437
fax: (416) 960-5437
info@kidscan.com (e-mail)

Kids Can Press is a children's publisher producing quality fiction and nonfiction titles. Kids Can books are published for a range of readers from pre-school to young adult. The house concentrates on information picture books, poetry, novels, sports, games, how-to, crafts, nature, and science.

Many Kids Can books have been recognized for excellence, including: *The Kids Book of Canada* by Barbara Greenwood (illustrated by Jock McRae); *The Kids Guide to the Millennium* by Ann Love and Jane Drake (illustrated by Bill Slavin); *At Grandpa's Sugar Bush* by Margaret Carney (illustrated by Janet Wilson); *Emma and the Silk Train* by Julie Lawson (illustrated by Paul Mombourquette). Other Kids Can notables: *I Went to the Bay* by Ruth Miller (illustrated by Martine Gourbault); *I Heard a Little Baa* by Elizabeth MacLeod (illustrated by Louise Phillips); *The Runaways* by Kristin Butcher; *Dead Water Zone* by Kenneth Oppel; *Superstars on Ice* by Patty Cranston. Kids Can also publishes the bestselling *Franklin* series, now an animated series on television in Canada and the United States.

Kids Can Press does accept unsolicited manuscripts, but requests that no original art or other materials you'd like returned be included. All submissions should include a self-addressed envelope with sufficient Canadian or international postage to return all materials. Direct manuscripts to:

Acquisitions Editor

LOBSTER PRESS LIMITED/LES ÉDITIONS HOMARD LTÉ

1250 René-Lévesque Boulevard West
Suite 2200
Montréal
Quebec H3B 4W8
Canada
(514) 989-3121
fax: (514) 989-3168

Lobster Press is a bilingual children's publisher that focuses on children's fiction, picture books, and travel books. This season, Lobster published English and French versions of *12 Months of Fun! The Lobster Kids' Guide to Exploring Montreal 1998–99*. This is the first in a series of city guides for parents, teachers, and tourists traveling with children.

Manuscripts and SASEs should be directed to the **Children's Editor**. Lobster Press does not accept multiple submissions. For author guidelines, contact **Kathy Tompkins**.

LONE PINE PUBLISHING

10426-81 Avenue, Suite 206
Edmonton
Alberta T6E 1X5
Canada
(403) 433-9333
fax: (403) 433-9646

Established in 1980, Lone Pine Publishing is dedicated to publishing multiregional works of merit. By publishing titles of "local relevance," Lone Pine seeks to enrich

Canadians' appreciation of their own landscape and people. Lone Pine publishes 20 books annually, specializing in nature, gardening, and the outdoors.

Titles representative of the list: *B.C. Trivia* by Don Blake; *Banff's Best Dayhikes* by Heather Elton; *Gardening in Toronto* by Pat Tucker; *Ontario Birds* by Chris Fisher; *Plants of the Rocky Mountains* by Linda Kershaw with Andy MacKinnon and Jim Pojar.

Submissions should include a cover letter, outline, sample chapter, and copies of illustrations (not originals). Include a SASE if you wish material to be returned. No phone calls please.

Direct queries and submissions to **Acquisitions**.

MACFARLANE WALTER & ROSS

37A Hazelton Avenue
Toronto
Ontario M5R 2E3
Canada
(416) 924-7595

Macfarlane Walter & Ross, founded in 1988, bases it publishing program on four elements: to publish a small, select list of quality nonfiction; to offer an extraordinary degree of editorial support to writers; to produce books of high design and production values; and to give every book a strong and vigorous marketing effort.

MW&R publishes between 8 and 12 works of quality nonfiction annually, with particular emphasis in the areas of politics, history, biography, business, sports, and popular culture. MW&R also publishes several literary anthologies.

MW&R books have won many awards and at least one title has appeared on the national bestseller lists in every season since the company's inception. Their 1996 title, *Boom Bust & Echo: How to Profit from the Coming Demographic Shift*, has sold over a quarter of a million copies in hardcover.

After 10 years of operation, MW&R has achieved a number of its early goals: a stable of gifted authors, a reputation for excellence in editorial and literary accomplishment, and a list that is known for the topical, the original, the controversial, and the new.

Query letters and SASEs should be directed to:

Paul Woods, Assistant Editor

MACMILLAN CANADA

29 Birch Avenue
Toronto
Ontario M4V 1E2
Canada
(416) 963-8830

Macmillan Canada, established in 1905, is one of the larger Canadian houses. It publishes a wide-ranging list of nonfiction trade books. Macmillan seeks to publish books that will appeal to the Canadian public, by Canadian authors, with a Canadian focus. Macmillan does not publish fiction, nor does it produce children's books.

Areas of interest include health, environment, food, business, and popular biography.

A sampler of Macmillan successes: *The Living Beach* by Silver Donald Cameron; *The Learning Paradox* by Jim Harris; *The Healthy Type A* by Dr. Kerry Crofton. Macmillan also publishes the ever-popular Anne Lindsay cookbook series.

Submit a query letter along with an outline, sample chapter, and SASE to:

Editorial Department

MALCOLM LESTER BOOKS

25 Isabella Street
Toronto
Ontario M4Y 1M7
Canada
(416) 944-3634
fax: (416) 944-3122
http://gutenberg.com/malcolmlesterbooks/

Malcolm Lester Books is a new arrival on the Canadian scene, publishing "highly visible trade books focusing on special and important non-fiction." Though the press is young, publisher Malcolm Lester has been in the industry for 34 years and promises to showcase writers with a highly personal publishing service. Central to the vision of his press is a commitment to quality books and a belief in their cultural importance.

Areas of specialty: history, autobiography, biography, science, philosophy, and Judaica. Malcolm Lester emphasizes books dealing with issues of social and political consequence. The press will also be publishing a few fiction titles each year.

The inaugural list features: *Chips & Pop: Decoding the Nexus Generation* by Robert Barnard, Dave Cosgrave, and Jennifer Welsh; *Ashes and Miracles: A Polish Journey* by

Irena F. Karafilly; *The War to End All Wars* by Morley Torgov; *The Ends of Our Exploring: Ethical and Scientific Journey to Remote Places* by Hooley McLaughlin; *Travesty of Justice: How Canada Became a Safe Haven for Nazi War Criminals* by Alti Rodal; *The Healing Heart* by Eleanor Koldofsky; *100 Cigarettes and a Bottle of Vodka* by Arthur Schaller.

Submission guidelines: Query letter or phone call first; no unsolicited manuscripts without first querying. All submissions should be directed to:

Malcolm Lester, Publisher

McGILL-QUEEN'S UNIVERSITY PRESS

Montreal office:
McGill University
3430 McTavish Street
Montreal
Quebec H3A 1X9
Canada
(514) 398-3750
fax: (514) 398-4333
www.mcgill.ca/mqup/

Kingston office:
Queen's University
Kingston
Ontario K7L 3N6
Canada
(613) 533-2155

McGill-Queen's University Press, founded in 1969, produces trade books with scholarly market crossover, as well as titles geared specifically for the academic market. The press is a joint publishing endeavor of Queen's University (Kingston) and McGill University (Montreal). Many McGill-Queen's books have a Canadian subject slant; in addition, the house is strong in a variety of fields in the international arena as well as the social sciences and humanities. McGill-Queen's publishes in French and English.

Publications from McGill-Queen's include works in African studies, anthropology, architecture, art history, Asian studies, biography, British studies, business history, Canadian history, Canadian politics, communications, cultural studies, ecology, economics, environment, ethnic studies, French history, geography, housing policy, international history, Irish history, Judaica, labor studies, literature and literary criticism, loyalist history, history of medicine, native studies, philosophy, photography, political economy, political science, Quebec history, religion, sociology, urban geography, women's studies, and general-interest books primarily in areas of current interest in international and cultural affairs. McGill-Queen's does not publish hard science.

Titles representative of the list: *Moshe Safdie* edited by Irena Zantovska Murray; *Surpassing Wonder* by Donald Harman Akenson; *The World of the Gift* by Jacques T. Godbout with Alain Caille; *The Excluded Wife* by Yuen-fong Woon; *Dublin's Literary Pubs* by Peter Costello; *The Road to Egdon Heath* by Richard Bevis; *On Their Own* by Stewart Crysdale, Alan J. C. King, and Nancy Mandell.

The McGill-Queen's literary purview embraces criticism, memoir, biography, and letters. Offerings here: *Reading Mansfield and Metaphors of Form* by W. H. New; *New World Myth* by Marie Vautier; *Herman Melville: Stargazer* by Brett Zimmerman; *Joseph Brodsky and the Baroque* by David MacFayden.

Distribution for McGill-Queen's University Press is handled by **General Distribution Services.**

Query letters and SASEs should be directed to:

Philip J. Cercone, Senior Editor (Montreal)

Aurele Parisien, Editor (Montreal)

John Zucchi, Editor (Montreal)

Donald H. Akenson, Senior Editor (Kingston)

Joan Harcourt, Editor (Kingston)

Roger Martin, Editor (Kingston)

McGraw-Hill Ryerson Limited

300 Water Street
Whitby
Ontario L1N 9B6
Canada
(905) 430-5143

McGraw-Hill Ryerson Limited prides itself on being one of the "liveliest Canadian publishers." Though founded on its educational division, McGraw-Hill Ryerson also has a thriving trade arm. This division publishes general interest books by, about, and for Canadians.

McGraw-Hill Ryerson concentrates on personal finance, management, and small business books. The *SOHO* series offers solutions for those in the small office/home office sector.

Notables from the McGraw-Hill fall 1998 list: *The Bagel Effect* by Paul Hoffert; *201 Easy Ways to Reduce Your Taxes* by Evelyn Jacks; *Guarantee Your Child's Financial Future* by Ben McLean.

McGraw-Hill Ryerson does accept unsolicited manuscripts, but suggests that authors call for proposal guidelines before submitting. Queries should be directed to:

Lynda Walthert, Assistant to the Publisher

THE MERCURY PRESS
22 Prince Rupert Avenue
Toronto
Ontario M6P 2A7
Canada
(416) 531-4338
fax: (416) 531-0765
www.lpg.ca/publishers/mercury.htm

The Mercury Press was established in 1990. It describes itself as "an eclectic house with a core dedication to cutting-edge fiction and poetry in fine trade editions." It is also a publisher of trade nonfiction titles. Mercury publishes a murder mystery imprint, **Midnight Originals.** Many Mercury titles have been nominated for prestigious Canadian and international awards.

Titles on the literary list: *Tommy's Farm* by Douglas Ord; *Childforever* by Ian McCulloch; *Laurence* by France Theoret; *City of Forgetting* by Robert Majzels; *Connie Many Stories* by Sarah Murphy; *The Flesh So Close* by Kenneth J. Harvey; *The Little Black Dress* by Cary Fagan.

Nonfiction highlights: *She Would Be the First Sentence of My Next Novel* by Nicole Brossard; *The Power to Bend Spoons: Interviews with Canadian Fiction Writers* edited by Beverley Daurio; *Such Melodious Racket: The Lost History of Jazz in Canada, 1914–1949*; *Dancing Naked: Narrative Strategies for Writing Across Centuries* by Di Brandt; *Broken Entries: Race. Subjectivity. Writing.* by Roy Mikki; *A Genealogy of Resistance* by M. Nourbese Philip; *Impossible Nation: The Longing for Homeland in Canada and Quebec* by Ray Conlogue.

Mercury accepts unsolicited manuscripts, but only publishes Canadian writers. All correspondence should be by mail; Mercury does not accept electronic submissions.

Direct manuscripts to:

The Editor

NeWest Press

201, 8540 109 Street
Edmonton
Alberta T6G 1E6
Canada
(403) 432-9427
fax: (780) 433-3179
newest@planet.eon.net (e-mail)

NeWest, established in 1977, is a small press with a distinctive Western Canadian focus. The press publishes eight titles annually, producing a mixed list of literary fiction and nonfiction. The house only considers manuscripts that are by Western Canadian authors or relate to Western Canada. Currently, NeWest is not considering poetry, short stories, children's, or young adult fiction.

NeWest has a popular *Prairie Play* series, as well as a fiction imprint, **Nunatak New Fiction**, which produces select, outstanding works by emerging Western Canadian writers. The *Writer as Critic* series features critical works by preeminent Canadian authors.

Areas of interest: literary fiction, drama, creative nonfiction, autobiography, and other works in the areas of Western Canadian history and social concerns.

Titles from NeWest: *Icefields* by Thomas Wharton; *The Doomed Bridegroom* by Myrna Kostash; *Martin Yesterday* by Brad Fraser; *Readings from the Labyrinth* by Daphne Marlatt; *Chorus of Mushrooms* by Hiromi Goto; *Misshapen* by Robert Budde; *The Blood Girls* by Meira Cook.

Send a query letter or a proposal with a book outline, and a SASE to the address listed above.

Orca Book Publishers

P.O. Box 5626, Station B
Victoria
British Columbia V8R 6S4
Canada
(250) 380-1229
fax: (250) 380-1892
orca@pinc.com (e-mail)
www.swifty.com/orca/

Orca publishes an eclectic mix of children's picture books, juvenile and young adult fiction. At the present, Orca only considers manuscripts by Canadian authors.

Pick of the Orca list: *Draugr* by Arthur G. Slade; *The Moccasin Goalie* by William Brownridge; *A Fly Named Alfred* by Don Trembath; *A Time to Choose* by Martha Attema; *Belle's Journey* by Marilyn Reynolds.

Orca is eagerly seeking picture book manuscripts in the following areas: stories derived from the author's own childhood experiences, carefully researched historical tales, and modern stories situated within Canada, but with universal appeal. Manuscripts should be limited to 2,500 words in length.

In the juvenile and young adult fiction genres, Orca seeks manuscripts that meet the following criteria: regional stories, challenging language and themes, stories based on historical subjects, or contemporary stories that are issue-oriented. These manuscripts should be between 20,000 and 45,000 words in length.

For picture books, submit a manuscript *without* artwork unless you are a trained artist; do not send any originals. For juvenile or young adult projects, send a query first, along with a synopsis and the first few chapters. All submissions should include a SASE. Do not query by e-mail or fax.

These and other guidelines can be found on the Orca Web site.

Direct queries and submissions to:

Bob Tyrrell, Publisher (juvenile and young adult, adult nonfiction)

Ann Featherstone, Children's Book Editor (picture books)

OXFORD UNIVERSITY PRESS

70 Wynford Drive
Don Mills
Ontario M3C 1J9
Canada
(416) 441-2941
www.oupcan.com

Oxford University Press Canada is the equivalent of a wholly owned subsidiary of Oxford University Press. The Canadian branch (established in 1904) was the second overseas office opened, after New York. Oxford University Press Canada has a modest trade publishing program, producing a select list of history and reference books. These books are all intended for a general readership; manuscripts of a more specialized, academic nature will not be considered for publication in the trade division. Everything on the

OUP Canada list is topically Canadian or tackles the given subject from a Canadian perspective. The press does not consider novels, short story collections, how-to or self-help books, cookbooks, photographic books, or books for young readers. At the present time, OUP Canada is not accepting poetry manuscripts.

Titles representative of the list: *The Canadian Oxford World Atlas* edited by Quentin Stanford; *True North* (an illustrated history of Canada's north; edited by William Morrison); *Forging the Prairie West* by John Herd Thompson; *The Canadian Oxford Dictionary; The Canadian Oxford Junior Atlas* (edited by Quentin Stanford).

Send a brief synopsis, accompanied by a summary of the author's background and previous publications, along with one or two sample chapters and a SASE to:

Anne Erickson, Director, Trade, Medical, and Professional Division

PENGUIN BOOKS CANADA LIMITED

10 Alcorn Avenue, Suite 300
Toronto
Ontario M4V 3B2
Canada
(416) 925-2249

Founded in 1974, Penguin Canada's mandate is to publish Canadian authors. The house does so with style, covering a wide range of original trade nonfiction as well as mainstream and category fiction and literary works. Canadian authors whom Penguin Canada publishes include John Ralston Saul, Peter C. Newman, Guy Gavriel Kay, Jack Whyte, and Anita Rau Badami. As well at its Canadian authors, Penguin Canada publishes works by a wide range of international authors from John Le Carré to Anne Tyler to Nadine Gordimer. Hardcovers are published under the **Viking** imprint; paperbacks under the **Penguin** imprint. Children's hardcovers are published under the **Viking** imprint; children's paperbacks under the **Puffin** imprint.

Penguin Books also purveys via its catalog and distribution network featured titles from the company's various international divisions, as well as over forty lines including Faber and Faber, Ladybird, and W. W. Norton.

In accordance with its current acquisitions policy, Penguin Books Canada does not accept unsolicited manuscripts. Query letters and SASEs should be directed to:

Editorial Department

PLAYWRIGHTS CANADA PRESS

54 Wolseley Street
Toronto
Ontario M5T 1A5
Canada
(416) 703-0201
fax: (416) 703-0059
cdplays@interlog.com (e-mail)

Playwrights Canada Press is an award-winning drama publisher. The press publishes six to seven titles annually, specializing in Canadian plays and selected drama theory and history.

Recent titles include *Mad Boy Chronicle* by Michael O'Brien; *Colonial Tongues* by Mansel Robinson; *Clever as Paint: The Rossettis in Love* by Kim Morrissey; *Office Hours* by Norm Foster.

Please direct manuscripts with a SASE to:

Angela Rebeiro, Publisher

POLESTAR BOOK PUBLISHERS

P.O. Box 5238, Station B
Victoria
British Columbia V8R 6N4
Canada
(250) 361-9718
fax: (250) 361-9738

Polestar Book Publishers produces literary and commercial titles aimed at a wide readership. Polestar encourages "culturally significant writing" through its *First Fiction* series, which publishes the work of new authors. Polestar also maintains a poetry list. Popular nonfiction rounds out the Polestar catalog, with an emphasis on sports, dogs, science, and food.

Books representative of the trade list: *Country on Ice* by Doug Beardsley; *Home Run* by Michael McRae; and *Great Canadian Scientists* by Barry Shell.

Literary line-up: *Love Medicine* by Gregory Scofield; *Diss/Ed Banded Nation* by david nandi odhiambo; *Pool-Hopping* by Anne Fleming.

Polestar publishes Canadian authors only. It does not accept illustrated children's books. Direct queries and SASEs to:

Lynn Henry, Managing Editor

THE PORCUPINE'S QUILL

68 Main Street
Erin
Ontario N0B 1T0
Canada
(519) 833-9158
www.sentex.net/~pql/new.html

The Porcupine's Quill is a leading Canadian small press producing a hand-picked list of literary works (short story collections, novels, juvenile fiction, and poetry) by both emerging and veteran writers. The press is proud to have produced several books that have been shortlisted for awards, including the prestigious Governor General's Award. The Porcupine's Quill also produces a selection of trade and critical works, as well as a handful of books on the visual arts.

The Porcupine's Quill roster includes: *Noise* by Russell Smith; *Small Change* by Elizabeth Hay; *Ripostes* by Philip Marchand; *Learning to Live Indoors* by Alison Acheson; *Storm Glass* by Jane Urquhart.

Now a popular destination for submissions, The Porcupine's Quill is swamped with manuscripts; as such, it does not accept unsolicited work. Instead, the Porcupine's Quill often seeks out writers whose work has appeared in literary magazines such as *The New Quarterly*. All submissions should include a SASE, short biography, and bibliography. They should be directed to:

Tim Inkster, Publisher

John Metcalf, Senior Editor

PRENTICE HALL CANADA, INC.

PTR Division
1870 Birchmount Road
Scarborough
Ontario M1P 2J7
Canada
www.phcanada.com
(800) 223-2336
fax: (800) 943-9831

Prentice Hall Canada, a division of Simon & Schuster, is one of the largest trade and educational publishers in Canada. Prentice Hall currently publishes about 100 titles annually. The house has a broad line of trade publications, specializing in the areas of technology, personal finance, business, health, computer technology, pop culture, and self-help. Some Prentice Hall imprints: **Allyn and Bacon Canada, Prentice Hall Ginn,** and **Appleton & Lange Canada**.

Prentice Hall offers detailed advice for potential authors on its Web site, www. phcanada.com. A summary follows.

Writers should submit a prospectus, book outline, three sample chapters, and SASE. The prospectus should contain a brief description of the project, the unique features of the work (as well as art and text features), and the target level of the book. The prospectus should also indicate the potential market, list any competing titles, and provide a background of the author. Direct all submissions to:

Acquisitions Editor

RAINCOAST BOOKS
8680 Cambie Street
Vancouver
British Columbia V6P 6M9
Canada
(604) 323-7100
fax: (604) 323-2600
info@raincoast.com (e-mail)
www.raincoast.com

Raincoast Books publishes an eclectic mix of topical and beautifully designed books. They produce books of a regional, national, and international nature in the areas of food, travel, antiques, architecture and interior design, arts and photography, crafts, pop culture, New Age, sports, and the outdoors. Raincoast also publishes a select list of fiction and literature, as well as children's picture books.

Titles published by Raincoast: *The Canadian Traveller's Diary*; *Haida Gwaii* by Ian Gill and David Nunuk; *Irresistible Waters* by Art Lingren; *Calling the Maritimes Home* by Julie V. Watson; *Tin Fish Gourmet* by Barbara-Jo McIntosh; *A Dreamspeaker Cruising Guide* by Anne and Laurence Yeadon-Jones; *The Sensualist* by Barbara Hodgson; *My Leafs Sweater* by Mike Leonetti and Sean Thompson; *CraftScapes* by Sue Warden.

Queries and SASEs should be directed to:

Brian Scrivener, Editorial Director

SECOND STORY PRESS

720 Bathurst Street, Suite 301
Toronto
Ontario M5S 2R4
Canada
(416) 537-7850
fax: (416) 537-0588
www.secondstorypress.on.ca

Second Story Press, feminist publishers, produces fiction and nonfiction titles for adults and younger readers. The press's Women's Issues Publishing Program presents works of interest to students of women's studies as well as to the general reader. Each year, Second Story develops a list that seeks to "challenge, inform, stimulate, delight, and entertain."

Representative of the Second Story nonfiction list: *From Memory to Transformation: Jewish Women's Voices* (edited by Sarah Silverstein Swartz and Margie Wolfe); *Cracking the Gender Code* by Melanie Stewart Millar.

Fiction titles: *The Other Side* by Cynthia Holz; *Aurat Durbar* (edited by Fauzia Rafiq); *Double Negative* by Leona Gom.

Children's titles: *The Girl Who Hated Books* by Manjusha Pawagi (illustrated by Leanne Franson); *A Gift for Gita* by Rachna Gilmore (illustrated by Alice Priestley); *Miracle at Willowcreek* by Annette LeBox.

Submissions guidelines: only manuscripts commensurate with the mandate of the press will be considered.

SELF-COUNSEL PRESS

1481 Charlotte Road
North Vancouver
British Columbia V7J 1H1
Canada
www.self-counsel.com
(604) 986-3366
(800) 663-3007
fax: (604) 986-3947

Self-Counsel Press publishes quality self-help titles throughout North America by reputable professionals in the areas of business, legal, and writing. Books offer guidance in the following subjects: business, marketing, sales, personal finance, law (including divorce, incorporation, wills, probate and family trusts), and writing.

Representative of the Self-Counsel publishing program: *Computer Crisis 2000* by W. Michael Fletcher; *Writing for Science Fiction and Fantasy* by Crawford Kilian; *Writing for Kids and Teens* by Marion Crook; *Investing Offshore* by Peter Sabourin, David Schincariol, and Alec MacLennan; *Start and Run a Profitable Consulting Business* by Douglas Gray; *Divorce Guide and Forms for Oregon* by Herb Weisser; and *Preparing a Successful Business Plan* by Rodger D. Touchie.

Direct queries and SASEs to:

Lori Ledingham, Managing Editor

SOMERVILLE HOUSE BOOKS LIMITED

3080 Yonge Street, Suite 5000
Toronto
Ontario M4N 3N1
Canada
(416) 488-5938
fax: (416) 488-5506
sombooks@goodmedia.com (e-mail)
www.sombooks.com

Somerville House publishes children's titles, as well as a select line of adult fiction and nonfiction. In November 1997, Somerville announced a joint-venture partnership with Penguin Putnam Inc. This new effort will produce the same kind of fun and educational children's titles typical of the Somerville list. The house specializes in interactive books and kits for young readers. Of note are Somerville's **Eye to Eye** books, which feature stereographic cards and a 3-D viewer.

Areas of interest: natural sciences, activity books, cooking, sports, arts and crafts, games, early education, and books plus interactive packages.

Titles typical of the list: *Wild Cats* by Andrea Holden-Boone; *Chew on This* by Susan Devins; *Environmental Detective* by Doug Herridge and Susan Hughes; *The Tree Suitcase* by Dr. David Suzuki; and *The Bones Book & Skeleton* by Stephen Cumbaa.

Somerville House does not accept unsolicited adult manuscripts. Children's nonfiction submissions are welcome; include a SASE. Due to the volume of submissions, Somerville House discards materials after three months if insufficient postage is enclosed. Direct all queries to:

Linda Pruessen, Editor, Acquisitions and Development (Children's)

STODDART PUBLISHING CO. LIMITED

34 Lesmill Road
Toronto
Ontario M3B 2T6
Canada
(416) 445-3333

Stoddart Publishing (established in 1984) produces a wide range of commercial Canadian nonfiction and fiction titles. Stoddart nonfiction categories include humor, history, military history, politics, biography, cooking, the environment, nutrition, and business and consumer guides. The Stoddart fiction line, while smaller, encompasses literature, mainstream novels, mysteries, and thrillers. Stoddart Publishing is the trade-publishing arm of General Publishing Co. Limited.

Recent nonfiction from Stoddart: *The Eatons: The Rise and Fall of Canada's Royal Family* by Rod McQueen; *In My Own Key: My Life in Love and Music* by Liona Boyd; *Seacoasts* by Pierre Berton (photographs by André Gallant); *Valley of the Grizzlies* by Robert H. Busch; *The Beatles: An Oral History* by David Pritchard and Alan Lysaght; *Remembering the Rocket: A Celebration* (compiled by Craig MacInnis); *Charest: His Life and Politics* by André Pratte (translated by Fred Reed); and *Earth Time: Essays* by David Suzuki.

Recent Stoddart fiction: *Save Me, Joe Louis* by M. T. Kelly; *The Bull Is Not Killed* by Sarah Dearing; and *In the Wings* by Carole Corbeil.

Query letters, sample chapters, and SASEs should be directed to:

Donald G. Bastian, Managing Editor

TURNERBOOKS.

1670 Bayview Avenue, #310
Toronto
Ontario M4G 3C2
Canada
www.turnerbooks.com

Turnerbooks., formerly Lester publishing, produces a compact list of trade nonfiction. This small book-publishing company seeks to give Canadians their own unique titles, producing approximately a dozen titles a year. Turnerbooks. is committed to supporting and promoting the authors it publishes. One unique feature of Turnerbooks. is its desire to synchronize with the new media. In this regard, Turnerbooks. has developed a Web site where readers can browse through titles and submit reviews.

This small press seeks outstanding manuscripts in the areas of personal finance, current affairs, management, and business.

Titles from Turnerbooks.: *The Manager's Mentor* by Les McIlroy; *Leaders* by Gary Tannyan; *The First Book* by Gordon Bell; *Money Is a Girl's Best Friend* by Linda Leatherdale; *Israel, a History* by Martin Gilbert; *Second Chances* by Tom Koch; and *Chretien: The Will to Win* by Lawrence Martin.

Send a query, manuscript, or synopsis, along with a SASE to:

Annette Geldbert, Executive Administrator

UNIVERSITY OF BRITISH COLUMBIA PRESS

6344 Memorial Road
Vancouver
British Columbia V6T 1Z2
Canada
(604) 822-3259
fax: (604) 822-6083
orders@ubcpress.ubc.ca
www.ubcpress.ubc.ca

University of British Columbia Press, founded in 1971, publishes scholarly books as well as general interest works, with an emphasis on Canadian subjects.

UBC Press' areas of interest include Canadian culture and history, political science, archeology, international law, race and gender studies, Asian studies, native studies (specifically the Northwest Coast), Pacific Rim studies, global geography, fisheries and forestry, environmental studies, Northern studies, and Canadian sociology.

Titles on the UBC list include: *Imaging the Arctic* (edited by J. C. H. King and Henrietta Lidchi); *Gamblers and Dreamers* by Charlene Porsild; *Clearcutting the Pacific Rain Forest* by Richard A. Rajala; *Chinese Opera* by Siu Wang-Ngai with Peter Lovrick; and *The First Nations of British Columbia* by Robert J. Muckle.

University of British Columbia Press handles its own distribution.

Query letters and SASEs should be directed to:

Jean Wilson, Senior Editor

UNIVERSITY OF TORONTO PRESS

10 St. Mary Street, Suite 700
Toronto
Ontario M4Y 2W8
Canada
(416) 978-2239

University of Toronto Press produces titles for the general trade as well as academic works. UTP also issues a series of specialist journals of note, including *Canadian Theatre Review.*

University of Toronto Press publishes in a range of fields including history, politics, women's studies, health, family, social science, law and crime, economics, workplace communication, cultural theory, literary studies, education, business, semiotics, drama, medieval studies, Renaissance studies, native studies, modern languages, urban studies, anthropology, sociology, and music. University of Toronto Press also publishes travel and touring guides, as well as atlases. The house produces no original contemporary fiction or poetry.

Representing the UTP list: *A Season of Opera* by M. Owen Lee; *David B. Milne* by David Milne, Jr., and David P. Silcox; *The Concise Historical Atlas of Canada*; *Closely Guarded* by John Starnes; *Globalization and the Meaning of Canadian Life* by William Watson; *Against the Odds* by Bruce Muirhead; *The Future of Aesthetics* by Francis Sparshott; *For a New Political Economy* by Bernard Lonergan; *Writing the Social* by Dorothy E. Smith; *Inside the Academy and Out* (edited by Janice L. Ristock and Catherine Taylor); *Playing with Desire* by Fred B. Tromly; *Design with Type* by Carl Dair; *The Gutenberg Galaxy* by Marshall McLuhan.

University of Toronto Press oversees a distributional network encompassing offices and sales agents worldwide; the house handles titles from The British Library, Royal Ontario Museum, Canadian Museum of Nature, and University of Ottawa Press.

Query letters and SASEs should be directed to:

Bill Harnum, Senior Vice-President, Scholarly Publishing

WHITECAP BOOKS

351 Lynn Avenue
North Vancouver
British Columbia V7J 2C4
Canada
(604) 980-9852
fax (604) 980-8197
whitecap@pinc.com
www.whitecap.ca

Whitecap Books, established in 1977, was created with one thing in mind: "survival." As such, Whitecap Books is a commercial press, with a strong marketing program to showcase its publications.

Whitecap produces trade nonfiction, with a strong focus on cookbooks by chefs, gardening, large-format photography, and books on local interest subjects. Whitecap also maintains a children's list of nonfiction and fiction.

Titles representative of the list: *The Girls Who Dish: Top Women Chefs Cook Their Best; Ducks* by David Jones; *Journeys Through the Garden* by Paddy Wales; *The Yukon Fact Book* by Mark Zuehlke.

Books from the children's list: *Animals Eat the Weirdest Things* by Diane Swanson; *Dog Tales* by Jennifer Rae (illustrated by Rose Cowles).

Send a sample chapter and one-page synopsis of the project with a SASE (U.S. submissions should include an international reply coupon) to:

Robin Rivers, Editorial Director

WOMEN'S PRESS

517 College Street, Suite 302
Toronto
Ontario M6G 4A2
Canada
(416) 921-2425

As its name suggests, Women's Press publishes inspiring feminist books by and about women. Women's Press seeks to bridge differences by selecting a list that covers a full spectrum of women's experiences, from disability to immigration to lesbianism.

Women's Press emphasizes fiction, biography, lesbian studies, Caribbean studies, psychology, political theory, sociology, health, women's studies, native studies, cultural studies, literary theory, history, and Latin American studies.

Of note are Women's Press's anthologies, *Curaggia: Writing by Women of Italian Descent* and *Out Rage.* Other titles from the Women's Press catalog: *Tongues on Fire* (edited by Rosamund Elwin); *Exile and the Heart* by Tamai Kobayashi; *Petticoats & Prejudice* by Constance Backhouse; *Out of Bounds* by Helen Lenskyj; *Marxism and Feminism* by Charnie Guettel.

Submissions guidelines: query letter, one-page description of project, brief biography, and SASE.

England

ABSOLUTE PRESS

Scarborough House
29 James Street West
Bath BA1 2BT
England
(44) 1225 316013
fax: (44) 1225 445836
sales@absolutepress.demon.co.uk (e-mail)

Absolute Press publishes mainly cookery and cultural lifestyles titles, including the established *Outlines* series, about gay and lesbian creative artists. The cookery titles, which include award-winners, are not your run-of-the-mill cookbooks. They include unusual or otherwise generally unknown styles of international cuisine. Absolute also takes a delight in publishing culinary experts who have a lively and entertaining story to tell as they educate. Examples include: *Street Food from Around the World* by James Mayson; *South African Cape Malay Cooking* by Sonia Allison and Mynra Robins; *Mexican Kitchen* by Rick Bayless (The Julia Childs Cookbook Awards "Book of the Year").

The *Outline* series, whose backlist includes biographies on David Hockney, Bessie Smith, and Benjamin Britten, has attracted impressive mainstream reviews. Forthcoming titles include three more Outlines—Tallullah Bankhead, Armistead Maupin, and k.d. lang—as well as a large-format fully illustrated book on *20th Century Gay Icons*.

And for the travel-minded, Absolute publishes a popular map series: *Streetwise Maps*. The series covers all the major U.S. cities, major European cities, plus major cities in Canada, Australia, and the Middle East. The *Artwise* titles promote museums and cultural institutions around the world.

Direct query letters and SASEs to:

Jon Croft, Publisher (Cookery and Lifestyle titles)

Nick Drake, Outlines titles

Camilla Ford, Illustrated books

AIRLIFE PUBLISHING LIMITED

101 Longden Road
Shrewsbury
Shropshire SY3 9EB
England
(44) 1743 235651
fax: (44) 1743 232944

This is the house for the outdoors enthusiast, whether a flier, a mariner, or a naturalist. Most prominently, it specializes in all things avionic, with an excellent range of titles —often generously illustrated—covering: military aviation, military history, civil aviation, general interest aviation, naval air history, aircraft modeling, biographies, and monographs. There is also a quite spectacular range of books for pilots.

Airlife also owns the **Swan Hill Press** imprint for the outdoor sportsman, and the **Waterline** imprint for the naturalist. **Swan Hill** covers: natural history, Africana, fishing, falconry, country sports, equestrian topics, travel and climbing, diving, country interest, books on deer and dog training, wildlife art, and titles featuring art from historical journeys of explorers.

Airlife has a considerable stocklist, an indication of the scope and scale of its publications follows: *Cockpit: An Illustrated History of WWII Aircraft Interiors* by Donald Nijboer; *The International Directory of Military Aircraft 1998–99* by Gerard Frawley; *The Second Battle of The Marne——1918* by Paul Greenwood; *Silvered Wings: The Aerial Photography of Gordon Bain* by Gordon Bain; *Flying the Big Jets, 3rd edition* by Stanley Stewart; *Ship Strike: A History of Air-Launched Anti-Ship Missile Systems* by Peter C. Smith; *Detailing Scale Model Aircraft* by Mike Ashey; *Man Is Not Lost* by Grp. Capt. Dickie Richardson; *Wellington: The Geodetic Giant* by Martin Bowman; and *Air Pilot's Practical and Theoretical Weather Manual* by David Bruford.

The **Waterline** imprint features a rich and varied range of technical and "how-to" handbooks and guides for the yachtsman and sailor, substantial listings for the international mariner, rowing, ship and boat modelling, and maritime historian. Recent Waterline titles include: *GMDSS Handbook: Understanding the Global Maritime Distress and Safety System* by John Campbell; *Do It Yourself Yacht Improvements* by Reg Minal; *Boats with an Open Mind: Seventy-Five Unconventional Designs and Concepts* by Philip Bolger; *The International Marine Boat Manager* by Bob Payne and Nick Ellison; *The Essential Sea Kayaker* by David Seidman; *Ship Modelling from Scratch* by Edwin B. Leaf; and *The American-Built Clipper Ship, 1850–1856: Characteristics, Construction and Details* by William L. Crothers.

Swan Hill features: *The Last of the Hunter Gatherers: Fisheries Crisis at Sea* by Michael Wigan; *Africa's Vanishing Wildlife* by Chris and Tilde Stuart; *Love of Labs:*

The Ultimate Tribute to Labrador Retrievers; Falconry for Beginners by Lee William Harris; *Open Season: An Artist's Sporting Year* by Rodger McPhail; *Mountaineering: The Freedom of the Hills, 6th edition* by Don Graydon; *Beneath British Seas* by Alan James; and *Hummingbirds* by Connie Toops.

Airlife maintains a solid network of overseas stockholding agents.

Query letters and SASEs should be directed to:

Anne Cooper, Rights Director

IAN ALLAN PUBLISHING

Riverdene Business Park
Molesey Road
Hersham
Surrey KT12 4RG
England
(44) 1932 266600
fax: (44) 1932 266601

When, in 1942, Ian Allan published his first book, *"The abc of Southern Locomotives,"* he had little idea that this was the first step to a multi-million dollar organization. From the initial 2,000 print run—snapped up by enthusiasts within the first week—Ian Allan's faith in his innovative product spawned the largest independent transport publisher in the world. The company's product range encompasses videos, magazines, and an extensive book publication list. "Diverse" is the word that best describes the Ian Allan group of companies, and no company within the group demonstrates this attribute more than Ian Allan Publishing. Its publications were originally aimed at railway enthusiasts, but grew to include road, sea, and air transport, with a further expansion in the 1970s into military and topographical publications. The name Ian Allan has become synonymous with transport and military subjects, but through the launch of the **Dial House** imprint in 1992, it has diversified into the general nonfiction markets, particularly those of leisure and sports. The experienced national and international sales force presently represents some 4,000 individual product lines. A distinct and major feature of the Ian Allan is its direct-selling operation, which includes bookshops, an extensive mail-order program and an expanding subscriptions service. The growing retailing sector of Allan's also offers a complete distribution service to other publishers.

From its superlative current listings: *A History of the Great North of Scotland Railway* by Sir Malcolm Barclay-Harvey; *The Engine Driver's Manual: How to Prepare, Fire and Drive a Steam Locomotive* by Brian Topping; *Tracks on Canvas: The Railway Paintings of Philip D. Hawkins* by Philip Hawkins (from its **OPC** imprint); *abc Bus &*

Coach Recognition (4th edition) by Alan Millar; *Afrika Korps at War* (in two volumes.) by George Forty; *Glory Days: Cunard* by David L. Williams; *Aerofilms Guide: Football Grounds* (6th edition); *Boeing Airliners: 747/757/767 in Colour* by Alan J. Wright and Robbie Shaw.

Allan's extensive backlist includes: *British Railway Disasters*; *Fire Engines in Colour* by S. W. Stevens-Stratten; *abc Civil Airliner Recognition* by Peter R. March; *U.S. Carriers at War* (reprint) by Peter Kilduff; *D-Day: Piercing the Atlantic Wall* by Robert Kershaw.

Query letters and SASEs should be directed to:

David Allan, Chairman

Tony Saunders, Managing Director

Bill Lucas, Director of Publishing

Wendy Myers, Sales Support Manager

Peter Waller, Publishing Manager

Zoe Schofield, Marketing Manager

Nigel Passmore, Sales Manager

J. A. ALLEN & CO. LTD.

The Horseman's Publisher
1 and 4 Lower Grosvenor Place
Victoria
London SW1W 0EL
United Kingdom
(44) 171 834 0090
fax: (44) 171 976 5836
sales@allens-books.com (e-mail)

J. A. Allen is a specialist publisher of a rich variety of high-quality titles on all things equine. Their products cover anatomy, farriery, psychology, veterinary care, breaking and schooling, breed books, breeding and stud management, care and general management, dressage and classical riding, driving and carriages, dictionaries, poetry and history, humor, hunting, jumping and eventing, polo, racing and bloodstock breeding, riding and horsemanship, saddlery, harness and horse clothing, shows and showing, teaching, Allen junior, The Pony Club, books for students, Allen photographic guides, and a selection of titles on dogs.

A sample of J. A. Allen's latest: *The Allen Illustrated Guide to Bits and Bitting* by Hilary Vernon (a fully comprehensive guide to bits and bitting for the modern rider that covers types of bits, their correct fitting and action with a section on nosebands, reins, and martingales); *Inside Your Horse's Mind* by Lesley Skipper (a challenging, in-depth study of the less-explored aspects of equine psychology and behavior—emotions, mental processes, and social relationships; also examines and questions scientific attitudes to equine behavior, evolutionary ideas, and anthropomorphism); *The Equine Body* by Beth Maloney (provides easy-to-understand equine physiology via innovative use of full-color, easy-to-assemble three-dimensional and moveable models and illustrations); *The Welsh Cob* by Wynne Davies (traces the origin and development of one of the most popular breeds for riding and driving in the world; beautifully illustrated with color pictures); *The Horse Shoeing Book* by Martin Humphrey (a pictorial guide to farriery from basics to advanced-level corrective and therapeutic shoeing).

Also new: *Competition Carriage Driving on a Shoestring* by Jinny Johnson (an introductory handbook on competitive driving trials for single horse or pony); *The International Horseman's Dictionary* (an illustrated English/French/German/Italian/Spanish dictionary of the horse, its types and breeds, equipment, care and activities, prepared for the international horseman and those engaged in equestrian business); *The Poetry of Horses* by Olwen Way (first major anthology of nearly 300 poems from classical Greek to modern day about every aspect of this marvelous animal; each poem is linked in subject, atmosphere, or thought to the one that follows); *The Pony Hobby Book* by Karen Bush and Claire Colvin (inventive and irresistible ideas for young pony enthusiasts to collect, make, and do; with step-by-step instructions, diagrams, and cartoons); and *The Holistic Management of Dogs* by veterinary adviser Keith Allison and Christopher Day (benefits of a holistic approach to health and welfare of the domestic dog; covers the dog's evolution, relationship with man, common breeds, general management, common ailments and treatments with holistic therapies, and many controversial topics).

Query letters and SASEs should be directed to:

Editorial (see previous page)

ANTIQUE COLLECTORS' CLUB

5 Church Street
Woodbridge
Suffolk IP12 1DS
England
(44) 1394 385501
fax: (44) 1394 384434
accbc@aol.com (e-mail)
www.antique-acc.com

The declared intention and editorial policy of the Antique Collectors' Club is to publish only the best books on the subject. Consequently it has been able to ensure that its imprint is respected throughout the world of arts and antiques. To date over 300 titles have been published, written by distinguished experts, covering: art reference, furniture, silver and jewelry, metalwork, horology, collectibles, textiles, specialist gardening, garden history and design, architecture and children's classics. It has recently announced the launch of the **ACC Children's Classics** list. Its aim is to give new life to unjustly neglected or overlooked titles of real quality by reissuing them with the best of contemporary new illustrations, fine printing, good paper, and traditional cloth bindings with dust jackets—at an affordable price. A prime motivation for this project is the belief that children deserve the same level of quality that adults are accustomed to receiving.

The outstanding quality demanded by the Antique Collectors' Club is indeed matched by the beautiful quality of its current catalog. New and backlist tiles include: *Fountain Pens: History and Design* (edited by Giorgio Dragoni and Giuseppe Fichera; 100 detailed examples of the fountain pen dating from 1890 to 1997); *Peter Pan* by J. M. Barrie (a beautifully illustrated new edition of one of the greatest children's stories ever written); *The Directory of Gold & Silversmiths, Jewellers and Allied Traders* by John Culme (leading reference on British nineteenth-century silver with 4,000 biographies and 15,000 makers' marks; illustrated and arranged for easy identification); *Victorian and Edwardian Furniture: Price Guide and Reason for Values* by John Andrews; *Brass Dial Clocks* by Brian Loomes; *Fire & Light in the Home, Pre-1820* by John Caspall (treasury of information on the vast array of highly collectible, decorative and interesting paraphernalia, from early tinder boxes, lanterns, and candlesticks to the home-lighting inventions of the early nineteenth century); *Dictionary of Sea Painters* by E. H. H. Archibald; *The Master Architect Series II: Norman Foster* by Dobney; *The Last Wanderers: Nomads and Gypsies of India* by T. S. Randhawa; and *Outstanding Shop Designs* by Olivier Boissere.

Trade orders are handled by **TBS Distribution Centre,** Colchester Road, Frating Green, Colchester, Essex CO7 7DW, England. Tel: (44) 1206 255679, Fax: (44) 1206 255930.

Query letters and SASEs should be directed to:

Diana Steel, Managing Director

Brian Cotton, Director

Jenny Gosling, Sales Director

Sarah Smye, Sales and Marketing Manager

Clare Trickett, Sales Office Manager

ANVIL PRESS POETRY LTD.

Neptune House
70 Royal Hill
London SE10 8RT
England
(44) 181 469 3033
fax: (44) 181 469 3363
anvil@cix.compulink.co.uk (e-mail)

A very small independent publisher of poetry in paperback and hardback, Anvil produces only 10 to 12 titles per year. However, it does accept unsolicited material provided that it is accompanied with the appropriate return postage.

Despite its modest scale, Anvil Press Poetry possesses a sizeable stocklist in addition to current titles. Newly offered: *Beyond Bedlam: Poems Written out of Mental Distress* (edited by Ken Smith and Matthew Sweeney); *Asleep in the Garden* (new and selected poems by Stanley Moss); and reprints such as *Selling Manhattan* by Carol Ann Duffy. Stocklist titles: *Poems in Prose* by Ana Blandiana; *The Truth of Poetry* by James Harpur; *Quality Time* by O. Paz/C. Tomlinson; and *Inveting the Fishes* by Tu Fu.

Distribution is handled by **Littlehampton Book Services,** (see **Aurum Press**). Query letters and SASEs should be directed to:

Peter Jay, Editor

ASLIB, THE ASSOCIATION FOR INFORMATION MANAGEMENT

Staple Hall
Stone House Court
London EC3A 7PB
England
(44) 171 903 0000
fax: (44) 171 903 0011
aslib@aslib.co.uk (e-mail)
www.aslib.co.uk

Aslib actively promotes best practice in the management of information resources worldwide. The Aslib Publications Department, as part of Aslib's wider mission, aims to produce practical, informative titles to help everyone in the practical and strategic use of knowledge. Its wide range of books, journals, and reference sources supports its organizational objective.

Aslib's highly regarded titles cover specialized areas such as information management for business, and for the voluntary sector; information policy, science and sources; records management; quality management; and translations and thesauri among numerous others. Aslib also produces the *Know How Guide* series, set up in 1994, which has proved to be a resounding success. Together with the new titles in its current catalog, Aslib now has an impressive total of 24 titles in this practical and popular series and is continuing to make further announcements of new products through its Web site.

Key new titles among the current listings are: *Copyright Made Easier* (an easily accessible guide to modern copyright law), and a new series of *Managing Information* reports. These reports include *Meeting Manager's Information Needs, The Internet and the Changing Information Environment,* and *Document Delivery.*

Aslib boasts a solid stable of active authors. However, it does welcome inquiries from anyone interested in writing or contributing to Aslib publications that addresses the growing and important field of information resource management.

Query letters and SASEs should be directed to the:

Head of Publications, Aslib (see previous page)

THE ATHLONE PRESS LIMITED

1 Park Drive
London NW11 7SG
England
(44) 181 458 0888
fax: (44) 181 201 8115
athlonepress@btinternet.com (e-mail)

Athlone, an academic press, publishes across the social sciences and humanities, as well as in the fields of law and science for the international market. Its publications (which include works of reference, monographs, upper-level paperbacks, and introductory texts) appear in the following wide range of categories: social science (sociology, political science, economics), cultural studies, film studies, architecture/planning, art history, classics, philosophy, English literature and literary studies, European and world literature and literary studies, social/cultural history, history of science, psychiatry, psychology and psychoanalysis, history of medicine, anthropology, museum studies, Asian studies, business and economic history, education and education history, and law and science.

Query letters and SASEs should be directed to:

D. Southam, Managing Director

B. Southam, Chairperson

T. Palmer, Editorial Director

AURUM PRESS

25 Bedford Avenue
London WC1B 3AT
England
(44) 171 637 3225
fax: (44) 171 580 2469
aurum@ibm.net (e-mail)

Aurum publishes neither fiction nor children's books. However, the range of categories under which it publishes in both hardback and paperback is impressively broad. Here you find interests ranging from the military, biography, history and current affairs to poetry and literature; from the arts, architecture, and crafts to business, popular science, and health. Titles also appear under sports and games, food and drink, entertainment and travel.

A sample from Aurum's current list: *The Road to Reading: A Practical Guide to Teaching Your Child to Read* by Theodore H. McDonald; *Little Black Dress* by Amy Holman Edelman; *Banker to the Poor: The Autobiography of Muhammad Yunus, Founder of the Grameen Bank* by Muhammad Yunus with Alan Jolis; and *Irish Country Style* by Bill Laws.

Aurum's substantial and varied stocklist includes: *Hair: An Owner's Handbook* by Philip Kingsley; *The Ultimate Mountain Bike Book* by Nicky Crowther; *Mustards, Pickles and Chutneys* by Margaret O'Sullivan; *Perfume: The Creation and Allure of Classic Fragrances* by Susan Irvine (with 220 color photographs and illustrations); *The New Apartment Book: Inspiring Ideas and Practical Projects for Decorating Your First Home* by Michele Michael with Wendy Israel; *Wolfpack: U-Boats at War 1939–1945* by Philip Kaplan and Jack Currie; *Rasputin: The Saint Who Sinned* by Brian Moynahan; *The Song of Eve* by Manuela Dunn Mascetti; The National Trail Guides series (for example: *Offa's Dyke Path South* by Ernie and Kathy Kay and Mark Richards), The Recreational Path Guides series (for example: *The Southern Upland Way* by Anthony Burton), and *The Wild Guides* series (for example: *Wild Italy* by Tim Jepson).

Also of note is the creation of a specialized new imprint, the **Argentum** banner, "established to publish the very best in practical photography books, written by a variety of top photographers from around the world." All rights inquiries should be addressed to Aurum Press. Sales and distribution inquiries are taken either by **Aurum** or **Littlehampton Book Services**, 10–14 Eldon Way, Lineside Estate, Littlehampton, West Sussex BN17 7HE, England. Tel: (44) 1903 828 800; fax: (44) 1903 828 801.

Query letters and SASEs should be directed to:

Sheila Murphy, Acquisitions Editor

Anica Alvarez, Acquisitions Editor

Piers Burnett, Acquisitions Editor and Editorial Director

A & C BLACK (PUBLISHERS) LTD.

35 Bedford Row
London WC1R 4JH
England
(44) 171 242 0946
fax: (44) 171 831 8478
enquiries@acblack.co.uk (e-mail)

A & C Black was founded in 1807 and is one of the few remaining independent medium-sized United Kingdom publishers. Charles Black, of the founding family, is at the helm as chairman. A & C Black markets titles across a wide range of subject matters, but clearly defines the scope of interest within each category: travel, drama, visual arts, music, sports, ornithology, reference, children, exhibitions, and sailing.

This house's output appears under two imprints: **Adlard Coles Nautical** (books for the seafarer, boatbuilder, and inland waterway user) and **Christopher Helm** (reference works for birdwatchers). Their listings also include publications by **Applause Books, Magi Publications, Sunflower Books,** and **V & A Publications**, since A & C Black acts as seller and distributor for these companies as well.

Examples of A & C Black publications: *Who's Who* (the famous standard reference source on people of influence and interest, now in its 151st annual edition); *New World Blackbirds: The Icterids* by Alvaro Jaramillo and Peter Burke (an identification guide from the Helm imprint); *Blue Guide Florence,* 7th edition, by Alta Macadam (a best-selling guidebook); *Acting Skills,* 2nd edition, by Hugh Morrison (a practical analysis of acting techniques essential for thespians keen to understand and improve their craft); *The Soccer Referee's Manual,* 2nd edition, by David Ager (a valuable work of reference for "in-training" and qualified referees); *Learning to Crew* by Basil Mosenthal (from the Adlard imprint).

Also current: *The Other Way: An Alternative Approach to Acting and Directing* by Charles Marowitz; *Introduction* by Frank Langella (from Applause Books); *Mouse, Look Out!* by Judy Waite (illustrated by Norma Burgin, from Magi Publications); *Landscapes of Samos,* 3rd edition, by Brian and Eileen Anderson (from the Sunflower pocket guides series); and, *British Textile Design from 1940 to the Present* by Ngozi Ikoku (from Victoria and Albert Museum Publications).

Query letters and SASEs should be directed to:

Gemma Davies, Travel

Jane Harris, Children's Books

Tesni Hollands, Theatre, Writing Reference

Robert Kirk, Ornithology

Linda Lambert, Ceramics, Art, and Design

Janet Murphy, Nautical subjects

Sheena Roberts, Music

Jonathan Taylor, Sports

BLAKE PUBLISHING LIMITED

3 Bramber Court
2 Bramber Road
London W14 9PB
England
(44) 171 381 0666
fax: (44) 171 381 6868
words@blake.co.uk (e-mail)

The Blake catalog strongly features biographies—in particular a fascinating variety of entertainment biographies of the rich and famous—in both hardback and paperback. Its nonfiction interests also cover politics and the military, the Royal Family, pets, health and fitness, and a lengthy list of true crime titles. Moreover, the house produces works of fiction by such well-known individuals as Judge James Pickles.

In terms of subject matter, Blake books are well aimed at the mass and popular market, a fact indicated by the solid distribution network that extends into Australia, South Africa, Canada, and New Zealand, as well as Europe and the U.S.

Indicative of Blake: *Ian Gillan: The Autobiography of Deep Purple's Lead Singer* by Ian Gillan; *Tom Cruise: Unauthorised* by Wensley Clarkson; *Clint Eastwood: Sexual Cowboy* by Douglas Thompson; *The Nemesis File* by Paul Bruce (a controversial and sensational story about Britain's legendary special force, the SAS); *A Deadly Kind of Love* by Nicholas Davies (a true crime love story about two army personnel that ended in murder); *How to Talk to Your Cat* by Claire Bessant (a jargon-free guide for all cat owners keen to unravel the mysteries of feline behavior); *The Art of Sensual Aromatherapy* by Nitya Lacroix with Sakina Bowhay (a uniquely holistic approach to sensual massage and aromatherapy); and *Double Exposure* by Jilly Johnson (Britain's first page-three girl's sizzling fiction debut, set in the world of modeling).

Query letters and SASEs should be directed to:

David Blake, Chairman

Adam Parfitt, Executive Editor

THE BREEDON BOOKS PUBLISHING COMPANY LTD.

Breedon House
44 Friar Gate
Derby DE1 1DA
England
(44) 1332 384235
fax: (44) 1332 292755
breedonbooks@netmatters.co.uk (e-mail)

Groundbreaking oral histories of Arsenal, Aston Villa, Wolves, and Sheffield Wednesday; a superb full-color history of the County of Durham; the story of the Royals in Kent; and additions to the highly acclaimed *Images of . . .* series with titles on Bristol, Swansea, Guildford, Ashford, and Aldershot are just a few from the recent list announced by Breedon.

Since its formation in 1982, Breedon has consistently produced bestselling local titles as well as made its name with some of the best football titles to be published in Britain. No wonder the *Independent* newspaper said, "No one does all our Saturdays better than Breedon." Most of Breedon's early soccer club histories are now out of print—and some copies are now changing hands for three-figure sums as collectors chase those first titles. The number of titles in the *Illustrated History* series of British soccer clubs will be increased over the next 2 years, and Breedon is currently launching *Talking to . . .* a new series of oral histories where the players of yesterday and today, as well as supporters young and old, recall memories of their favorite club. *Images of . . .* now cover over 70 British towns and cities, and although many titles are now out of print, there are some exciting new titles and a healthy backlist that keeps on selling.

Two great favorites—*Images of Teeside* and *Images of Merseyside*—will this year be reissued in softback to reach a new market. Breedon's partnership with the Kent Messenger Group sees the publication of *Images of Royal Kent*, a century of royal visits to that county captured on film. And *Walks Through History: Kent* marks the launch of another series.

New titles: *Arsenal in the Blood* by David Lemmon; *The Rugby League Challenge Cup: An Illustrated History* by Les Hoole; *A Taste of Leeds* by Peter Brears; and *Derbeians of Distinction* by Maxwell Craven. On the substantial stocklist: *Images of Nuneaton* (Nuneaton Tribune); *Images of World War II* by Rupert Matthews; and *She Knows You Know! The Remarkable Story of Hylda Baker* by Jean Fergusson.

Breedon is currently looking for sports (autobiographies/biographies), soccer (especially club-oriented), and local history/nostalgia titles.

Query letters and SASEs should be directed to:

Anton Rippon, Editorial Director

THE BRITISH LIBRARY

Publishing Office
96 Euston Road
London NW1 2DB
(44) 171 412 7535
fax: (44) 171 412 7768

The British Library at St. Pancras, one of the most important public buildings erected in the United Kingdom in the twentieth century, opened to the public in April 1998. The story of this national institution and its new construction is told in one of their own titles by Professor Colin St. John Wilson.

The British Library's publishing division offers an extensive range of titles in history, medieval history, book/arts history, oriental art, bibliography, manuscript studies, cartography, map history, monastic history, conservation science, electronic reference, literature, gift titles, as well as specialist guides on writing and scripts, bookbinding, and printing, to name just some of their academic and reference categories.

Here is a small sample of new and stocklist books from the Library: *Towards the Digital Library* (edited by Leona Carpenter, Andrew Prescott, and Simon Shaw; foreword by Sir Anthony Kenny); *Between France and Flanders: Manuscript Painting in Amiens in the Fifteenth Century* by Susie Nash (from the Studies in Medieval Culture Series); *Glaister's Encyclopedia of the Book* (a reissue of the 1979 second edition containing over 3,000 definitions of the terms used in bookbinding, printing, papermaking, and the book trade); *Dictionary of British Comic Artists, Writers and Editors* by Alan Clark; *Mapping Time & Space: How Medieval Mapmakers Viewed the World* by Evelyn Edson; *English Short Title Catalogue 1473–1800 on CD-ROM* (a "must have" reference for academic libraries); *Alice's Adventures Under Ground Address Book* (one of a number of gift address books); *British Bird Sounds on CD*; *The Mythical Quest: In Search of Adventure, Romance & Enlightenment* (introduction by Penelope Lively; stories retold by Rosalind Kerven).

The British Library welcomes trade orders with delivery carried out by **Turpin Distribution Services.**

Query letters and SASEs should be directed to:

Catherine Brittan, Sales and Marketing

Dana Way, Editorial and Rights

Anne Young, Non-Book Publishing

CONRAN OCTOPUS LTD.

224 Heron Quays
London E14 4JP
England
(44) 171 531 8400
fax: (44) 171 531 8627
ISDN: (44) 171 379 1061
conran.octopus@co.uk (e-mail)

Conran Octopus is a niche specialist publisher of beautifully designed and lavishly illustrated nonfiction titles on cookery, crafts, gardening, interiors and design, general design, and travel.

New from Conran Octopus: *The Family Home: Relaxed, Informal Living for All Ages* by Jo Copestick (shows how to adapt your home, with style, to create the safe, welcoming haven away from the rigors of everyday life); *Furniture and Furnishings* by Melanie Paine (from a new series of four focused, stylish titles by experts in their fields, each book takes a feature of the home and explores its decorative possibilities; contains illustrated product directories, essential advice on estimating quantities, lists of tools and equipment to buy or rent for each job, and notes on problem-solving. Also gives up-to-the-minute ideas to suit all tastes and budgets; picture captions analyze the reasons for the success of each room scheme); *Vietnamese Street Food* by Annabel Doling with photography by Jeremy Hopley (light cuisine with sophisticated but simple flavors—between Chinese and Thai—from the stalls of Hanoi and Saigon; many recipes are assembled by the diners themselves, with fresh herbs, chili and seasoning added to taste); and *Lorna Wing's Party Food: Simple and Stunning Ideas for Fingers and Forks* by Lorna Wing with photography by Jan Baldwin (combines Lorna Wing's innovative approach to food with her confidence and knowledge of organizing successful events).

Gardening, crafts, and general: *The Essential Garden Book* by Terence Conran and Dan Pearson tackles design in a common-sense way, showing how to decide what you want from your garden, and then how to achieve those aims; *Secret Gardens* by Jennifer Potter (techniques for designing retreats, with hints for creating surprise and heightening suspense, and planting ideas for the perfect hideaway); *Shane Connolly's Wedding Flowers* by Shane Connolly with photography by Jan Baldwin (a personal approach to wedding flowers that reflect the individuality of today's brides by insisting that all floral decisions should flow from the bride and her dress; provides twenty interpretations based on classical, romantic, and alternative themes that embrace the eclecticism of the international fashion scene); and *Up in Smoke* by Jonathan Futrell with photography by Lisa Linder (takes an upbeat look at today's cigar-smoking lifestyle, an exciting look at cigar paraphernalia, gives profiles of the different types of cigars; and atmospheric images of the clubs in which to smoke).

Query letters and SASEs should be directed to:

Denny Hemming, Acquisitions Editor, Interior Design, General Design, Architecture, Crafts and Popular Culture

Stewart Cooper, Acquisitions Editor, Garden Design, Gardening, Flower Crafts, Cookery and Travel

EGMONT CHILDREN'S BOOKS

Michelin House
81 Fulham Road
London SW3 6RB
England
(44) 171 581 9393
fax: (44) 171 225 9726

Egmont became a power to reckon with in the United Kingdom market for children's books in April 1998. The acquisition of Reed Children's Books, which recorded sales of a quarter billion DKK in 1997, makes Egmont Books a significant presence in the UK. The new company, called **Egmont Children's Books,** is one of the leading publishers of fiction and picture books for children in the UK.

Egmont Children's Books comprises six companies and several imprints, including **Methuen, Mammoth,** and **Heinemann.** The 87 employees publish numerous children's books, with an annual total of 230 titles and 10 million books sold in the UK market. They also sell the publishing company's rights through 80 partners in twenty-six countries, including several Egmont companies.

Egmont Children's Books now has publishing rights to numerous characters known by children and young TV viewers and readers all over the world. These include names such as Winnie-the-Pooh, Postman Pat, Bananas in Pyjamas, Barbie, Thomas the Tank Engine, Sesame Street, Muppets, Action Man, Disney Playbooks, Lego Duplo and Lego Primo.

A sample of Egmont Children's specialties: *A Hole at the Pole* by Chris d'Lacey, illustrated by Joanna Carey (story about Billy, who wants to mend the hole at the North Pole with sticky tape, but everybody laughs at him until a magical ice bear shows him how to set about mending the hole properly and Billy is able to tell everyone at school that cars and aerosols are causing the problems); *Twist of Gold* by Michael Morpurgo (when the potato famine of 1847 strikes Ireland, whole families are wiped out. Sean and Annie have been taught not to trust the English, but an English dragoon befriends them and encourages them to leave Ireland as the fever claims more lives. They set off in search of their father in America, making the epic journey from Cork to California); *Rise and Shine* (a Sesame Street storybook designed to help children learn words and language and to take the first steps towards reading proficiency); *Winnie-the-Pooh's Teatime Cookbook* (inspired by A. A. Milne and with decorations by Ernest H. Shepard, from the prestigious Methuen *Wisdom of Pooh* list); *Thomas the Tank Engine* (the famous set of 105 stories within 26 little books by The Rev. W. Awdry; now revised by Wilbert Awdry's son Christopher into a 40-book series that has sold 8 million copies worldwide to date); *Barbie Secrets Journal* (designed with a special flap on each page behind which users can record and hide their most personal thoughts and wishes); *Build A Book* by Cherry Denman, author/illustrator (includes themed stickers and a blank book to help children create their very own story book); and *Sun Snow Stars Sky* by Catherine and Laurence Anholt (one of the UK's top author and artist teams for children's picture books produce a series of books to help children learn all about the weather; delightfully illustrated introduction to the seasons for the very young).

Query letters and SASEs should be directed to:

Jane Winterbotham, Managing Director

Gill Evans, Publishing Director, Mammoth (Fiction, Picture Books, and Hamlyn)

Sara Domville, Rights Director

FOLENS LIMITED

Albert House
Apex Business Centre
Boscombe Road
Dunstable
Bedfordshire LU5 4RL
England
(44) 1582 478110
fax: (44) 1582 475524
folens@folens.com (e-mail)
www.folens.com

Folens, founded in 1988, is a specialized producer of a wide variety of materials for the teaching profession. Its curriculum resources include high-quality, superbly illustrated books for primary education covering art, English, geography, history, mathematics, music, physical education, religious education, technology, and science, with some titles featured under a **Belair** imprint. It offers teaching resources such as the "ideas bank," lesson-plan materials, poster and display items, software, and a range of professional development titles. Secondary-level education materials include books on English and religious education, and a special needs catalog offers materials for the specialist teacher.

Folens is interested in new ideas and welcomes new authors, but by and large these authors tend to be teachers. This fact is reflected in the imaginative excellence of their products, which show that a great deal of hands-on "frontline" experience has contributed to the development, layout, and presentation of their books.

Emblematic of Folens: *Basic Rules of English Grammar* (a series of structured textbooks to help develop children's understanding of the basic rules of grammar, for ages 6–11 years); *PE in Action: The Complete Physical Education Programme* (a comprehensive scheme of physical education activities designed to provide a well-planned, progressive, flexible, and stimulating approach to the teaching of PE across the primary age range); *Brain Waves: The Leading Photocopiable Teacher Idea Books* (a series of teaching resource books on a range of subjects, customizable for class, group, or individual activities). From the **Belair** imprint: *Maths on Display* (covers all main areas of math with emphasis on activities and creative ideas); *Stress Management for the Individual Teacher* by Sandra H. Mills (a professional development handbook); *The Inspectors Call: A Guide to Managing the School Inspection Week* by Jim Donnelly; *Hinduism* (from the photopacks book series in secondary religious education); and *Writing Skills* by Maureen Mills and Margaret Underhill (a special needs title for secondary education).

Query letters and SASEs should be directed to:

Steve Harrison, Director of Publishing

FOULSHAM

The Publishing House
Bennetts Close
Cippenham
Slough
Berkshire SL1 5AP
England
(44) 1753 526769
fax: (44) 1753 535003

Foulsham is essentially one of the "older guard" of the publishing world, having been in business since 1819. The house produces titles for the mass market over a wide range of popular interests that include family health, dieting, beauty and fashion, food and drink, babies' names, sport and leisure, mind, body and spirit, the paranormal, divination, dreams, astrology, personal psychology, ancient history, collectibles, careers, driving, gambling, humor, hobbies and pastimes, languages, mind games and puzzles, finance, and family reference.

As may be expected with such an established house, it has a solid network of international representatives with distribution handled by **Macmillan Distribution Ltd.**

Some of Foulsham's latest offerings: *Mind Over Cancer: Reposition Your Attitude, Use the Advice You Receive and Grow Into Good Health*; *Family Aromatherapy* by Joan Radford (an extensively updated edition of a bestselling title); *The Rambler's Yearbook and Accommodation Guide 1999* (a brand leader and the official Rambler's Association Guide with over 2,300 guesthouses and 400 self-catering cottages, flats, and farmhouses, as well as the best walks); *Intelligent Puzzles* by Ken Russell and Philip Carter (the Mensa UK puzzle editors); *Winning Horse Racing Formulae: Betting to Win: The 12 Golden Rules of Successful Betting, Stake Right, Win More and Lose Less,* and *7*

Steps to a Better Selection Strategy by David Duncan; *The Complete Book of Dreams* by Edwin Raphael; *Every Woman a Witch: Take Advantage of the Natural Forces of Life* by Cassandra Eason; *101 School Assembly Stories: True Stories, Fables, Poems, Folk Tales* by Frank Carr; and *The Complete Book of Indian Cooking* by Premila Lal.

Query letters and SASEs should be directed to:

Editorial, as on previous page.

GARNET PUBLISHING, LTD.

8 Southern Court
South Street
Reading
Berkshire RG1 4QS
England
(44) 118 959 7847
fax: (44) 118 959 7356
inquiry@garnet-ithica.demon.co.uk (e-mail)
www.garnet-ithaca.demon.co.uk

Since its foundation in 1990, Garnet Publishing has expanded its list to 160 titles to date, on a wide range of subjects from translated fiction to high-quality illustrated books designed to offer readers enriching cross-cultural insights. Art, architecture, travel, and photography continue to feature strongly on their list, as does religious studies. Garnet's program boasts a number of new highlights, including *Jerusalem* (an addition to their successful *Caught in Time: Great Photographic Archives* series). Two important additions to the growing architecture list are *The Story of Islamic Architecture* and *The Architecture of Oman*. The latter, whose foreword is written by HRH The Prince of Wales, is the culmination of 4 years of dedicated, original research by Dr. Salma Samar Damluji and was featured at an exhibition of Omani Architecture at the Royal Institute of British Architects (RIBA). Garnet Publishing also recently completed and published a huge project on behalf of the Sultan Qaboos University in Oman—J.G. Lorimer's *Gazetteer of the Persian Gulf, Oman and Central Arabia*—in a nineteen-volume dual language (English/Arabic) edition. This, too, is featured in the RIBA exhibition. Also increasing is the series published for the Center for the Muslim Contribution to Civilization with the publication of two volumes of the four-volume *Life of the Prophet Muhammad*, while Garnet's educational division continues to expand its TEFL activities.

Ithaca Press, an academic imprint now belonging to Garnet, was established in 1973. Ithaca publishes books mainly on the Middle East, in the fields of history, politics, and international relations, economics, social anthropology, religion, and literature; the imprint also has an extensive backlist. Ithaca has expanded rapidly in recent years and broadened its range of academic books to include subjects of more general interest, such as women's studies, legal studies, and biography. A new series, *Ithaca Press Paperbacks,* was launched in autumn 1996 to reach a wider audience, including in particular students of the social sciences.

Also from Garnet: *The Day It Rained Bricks and Bats: And Other Tales from the Gulf* by Maruf Khawaja (a book of humorous articles on cultural diversity in the Gulf); *Petra: Jordan's Most Famous Historical Attraction: A Travellers' Guide* by Rosalyn Maqsood; *The Bretschneider Albums: 19th Century Paintings of Life in China* (introduced by K. Y. Solonin, annotated by Frances Wood); *Patchwork Quilts for Beds: New Techniques for Classic Design* by Pippa Abrahams; *The Fires of Excellence: Spanish and Portugese Oriental Architecture* by Miles Danby (photographs by Matthew Weinreb); and *Scheherezade Presents . . .* adapted by Jo Deighton (international children's stories in a multi-volume series).

Ithaca titles: *Political Islam and the United States: A Study of U.S. Policy Towards Islamist Movements in the Middle East* by Maria do Ceu Pinto; *The Last Khedive of Egypt: Memoirs of Abbas Hilmi II* (translated and edited by Amira Sonbol); *Islamic Fundamentalism: Myths and Realities* (edited by Ahmad S. Moussalli); *Palestine and the Law: Guidelines for the Resolution of the Arab-Israel Conflict* by Musa Mazzawi; *Water Resources Development in Ethiopia: An Evaluation of Present Experience and Future Planning Concepts* by Zewdie Abate.

Query letters and SASEs should be directed to:

Emma Hawker, Acquisitions Editor, Garnet Publishing

Adel Kamal, Acquisitions Editor, Ithaca

GOLDEN COCKEREL PRESS

ASSOCIATED UNIVERSITY PRESSES
CORNWALL BOOKS
CYGNUS ARTS

16 Barter Street
London WC1A 2AH
(44) 171 405 7979
fax: (44) 171 404 3598
lindesa@ibm.net (e-mail)

Associated University Presses is, in fact, an American New Jersey-based company; **Golden Cockerel** acts as its United Kingdom office and branch. Current member presses of the parent company are: **Bucknell University Press, University of Delaware Press, Fairleigh Dickinson University Press, Lehigh University Press,** and **Susquehanna University Press.** This press shows a particularly strong and rich interest in literature, whether English or foreign (for example: Russian, Scandinavian, and Portugese) from medieval to modern. However, Golden Cockerel also markets titles in the Arts and Humanities in general, with music, cinema, film, art history, fine and decorative arts, theology, philosophy, social studies, history, and politics all finding representation. A somewhat smaller number of books appear in the science and technology category.

Also of note is that, aside from its current new offerings, Associated maintains a very considerable and substantial backlist of academic tomes. Some of its latest: medieval and renaissance English literature, *Sex, Gender and Desire in the Plays of Christopher Marlowe* by Sara Munson Deats; American literature, *The Turn of the Mind: Constituting Consciousness in Henry James* by Adre Marshall; Spanish, Portugese, and Latin American literature, *A Star-Crossed Golden Age: Myth and the Spanish Comedia* (edited by Frederick A. De Armas); cinema, *French-Speaking Women Film Directors: A Guide* by Janis L. Pallister; education, *Western Perspectives on Chinese Higher Education: A Model for Cross-Cultural Inquiry* by Xiuwu R. Liu.

And from the backlist: Italian literature, *Boiardo's Orlando Innamorato: An Ethics of Desire* by Jo Ann Cavallo; world literature, *John Edgar Wideman: Reclaiming the African Personality* by D. D. Mbalia; fine and decorative arts, *John Hutton: Artist and Glass Engraver* by M. Brentnall; European history and politics, *The Moral Treatment of Returning Warriors in Early Medieval and Modern Times* by B. J. Verkamp; North and South American history, *The Social Ideas of American Physicians (1776–1976): Studies of the Humanitarian Tradition in Medicine* by Eugene Perry Link; world history and politics, *The Mind of African Strategists: A Study of Kalabari* by Nimi Wariboko; theology, *Between Reformed Scholasticism and Pan-Protestantism: Jean-Alphonse Turretin (1671–1737) and Enlightened Orthodoxy at the Academy of Geneva* by Martin I. Klauber; philosophy, *Giles Deleuze and the Question of Philosophy* by Philip Goodchild; social studies, *The World Bank and the Environmental Challenge* by

P. Le Prestre; and science and technology, *The Rainbow Makers: The Origins of the European Synthetic Dyestuffs Industry* by Anthony Travis.

Cygnus Arts, a hardback division of Golden Cockerel, specializes in the categories of art, antiques and collecting, cinema, dance, media studies, crime, and music. A current antiques title: *The Scottish Pistol: Its History, Manufacture and Design* by Martin Kelvin. And from media studies: *Uneasy Pleasures: The Male as Erotic Object* by Kenneth MacKinnon.

Query letters and SASEs should be addressed to:

Andrew Lindesay, Director

Tamar Lindesay, Director

GOWER PUBLISHING LTD.

Gower House
Croft Road
Aldershot
Hampshire GU11 3HR
England
(44) 1252 331551
fax: (44) 1252 344405
gower@gowerpub.demon.co.uk (e-mail)

Gower is the original imprint of **Ashgate Publishing.** Founded in 1967 by Nigel Farrow, the chairman of Ashgate, Gower is today one of the world's leading publishers on management and business practice. Its program ranges from 1,000-page handbooks to practical manuals to popular entertaining books on the practicalities of coping with working life, shelf references, and inspirational books that help organizations plan for their future creatively. In particular, Gower covers the main functions of management, including human resource development, sales and marketing, project management, finance, as well as produces training videos and activities manuals on a wide range of management skills. Gower books are aimed at the real manager facing real issues and juggling a busy schedule.

Some representative titles: *Don't Put Socks on the Hippopotamus—and Other Rules of Business Life* by Terry Kelley; *The Gower Handbook of Management,* 4th edition (edited by Dennis Lock); *Creating a Stress-Free Office* by Simon Priest and Jim Welch; *Customer Clubs and Loyalty Programmes: A Practical Guide* by Stephen A. Butscher; *Flip Chart Games for Trainers* by Graham Roberts-Phelps; *Organisations & People,*

Volume 5, Issues 1–4 (Quarterly Journal of the Association for Management Education and Development); *The Assertive Social Worker* by Patricia McBride; *Strategic Supply Chain Integration* (edited by John Gattorna); and *The Student Skills Guide* by Sue Drew and Rosie Bingham.

Query letters and SASEs should be directed to:

Jonathan Norman, Projects Director

GRANTA BOOKS

2/3 Hanover Yard
Noel Road
London N1 8BE
England
(44) 171 704 9776
fax: (44) 171 354 3469
info@granta.com (e-mail)
www.granta.com

Granta publishes literary fiction and a range of topical nonfiction titles. It also produces its own magazine, *Granta: The Magazine of New Writing,* which has attracted acclaim for its contribution to contemporary literature and political writing with pieces by such authors as Martin Amis, Hilary Mantel, Linda Grant, Ariel Dorfman, Joyce Carol Oates, and Julia Blackburn.

Fiction from Granta: *Paper* by John McCabe, an anarchically comic exploration of logic, fallibility, obsessive behavior, science, and manslaughter; *The House of Mathilde* by Hassan Daoud, translated by Peter Theroux (a story of human survival in Lebanon set amid the murderous simplicities of civil war); *Winter in Lisbon* by Antonio Munoz Molina, translated by Sonia Soto (a haunting exploration of the lethal extremes to which we can be driven by love, art, and money).

Nonfiction: *Having None Of It: Women, Men and the Future of Work* by Suzanne Franks; *The First and the Last* by Isaiah Berlin with an introduction by Henry Hardy (the earliest known story and the last essay by Sir Isaiah Berlin); *As We Know It: Coming to Terms with an Evolved Mind* by Marek Kohn (an analytical survey of social biology and a sympathetic attempt to reconcile "nature and nurture").

Query letters and SASEs should be directed to:

Granta, as above

GREENHILL BOOKS/LIONEL LEVENTHAL LIMITED

Park House
1 Russell Gardens
London NW11 9NN
England
(44) 181 458 6314
fax: (44) 181 905 5245
lionelleventhal@compuserve.com (e-mail)
www.greenhillbooks.com

This publishing house, together with its imprints, is a specialized publisher of books on all aspects of warfare and the military. Here both the expert historian and the generally fascinated will find something of interest and value.

Greenhill and its imprints—**Stackpole Books, Combined Publishing, Presidio Press, Emperor's Press, Savas Publishing, Concord Publications,** and **Medals of America Press**—cover the art of war and early history, the major twentieth-century wars, The American Revolution and Civil War, wars of the Middle Ages, Napoleonic wars, Zulu wars, naval warfare, aviation, special forces, equipment, uniforms and guns, strategy, tactics, and leadership, as well as guides, and reference books.

Greenhill's tremendous range of material, which comes both from new title offerings and a substantial stocklist, includes: *On Wellington: The Duke and His Art of War* by Jac Weller (edited by Andrew Uffindell, with an introduction by the present Duke of Wellington); from the *Greenhill Military Manuals* series, *Ammunition: Small Arms, Grenades and Projected Munitions* by Ian V. Hogg; *A History of the Art of War in the Middle Ages* by Sir Charles Oman (a classic history of warfare); *Don Troiani's Soldiers in America, 1754–1865* by Don Troiani, Earl J. Coates, and James L. Kochan (foreword by Brian Pohanka: a lavishly illustrated guide to the uniforms and equipment of troops on all sides); *The Deadly Brotherhood: The American Combat Soldier in World War II* by John C. McManus; *Into the Tiger's Jaw, America's First Black Marine Aviator: The Autobiography of Lt. Gen. Frank E. Peterson* by Frank E. Peterson with J. Alfred Phelps; *The Principles of War for the Information Age* by Robert R. Leonhard; *Death Valley: The Summer Offensive, I Corps, August 1969* by Keith William Nolan; *The Generals of Gettysburg: An Appraisal of the Leaders of America's Greatest Battle* by Larry Tagg; *The Illustrated Guide to the World's Top Naval Special Forces Units* by Samuel M. Katz.

Query letters and SASEs should be directed to:

Editorial, as above

GRUB STREET

The Basement
10 Chivalry Road
London SW11 1HT
England
(44) 171 924 3966
fax: (44) 171 738 1009

This small publisher is immediately distinctive for the nature of its interests in two highly focused and completely unrelated nonfiction areas: food and wine books, and military aviation history. The food and wine titles cover the entire gastronomic gamut, from general basic "how-to" to books on the cuisine of individual countries or cultures. In the case of the latter, Grub Street offers a list consisting of biographies and auto-biographies of pilots who have flown in the major wars of the twentieth century, with a number of the books being authored by famous former aviators. The result is a collection with general and popular appeal dealing with one specific aspect of warfare experience.

Grub Street Aviation: *Above Flanders' Fields: A Complete History of the Belgian Air Force in World War I* by Walter Pieters; *Hunting with Richthofen, The Bodenschatz Diaries: Sixteen Months of Battle with J. G. Freiherr Von Richthofen No. 1* (translated by Jan Hayzlett); *Duel for the Sky: Ten Crucial Air Battles of World War II Vividly Recreated* by Christopher Shores; *To Hell and Back: True Life Experiences of Bomber Command at War* by Mel Rolfe; *Who Downed the Aces in WWI?* by Norman Franks.

Grub Street Food and Wine: *Moroccan Cuisine* by Paula Wolfert; *Simply Seaweed: Tempting Recipes for Samphire, Seaweed and Sea Vegetables* by Lesley Ellis; *Classic Indian Vegetarian Cooking* by Julie Sahni; *The Cook's Encyclopedia: Ingredients and Processes* by Tom Stobart (an acclaimed reference source for cooks, students, and all lovers of food); *Lebanese Cuisine* by Anissa Helou; *The Everyday Wholefood Cookbook* (edited by Ruth Lea).

Query letters and SASEs should be directed to:

John Davies, Acquisition Editor, Aviation/Military History

Anne Dolamore, Acquisition Editor, Food and Wine

ROBERT HALE PUBLISHERS

Clerkenwell House
45–47 Clerkenwell Greeen
London EC1R 0HT
England
(44) 171 251 1661
fax: (44) 171 490 4958

Robert Hale is a publisher of mainstream fiction and nonfiction across a broad range of categories, and the exclusive distributor of the distinguished photography list *Aperture.*

Newest highlights from Robert Hale: *The English Village Church* by R. J. Brown (study of the village church, England's richest legacy of medieval architecture and art); *Breadmaking at Home: The Ultimate Instruction Guide* by Harold Bagust (invaluable guide for both beginners and those who want to improve their breadmaking skills); *Let Me Hear Your Voice: A Family's Triumph over Autism* by Catherine Maurice (a mother's profoundly moving story of how her two children were rescued from the tragedy of autism; first account in which diagnosis, therapy, and authentic recovery are fully documented); *Gemmologists' Compendium* by Robert Webster, FGA (revised by E. Alan Jobbins, FGA; the seventh edition of the "bible" of professional and amateur gemmologists, as well as retail jewellers); *A Cynic's Guide to Management* by Stuart McKibbin (introduces the "signal manager," who is governed by mortal fear of "sending the wrong signals," the "evangelical manager," who tenaciously clings to the missionary position, the "ballcock manager," kept afloat by the energies and talents of subordinates—and many, many more).

Also: *The Craft of the Media Interview* by Dennis Barker (comprehensive and practical guidebook to interview practice, with a detailed examination of the various techniques); *The Dreadful Debutante* by Marion Chesney (fictional story of Mira who, undaunted by her town and its ridiculous marriage market, knows her heart belongs to Lord Charles, subject of her dreams since she was a child—despite the fact that Charles had eyes only for her ever-perfect sister Drusilla); and *A Witch's Spell* by Barbara Cartland (Hermia, the beautiful daughter of the vicar of Little Millbrooke who meets a cynical and sardonic gentleman who is having difficulty removing a shoe from his horse's hoof . . .).

Query letters and SASEs should be directed to:

John Hale, Director

HARCOURT BRACE & COMPANY LIMITED

24–28 Oval Road
London NW1 7DX
England
(44) 181 308 5710
www.hbuk.co.uk

Harcourt Brace is another of the larger publishing operations whose titles are marketed and distributed under a variety of specialist imprints.

The **W. B. Saunders Company** is a Harcourt Brace division publishing high-quality text books, references, periodicals, and electronic products in the fields of medicine, nursing, dentistry, veterinary medicine, and the health-related professions. It has a spectacular bank of new and stocklist titles and is quite probably correct in its claim to be "a world leader in health-care publishing."

From Saunders: *Dorland's Electronic Medical Dictionary*, 28th edition (new CD-ROM version of a classic medical reference); *Legal Aspects of Emergency Medical Services* by Bruce M. Cohn and Alan J. Azzara; *Drug Therapy Decision Making Guide* (edited by James McCormack, Glen Brown, Marc Levine, Robert Rangno, and John Ruedy); *Textbook of Physical Diagnosis: History and Diagnosis,* 3rd edition, by Mark H. Swartz; *Textbook of Neuroanatomy* by Alvin M. Burt; *An Atlas of Head and Neck Surgery,* 3rd edition, by John M. Lore; *Plastic and Reconstructive Surgery of the Nose* by Nabil I. Elsahy; *Dermatology in Emergency Care* by Libby Edwards; *Obstetrics: Normal & Problem Pregnancies,* 3rd edition (edited by S. G. Gabbe, J. R. Niebyl, and J. L. Simpson); *Community Health Nursing: Promoting the Health of Aggregates,* 2nd edition, by Janice M. Swanson and Mary Nies; and *Clinical Textbook for Veterinary Technicians* by Denis M. McCumin.

Harcourt's **Academic Press** is itself an award-winning publisher of major works of reference. These books are designed to inform, educate, and enlighten by providing necessary sources for researchers, professionals, and students, and are intended to become, as comprehensive and authoritative works, the leading references in their field.

From AP: *Encyclopedia of the Solar System* (edited by Paul Weissman, Lucy-Ann McFadden, and Torrence Johnson; with foreword by Sally Ride, America's first woman in space); *Encyclopedia of Toxicology* (editor-in-chief Philip Wexler; a comprehensive collection of toxicological principles and chemical hazards); *Encyclopedia of Mental Health* (editor-in-chief Howard S. Friedman; a three-volume set containing almost 170 articles written by more than 250 leaders in the field); *Encylopedia of Creativity* (edited by Mark A. Runco and Steven Pritzker; a sourcebook of specialized information about creativity and motivation); and *Academic Press Dictionary of Science and Technology* (new CD-ROM version).

In association with its own imprints—**T & AD Poyser, Poyser Natural History, AP Natural World**—Academic Press also publishes a wide range of books on ornithology and natural history subjects for both the keen amateur and professional ecologist. This range of works has acquired an international reputation for high quality as they are also designed to appeal to the widest possible audience, packed with fascinating detail, and beautifully illustrated by leading ornithological and natural history artists.

A sample of the latest from this collection: *A Naturalist's Shetland* by J. Laughton Johnston (the only full description of the natural history of Shetland in print from T & AD Poyser); *Sperm Competition and Sexual Selection* (edited by Tim Birkhead and Anders Moller, from AP); *A Photographic Guide to North American Raptors* by Brian Wheeler and William Clark (also from AP); *A Natural History of Australia* by Tim M. Berra (from AP Natural World); and *Newts and Salamanders of Europe* by Richard Griffiths (illustrated by Bas Teunis, from Poyser Natural History).

Query letters and SASEs should be directed to:

Editorial, as on previous page

HOLLIS DIRECTORIES

Harlequin House
7 High Street
Teddington
Middlesex TW11 8EL
England
(44) 181 977 7711
fax: (44) 181 977 1133
hollis@hollis-pr.demon.co.uk (e-mail)
www.hollis-pr.co.uk

Hollis is an expert specialist producer of authoritative and comprehensive information directories and reference sources. It has carved out a distinctive niche for itself and established an international reputation specifically for the publication of directories on national and international print media, public relations, marketing, corporate hospitality, direct mail, the advertising industry, and the field of sponsorship and donations.

Leading Hollis titles include: *Willings Press Guide* (a national and international guide in two volumes now in its 124th edition; provides extensive professionally researched coverage of the UK and international print media—national and regional newspapers, magazines, periodicals, and special interest titles); *Advertisers Annual: The Blue Book* (a huge compendium providing data on every aspect of the advertising industry, including agencies and clients, advertisers and brands, media owners, and league tables); *Hollis Sponsorship & Donations Yearbook* (the definitive guide to the sponsorship market and to thousands of sponsorship and fundraising opportunities); *Hollis UK Press & Public Relations Annual* (the bible of the industry now out in a special 30th anniversary edition); and *Hollis Europe: The Directory of European Public Relations & PR Networks* (an essential guide to PR and corporate communications across the entire continent).

Query letters and SASEs should be directed to:

Gary Zabel, Managing Director

INTER-VARSITY PRESS

Norton Street
Nottingham NG7 3HR
England
(44) 115 978 1054
fax: (44) 115 942 2694
ivp@ivpnottm.compulink.co.uk (e-mail)
www.ivpbooks.com

IVP aims to publish Bible-based books that build faith and help the church to grow worldwide. With its highly qualified editorial team, IVP commissions a wide range of quality titles from reference and study guides to lifestyle and devotional books. It continues to publish well-known and respected authors, such as John Stott, Alister Mc-Grath, and Becky Manley Pippert, while seeking to develop new authors such as Steve Ayers, Al Hsu, and Nick Pollard. Categories of special interest include: Bible background and commentaries, Bible study guides, biography, Christian classics, Christian life, church life, contemporary social issues, contours of Christian theology, dictionaries and encyclopedias, doctrine and theology, evangelism and follow-up, gifts, love, sex and marriage, world missions, and world religions and cults.

IVP titles: *Arguing with God: The Problem of Evil* by Hugh Silvester; *At the Heart of the Universe: What Christians Believe* by Peter Jensen; *Dictionary of Paul and His Letters* (edited by Ralph P. Martin, Gerald F. Hawthorne, and Daniel G. Reid); *End of Story? What Jesus Said About the Future of the World* by Stephen H. Travis; *Sex and Sensibility* by Steve Ayers; *Testing Darwinism: An Easy to Understand Guide* by Phillip E. Johnson; *The Message of the Thessalonians: Preparing for the Coming King* by John Stott (from the large *The Bible Speaks Today* series); and *Joshua* by Richard Hess (a volume from the IVP *Tyndale Old Testament Commentaries* series).

IVP also publishes under the imprint names of **Apollos** and **Crossway.**

Apollos is an academic imprint whose books are designed to be used by teachers and scholars working at more advanced levels. Its titles are drawn from all parts of the world and cover a range of disciplines. Typical of Apollos: *Human Nature at the Millennium: Reflections on the Integration of Psychology and Christianity* by Malcolm A. Jeeves; *The Moral Quest: Foundations of Christian Ethics* by Stanley J. Grenz; *God & The Biologist: Faith at the Frontiers of Science* by R. J. Berry; and *Dictionary of the Later New Testament & Its Developments: A Compendium of Contemporary Biblical Scholarship* (edited by R. P. Martin and P. H. Davids).

Crossway publishes books for churches on the cutting edge of modern society, stimulating growth and personal discipleship. It specializes in three areas: Bible resources—for housegroups and individuals (spearheaded by the popular Crossway Bible Guides series); church development—books on evangelism, discipleship, and Christian living; and home life—books on parenthood and other family relationships, and tools for practical Christian living. These are complemented by contemporary biography, real stories of faith in the modern world; Christian fiction, conveying wholesome values and exploring questions of faith; and devotional books, direct, heartwarming, and encouraging true spirituality.

From the latest Crossway offerings: *The Bible with Pleasure: How to Get the Most out of Reading Your Bible* by Stephen Motyer; *Jesus: A Biblical Defence of His Deity* by Josh McDowell and Bart Larson (a church development title); *Pollution and the Death of Man* by F. A. Schaeffer and U. Middleman (on how the answer to the ecological crises of our day is found only in the truths of biblical Christianity); *The 77 Habits of Highly Ineffective Christians* by Chris Fabry; *Held by the Watchtower: Set Free by Christ* by Susan Thorne (a dramatic autobiographical account); *Then the Curtain Opened: Christian Witness in Eastern Europe* by Clive Doubleday.

IVP and its imprints welcome new authors. Query letters and SASEs should be directed to:

Brian Wilson, Commercial Director, IVP

Colin Duriez, Editor, Apollos

Dr. Mark Smith, Editor, Apollos

Derek Wood, Editor, Crossway

JANE'S INFORMATION GROUP

Sentinel House
163 Brighton Road
Coulsdon
Surrey CR5 2NH
England
(44) 181 700 3700
fax: (44) 181 763 1005
info@janes.co.uk (e-mail)
www.janes.com

Jane's is a specialist information service provider with over a hundred years of experience devoted to editorial accuracy and worldwide coverage. Its mission is "to provide rapid, accurate, and impartial military, security, transportation and technical information." It achieves this primary aim by providing information across a range of categories through a variety of media including yearbooks, magazines, or newsletters, binders and updates, electronic delivery systems such as e-mail, microfiche, and CD-ROM, and dynamic tailored combinations of all of these formats.

Jane's publishing output covers defense, research studies, and special reports, U.S. market intelligence, geopolitical issues, the police, and transport. Recently, Jane's expanded its publishing operation by adding an Asian office to two existing centers in London and Washington. With its strengthened international outlook, Jane's is confident that it can help industry, military, government, and university professionals around the world make the most of the coming new millennium.

In the current Jane's program: *Jane's Helicopter Markets and Systems* (a clear view of the specifications and market positions of 150 main models); *Jane's Fighting Ships* (the world's most authoritative naval encyclopedia); *Jane's Radar and Electronic Warfare Systems* (a one-stop guide to development programs, specifications, and operational status); *Jane's World Insurgency and Terrorism* (a vital tool in the battle to understand and combat world terrorism); *International Police Review* (a new magazine on the latest developments in law enforcement throughout the world); *Jane's World Railways* (in its 41st year; the foremost information source on railway manufacturers and operators); and *Jane's Airports and Handling Agents* (essential flight-planning data on more than 1,600 airports worldwide).

Query letters and SASEs should be directed to:

Alfred Rolington, Group Managing Director

KOGAN PAGE LTD.

120 Pentonville Road
London N1 9JN
England
(44) 171 278 0433
fax: (44) 171 837 6348
kpinfo@kogan-page.co.uk (e-mail)

Kogan Page is a mid-size publisher with a substantial catalog of titles specializing in the fields of business, training, and education.

Kogan Page publishes books about business and management, finance and banking, marketing and public relations, training and development, careers advice, education, health care, economics and social science, and transport and logistics. Its established expertise in these fields means that Kogan Page is able to attract a substantial number of well-known and talented authors to its program. In addition to distributing its own products, Kogan Page also acts as distributor to other publishers, including American Banking Association, AP Information Services—London, Earthscan Publications Ltd.—London, Island Press—USA, Jessica Kingsley Publishers—London, and Tudor Business Publishing.

Highlights and new books from Kogan Page: *Connected Intelligence: The Arrival of the Web Society* by Derrick de Kerckhove; *Great Myths of Business* by William Davis (revised edition of an acclaimed work); *The Making of a Manager: How to Launch Your Career on the Fast Track* by Donald A. Wellman (a bestseller); *United Kingdom: Business Gateway to Europe* (consultant-editor Timothy Foster; published in association with the Department of Trade and Industry with the endorsement of the British-American Chamber of Commerce and the Canada-United Kingdom Chamber of Commerce); *Your Bank: Make It Work for Your Business: A Practical Guide for the Small and Growing Business* by Iayn G. Clark and Penelope Kimber; *Your Child's Education* by Niki Chesworth (from the *Lifeplanner* series); *Marketing Communications: An Integrated Approach,* 2nd edition, by Paul Smith; *Using Presentations in Training and Development* by Leslie Rae; *Net That Job! Using the World Wide Web to Develop Your Career and Find Work* by Irene Krechowiecka; *A Handbook for Teachers in Universities & Colleges: A Guide to Improving Teaching Methods,* 3rd edition, by David Newble and Robert Cannon; *Dealing with Difficult Staff in the NHS* by Robin Gourlay; and *Crawford's Directory of City Connections,* 20th edition.

Query letters and SASEs should be directed to:

Philip Kogan, Managing Director

FRANCES LINCOLN LTD.

4 Torriano Mews
Torriano Avenue
London NW5 2RZ
England
(44) 171 284 4009
fax: (44) 171 485 0490

Frances Lincoln has proudly celebrated more than 20 years in the publishing business. And with some of its achievements, particularly awards and recommendations for children's books, this publisher has had much to celebrate. Frances Lincoln Publishing produces quality illustrated books for both adults and children. Its adult listing covers gardening, interiors, cookery, travel, health, and stationery. It is currently in the process of launching the new "Mind, Body and Spirit" list, including illustrated translations of the Tao Te Ching, the poetry of Rumi, and the Perfection of Wisdom in 8,000 lines. The children's list caters to children aged one to 12. The house specializes in photographic books for the very young, multicultural picture books, educational picture books, and traditional picture books. Frances Lincoln also maintains an art and gift-book list that combines fine art, poetry, and religion for both adults and children.

Hot titles from Frances Lincoln: *The Low Maintenance Garden* by Graham Rose; *The Rice Book: The Definitive Book on the Magic of Rice Cookery* by Sri Owen (winner of the Andre Simon Award for best food book and shortlisted for the James Beard award); *Rooms to Remember: Interiors Inspired by the Past* by Barbara Stoeltie with photographs by Rene Stoeltie; *The New Fabric Magic* by Melanie Paine (an authoritative guide to soft furnishings that no aspiring designer should be without); *Easy Exercises to Relieve Stress* by Hussein Eshref (with photographs by Anthea Sieveking); *Good Planting* by Rosemary Verey (with photographs by Andrew Lawson; practical guide to planting with an eye to shape, texture, and color a garden that interests throughout the seasons); *The Patio Garden* by Hazel Evans (how to design, construct, plant, and furnish the perfect patio); *Through the Woods* by H. E. Bates with wood engravings by Agnes Miller Parker (H. E. Bates' evocation of a year in the life of an English woodland); *Women of the Bible* by Carole Armstrong (illustrated with paintings from the great art museums of the world); *Since Dad Left* by Caroline Binch (a children's picture book); *A Zoo in the Sky* by Jacqueline Mitton and illustrated by Christina Balit (an educational book of animal constellations by a Fellow of the Royal Astronomical Society); *The Drop in My Drink: The Story of Water on Our Planet* by Meredith

Hooper and illustrated by Chris Coady; *My Grandfather Is a Magician: Work and Wisdom in an African Village* by Ifeoma Onyefulu (a children's information book); *Rhymes and Reasons* by Opal Dunn and illustrated by Sally Anne Lambert (learning through rhyme from birth to age 3).

Query letters and SASEs should be directed to:

Kate Cave, Editorial Director, Adult Books, "Mind, Body and Spirit" list

Janetta Otter-Barry, Editorial Director, Children's

LION PUBLISHING PLC

Peter's Way
Sandy Lane West
Oxford OX4 5HG
England
(44) 1865 747550
fax: (44) 1865 747568

Lion offers a broad range of informative and inspiring books for adults, beautifully illustrated gift books, and a wide variety of children's books. All of Lion's books are written for the general reader by Christian authors. The adult religious and spiritual titles cover information and reference, spirituality and spiritual heritage, literature, biography, social issues, gift series and special occasions, body and soul, pocket guides, and fiction. The children's range is also large and its subjects, also typically with a Christian slant, include: Bible stories and prayer, picture books for the very young, activity and novelty books, information and educational books, anthologies and poetry books, fiction for different age groups, texts for secondary level religious education, and a range of titles dealing particularly with Christmas and Easter.

Two of Lion's top-sellers recently appeared in paperback: Walt Wangerin's epic novelization of the Bible, *The Book of God,* and Stephen Lawhead's *Grail,* the fifth and concluding volume of his Arthurian epic. The new *The Lion Christian Meditation Collection* adds to an already popular range of companions and collections successfully designed to become lasting resources. A major feature in the children's range of Bibles and prayer books is the *Lion First Bible* and its new companion volume *The Lion Book of First Prayers.*

Other titles from Lion: *The New Lion Encyclopedia of the Bible* (edited by John Drane; a new edition); *Magdalene: Jesus and the Woman Who Loved Him* by Gordon Thomas; *The Fear Not Angel and Other Stories* by Walter Wangerin (a collection of evocative, powerful stories for older children by a winner of the American Book Award); *The Lion Concise Book of Bible Quotations* (edited by Martin Manser); *Billy Graham in Conversation* by David Frost (interview with Billy Graham); *Our Wedding: A Keepsake Album* (compiled by Sandra Carter; a popular book for recording the events, joys, and highlights of your wedding day; beautifully illustrated and interspersed with thoughts and quotations on love and marriage); *Trying for a Baby* by Dr. Pete Moore; *The Omega Network* by Thomas Locke (fiction); *365 Children's Prayers: Prayers Old and New for Today and Everyday* (compiled by Carol Watson); *Miracle Maker* by Mary Joslin and illustrated by Franscesca Pelizzoli (a treasury of stories about the life of Jesus); *Colouring Book: Rainforest* (a children's activity book); and *God Talk: Science Talk—A Teacher's Guide to Science & Belief* by Adrian Brown, Sue Hookway, and Michael Poole.

Query letters and SASEs should be directed to:

Philip Law, Publishing Manager

LITTLE, BROWN (UK)

Brettenham House
Lancaster Place
London WC2E 7EN
England
(44) 171 911 8000
fax: (44) 171 911 8100

This is another one of the bigger players in the publishing world, producing a great variety of nonfiction titles across mainstream and mass-market categories as well as popular fiction genres such as crime fiction, science fiction and fantasy, horror, war fiction, thrillers and erotica, and books for children.

Typical of the nonfiction subjects are autobiographies/biographies, popular science, health and fitness, garden and DIY, crafts and hobbies, war, history, fine arts, cinema, music, travel, management and business, humor and puzzle books, photography, politics and current affairs, sports, reference and dictionaries, mind and body, as well as books on gender studies and science subjects like anthropology, psychology, and sociology. The house also produces stationery and gift books, posters, and calendars.

A sample of Little Brown fiction: *Mayday* by Nelson Demille and Thomas Block (billed as "the most terrifyingly realistic air-disaster thriller you will ever read"); *There's a Hair in My Dirt: A Worm's Story* by Gary Larson (with foreword by Edward O. Wilson, the creator of the *Far Side* cartoons first "fable"); *The Uncanny* by Andrew

Klavan (a gothic ghost story from the bestselling author of the award-winning *True Crime*); *Point of Origin* by Patricia Cornwell (a novel of high suspense from the mistress of the forensic thriller); *Trophy Wives* by Karren Brady (a story of what really goes on behind the scenes in Britain's favorite sport).

From the nonfiction listing: *Anatomy of Desire: The Science and Psychology of Sex, Love and Marriage* by Simon Andreae; *The Inward Revolution: Discover the Secrets of the Greatest Human Power* by Storm Constantine and Deborah Benstead; *Fit for Action* by Ranulph Fiennes (a guide to maximizing fitness potential from one of the world's most famous explorers); *The Assassination of Marilyn Monroe* by D. H. Wolfe; *Bloodlines: Real Lives in a Great British Hospital* by Andrew Davidson (a compelling portrait of the medical world in action as seen in one of the country's oldest teaching hospitals); *Consilience* by Edward O. Wilson (groundbreaking book on the fundamental unity of all knowledge); *Letters from a Prince: The Letters of Edward, Prince of Wales to Mrs. Freda Dudley Ward* by Rupert Godfrey; *The Body Shop Book* by The Body Shop Team; *Ansel Adams California Postcard Book* by Ansel Adams.

Query letters and SASEs should be directed to:

Editorial, as on previous page

LITTLE TIGER PRESS

22 Manchester Street
London W1M 5PG
England
(44) 171 486 0925
fax: (44) 171 486 0926
MB@magi-publication.demon.co.uk (e-mail)
www.littletiger.okukbooks.com

Little Tiger Press is the new name for a company that until recently was known as **Magi Publications.** The name change from "Magi" harmonizes with the name already established for the company in the United States. Magi started out as publisher of dual-language picture books, mostly brought in from other publishers and translated into different languages. However, for more than 10 years, the company has been producing its own superbly illustrated and high-quality picture books for children in the British market. Little Tiger's principal aim is to encourage new talent, both writers and illustrators, and to build them up into leading names in the picture-book field. In consequence, Little Tiger is now able to boast many exciting new names that are exclusive to them and so do not appear on other lists in the UK.

A development in process is the launching of a new list for pre-school and novelty categories to be entitled **Little Rocket Press.** In addition to the established and growing picture-book range, Little Tiger's recent introduction of posters has proved to be extremely popular with schools and libraries, both for their colorful appeal and their educational value.

Emblematic of Little Tiger Press: *Look Out for the Big Bad Fish!* by Sheridan Cain and Tanya Linch ("a gem for pre-school and younger primary children—an adventurous 'life lesson'"—*Times Educational Supplement)*; *Dora's Eggs* by Julie Sykes, pictures by Jane Chapman ("Here is an absolute treat for the very young . . . Julie Sykes' satisfying tale is illustrated in bold painterly style. Jane Chapman has an inspired sense . . . of composing pictures for double spreads"—*School Librarian)*; *The Sleepy Dormouse* by Mark Ezra, pictures by Gavin Rowe ("The details of flowers, birds and insects are minutely observed yet never overpowering"—*Practical Parenting)*; *Mouse Look Out!* by Judy Waite, pictures by Norma Burgin (the stunning, atmospheric illustrations to this cat-and-mouse tale accompany a spare and suspenseful text); *Tom's Tail* by Linda Jennings and Tim Warnes ("It reads well aloud. There is a real charm about the high-quality illustrations"—*School Librarian)*; *The Storm Seal* by Judy Waite and illustrated by Neil Reed (dramatic seascapes are the background to this story about rearing a wild creature, yet learning to give it its dignity and freedom); *The Whales' Song* by Dyan Sheldon and Gary Blythe; *Owl Babies* by Martin Waddell and Patrick Benson (an engagingly simple text is accompanied by gentle and atmospheric pictures, conveying exactly the anxiety of three baby owls left all alone); *Guess How Much I Love You* by Sam McBratney and illustrated by Anita Jeram (this simple story, already a classic, is told with great tenderness and illustrated with gentle charm); and from the posters series, *Ten Ways to Improve Your Reading.*

Query letters and SASEs should be directed to:

Linda Jennings, Editor

LUND HUMPHRIES PUBLISHERS LTD.

Park House
1 Russell Gardens
London NW11 9NN
England
(44) 181 458 6314
fax: (44) 181 905 5245

Lund Humphries Publishers Limited began life as Percy Lund, Humphries & Co. Ltd, a Bradford printing company founded in 1884. The publishing side of the original business developed from within the printing company and its first publication was *The Penrose Annual* in 1897. In 1969 Lund Humphries Publishers Limited was itself formed as a subsidiary of Percy Lund, Humphries & Co. The latter met its demise and went into receivership in 1995; the former continues to thrive under a new parent company (Lionel Leventhal) as a successful specialist publisher of books on fine art, architecture, design and typography, photography, and decorative arts.

Sculpture is an important part of Lund Humphries list and, with the Henry Moore Foundation, it publishes the *British Sculptors and Sculpture* series, which has volumes on sculptors such as Austin Wright, Bernard Meadows, and David Nash. The most distinctive quality of the company, however, is its identification of subjects not explored elsewhere. It is not likely to publish surveys of the works of Monet or Picasso, leaving such mainstream titles to the likes of Thames and Hudson and Phaidon or, at the more popular end of the market, Taschen. But it can score over larger rivals in tackling artists such as the Belgian painter and engraver James Ensor—*James Ensor 1860–1949: Theatre of Masks*—previously unrepresented in book form and recently featured in a Barbican exhibition. Tie-ins such as the one at the Barbican are another Lund Humphries specialty. "We spend a lot of time working on our relationship with galleries," Editorial director Lucy Myers said. "Because we're small, we can take on a project at short notice. That's where we have an advantage over Thames and Hudson and Phaidon." And in order to help promote itself to galleries, Lund Humphries began publishing *A Calendar of Art Exhibitions*, an annual (which now sells about 4,000 copies each year).

Lund Humphries has published titles in association with, among others, The Irish Museum of Modern Art (*The Pursuit of Painting*), Central St. Martin's College of Art and Design *(Ralph Koltai: Designer for the Stage)*, the National Museum of Wales, the South Bank Centre, and the Royal Academy. It is also the trade representative of the National Galleries of Scotland. Recently, Lund Humphries has also published Dorothy Bohm's images of *Sixties* London, and is looking "cautiously" to develop its photography list while it also publishes "selectively" in the graphic arts. Here it has most recently brought out Ruari McLean's study *Jan Tschichold: A Life in Typography*.

Other titles on the Lund Humphries list include: *Made to Wear: Creativity in Contemporary Jewellery* by Janice West (accompanying a Central St. Martin's exhibition); *Eric Fraser: Designer and Illustrator* (celebration of an artist best known for his drawings for *Radio Times*); *A Short History of the Printed Word* (a classic by Warren Chappell, updated by Robert Bringhurst); *After the Party: Andy Warhol: Works 1956–1986* essay by Thomas Crow and introduction by Declan McGonagle; *Effigies and Ecstasies: Roman Baroque Sculpture and Design in the Age of Bernini* and *Shoji Hamada: Master*

Potter (edited by Timothy Wilcox; essays by Yuko Kikuchi, Julian Stair, and Timothy Wilcox, with a memoir by Janet Leach).

Distribution of Lund Humphries titles in the U.S. is by *Antique Collectors Club.*

Query letters and SASEs should be directed to:

Lucy Myers, Editorial Director

THE LUTTERWORTH PRESS

P.O. Box 60
Cambridge CB1 2NT
England
(44) 1223 350865
fax: (44) 1223 366951
publishing@lutterworth.com (e-mail)
http://dialspace.dial.pipex.com/lutterworth.pr/

The Lutterworth Press, one of the longest-established and best-known independent publishers in the United Kingdom, has been publishing educational and children's books since the eighteenth century. The Lutterworth Press was originally founded as the Religious Tract Society to publish religious and children's literature, and soon added educational and general books. In the nineteenth century it became one of the leading publishers of children's books and magazines, of which the most prominent were *The Girl's Own Paper* and *The Boy's Own Paper*. Lutterworth was the first British publishing house to open branches abroad (in Africa and Asia) and published literature, dictionaries, and children's and religious books in local languages. Many leading children's authors have been associated with Lutterworth since its foundation: Hesba Stratton, Kathleen Fidler, W. E. Johns, Enid Blyton, Laura Ingalls Wilder, and Meindert deJong as just a few examples from the past. More recently, Lutterworth has published books by Helen Cresswell, Joan Aiken, Pauline Baynes, and other well-known children's writers and illustrators. Lutterworth has helped to develop the careers of many writers, such as Sir David Attenborough and Patrick Moore, by publishing their early works.

Lutterworth continues to publish works in its main areas: children's, religious, educational, and adult nonfiction; and though the scope has widened, the general, moral tone has remained since the early missionary days. In educational books this influence is evident in books for GCSE R.E. and "A"-level philosophy courses. The children's books cover a wide range reflecting the concerns of teachers, children, and society at large; thus, for example, environmental and conservation issues are dealt with in both fiction and information books. There is a wide-ranging fiction list that has a great deal to offer to school libraries as well as likewise suitable works of reference on topics as varied as the Bible and medicinal herbs. And under the **James Clarke & Co. Ltd.** imprint, religious titles with a more scholarly appeal are marketed. In essence, the publishing program of Lutterworth reflects the view that much of the material on the market is of questionable literary and educational quality. The press aims to present the best of children's literature, both fiction and nonfiction, in a form that will appeal to librarians and library users, and is selected to offer children both entertainment and information.

Typical of Lutterworth: *Time, Science and Philosophy* by Hector C. Parr; *Painting the Warmth of the Sun* by Tom Cross (the story of the St. Ives colony of artists); *Clocks and Clock Repairing* by Eric Smith; *Making Paper Toys* by Carson I. A. Ritchie; *Armies of Pestilence: Pandemics in History* by R. S. Bray; *A Handbook of Christian Theologians* by Martin E. Marty and Dean G. Peerman (coherent and concise portraits of the major theologians of the past 200 years); *Journey Round the Arctic Circle* by Christopher Hill (an illustrated children's information book); *Mists and Magic* by Dorothy Edwards (a children's poetry book); and *God Is Always with Me* by Helen Caswell (a children's picture book).

Examples from James Clarke: *Counting the Days to Armageddon: Jehovah's Witnesses and the Second Presence of Christ* by Robert Crompton (the only academic work on the Jehovah's Witnesses movement, studying its views on Biblical prophecy of the end of the world); *Dark Night of the Soul* by Soren Kierkegaard (the only English translation of one of Kierkegaard's most important spiritual writings); *Sexual Desire & Love: Origins and History of the Christian Ethic of Sexuality and Marriage* by Eric Fuchs.

Query letters and SASEs should be directed to:

Colin Lester, Commissioning Editor

MARTIN BOOKS

Simon & Schuster Consumer Group
Grafton House
64 Maids Causeway
Cambridge CB5 8DD
England
(44) 1223 366733
fax: (44) 1223 461428
Linda_Lumley@prenhall.co.uk (e-mail)

Martin Books is a niche specialist division of the publishing giant Simon & Schuster. Martin, which has been in business for over 25 years, specializes in sponsored and promotional publishing, offering titles that help to promote companies, their products and services. Its success in carving out a distinctive publishing niche stems from a clear conception of the advantages that books can present over other types of promotional material. From Martin's viewpoint, books have the most prestige and the most credibility; they last, being read and re-read; and, of course, they are often kept for years. Moreover books are still the most widely accepted way of packaging detailed information. Having developed an expert understanding of the importance of projecting the right image of a company and its brand, the house believes that it can offer its clients the best of both worlds—the flexibility and customer-led approach of a small creative unit and the global resources of the parent publisher.

They have produced leisure and travel guides, good driving guides, pocket guides to World Cup football, cookbooks, business titles, guides to personal finance and family health care, baby-care books, and numerous "how-to" titles on topics such as dressmaking, kitchen design, garden, and party-planning. Martin produces all for a wideranging list of big-name national and international clients including the likes of the BBC and H P Foods.

Examples from Martin: *Complete Motoring Guide* by Sue Baker (an own-brand book for Halfords); *Imaginative Gardening: A Practical Handbook* by David Stevens (an own-brand title for B & Q); *Quick and Easy Fish* by Antony Worrall Thompson (one in a long-running own-brand series for J Sainsbury's); *Mediterranean Cooking* by Carla Capalbo (a book for Le Creuset accompanying their cookware range); *Savlon Guide to Baby Skincare* by Isobel McKenzie-Price; *The Oxo Book of Food and Cooking* and *My Story: Sarah the Duchess of York* (with Jeff Coplon).

Martin's editors are always happy to discuss concepts, schedules, and costs without obligation.

Query letters and SASEs should be directed to:

Janet Copleston, Editorial

KEVIN MAYHEW PUBLISHERS
Rattlesden
Bury St. Edmunds
Suffolk IP30 0SZ
England
(44) 1449 737978
fax: (44) 1449 737834
KevinMayhewLtd@msn.com (e-mail)

Kevin Mayhew Ltd., now established for over 20 years, is one of the foremost special-ist producers of Christian books and music. Mayhew, an independent house still run by its founder and chairman Kevin Mayhew, has enjoyed considerable success from its original publishing vision, continues to expand steadily and soon expects to move into a new custom built £1 million development. Along with expansion has come diversifi-cation into new product ranges which include a now-extensive list of secular, instru-mental, and vocal music. The house also now has an agreement with the major American music publisher Mel Bay, to market and distribute its products in the UK and Eire. With over 2,000 titles on the Mel Bay lists, this gives Mayhew the chance to be-come more deeply involved in the instrumental market.

Existing Mayhew products fall into these broad categories: Christian books, young people and children's books, choral music, organ music, instrumental and piano music, and greetings cards. On the books side, the company has a vast range of titles and au-thors, including established titles such as *The Palm Tree Bible Stories* (which have sold millions of copies in numerous languages); the famous *Instant Art* series (which contin-ues to expand); and authors like Susan Sayers. Sayers' *Springboard to Worship* ar-guably changed the direction of worship in many Anglican parishes. Other prominent authors, who come from every perspective of the Christian churches and write books that appeal to a variety of audiences, include Susan Hardwick, Michael Forster, Gra-ham Jeffery, David Gatward, Ray Jackson, and Margaret Rizza.

Also noteworthy are the Roman Catholic range of titles. Large numbers of resource books have been produced for the Catholic Liturgy, with *The Sacraments Explained* se-ries and the *Focus on the Sacraments* series proving to be very popular. The continued expansion of both Mayhew's titles lists and house authors is most evident with the books for young people. The young "Christian Fiction" series has been developed, the comedy and cartoon titles have grown, ground-breaking youth-work resources have been introduced, and Mayhew is soon to offer a selection of books on difficult teenage issues that many other publishers have avoided. The music catalog also is very strong, with an impressive list of composers. This includes famous names such as Malcom Archer, the master of the music at Wells Cathedral, and Colin Mawby, the director of the Irish National Choir. And there are cathedral organists including Donald Hunt, Richard Lloyd, and Philip Moore, as well as younger composers rapidly making their mark such as Chris Tambling, Andrew Gant, and Andrew Moore. In the eyes of the chairman Kevin Mayhew, the success of the company in its continued development is down to the enthusiasm of the house team and the fact that the company produces for the entire Christian church.

From the Mayhew range: *Hymns Old & New: New Anglican Edition* (an exhaustive collection of nearly 600 fine hymns); *Godsearch* by Eleanor Watkins (a children's and young people's title); *Instant Art for Bible Action Models* (a popular children's annual reprint); *Sunday Psalms: Musical Settings for the Revised Common Lectionary* by Andrew Moore; *Quotes and Anecdotes: The Essential Reference for Preachers & Teachers* by Anthony P. Castle; *The Complete Organist—Book One: One Hundred Pieces from Across the Centuries*; *The Oboist's Collection—Book One* (selected and edited by Roy Carter); *The Pianist's Collection* (fourteen volumes to date of beautiful music from across the centuries); *Why, God?* by Susan Hardwick (a Christian response to the death of Diana, Princess of Wales); and *Fast-Track Guitar: A Quick and Easy Playing Method for Musicians Who Already Read Music* by Chris Kilvington.

Query letters and SASEs should be directed to:

Katherine Laidler, Managing Editor

Jonathan Bugden, Commissioning Editor, Young People's and Children's Books, Praise and Worship Music

Donald Thompson, Music Editor

Janet Simpson, Hymn Music Submissions

METHODIST PUBLISHING HOUSE

20 Ivatt Way
Peterborough PE3 7PG
England
(44) 1733 332202
fax: (44) 1733 331201

Methodist is another specialist Christian publishing house that proudly values the role it plays in the mission and ministry of the entire church.

Methodist publishes a wide range of titles and greetings cards. Methodist subjects include: Bible theology and church history, education training and ministry, church mission, church organization, and worship.

A sample from Methodist: *The Making of Methodism* by Barrie Tabraham; *An Evangelical Theology of Preaching* by Donald English; *Under Fives Alive* by Jane Farley, Eileen Goddard, and Judy Jarvis (25 themes to help children learn about God); *Tuck In! A Feast for Christian Youth Workers and Young People* by Michael Jebson (a full and lively program of ideas and involvement methods catering for youth groups of any size); *Don't Panic! The Training Pack for Church Stewards* by Chris Kitchin and Roger Walton; *Getting on the Map: A Study Guide to Help Churches Respond to Mission Alongside the Poor* by The Methodist Church; *Ripples* (a collection of poems and meditations for personal and group use); *Singing Faith* by Brian Hoare (a new collection of hymns and songs); *Let Me Say That Again: Maxims for Spiritual Living* by Maxie Dunnam; and *The New Handbook of the Christian Year* (a rich sourcebook of worship materials containing lessons, prayers, responses, and service.

Query letters and SASEs should be directed to:

Brian Thornton, Chief Executive

MILESTONE PUBLICATIONS

62 Murray Road
Horndean
Waterlooville
Hampshire PO8 9JL
England
info@gosschinaclub.deman.co.uk

Milestone is very much a niche specialist publisher whose subject interest is extremely narrowly focused. Milestone is the publishing and bookselling division of Goss and Crested China Ltd., and while Milestone has published local history, military, finance and personal investment, and other trade titles, it now only publishes books on Goss and Crested china or other heraldic porcelain.

Goss was a family-owned business whose factory produced a unique kind of souvenir porcelain to meet the needs of the newly born tourist industry towards the end of the last century. The company began producing heraldic porcelain and supplying retail agents in each town and seaside resort with pieces bearing the coat of arms relating to the district, thus meeting the demands of tourists for little holiday mementos of towns and cities they visited. After only about 70 years of production and despite commercial success, the business ended owing to reasons basically stemming from the advent of the Great War. Consequently, there is now a tremendous and rapidly growing interest in this kind of porcelain as a collector's item, both because of the finite number of pieces and the quality and sheer variety of the genuine articles. Numerous other factories in the famous Stoke-on-Trent potteries region copied Goss's original lead in producing crested ware but such is the prestige of the Goss name that the term "Goss china" is often used to describe all crested ware.

Milestone's current publications, authored by the resident expert Nicholas Pine, all address this quite unique little field of interest. Titles include: *The Concise Encyclopaedia and Price Guide to Goss China, The Price Guide to Arms and Decorations on Goss China,* and *The Price Guide to Crested China, Including Histories and Marks for over*

300 Factories—three essential titles that tell collectors all they need to know about Goss and Crested China, including how to spot bargains and avoid mistakes.

Hence, Milestone is interested only in receiving submissions in this very narrow field. Would-be authors or their agents should, however, write first with an outline and not submit manuscripts.

Query letters and SASEs should be directed to:

Nicholas Pine, Managing Director

MQ PUBLICATIONS LTD.

254–258 Goswell Road
London EC1V 7EB
England
(44) 171 490 7732
fax: (44) 171 253 7358
mqp@btinternet.com (e-mail)

MQP produces titles with popular appeal across a range of mainly nonfiction categories that deal with the pleasures of life and its finer side. Notably distinctive of MQP's approach is its creation of a variety of different series for many of its titles, a move that has clearly brought them success by encouraging the desire in readers to form collections of material. MQP also places great importance upon, and puts much energy into, the design and lavish illustration of its titles and this is another factor that undoubtedly explains the company's growth and continued ability to increase its listing.

The *Infatuations* series, for example, features beautifully designed eye-catching books on a range of popular subjects from mother to love to food. There is a superbly illustrated new gardening series on the list with such titles as *The Cottage Gardener*, *The Herb Gardener et al.* Three new gift series make their appearance: *Attitude!*, a stylish pop culture photographic range of books; *Suitcase Books,* which bring together classic stories from the world of murder, mystery, and romance; and *Simple Thoughts,* an inspirational range of little books. A new range of fine art gift books produced in association with The National Gallery includes the likes of *Angels in Art*, *Costume in Art*, *People in Art*, and others; and a new series of eight books entitled *Simple Style* features craft and lifestyle titles. Certainly by adding to established series and introducing new ones in this way, MQP can expect their catalog to continue to grow.

From the latest listing: *The Secret History of Food* by Susan Tomnay with illustrations by Nadine Wickenden (a fascinating insight into the little-known facts, folklore, fashions, and traditions that surround food; from the *Infatuations* series in which each title is written by an authority in the field and contains specially commissioned color illustrations and charming line art work); *Dreams* (also from the Infatuations series); *Heaven in Art* (a Fine Art series title in association with the National Gallery); *Shoes: Attitude!* (from the *Attitude!* series, each of which boasts more than 50 of the most sought-after photographs while a provocative and informative text explores history and eccentricities, producing a quirky and fascinating combination of visual imagery, facts, and fashion); *Love: A Pillow Book to Dream On* (from the *Pillow Books* series of books that are carefully crafted to combine selected extracts from great literature with beautiful, sensitive images that will usher in an evening of pleasant dreams); *Little Expert: Rose Gardener* by Angela Kirby (from the new garden series; discusses the history and development of the rose as well as its cultivation); *Dublin & Ireland: Guide & Travel Journal* by Brian Lalor (from the established travel guides set); *Classic Romance Stories* (from the Suitcase Books series); *A Little Brown Notebook: Shakespeare at the Globe* (a title in the bestselling series of pocket books of popular authors and playwrights with specially commissioned artwork on high-quality craft paper reflecting the spirit of old world charm); *Simple Style: Wire & Metal* by Deborah Schneebeli-Morrell (20 accessible and beautiful projects achievable by everyone); and *Patchwork Quilting and Applique: The Complete Guide to All the Essential Techniques* by Jenni Dobson.

Query letters and SASEs should be directed to:

Ljiljana Baird, Editorial Director

MUSIC SALES LIMITED

8/9 Frith Street
London W1V 5TZ
England
(44) 171 434 0066
fax: (44) 171 439 2848
music@musicsales.co.uk (e-mail)
www.musicsales.co.uk

Music Sales offers an enormous catalog of printed music, songbooks and tutors, CD plus book packs, videos, MIDI files, CD-ROMs, classical titles, and educational products.

Music Sales' huge compendium of titles includes music books and tutors for guitar and all fretted instruments across all major music styles; songbooks, tutors, and music products from all the bestselling names in popular music for a wide range of instruments and in many formats; the most up-to-date and comprehensive range of music books for keyboard and organ, including a selection of outstanding busking books; the most up-to-date and comprehensive range of music and tutor books for woodwind, brass, strings, percussion, recorder, harmonica . . . both educational and ensemble; the most up-to-date and comprehensive listing of interactive MIDI software, CD plus book packs, tutorial videos, CD-ROMs . . . plus technical sequencing and sampling, home recording, and MIDI; the world's finest selection of classical music . . . including the full range of Dover publications, all the major titles from the Novello, Chester Music, Edition Wilhelm, Hansen, Curwen, and Union Musical Ediciones catalogs; the world's most comprehensive range of musical shows, chorals, classroom and ensemble music for all ages and occasions from Golden Apple, Chester, Novello, Shawnee Press, Kjos et al, and a superb range of selected titles from Hal Leonard, America's top publisher of printed music.

From the same stable, the sister catalog of **Omnibus Press,** a Book Sales imprint, offers its own range of titles and series in a variety of formats on the lives and lyrics of big names in the world of music, as well as songbooks, music tutors, and BBC (British Broadcasting Company) music guides.

A small representative selection from the *very* large Music Sales listing: *The Beatles: Guitar Techniques* (eighty songs transcribed by Jesse Gress, as recorded by The Beatles, complete with lessons); *Richard Clayderman: I Can Play That!* (seventeen pieces associated with the French performer and recording artist, arranged for easy piano); *Narada: New Age Piano Solos* (compilation of top piano artists from Narada records, a leader in New Age music); *The Busker's Fake Book: 1001 All Time Hit Songs* the mega-collection of hits for buskers; *Speed Mechanics for Lead Guitar* (the ultimate technique book with over 200 vicious exercises, including Troy's scorching version of "Flight of the Bumblebee"); *Solos for the Harp Player* (selected and edited by Lucile Lawrence); *Studio Recording for Musicians* by Fred Miller (an illustrated survival manual for every professional and aspiring musician, producer, engineer, arranger, and contractor); *Technical Manual and Dictionary of Classical Ballet* by Gail Grant (one of the most popular and effective ballet reference guides fully defining and describing over 1,100 ballet steps); and *Chester's Easiest Nursery Rhymes* by Carol Barratt (26 favorites to play and sing with the vocal range ideally suited to young children).

From Omnibus: *The Lyrics of Bob Marley* (a title from the Lyrics of . . . series); *The Doors: Moonlight Drive* by Chuck Crisafulli (the first book to explain the meaning behind their poetic song lyrics); *Sex & Drugs & Rock & Roll* by Chris Charlesworth (a collection of candid and suggestive photographs illustrating the seamier side of rock 'n' roll); *R.E.D. Classical Collector Catalogue,* 1st edition (a fully cross-referenced listing of over 16,000 currently available CDs that have been reviewed in *Gramaphone* magazine); and *The Lion King: Illustrated Songbook,* music by Elton John and lyrics by Tim Rice (one of a series of Disney songbooks).

Query letters and SASEs should be directed to:

Robert Wise, Managing Director, Music Sales

Chris Charlesworth, Editor-in-Chief, Omnibus Press

THE NATIONAL MUSEUM OF SCIENCE & INDUSTRY

Science Museum
Exhibition Road
London SW7 2DD
England
(44) 171 938 8211
fax: (44) 171 938 8169
publicat@nmsi.ac.uk (e-mail)
www.nmsi.ac.uk

The National Museum of Science & Industry is the world's preeminent museum devoted to the history and contemporary practice of science, technology, and medicine. The museum makes an important contribution to international scholarship in the fields of the history and public understanding of science. The NMSI comprises the Science Museum, the National Railway Museum, and the National Museum of Photography, Film & Television.

New from the NMSI: *Hutchinson Science Library: CD-ROM for Windows* (brings together seven science reference books from the Hutchinson reference range, forming a superbly comprehensive source with over 12,000 entries including definitions, biographies, key events, and discoveries in the form of articles, pop-up news flashes, quotations, tables, bibliographies, and features—all fully searchable by word or category); *Museum Collecting Policies: In Modern Science and Technology* (a collection of papers from a one-day seminar at the Science Museum); *Great British Locomotives: The National Railway Museum Locomotives in Action* by Michael Blakemore and David Mosley (a superb collection of color photographs showing a large selection of fabulous locomotives in a variety of settings); *Record of the Dawn of Photography: Talbot's Notebooks P & Q* by Larry J. Schaaf (the first publication of the two most important notebooks created by William Henry Fox Talbot [1800–1877], the inventor of negative-positive photography); *Early Plastics: Perspectives 1850–1950* (edited by Susan Mossman; an examination of aspects of the historical, technological, social, and design elements of plastics that punctures myths, explains developments, and shows how the modern industry is historically rooted); *Instruments of Science: An Historical Encyclo-*

pedia (edited by Robert Bud and Deborah Warner; awarded the Paul Bunge Prize for 1998 by the Hans R. Jenemann Foundation); and *Health Matters: Modern Medicine and the Search for Better Health* by Ghislaine Lawrence and Tim Boon (a souvenir gallery guide).

Query letters and SASEs should be directed to:

Astrid Ferszt, Publications Officer

THE NATIONAL TRUST

36 Queen Anne's Gate
London SW1H 9AS
England
(44) 171 222 9251
fax: (44) 171 222 5097
www.nationaltrust.org.uk

The National Trust has a small publications department whose titles in essence reflect or relate to the organization's aims. The Trust is a registered charity that exists to identify and help to safeguard and preserve places of historic interest and natural beauty. Its books are mostly nonfiction titles, although it has a small selection of children's titles. Topics cover photography, history, social history, gardening, cookery, education, handbooks, and books on great houses.

New National Trust books: *The National Trust: Countryside* (introduction by Richard Mabey and photographs by Joe Cornish, David Noton, and Paul Wakefield; a celebration of some of the beautiful places in England, Wales, and Northern Ireland in the care of the National Trust); *An Elizabethan Inheritance: The Hardwick Hall Textiles* by Santina M. Levey; *Household Management* by Margaret Willes (from the Trust's souvenir series—examines the life and tasks of the housekeeper, the nursery maids, the butler, and the cook, providing a fascinating insight into how a country house was run in earlier centuries); *Pots and Containers* by Sue Spielburg (on how to make the most of the natural microclimate of your garden); *Gardens of the National Trust* by Stephen Lacey; *Jams, Preserves & Other Edible Delights* by Sara Paston-Williams; *The National Trust Book of Fairy Tales* illustrated by Ian Penney; *Investigating Medieval Times* by Anita Ganeri and Alison Honey (from the *Investigating* series; using evidence from National Trust properties, presents fascinating facts about medieval times—where people lived, how they worked, what they wore, and what they ate); and *The National Trust Historic Houses Handbook*.

The National Trust's publications are delivered in the trade by **Derek Searle Associates Ltd.** The Trust asks that no unsolicited manuscripts be sent to them.

Query letters and SASEs should be directed to:

Sophie Blair, Publications

NEW HOLLAND PUBLISHERS (UK) LTD.

24 Nutford Place
London W1H 6DQ
England
(44) 171 724 7773
fax: (44) 171 258 1293
vobis@nhpub.u-net.com (e-mail)

Like many mainstream publishers, New Holland maintains a solid listing of titles across a broad range of popular nonfiction categories.

One factor that makes New Holland notable is its arrangement of many titles, particularly travel and natural history, into distinctive series and collections. For example, New Holland publishes a series of compact, easy-to-use photographic guides to birds, each of which covers approximately 250 species; a similar series covers mammals, fauna, et al. In the case of travel, the company offers a series on exotic travel destinations, a walking series of guides to major cities, the globetrotters pocket-sized guides (each dealing with a particular country, state, or city), the globetrotters travel maps series, atlases, and travel packs that combine both map and guide.

New Holland also produces an interesting list of diving books, books on adventure sports, general nonfiction, and a strong range of lifestyle titles that includes interiors and home style, DIY and gardening, practical home decorating, art and design, general crafts, contemporary crafts, New Age, needlecraft, cake decorating, food and drink, and general lifestyle reference.

A sample of New Holland's latest: *Design and Decorate Bathrooms* by Lesley Taylor; *Making Your Own Paper* by Marianne Saddington; *First Steps in Cake Decorating* by Janice Murfitt; *Natural Home Pharmacy: Natural Therapies for You and Your Family* by Linda Scott and Keith Scott; *Top Dive Sites of the Caribbean* by Lawson Wood; *The Mapping of the World: Early Printed World Maps 1472–1700* by Rodney W. Shirley (a magnificently illustrated cartobibliographical study); *An Identification Guide to the Birds of South-east Asia* by Craig Robson; *Wild China* by John MacKinnon (photographs by Nigel Hicks); *Guide to Southern African Safari Lodges* by Peter Joyce; and

Ibiza and Formentera by Sue Bryant (a pocket-guide crammed with essential and practical data, travel tips, and recommendations for the traveler).

New Holland also represents the lists of Map Studio, Stonebridge Press, Struik Publishers, and Weatherhill; their distribution is handled by **Littlehampton Book Services Ltd.**

Query letters and SASEs should be directed to:

John Beaufoy, Managing Director

MICHAEL O'MARA BOOKS LIMITED

9 Lion Yard
Tremadoc Road
London SW4 7NQ
England
(44) 171 720 8643
fax: (44) 171 627 8953
admin@michaelomarabooks.com (e-mail)

O'Mara produces mainly nonfiction, humor, and children's titles for the mainstream and popular markets. One of its notable coups was the now-famous Royal book by Andrew Morton, *Diana: Her True Story in Her Own Words*, which was the world's best-selling book in 1997 and has been updated since her death.

Subjects covered by O'Mara include, besides the Royals: poetry, biography, health and lifestyle, history, general nonfiction, crafts, gift, humor, children's, and fiction. As well as new titles, all of these categories are also well represented in a substantial backlist maintained by the house.

From O'Mara's current frontlist: *Favourite Poems* by Trevor McDonald (a special collection selected by one of Britain's leading television news presenters); *Charlotte in Love: The True Story of Charlotte Bronte's Courtship and Marriage* by Brian Wilks; *What Are You Eating? The Food Fact File* by Isabel Skypala; *Ailments Through the Ages: An Alarming History of Famous & Difficult Patients* by Richard Gordon; *Victorian Conundrums: A Nineteenth Century Puzzler* by Ken Russell and Philip Carter; *Best-Loved Dog Stories* (a gift collection for literature and dog-lovers everywhere, with contributions from some of the world's most accomplished authors including James Herriot, Virginia Woolf, D. H. Lawrence, and James Thurber); *Tailwinds: The Lore and Language of Fizzles, Farts and Toots* by Peter Furze; *Championship Paper Planes* by Paul Jackson (a unique collection of highly innovative designs for paper plane enthusiasts of all ages and abilities); *Stupid Sex: The Most Idiotic & Embarrassing Intimate Encounters of All Time* by Ross and Kathryn Petras; *Nature Craft* (a children's year-round guide to creating fabulous crafts with a little help from Mother Nature); and *Millennium Calendar 1999* (compiled by Mark Seaman of the Imperial War Museum).

Query letters and SASEs should be directed to:

Gabrielle Mander, Managing Editor

THE ORION PUBLISHING GROUP

Orion House
5 Upper Saint Martin's Lane
London WC2H 9EA
England
(44) 171 240 3444
fax: (44) 171 240 4822
nac@orionbooks.co.uk (e-mail)

The Orion Group is one of the larger fish in the publishing seas. It produces both fiction and a wide variety of nonfiction titles for the mass and popular market under a number of well-known high-profile imprints: **Weidenfeld & Nicolson, Phoenix House, J. M. Dent, Orion, Orion Media, Orion Business, Millenium, Orion Paperbacks, Phoenix Paperbacks, Everyman Paperbacks, Orion Children's Books,** and **Peter Halban.** The Group is able to count some big-selling names among its authorial ranks and in a variety of categories.

A sample, from the Orion stables, of new and recent titles: *The Green Mile* by Stephen King (first publication in one volume of King's "serial thriller"); *Blood Money: An SAS Novel* by Johnny "Two Combs" Howard (fiction based in experienced fact); *Bodyguard of Lightning* by Stan Nicholls (first volume of a science fiction fantasy epic); *Witness: The Making of Schindler's List* by Franciszek Palowski (exclusive interview with Steven Spielberg, foreword by Thomas Keneally); *The Astrology File: Scientific Proof of the Link Between Star Signs and Human Behaviour* by Gunter Sachs; *Walking on Thin Ice: In Pursuit of the North Pole* by David Hempleman-Adams; *Who's Who of Business Asia: The First Ever Directory of Asia's 400 Leading Business Tycoons* (co-published with *Asia Inc.*, the leading business magazine in Asia); *The Wisdom of Business: A Book of Maxims* by Eugene Weber; *The Lost Tomb: The Greatest Discovery at the Valley of the Kings Since Tutankhamen* by Kent Week; *Marilyn Monroe* by Barbara Leaming; *The Complete Body Foods Book: For Men, Women & Children* by Jane Clarke; from the Everyman Art Library, *The Body in Sculpture* by Tom

Flynn; *Ferocious Humanism: An Anthology of Irish Poetry from Before Swift to Yeats and After* (edited by W. J. McCormack); *The Nursery Storybook* by Georgie Adams, illustrated by Peter Utton; *The Human Brain: A Guided Tour* by Susan Greenfield; *After God: The Future of Religion* by Don Cupitt; *Descartes* by John Cottingham (one from the Great Philosophers series); and *Memoirs of a Fortunate Jew: An Italian Story* by Dan Vittorio Segre.

Query letters and SASEs should be directed to:

Orion, as above

PEN & SWORD BOOKS LTD.

47 Church Street
Barnsley
South Yorkshire S70 2AS
England
(44) 1226 734222/734555
fax: (44) 1226 734438
charles@pen-and-sword.demon.co.uk (e-mail)
www.yorkshire-web.co.uk/ps/

The **Leo Cooper** imprint, acquired by Pen & Sword Books 10 years ago, has a tradition stretching back over 30 years for publishing military history. Pen & Sword, which developed the Leo Cooper imprint in a number of areas—most notably into Battlefield Guides—publishes about 60 books a year, covering all aspects of military history. Its titles, which combine fascinating entertaining reading with solid history, make up both a substantial back catalog and front-list of the new and recent.

A Leo Cooper selection: *Major and Mrs. Holt's Battlefield Guide to the Somme* by Tonie and Valmai Holt (this updated and reprinted book is one of the bestselling guide books to the battlefields of the Somme); *Wilfred Owen: On the Trail of the Poets of the Great War* by Helen McPhail and Philip Guest (a guide to the battlefields that inspired the young and sensitive poet); *The Armed Forces of the UK 1999/2000* by Charles Heyman (covers all the vital aspects of the organization and equipment of the United Kingdom Army, Navy, and the Royal Air Force); *Shot at Dawn: Executions in World War One by Authority of the British Army Act* by Julian Putkowski and Julian Sykes (updated and revised to its 8th edition; the only comprehensive record of what happened to these soldiers that's available to the public); *The Fighting Commodores: Convoy Commanders in the Second World War* by Alan Burn; *Nine Battles to Stanley* by Nick van der Bijl (a soldier's account of the ground fighting on South Georgia and the

Falklands); *Chavasse Double VC* by Ann Clayton (the story of Noel Godfrey Chavasse, who was twice awarded the Victoria Cross during World War I); *Field Gun Jack Versus the Boers* by Tony Bridgland (the first account of how the British were forced to cannibalize Naval guns and use them on land); *The Men Behind the Medals* by Graham Pitchfork (the actions of 21 aviators during World War II); and *Storming St Nazaire* by James Dorrian (the story of the British raid on the giant Normandie dry dock in March 1942).

Query letters and SASEs should be directed to:

Brigadier Henry Wilson, Publishing Manager, Acquisitions, Military History

Charles Hewitt, Rights Manager

Penguin UK

27 Wrights Lane
Kensington
London W8 5TZ
England
(44) 171 416 3000
fax: (44) 171 416 3099
www.penguin.co.uk

Penguin UK is owned by Pearson PLC. It is undoubtedly one of the world's best-known book brands and a leading publisher for more than 60 years. Penguin's adult and children's lists include fiction, nonfiction, poetry, drama, classics, reference, and special interest areas. Its huge backlist and the cyclical interest in established works means that, aside from a steady stream of new work, there is always considerable demand for reprints. The company is structured into a number of specialist divisions that produce their titles under a variety of imprints.

Penguin General Books publishes adult fiction and nonfiction in hardback under the **Michael Joseph, Viking,** and **Hamish Hamilton** imprints, and in paperback under the **Penguin** imprint. This division does not accept unsolicited manuscripts and synopses.

The Penguin Press division produces adult nonfiction, reference, specialist titles, and classics under the following imprints: **Allen Lane; Arkana—Mind, Body and Spirit; Buildings of England; Classics;** and **Penguin Books.** Penguin Press will only respond to approaches made in writing.

Frederick Warne deals with classic children's publishing and merchandising including *Beatrix Potter*™, *Flower Fairies,* and *Orlando.* Warne also does not accept unsolicited manuscripts or synopses. More information can be found about this division on the World Wide Web at www.peterrabbit.com

Ventura is the producer and packager of Spot titles by Eric Hill. Again, they do not accept unsolicited manuscripts or synopses.

Penguin children's books are sold in hardback under the **Hamish Hamilton Children's** and **Viking Children's** imprints, and under the **Puffin** imprint in paperback. The latter is a leading children's paperback list, publishing in virtually all fields, including fiction, nonfiction, poetry, picture books, and media-related titles. While this division, too, does not accept unsolicited manuscripts, it does welcome ideas and synopses. It has a specialized Web site also, located at www.puffin.co.uk

Hot from the Penguin House (Michael Joseph): *Perfect Strangers* (a romantic novel by Robyn Sisman, asking: Can you fall in love with someone you've never met?); *A Certain Age* by Rebecca Ray (a first novel by an 18-year-old about the reality behind the problem pages; what *Just 17* never told you about growing up); *Heaven's Mirror: Quest for the Lost Civilization* by Graham Hancock and Santha Faiia (a major new piece of historical detective work from the author of *Fingerprints of the Gods* to accompany a four-part television series); *125 Best Recipes Ever* by Loyd Grossman (*Masterchef's* Loyd Grossman selects the classic, definitive recipes of world cooking).

From Viking: *Maurice or The Fisher's Cot* by Mary Shelley with an introduction by Claire Tomalin (a long-lost story for children by the author of *Frankenstein*, written in 1820 but never before published); *To the Last Man: Spring 1918* by Lyn Macdonald (seventh in a series of acclaimed histories by the leading chronicler of the First World War); *Boogie Man: The Adventures of John Lee Hooker in the American Twentieth Century* by Charles Shaar Murray (biography of one of the most influential blues musicians of the era); *The Little Book of Calm at Work* by Paul Wilson (author of the best-selling *The Little Book of Calm*).

Hamish Hamilton: *Manners* by Robert Newman (a new crime thriller from an award-winning writer and stand-up comic); *Princess Andrew of Greece* by Hugo Vickers (compelling biography of the mother of Prince Philip and great-granddaughter of Queen Victoria, written with the support of members of her family).

Query letters and SASEs should be directed to:

PENGUIN UK
Michael Lynton, Chairman
Anthony Forbes Watson, Managing Director

PENGUIN GENERAL BOOKS
Helen Fraser, Managing Director
Tony Lacey, Publishing Director, Penguin
Tom Weldon, Publishing Director, Michael Joseph/Penguin

Juliet Annan, Publishing Director, Viking/Hamish Hamilton/Penguin

Simon Prosser, Publisher, Hamish Hamilton

Louise Moore, Publisher, Michael Joseph/Penguin fiction

PENGUIN PRESS

Andrew Rosenheim, Managing Director

Alastair Rolfe, Publishing Director, Frederick Warne and Ventura

Sally Floyer, Publisher/ Managing Director

Diana Syrat, Chief Editor, Penguin Children's Books

Philippa Milnes-Smith, Managing Director

Jane Nissen, Publisher, Fiction, Poetry and Picture Books

Richard Scrivener, Publisher, Media and Popular Nonfiction

Anna Hopkins, Penguin Audiobooks

PHILLIMORE & CO. LTD.

Shopwyke Manor Barn
Chichester
West Sussex PO20 6BG
England
(44) 1243 787636
fax: (44) 1243 787639
bookshop@phillimore.co.uk (e-mail)
www.phillimore.co.uk

W. P. W. Phillimore (1853–1913) was the pioneer campaigner for the preservation of local records and the establishment of local record offices and already famous as the leading writer, editor, and publisher of local history and source material when he founded Phillimore & Co. in 1897. Prior to forming the company he had written, edited, and published more on family history than any of his contemporaries, including *How to Write the History of a Family.*

Since that time, Phillimore & Co. has celebrated its centenary. It has maintained its founder's record with an output over the past century unrivaled in the English-speaking world of "how-to-do-it" books, histories of specific families, and source material. For family historians writing up their research, Phillimore is the publisher of first choice.

Potential authors, or editors, of new books in Phillimore's field are invited to contact its editorial department at the earliest possible stage in the planning of their project. Rising publishing costs have made it increasingly important to shape books, in terms of length, detail, illustrations, and so on, with marketing considerations in mind from the outset; professional guidance on the preparation of the manuscript and illustrations can lead to great savings in production cost and thereby reduce the eventual retail price.

Emblematic of the Phillimore specialist niche: *Village Records* by John West (the Medlicott Medallist here gives detailed advice about the materials available for the study of local history and the best way to handle them); *Sources for English Local History* by W. B. Stephens (the standard work for all local history enthusiasts gives information on how to find, obtain, and use a variety of source material); *Signposts to the Past* by Margaret Gelling (popular work that remains the only modern study of the historical significance of English place-names); *The Craft of the Bellfounder* by George Elphick (a definitive history and description of the craft, from prehistoric China to the present day); *The Wigg Family* by J. L. Kirby, Jr.; *Domesday Book* (general editor John Morris, the only uniform English translation ever made, published in parallel text with the original Latin, county-by-county in 35 volumes); *Keighley: A Pictorial History* by Stuart Cardwell; *Princes Risborough Past* by Sandy McFarlane and Chris Kingham; *A Map of the County of Essex* by Chapman and Andre (first published in 1777, this is the first accurate and detailed map of the historic county, engraved from a full survey using "modern" methods); *A History of Bristol and Gloucestershire* by Brian Smith and Elizabeth Ralph; *Two Thousand Years in Exeter* by W. G. Hoskins; and *Balleine's History of Jersey, new edition* edited by Marguerite Syvret and Joan Stevens (first published in 1950, this book enjoys unrivalled preeminence in its field as a work of definitive scholarship; now completely revised and better illustrated by the Societe Jersiaise).

Query letters and SASEs should be directed to:

Editorial, as on previous page

PICCADILLY PRESS

5 Castle Road
London NW1 8PR
England
(44) 171 267 4492
fax: (44) 171 267 4493
books@piccadillypress.co.uk (e-mail)

Piccadilly Press, which has recently celebrated its fifteenth birthday, is a small, quintessentially English publishing house. It is situated in that "resolutely English bit of London called Kentish Town" and run by a native of Saskatoon, Saskatchewan. Brenda Gardner, Piccadilly's founder, arrived in the UK in 1972. After a number of years acquiring experience in the publishing business as a desk editor at Puffin, then as commissioning editor at E. J. Arnold on the then-new Pepper Press venture, she struck out boldly on her own and formed Piccadilly Press on the 1st July 1983—Canada Day! The house list focuses principally on pre-school books with its particularly solid range of picture books, teenage books for the 10–15 age range, and parenting books.

Gardner's first list, published in February 1984, included forward titles bought from the Pepper list after it was folded, such as Hawkins' *Mig the Pig* (the beginning of a series still in print), plus books by Charlotte Voake, Chris Winn, Terrance Dicks, and Sir Hugh Casson. "Because of the Hawkins and people like Sue Hellard, we had good contacts in the U.S. with Putnam and Little, Brown, and that gave us an in to do more of our own co-editions," says Gardner. "And those were the days when you could just show them some roughs and they bought the lot!" After coming through the turbulent recessionary years of the early nineties, Gardner believes one of Piccadilly's most important achievements and the role of the small publishing house is "developing people . . . with staying power.

The house has succeeded in its efforts to break into European markets, particularly Germany and Italy. It has extended its list of established writers with Rosie Rushton, Ros Asquith, Tony Maddox, and Lisa Stubbs, and is bringing on new talent like Kathryn Lamb, James Pope, and Sally Chambers. On the future shape of Piccadilly, Gardner said, "I see us staying small. We really do want to do fewer books and sell them better. We'll continue to hone our three main areas . . . more young, funny, character-based picture books, more contemporary and humorous teen fiction and nonfiction, and more growth for the parental titles."

Characteristic of Piccadilly's main areas: *The School from Hell? More Madness!* by Yvonne Coppard (humorous teen fiction that was Pick of the Year 1997 by The Federation of Children's Book Groups); *Boywatching! The Species, Their Characteristics and Behaviour* by Kathryn Lamb (the ultimate manual to school life); *Best Friends* by Rosie Rushton (as five very different teenagers struggle to cope with their changing lives, they fall into a friendship which surprises them all . . .); *Getting a Life: Letters and Diaries of an Aspiring Teenager* by Samantha Rugen; *Sonny's Treasure Hunt* by Lisa Stubbs (a full-color illustrated picture book for young children); *Fergus and Marigold* by Tony Maddox (from the Fergus picture books series); *Henrietta and the Jelly Fight* by Stan Cullimore (from the Starring Henrietta series). From the adult range: *Getting Pregnant & Staying Pregnant* by Diana Rabb; *Overcome Bullying for Parents* by Sheila Munro; and *What Worries Women Most?* by Dr. Sarah Brewer.

Query letters and SASEs should be directed to:

Brenda Gardner, Chief Editor

Jude Evans, Editor

THE POLICY PRESS

University of Bristol
34 Tyndall's Park Road
Bristol BS8 1PY
England
(44) 117 945 6800
fax: (44) 117 973 7308
tpp@bristol.ac.uk (e-mail)
www.bris.ac.uk/Publications/TPP/tpp.htm

The Policy Press, launched in 1996, is *the* specialist new policy studies publisher for academics, policy makers, and practitioners. It is an editorially independent publisher of research-based books, reports, practice guides, and journals spanning the broad range of policy issues. The Press publishes work from individuals and organizations internationally, satisfying rigorous academic and business criteria. Currently it works with the Joseph Rowntree Foundation, the Economic and Social Research Council, UK government departments and *Community Care* magazine among others. In the Press's view, findings from policy research should be read widely to impact on policy formation, implementation, and evaluation. The fast and effective specialist publishing service of The Policy Press aims to enable authors to achieve this.

The Press publishes titles on policy process, implementation, evaluation, and impact across a wide range of areas, and interdisciplinary work is encouraged. Areas of particular focus are child welfare, community and social care, environment, family policy and family justice, governance, health, housing, labor markets, unemployment and unpaid work, social justice and inequality, and urban policy.

Despite its newness, the house has grown very quickly. It is now beginning to produce some titles in both hardback and paperback in response to international library demands. Recently 38 new titles comprised a healthy addition to a backlist of almost 70 titles in just the first two years. New collections from The Policy Press include *The Dynamics of Modern Society* (edited by Robert Walker and Lutz Leisering) and *Trust and Contracts* (edited by Andrew Coulson). Also the *Community Care into Practice* series, bringing community care practitioners up-to-date with concise findings on new developments in their field, also is developing rapidly. The house also publishes *Policy and Politics,* now established as the key journal of public policy studies in the UK.

Policy Press output: *Beyond the Threshold: The Measurement and Analysis of Social Exclusion* (edited by Graham Room); *Making Partnerships Work in Community Care: A Guide for Practitioners in Housing, Health and Social Services* by Robin Means, Maria Brenton, Lyn Harrison, and Frances Heywood; *From Poor Law to Community Care: The Development of Welfare Services for Elderly People 1939–71* by Robin Means and Randall Smith; *Theorising Empowerment: Individual Power and Community Care* by Richard Servian; *Domestic Violence: A National Survey of Court Welfare and Voluntary Sector Mediation Practice* by Marianne Hester, Chris Pearson, and Lorraine Radford; *"I'll Tell You What I Need . . ." Identifying Local Housing Needs* by Paul Burton; *A Blueprint for Change: Construction Skills Training in Britain* by Linda Clarke and Christine Wall; *Mapping the Regions: Boundaries, Coordination and Government* by Brian W. Hogwood; *TECs and Racial Equality: Training, Work Experience and Ethnic Minorities* by Martin Boddy; and *Consumerism or Democracy? User Involvement in the Control of Voluntary Organisations* by Paul Robson, Michael Locke, and Jonathan Dawson.

The Press welcomes proposals for books, reports, guides, or journals. It specializes in collaborating with funding and research organizations to develop broad research dissemination strategies, from gaining high-profile media coverage of findings to publishing comprehensive books. The Press also is planning focused book series in its key areas. If authors have ideas for a series and would like The Policy Press to collaborate with their research program, or would like to submit an individual proposal, they are asked to either write for a proposal form, download one from the Web site, or telephone Alison Shaw (see below).

Query letters and SASEs should be directed to:

Alison Shaw, Publishing Manager

Dawn Pudney, Editorial Manager

Derek Hawes, Abstracts and Review Editor, *Policy and Politics* journal

Randall Smith, Editor, *Policy and Politics* journal

POLITY PRESS

65 Bridge Street
Cambridge CB2 1UR
England
(44) 1223 324315
fax: (44) 1223 461385
polity@dial.pipex.com (e-mail)
www.polity.co.uk

Polity is one of the world's leading social science and humanities publishers, committed to publishing intellectually exciting work from around the world. All of its titles are published in association with *Blackwell Publishers,* and it encompasses the following subject areas: sociology, politics, media and cultural studies, gender studies, philosophy, history, geography, psychology, linguistics, literary theory, anthropology, theology, and religion.

A small sample of highlights from Polity's very substantial academic collection: *Conversations with Anthony Giddens: Making Sense of Modernity* by Anthony Giddens and Christopher Pierson (an accessible and informal overview of the principal theories of "the key intellectual figure of New Labour"); *Salvos and Skirmishes: The State of Our Community* by Will Hutton (brings together the full range of Hutton's work as a journalist, pamphleteer, and essayist, advocate, and critic); *Freud 2000* edited by Anthony Elliott (a highly readable and bold defense of the relevance and importance of Freud's theories to contemporary culture); *Nature: Western Attitudes Since Ancient Times* by Peter Coates (introduction to the history of nature and the environment); *Prostitution, Power and Freedom* by Julia O'Connell Davidson (examines prostitution around the world, including sex tourism, and the power relations that affect the way that it is organized); *The MacIntyre Reader* edited by Kelvin Knight (the first comprehensive reader of MacIntyre's philosophical work); *Vigilant Citizens: Vigilantism and the State* by Ray Abrahams (a new approach to a topic that has been surprisingly little studied—vigilantism); *Language and Gender: An Introduction* by Mary M. Talbot (lively, highly accessible, and up-to-date textbook on language and gender); and *The Philosophy of Religion: A Critical Introduction* by Beverley Clack and Brian R. Clack (major new introductory textbook on the philosophy of religion and the only one to include all the areas traditionally covered plus a number of important alternative approaches).

Query letters and SASEs should be directed to:

Editorial, as above

PRIMA EDITIONS
Orleton Road
Ludlow Business Park
Ludlow
Shropshire SY8 1XF
England
(44) 1584 876737
www.pcsuk.com

Prima Editions is a division of Prima Creative Services, a wholly owned subsidiary of Prima Communications, Inc., Rocklin, California. Prima Editions is a co-edition publisher of illustrated books for the international market, focusing on general family reference titles on history, geography, lifestyle, crafts, and gardening of international interest. They welcome ideas in these areas, accompanied by a brief synopsis, a summary of the author's background and previous publications, along with a sample chapter. Only titles suitable for extensive illustrative treatment are of interest; series of titles considered also.

Representative titles: *History of Pirates, History of Shipwrecks* by Angus Konstam; *Atlas of Archaeology* by Nick Constable; *The Complete Guide to the Cat, The Complete Guide to the Dog, The Complete Guide to the Horse*; *Pipe—The Art & Lore of a Great Tradition* by Robin Crole.

Contact person:

Iain MacGregor, Commissioning Editor

PRION BOOKS LIMITED

Imperial Works
32 Perren Street
London NW5 3ED
England
(44) 171 482 4248
fax: (44) 171 482 4203
books@prion.co.uk (e-mail)

Prion Books—formerly known as Multimedia Books Limited—publishes titles across a wide range of categories with mainstream and popular appeal. It publishes books on drink, food, health, beauty, psychology, history, literature, travel, humor, popular culture, style, cinema, sport, martial arts, cars, contemporary issues, science, business, fiction, and a writers' Britain series.

Indicative of the Prion list: *Classic Spirits of the World: A Comprehensive Guide* by Gordon Brown; *Kenny's Cajun Creole Cookbook* by Kenny Miller (an insider tour of the flavors and culture of the Deep South by our leading Cajun Creole cook); *Nutrients A–Z: A User's Guide to Foods, Herbs, Vitamins, Minerals & Supplements* by Dr. Michael Sharon; *The Art of Makeup* by Kevyn Aucoin ("more than a book, a beauty bible"—*Clothes Show Magazine*); *Is There Life After Death? The Latest Evidence Analysed* by Robert Kastenbaum; *The River War* by Winston S. Churchill (this new abridged edition of Churchill's first large-scale historical work, written in 1899, contains a new foreword by Mr. Winston S. Churchill, the author's grandson); *The Atrocities of the Pirates* by Aaron Smith (with foreword and postscript by Robert S. Redmond); *Poets in a Landscape* by Gilbert Highet (a wonderful, lucid exploration of the world of the great Latin poets from one of the finest teachers of classics of recent times); *The Great Theatres of London* by Ronald Bergan (with foreword by Sir Anthony Hopkins); *Sex Lives of the Popes* by Nigel Cawthorne (from the Sex Lives of . . . series); *Hollywood: 60 Great Years* by John Russell Taylor, Jack Lodge, Adrian Turner, Douglas Jarvis, David Castell, and Mark Kermode (this massive and superb tome is the ultimate tribute to Hollywood from six of Britain's most eminent film critics); *The Man in Black: A History of the Football Referee* by Gordon Thompson; *The Martial Arts: Origins, Philosophy, Practice* by Peter Lewis (the fascinating cultural background to the martial arts is ignored by most books on the subject; here, in a fascinating review of how and why these arts developed, it takes center stage); *The Genius of China: 3000 Years of Science, Discovery and Invention* by Robert Temple (with introduction by Joseph Needham); and *The Red Pagoda* by Robert Mendelsohn (an American pilot and a Vietcong beauty flee across the world in an attempt to defy their past).

Query letters and SASEs should be directed to:

Barry Winkleman, Managing Director

Andrew Goodfellow, Editor

QUADRILLE PUBLISHING LTD.

5th Floor
Alhambra House
27–31 Charing Cross Road
London WC2H OLS
England
(44) 171 839 7117
fax: (44) 171 839 7118
enquiries@quadrille.co.uk (e-mail)

Quadrille is a young and groundbreaking publisher of beautifully presented and superbly illustrated books in the fields of cookery, gardening, interiors, crafts, magic, and health. The house's original intention and driving vision is to create a small list of books that would be sufficiently innovative to have serious front-list potential while simultaneously establishing themselves as core titles. Quadrille is currently offering new books from established house authors such as Tricia Guild, Nigel Colborn, Anne McKevitt, Judith Wills, and Titania Hardie, and welcoming new authors to their list, including Jean-Christophe Novelli and Stephen Woodhams.

Hot from Quadrille: *Sensual Home: Liberate Your Senses and Change Your Life* by Ilse Crawford (the founding editor of *Elle Decoration UK* looks at light, space, comfort, and texture; harmony and balance; sustenance, energy, and spirit; and shows, through evocative photography and concise informative text, how you can plan, decorate, and arrange your home to fulfill your needs); *Style on a Shoestring: How to Create Fantastic Rooms Quickly and Easily* by Anne McKevitt and Shelley Warrington; *Flower Power: A Colourful New Approach to Flower Arranging* by Stephen Woodhams; *The Food Bible: The Ultimate Guide to All That's Good and Bad in the Food We Eat* by Judith Wills; *Cooked to Perfection: An Illustrated Guide to Achieving Success with Every Dish* by Anne Willan (winner of the International Cookbook Review Award); *Bewitched: Titania's Book of Spells* by Titania Hardie ("If you've tried mysterious flowers, flirtatious glances, innocent invitations and still nothing, *Bewitched* could be just the thing" —*The Weekend Australian*); *Furniture Facelifts: A Sourcebook of Ideas, Techniques and Makeovers for Revamping Your Furniture* by Liz Wagstaff with Mark Thurgood; *Patchwork: Projects. Techniques. Motifs.* (text by Lucinda Ganderton, photographs by Linda Burgess; with a very contemporary use of color and pattern, Diane Crawford's original approach to patchwork has been given a whole new look in this beautifully illustrated book containing 20 irresistible projects); and *The Good Gift Guide: The Secret Formula for Choosing the Perfect Gift* by Susannah Constantine and Pia Marocco.

Query letters and SASEs should be directed to:

Stephanie Amor, Publicity and Marketing

QUARTET BOOKS LTD.

27 Goodge Street
London W1P 2LD
England
(44) 171 636 3992
fax: (44) 171 637 1866
quartetbooks@easynet.co.uk (e-mail)

Quartet books—a member of the **Namara Group**—is a small publisher of literary fiction, general fiction, popular culture titles, music books, biographies, and serious nonfiction, including science, history, and war studies.

Recent Quartet nonfiction and fiction offerings: *Bitch* by Elizabeth Wurtzel (in praise of difficult women, *Bitch* is the most searing feminist critique of contemporary gender relations to appear in the 1990s); *The Drifting of Spirits* by Gisele Pineau (set in the heart of Guadeloupe, this novel traces the rise and fall of man under the mocking eye of the spirits who roam the land, drifting between light and darkness, between happiness and misery, between love and death); *My Grandfather's Tale* by Ulfat Idilby (explores the close links between the Muslim Caucasus and the Arab world against a backdrop of conflict with the Russian empire); *Outremer* by Nabil Saleh (a novel of faith and heresy, loyalty and intrigue, set in the thirteenth century); *Have Gun Will Travel: The Spectacular Rise and Violent Fall of Death Row Records* by Ronin Ro ("Brimming with murder, mayhem, extortion and drug use . . . *Have Gun Will Travel* is meaty and bloody enough to enthrall both pop sociologists and armchair thrill seekers"—*Entertainment Weekly*); *DJ Culture* by Ulf Poschardt and translated from German by Shaun Whiteside with remix by Kodwo Eshun (filling the gap left by other pop histories this is a serious and visionary look at the transition of the DJ from record-spinner to musician beginning with the first-ever radio transmission in 1906 and taking us well into the next century); *Di Bella: The Man, the Cure, a Hope for All* by Vincenzo Brancatisano (the remarkable story of a man who rose from humble origins to pioneer a radical new treatment for cancer); and, now in paperback, *A Book of Your Own* by Anne Dickson, the long-established bestseller of inspirational statements.

Quartet trade orders are handled by **Plymbridge Distribution Services Ltd.**

Query letters and SASEs should be directed to:

Stella Kane, Publishing Director, Literary Fiction, Popular Culture, Music, Confessional Biography

Jeremy Beale, Managing Director, Serious Nonfiction, History, War Studies, and General Fiction

Piers Blofeld, Commissioning Editor, Science, Biography, History, and General Fiction

---

READER'S DIGEST CHILDREN'S BOOKS

King's Court
Parsonage Lane
Bath BA1 1ER
England
(44) 1225 312200
fax: (44) 1225 460942

Reader's Digest Children's Books is a division of **Victoria House Publishing**—itself a subsidiary of the Reader's Digest Association Inc. This house strives to publish a list of exciting and innovative children's books in inventive formats that inform and enrich as well as entertain and inspire the very young reader.

And these efforts clearly work effectively. The recent *Snap, Cuddle and Squeak* promotion, which brought together some of the world's bestselling novelty formats, included: *Squeeze and Squeak*—over 12 million copies sold; *Snappy Books*—over 800,000 copies sold to date; *Fluffy Tales*—over 3 million copies sold; *Tiny Hugs*—over a million copies sold; and *Window Acetate Books*—over 2 million copies sold. The *Playmobil Books* bring the world's favorite pretend-play figures and environments to an imaginative new book format, and this series follows on from the Fisher-Price Play Books launch that took place in 1997.

From Reader's Digest Children's: *The Enchanted Forest* by Shen Roddie and Tim Healey and illustrated by Paul Amesbury (a *Playmobil* title whose characters come to life in shaped board books that stand on their own two feet and have figures that bend at the waist and can sit, so that children can play with them as they read the stories); *Zoomers* by Claire Bampton and David Hawcock with illustrations by Ian Dicks, Nick Watton, Nadine Wickenden, Garry Walton, and Adam Abel (a revolutionary new format of high visual impact with strong contemporary art that combines fun with information and collectability); *Max's Train Ride* by Susan Hood and Judith Jango-Cohen with illustrations by the Thompson Bros (a unique new version of the bestselling *Squeak and Squeeze* format, creating a bright noisy book ideal for tiny hands); *Bloodhound Ben* by Stewart Cowley with illustrations by Sonia Canals (a *Waggy Tales* board book with bright, colorful illustrations and a simple, rhythmic text that encourages interaction with the story); *Surprise Spell* by Gill Davies with illustrations by Susi Adams, Gerry Hawksley, and Kate Davies (a *Little Spooky Window Book* where witches, bats, ghosts, and spiders in a "magic window" format provide exciting spooky characters and stories that all children will love); *The Learning Box* by Alison Boyle and illustrated by Lynn Breeze (a complete 36-book set of enjoyable first learning books for young children, in a full-color display folder with balcony for each book, and a formed carrying handle and Velcro closure that give a truly portable package); *The Reader's Digest Children's Atlas of the World* (prepared by an international team of cartographers, geographers, writers, editors, graphic designers, and specialist illustrators, the *Atlas* is designed to meet the needs of children living in today's information-rich and technology-led world); *The Human Body* by Dr. Luisa Dillner and illustrated by Graeme Chambers (from the unique acetate information series, which imaginatively uses acetates to overcome the limitations of conventional artwork and photography; gives clear detailed descriptions of how things work, backed up with experiments and amazing facts; and by interactively letting children see for themselves how things work, builds real enthusiasm for learning).

Distribution to the trade is by **Littlehampton Book Services Ltd.**

Query letters and SASEs should be directed to:

Stewart Cowley, Publishing Director

Peter Lawson, Art Director

ROUTLEDGE

11 New Fetter Lane
London EC4P 4EE
England
(44) 171 583 9855
fax: (44) 171 842 2298
info@routledge.co.uk (e-mail)
www.routledge.com

One of the bigger publishers, Routledge produces a substantial volume of nonfiction titles across a broad gamut of academic disciplines and maintains a very sizable stocklist in both paperback and hardback. Indeed, so extensive is the Routledge range that it produces 39 specialist subject catalogs per annum to advertise titles. The Routledge subject areas include: anthropology, archaeology, art, architecture and design, Asian studies, bilingual specialist dictionaries, business, classical studies, economics, education, environment, gender, geography, health and society, heritage and museum studies, history, language and linguistics, literature, philosophy, politics, psychology, media and cultural studies, religion, and sociology, as well as reference books and a range of specialist research journals.

Highlights and new titles from Routledge: *Women and Fascism* by Martin Durham (challenges the common assumption that fascism is a misogynist movement that has tended to exclude women); *The Facts of Causation* by D. H. Mellor (the culmination of Mellor's philosophical work over the last 30 years); *Now Read On: A Multicultural Anthology of Literature in English* edited by John McRae and Malachi Edwin Vethamani (the first anthology to bring together literature in English, from around the world, on an equal footing); *Punk Rock Revisited* edited by Roger Sabin (brings together a new generation of academics, writers, and journalists to provide the first comprehensive assessment of punk and its place in popular music history, culture, and myth); *The Colour of Angels: Cosmology, Gender and the Aesthetic Imagination* by Constance Classen (using a wide variety of examples, ranging from the sensuous religious visions of the middle ages through to nineteenth-century art movements, uncovers the gender politics behind our attitude to the senses); *The Atlas of the Future* edited by Ian Pearson, Futurologist, BT, UK (drawing on the most up-to-date research, an international team of leading analysts attempts to predict global developments over a range of diverse topics such as population, space exploration, and technology); *The Psychological Assessment of Presidential Candidates* by Stanley A. Renshon; *Essential Psychology for Nurses* by Graham Russell (an introductory text for health-care workers); and *The Economics of Fire Protection* by Ganapathy Ramachandran.

Query letters and SASEs should be directed to:

Editorial

SAGE PUBLICATIONS

6 Bonhill Street
London EC2A 4PU
England
(44) 171 374 0645
fax: (44) 171 374 8741

Sage, along with its imprints—**Alta Mira Press**, **Pine Forge Press,** and **Corwin Press**—is another major publisher of academic titles with a particularly solid showing in the humanities and social sciences. Sage books, many of which are interdisciplinary in nature so transcend specific subject categories, cover topics relating to addiction, anthropology, archaeology, communication and media studies, counseling and psychotherapy, criminology and law, development studies, education, family studies, gender studies, gerontology, interpersonal violence, linguistics and discourse studies, management and organization studies, marketing and sales, medicine, nursing and health, politics and international relations, psychology, public administration, race and ethnic studies, research methodology, sacred literature studies, social policy and social work, sociology and cultural studies, and urban studies. Moreover, Sage produces a very strong research journals list that, like its book output, also covers a substantial chunk of the academic spectrum.

Recent offerings and featured titles: *Theories of Communication: A Short Introduction* by Armand Mattelart and Michele Mattelart (translated by James Alan Cohen and Susan Gruenheck; a concise introduction to the development of communication theory); *Qualitative Methods and Analysis in Organizational Research: A Practical Guide* edited by Gillian Symon and Catherine Cassell (an invaluable resource that brings together and describes a wide range of qualitative methods in organizational research and shows how they can be used in practice); *Athletes and Acquaintance Rape* by Jeffrey R. Benedict (takes a provocative look at specific aspects of professional athletic life that contribute to a climate favorable to athletes sexually assaulting women—a climate that also protects offenders from conviction or punishment); *The Future of Terrorism: Violence in the New Millennium* edited by Harvey W. Kushner; *The Recorded Sayings of Zen Master Joshu: The First Full English Translation* translated by James Green (this first full English translation gives the odd, outrageous, and illuminating replies of this founding Zen [Ch'an] master from North China to the questions of eighth- and ninth-century Buddhist monks); *Every Living Thing: Daily Use of Animals in Ancient Israel* by Oded Borowski; *The Landscape of Qualitative Research* edited by Norman K. Denzin and Yvonna S. Lincoln (one of three new paperback volumes comprising the state-of-the-art *Handbook of Qualitative Research);* and *Promoting Teen Health: Linking*

Schools, Health Organizations, and Community by Sally Champlin, Alan Henderson, and William Evashwick (demonstrates how some of the most serious problems and dangers confronting teenagers today—tobacco, alcohol, substance abuse, pregnancy, sexually transmitted diseases, mental health problems, and youth violence—can be addressed through health promotion and practice).

Query letters and SASEs should be directed to:

Editorial, as on previous page

THE SCOUT ASSOCIATION

Baden-Powell House
65267 Queen's Gate
London SW7 5JS
England
(44) 171 584 7030
fax: (44) 171 590 5103
ukbphscout@aol.com (e-mail)
www.scoutbase.org.uk/

Scouting began when 20 boys went on an experimental camp during the first nine days of August 1907 to Brownsea Island, Dorset. The camp, which was a great success, was organized by Robert Baden-Powell, who taught them skills and methods he had learned as a young army officer in India where he specialized in scouting, map-making, and reporting. Today, the Scout Movement has an international membership of approximately 25 million in over 200 countries, with well over half a million in the UK alone, and is the world's largest voluntary organization for boys and girls.

Baden-Powell sought, through his methods, to prepare young boys to take a responsible and helpful role in society. The fundamental soundness of his original vision has blossomed as the Scout Movement has itself never stayed introspective and static, but adapted and changed with succeeding generations to remain ever relevant in a modern context. But while the image, activities, and membership have changed—for instance, the doors were opened to young girls in 1991—at its core, the Scouting Movement continues to offer young people a sense of membership, stimulate their loyalties, provide activities they might never otherwise experience, and encourage them to grow spiritually and develop within their own faith and denomination.

In January 1908, Baden-Powell published the first edition of *Scouting for Boys,* issued in fortnightly parts; it was an immediate success. Today, the Scout Association's publications—essentially training manuals and teaching aids, but also including many factsheets and charts—number some 80 "live" titles.

A small sample from the Scout Association: *Scouting Magazine* (monthly from the association); *The Beaver Scout Leaders' Manual* (the essential guide for anybody involved in Beaver Scouting, containing everything you need to know to run and support a successful Beaver Scout Colony); *The Cub Scout Handbook* (essential for every Cub Scout, this book covers every aspect of Cub Scouting, including the requirements for all the Progressive Training Awards and the Activity Badges); *Welcome to Scouts* (a colorful leaflet for youngsters new to scouting); *Starting a Venture Scout Unit* (how to set up a Venture Scout Unit and run it successfully); *Expeditions in Hot Climates* and *Dinghy Sailing* (both from the factsheets stock); *If I Push Him Will He Break?* (an excellent 40-page reprint of articles on Scouting for those with special needs), and *Really Wet Games* (a splendid collection of crazy games, with water as a central ingredient).

Query letters and SASEs should be directed to:

Mike Brennan, Publications Editor

Stephen Nixey, Assistant Publications Editor

SEARCH PRESS LTD.

(Incorporating **Burns and Oates**)
Wellwood
North Farm Road
Tunbridge Wells
Kent TN2 3DR
England
(44) 1892 510850
fax: (44) 1892 515903
searchpress@searchpress.com (e-mail)

Search Press publishes a very comprehensive range of outstandingly illustrated and beautiful arts and crafts titles, while its **Burns and Oates** imprint produces a wide-ranging religious listing. Search house-specialties include textile crafts, general crafts, silk painting, papercrafts, illumination and calligraphy, art, leisure arts and drawing, embroidery, knitting, gardening, cookery, Guild of Master Craftsmen titles, David Porteous Editions, and gift books.

New from Search: *How to Paint on Glass: Capture the Look of Genuine Stained Glass* by Julia Bottrell (recently one of the bestselling titles in what is now one of the hottest craft subjects); *Decoupage: Transforming Junk into Stunning Items for the Home* by Jane Gordon-Smith (learn how to transform everyday furnishings and objects into beautiful, decorative items—with just scissors, glue, paint, and varnish); *Friendship Bracelets* by Veronique Follet (step-by-step, easy-to-follow diagrams for twenty-two different designs—chevrons, stripes, diamonds, and a host of others in a carnival of colors); *Marbling on Paper Using Oil Paints* by Anne Chambers (the magical and mysterious process of marbling is shown clearly with step-by-step photographs and illustrations for effects such as marble cutting, patterning, and combing); *Colour Calligraphy* by David Graham (demonstrates how to produce brightly colored bookmarks, nameplates, letters, and cards and professional-looking designs); *Wet-into-Wet* by Bryan A. Thatcher (the "wet-into-wet" secrets of turning atmospheric skies, rivers, and landscapes into watercolor); *Inspirational Ideas for Embroidery on Clothes and Accessories* by Gail Lawther; and *Muck and Magic: Start Your Own Natural Garden with Colourful Simple Projects* by Jo Readman (winner of the Sir Peter Kent Prize for Nature Conservation Writing for Children; truly practical book on gardening with questions, quizzes, and projects such as growing potatoes in a tire).

The Burns and Oates list covers: lives of the Saints, prayer, mysticism and spirituality, Christian history, Christian doctrine and life, philosophy, theology, Bible reading and commentary, Christianity and society, gift books, arts and crafts, travel, and children's books.

Burns and Oates highlights: *The World of Hildegard of Bingen: Her Life, Times, and Visions* by Heinrich Schipperges and translated by John Cumming; *The Cloud of Unknowing: Reflections on Selected Texts* by Austin Cooper, O.M.I. (contains a series of short reflections on the writings of the anonymous author of *The Cloud of Unknowing* and shows how they relate to the wider Catholic traditions of both East and West); *Spiritual Writings* by Columba Marmion, O.S.B. (the principal spiritual works of the third abbot of Maredsous); *Mary Ward: Pilgrim and Mystic* by Margaret Mary Littlehales (the life of the foundress of the Institute of the Blessed Virgin Mary, born in Yorkshire in 1585); *A History of Philosophy* by Frederick Copleston (an unrivalled nine-volume work); *Encyclopedia of Theology: A Concise Sacramentum Mundi* (edited by Karl Rahner, offers over 1,800 pages of thought and information on the major themes of traditional and modern theology); *Christian Cross Stitch* by Gisela Banbury (using symbolism as a theme, the author shows how to create a selection of pictures and samplers); and *The Christian's Guide to Rome* by S. G. A. Luff (revised and updated for the modern-day pilgrim and ordinary visitor, offers a chance to explore this fascinating city in detail).

Query letters and SASEs should be directed to:

Rosalind Dace, Editorial Director, Search Press

Paul Burns, Acquisitions Editor, Burns and Oates

SERPENT'S TAIL

4 Blackstock Mews
London N4 2BT
England
(44) 171 354 1949
fax: (44) 171 704 6467
info@serpentstail.com (e-mail)
www.serpentstail.com

Serpent's Tail is a small and successful independent publisher of provocative and cutting-edge fiction and nonfiction titles. Its fiction interests particularly include crime and horror, cult fiction, anthologies, and translations of outstanding foreign literary fiction such as *Symmetries* by Luisa Valenzuela.

The house has just had its best year to date, with Jon Stock's *The Riot Act* being short-listed for the John Creasy Award for Best First Crime Novel of the year, the publication of *The Silent Cry* by Nobel-prizewinning Kenzaburo Oe, and the launch of the new **Five Star** paperback imprint.

Some of Tail's latest features: *Intoxication: An Anthology of Stimulant-Based Writing* edited by Toni Davidson (featuring some of the best new fiction exploring the themes and preoccupations of the "chemical generation," from British and American writers such as Irvine Welsh, Lynne Tillman, Jeff Noon, and Gary Indiana); *Dirty Laundry* by Don Taylor (set in the contemporary northeast of England, a unique modern comedy of sex and crime, and also an impressionistic tale of memory, madness, and abuse); *King Suckerman* by George P. Pelecanos (set in Washington D.C., an unforgettable crime novel of morality, friendship, and unexpected consequences); *Altered State: The Story of Ecstasy Culture and Acid House* by Matthew Collin with contributions by John Godfrey (the definitive inside story of a generation); *Wait for Me at the Bottom of the Pool: The Writings of Jack Smith* edited by J. Hoberman and E. Leffingwell (bringing together long unavailable essays, performance scripts, interviews, and a wealth of other material, reveals Jack Smith's ideas and personality); *Pornucopia: Porn, Sex, Technology and Desire* by Laurence O'Toole (argues that the expansion of the new technologies of video, cable, and the Internet is allowing pornography to emerge from the shadows); *Who's a Pretty Boy, Then? One Hundred and Fifty Years of Gay Life in Pictures* by James Gardiner (a remarkable collection of images that make up a personal and highly idiosyncratic view of gay history since the invention of the camera).

Distribution is now handled by **Littlehampton Book Services Ltd.**

Serpent's Tail welcomes approaches from authors who have made themselves familiar with the house's interests. Writers should send a synopsis together with a couple of sample chapters.

In the first instance, query letters and SASEs should be directed to:

Editorial, as on previous page

SHIRE PUBLICATIONS LTD.

Cromwell House
Church Street
Princes Risborough
Buckinghamshire HP27 9AA
England
(44) 1844 344301
fax: (44) 1844 347080
shire@shirebooks.co.uk (e-mail)
www.shirebooks.co.uk

Shire is a small publishing house producing a broad range of beautifully illustrated and informative nonfiction titles.

House interests include antiques and collecting, archaeology, architecture and buildings, biographies, canals and inland waterways, church history, Egyptology, ethnography, firefighting, garden history, genealogy, local history and folklore, guide books, horse power, industrial history, London, maritime, military history, motoring, music, natural history, photography, railways and steam, road transport, rural crafts, history and bygones, Scottish heritage, social history, textile history, and walking.

Recent house highlights: *Medieval Bridges* by Martin Cook (examines the Roman, Saxon, and Norman origins of the medieval bridge, including its broader national and international context, and considers the engineering techniques and social background that led to its development during the twelfth, thirteenth, and fourteenth centuries); *Dolls' House Furniture* by Halina Pasierbska (an historical overview of dolls' house furniture and furnishings from the sixteenth century to the present day, set against the social and economic conditions of the period in which they were made); *Discovering, English Customs and Traditions* by Margaret Gascoigne (a gazetteer of traditional customs with the history of each); *Victoria's Wars* by I. F. W. Beckett (this selection of campaign photographs shows the Victorian army in a variety of climes and conditions over 50 years from Burma in 1852 to Tibet in 1904); *Firefighting Equipment* by Brian Wright; *Shoemaking* by June Swann; *Old Television* by Andrew Emmerson (a Shire Album that explores the heritage of the black-and-white era and traces the development of television broadcasting); and *Walled Kitchen Gardens* by Susan Campbell (another of the Shire Album range that describes the layout, organization, planting, and maintenance of the gardens that supplied large households with their vegetables and fruit throughout the year).

Query letters and SASEs should be directed to:

Suzanne C. Ross, General Manager

SIMON & SCHUSTER (UK)

Africa House
64–78 Kingsway
London WC2B 6AH
England
(44) 171 316 1900
fax: (44) 171 316 0331

One of the larger players in the publishing world, Simon & Schuster books (parent company VIACOM) represent most nonfiction categories as well as a wide range of adult and young adult fiction. Titles also appear under the **Free Press, Earthlight,** and **Touchstone** imprints.

A selection from Simon & Schuster: *The Spider's Web* by Nigel McCrery (a third crime thriller in the Doctor Sam Ryan mystery series, now a major television drama starring Amanda Burton); *The Devil's Garden* by Ralph Peters (the new military thriller from the bestselling author of *Twilight of Heroes)*; *Cilla Black: Bobby's Girl* by Douglas Thompson (details the excitements, tragedies, and triumphs of Priscilla White, the woman who, 30 years ago, created a new persona for herself); *Confirmation: The Hard Evidence* by Whitley Strieber (attempts to posit hard evidence for the reality of his own abduction experience and close encounters that many he has been in contact with have experienced; both a quest for understanding and a thorough and rational examination of facts, particularly of what may be tangible evidence—explosive new detail on implants removed from people's bodies and material from crash sites); *Noah's Flood: The New Scientific Discoveries about the Event That Changed History* by Walter Pitman and William Ryan (part modern-day scientific detective story and part reconstruction of pre-modern history that gives fresh meaning to ancient myths); *Customer Centered Selling: Eight Steps to Success from the World's Best Sales Force* by Robert L. Jolles (a cutting-edge guide to selling, from one of the world's leading hands-on practitioners); *Easy Meals with Meat* by Sue Ashworth (an S & S *Weight Watchers* practical guide to eating meat and losing weight, too); *Savage Sky* by Emma Drummond (a wartime romance novel from the author of *The Knightshill Trilogy)*; *Diana and Dodi: A Love Story* by Rene Delorm with Barry Fox and Nadine Taylor (the final word on the relationship that took the world by storm, written by the only insider who really knew the full story); and *Star Trek: Q's Guide to the Continuum* by Michael Jan Friedman and Robert Greenberger (from Pocket Books—the Official Star Trek publishers).

Query letters and SASEs should be directed to:

Nick Webb, Managing Director

Clare Ledingham, Fiction Director

Helen Gummer, Nonfiction Director

Martin Fletcher, Editorial Director, Pocket Books/Scribner and Simon & Schuster

John Jarrold, Earthlight

Martina Challis, Publisher, Children's/Young Adults' Books

Diane Spivey, Rights Director

Darren Nash, Audio Books Manager

SOUVENIR PRESS LTD.

43 Great Russell Street
London WC1B 3PA
England
(44) 171 580 637 5711
fax: (44) 171 580 637 5711

Ernest Hecht founded Souvenir in 1952 in the bedroom of his parents' flat after graduating from the University of Hull and running its football teams in the pre-Larkin days—when the library was famed for its card schools as well as the books on its shelves. The first bestseller arrived with *The Password Is Courage*, the story of Charles Coward, a key witness in the War Crimes trial of I. G. Farben. Believing strongly in Sir Stanley Unwin's dictum that the publisher's first duty to his authors is to remain solvent, the list has always been an eclectic mixture of the commercial—bestsellers and books intended for more limited audiences.

Hecht's love affair with Brazilian football and consequent visits resulted in Souvenir becoming the official publisher of the great soccer teams of Brazil, Real Madrid, Matt Busby, and Bobby Charlton, as well as leading to the publication of many major Latin American writers, including Jorge Amado, Julio Cortazar, Jorge Luis Borges, and Pablo Neruda. In 1959 the magazine *Book Collector* asserted that Souvenir was responsible for bringing Rock and Roll publishing to Britain, and in the same year Hecht managed to persuade Arthur Hailey to try his hand as a novelist. Starting with *Flight into Danger,* this led to a whole series of major worldwide bestsellers. Less known is the fact that the Souvenir list includes five Nobel Prize winners and that, among its more esoteric books, Souvenir has published most of the leaders of the humanistic school of psychology. On the literary front Souvenir undertook a new series of translations of Knut Hamsun that *The Times Literary Supplement* has compared to the New Oxford editions of Ibsen, and brought back into print eleven novels of Neil M. Gunn that Hugh McDiarmid hailed as a major contribution to Scottish literature. Also, a personal experience involving a friend seeking advice for a disabled child led to the creation of the *Human Horizons* series of books for the disabled, a specialist list, now of some 100 titles, that has become preeminent in its field.

House authors who have figured on the international bestseller lists include Erich von Daniken, Laurence Peter, Charles Berlitz, John G. Fuller, Betty Edwards, Alexander McKee, Ronald Searle, Elaine Morgan, Jose Carreras, Rosemary Hawthorne, and Peter O'Donnell among others. With its bold independent approach to publishing, over the years Souvenir has had the satisfaction of seeing many of the general titles, seemingly offbeat at first publication, become standard so that to date Souvenir keeps some 700 individual titles in print.

Also from Souvenir: *Hen Frigates: Wives of Merchant Captains Under Sail* by Joan Druett (throughout the nineteenth century, many merchant ships plying the Atlantic, and farther afield to Europe and the far East, carried not only the captain and his crew but the captain's wife and children; the amazing, largely untold story of these "hen frigates" is more fascinating than any sailor's yarn); *Odd Dates Only: The Bizarre Birthday Book* by William Hartston (this eccentric almanac of really interesting things that happened on each day of the year is the perfect reference for all players of Trivial Pursuits and pub quiz games, and for every public speaker); *Yesterdays: The Way We Were, 1919–1939* by Eric Midwinter (the perfect souvenir for anyone who lived in the inter-war years—an album of memories); *Sum Hope: Breaking the Numbers Barrier* by Steve Chinn (this practical sympathetic book sets out to break the numbers barrier, to prove to people that they know more than they think, and to help them gain confidence in using numbers); *Magic and Mystery in Ancient Egypt* by Christian Jacq, translated by Janet M. Davis (an enthralling book that takes us on a journey into a secret world where magic was an exact science, its mysteries closely guarded by the temple priests); *The World of the Castrati: The History of an Extraordinary Operatic Phenomenon* by Patrick Barbier, translated by Margaret Crosland (entertaining and authoritative, this is the first study of the phenomenon of the castrati in relation to the baroque period, covering the lives and triumphs of more than sixty singers over three centuries when the fashion for castrati was at its peak); *Beyond Grief: A Guide for Recovering from the Death of a Loved One* by Carol Staudacher (a complete guide for anyone surviving the death of a loved one); and *Fairy Spells: Seeing and Communicating with the Fairies* by Claire Nahmad.

Query letters and SASEs should be directed to:

Ernest Hecht, Managing Director

SPELLMOUNT PUBLISHERS

The Old Rectory
Staplehurst
Kent TN12 0AZ
England
(44) 1580 893730
fax: (44) 1580 893731

Now entering its sixth year, Spellmount is a specialist publisher of high-quality titles that particularly focus on all aspects of military history. A strong and increasing interest in military heritage has helped Spellmount's list to grow rapidly at a time when Britain's modern armed forces are coming under the economic microscope.

Spellmount categories include, general military history, seventeenth- and eighteenth-century military history, Napoleonic times, nineteenth- and early twentieth-century military history, World War I, World War II and the modern era, as well as some more general history and nonfiction titles. Recently launched is the *Spellmount Classics* series, which offers classic works of military history in quality paperback editions at affordable prices. The first three *Classics* offerings are: *The Massacre of Glencoe* by John Buchan; *Sedgemoor 1685* by David Chandler; and *Thoughts on War* by B. H. Liddell Hart. An already established success for Spellmount is its facsimile series, *The Spellmount Library of Military History*, regarded as an important fund of source material for students of history and now with ten titles following its three newest additions.

Among Spellmount's latest: *Valour A History of the Gurkhas* by E. D. Smith (a lavishly illustrated history of the Gurkha regiments from their beginnings in 1815 through to the current day); *Soldiers of the Raj: The Indian Army 1600–1947* edited by Alan J. Guy and Peter B. Boyden (tells the fascinating story of the armies raised by Britain in India from the seventeenth century to independence, and the men and women, both Indian and British, who served in them); *Marlborough as Military Commander* by David Chandler with foreword by His Grace the Eleventh Duke of Marlborough (detailed, informed, and dispassionate analysis of the Duke of Marlborough's qualities as a military leader is set firmly against the military realities of the period); *In Hell Before Daylight:*

The Siege and Storming of the Fortress of Badajoz, 1812—2nd edition by Ian Fletcher (an epic action of the Peninsular War that involved Wellington's infantry in some of the most savage hand-to-hand fighting of the whole campaign); *Thunder Along the Mississippi: The River Battles That Split the Confederacy* by Jack D. Coombe (the story of the all-but-forgotten gunboat battles between the Union and Confederate navies up the small bayous and inlets along the Mississippi river); *A Noble Crusade: The History of the Eighth Army 1941–1945* by Richard Doherty (the first-ever history of one of the most famous British armies of all time); *The Jewish Brigade* by Morris Beckman (on the brigade that distinguished itself in action in Italy in the final months of the war, gave Jews worldwide pride at seeing a formation fighting under the Jewish flag, and which was to form the basis of the Israeli army); and *Mozart* by Martin Hoyle (covering all of Wolfgang Amadeus Mozart's operas from his early works to the masterpieces, the author maintains that they reveal, more than any other of his musical forms, how this child prodigy turned into a genius who could see into the human heart).

Query letters and SASEs should be directed to:

Jamie Wilson, Publisher

STAINER & BELL LTD.

P.O. Box 110
Victoria House
23 Gruneisen Road
Finchley
London N3 1DZ
England
(44) 181 343 3303
fax: (44) 181 343 3024
post@stainer.co.uk (e-mail)
www.stainer.co.uk

Founded in 1907, Stainer & Bell is a small, independent, family-run business, specializing in the publication of quality music and books. There was neither a Mr. Stainer nor a Mr. Bell. Tradition has it that the six original partners chose the firm's name because it had a credit-worthy ring to it. However, a direct family link with the present management team can be traced back to 1912.

Composers published in the early years included Charles Villiers Stanford, Percy Buck, Harold Darke, Thomas Dunhill, Gustav Holst, and Ralph Vaughan Williams;

works by all of these writers are still in print. Later the publishing pedigree was enhanced by the acquisition of Augener, famous for its practical editions of the classical master; Joseph Williams, one of the oldest British publishing houses, founded in 1808; and Galliard, which brought to the company a fine range of cello music. Carefully nurtured over many years, the catalog now contains some of the richest treasures from three centuries of British musical achievement, including works by Frank Bridge, Alan Bush, Geoffrey Bush, Frederick Delius, Edward Elgar, Herbert Howells, John Ireland, Gordon Jacob, Hubert Parry, Henry Purcell, and Peter Warlock, and acclaimed tutors and textbooks by Dorothy Bradley and Raymond Tobin, Adam Carse, Neil Mackay, Stewart Macpherson, and William Squire.

The house also has a long and distinguished association with a wide range of highly regarded scholarly publications, including the prestigious *Musica Britannica* series, published on behalf of the Musica Britannica Trust. Together with *The Byrd Edition*, *English Madrigalists*, *Early English Church Music,* and *Music for London Entertainment*, *Musica Britannica*, which has grown to well over sixty volumes since its conception in 1951, provides invaluable source material and authoritative texts for scholars worldwide.

All-in-all, the list is a stable of solid talent, rich archive, and extensive range of quality music from madrigals to musicals, concertos to choral music, hymn books and publications on liturgy, which easily account for Stainer & Bell's excellent international reputation.

A sample of the most recent listings: *Johann Christian Bach: Favourite Songs Sung at Vauxhall Gardens (c. 1760–65;* facsimile score with introductions by Stephen Roe and Christopher Hogwood); *Big Blue Planet: And Other Songs for Worship in God's World* edited by Judy Jarvis; *Travels with My Flute* by Tony Cliff (five pieces for flute and CD, featuring piano or full ensemble backing, plus complete recorded performances); *Hymnquest: A Dictionary of Hymnody—Volume I* (first lines, links, and book references); *New Horizons: Songs and Project Work for Primary Schools* edited by Richard Braley and June Boyce-Tillman; *Brendan Ahoy!* by Donald Swann (a musical play for stage or concert performance); *Touching the Pulse: Anthologies for Use in Worship* edited by Sandy Williams (worship where we live); *The Fiddle and I* by E. Markham Lee (violin and piano); *Manuscripts of Fourteenth Century English Polyphony* edited by Frank L. I. Harrison and Roger Wibberley (facsimiles of early English church music); and *Three Pieces for Small Orchestra* by Frederick Delius: *On Hearing the First Cuckoo in Spring, A Summer Night on the River, A Song Before Sunrise* (complete works, volume 27A, revised and edited by Thomas Beecham).

Query letters and SASEs should be directed to:

Nicholas Williams, Publishing Manager

SUMMERSDALE PUBLISHERS LTD.

46 West Street
Chichester
West Sussex PO19 1RP
England
(44) 1243 771107
fax: (44) 1243 786300
summersdale@summersdale.com (e-mail)

Summersdale was established in 1990 with the aim of producing high-quality books at competitive prices. Having published just 2 titles in the first year, Summersdale now has a backlist of about 100 titles, a most recent front-list of 46 new titles, and world-wide distribution. Indeed, a sales increase of 160% in the last 12 months made Summersdale Britain's fastest-growing independent publishing house.

House categories, including both fiction and a broad range of nonfiction, cover travel, true crime, gift, humor, cookery, science fiction/TV/film, health/self-help, reference, children's, popular psychology, EFL/languages, and militaria/self-defense.

New from Summersdale: *The Great British Festival Guide: Literature, Music, Food, Drink, Flowers, Sports, Traditional by Summersdale* (a comprehensive guide to Britain's large and small, weird and wonderful festivals encompassing everything from Worm Charming to Glastonbury, from Morris Dancing to Real Ale, and from Oysters to Shakespeare); *How to Say 'I Love You': 100 Ways to Show You Care* by Stewart Ferris (a collection of inventive, imaginative, incredibly impressive, and sometimes downright insane ways to say the three most important romantic words in the English language); *How to Chat-Up Men: Pocket Edition* by Kitty Malone (no one knows better than Kitty Malone how to get the guy you want and now she shares the secrets of her success); *The Student Grub Guide: Over 120 Favourite Recipes* by Alastair Williams, from the *Grub Guide* Series (a wide selection of popular and easy to prepare recipes—laid-back, witty, and user-friendly instructions); *The A–Z of Conspiracy Theories* by Robert Bircher (a comprehensive guide to alleged cover-ups, from JFK to UFOs, Men in Black to men on Mars; governments worldwide will tremble in their boots); *5 Minutes to De-Stress* by Fiona Burnett (a collection of visualization exercises and practical tips that provide instant relief from stress and tension, from the 5 Minute series); *Write Your Life: A Guide to Autobiography* by Ken Moon (guides aspiring writers through the process of researching, compiling and narrating an autobiography); and *Shaping Up: During and After Pregnancy* by Stavia Blunt (Dr. Stavia Blunt, mother of two young children, shows that it is not difficult to regain your pre-pregnancy figure or even achieve a better one!).

Summersdale books, backed up by strong publicity campaigns, including newspaper serialization, reviews, author interviews on television and radio, and signing tours, are distributed by **Littlehampton Book Services Ltd.,** currently Distributor of the Year.

Query letters and SASEs should be directed to:

Claire Richardson, Editorial

SUTTON PUBLISHING

Phoenix Mill
Thrupp
Stroud
Gloucestershire GL5 2BU
England
(44) 1453 731114
fax: (44) 1453 731117
editorial@sutton-publishing.co.uk (e-mail)

Sutton is a leading specialist publisher of history titles and has just celebrated its twentieth year in business.

The house's comprehensive history program is arranged into four divisions. The General History division includes British, European and international, archaeology and pre-history to twentieth century, history of battles and warfare, political history, genealogy, and heraldry. Its Biography and Heritage division covers biography and autobiography, literary classics and anthologies, history of art and architecture, the country house, and heritage nostalgia. The Military division ranges over British, European and international, nineteenth- and twentieth-century military, espionage and undercover operations, naval warfare and maritime, and air warfare and aviation. The Pictorial and Regional division deals with places, events and themes in old photographs, social history old photograph albums, illustrated local history, transport old photograph albums, and illustrated transport history.

On Sutton's newest listings: *A Deep Cry: First World War Soldier-Poets Killed in France and Flanders* edited and introduced by Anne Powell (arranged by dates of death, this book gives the short life-and-death stories of 66 British poets, beginning with R. W. Sterling, killed in April 1915, and ending with Wilfred Owen, killed a week before the armistice in 1918); *The Crusades* by Bernard Hamilton (from the *Sutton Pocket Histories* series edited by Asa Briggs; a masterful overview by a leading historian, this survey investigates why the crusading movement, launched in 1095 to liberate the Holy Places, became so popular and successful); *War: Themes in History—Identities in Conflict 1300–2000* edited by Bertrand Taithe and Tim Thornton (leading scholars address the concepts of warfare and identity from the fourteenth century to modern days. Four thematic and chronological sections cover some of the major historiographical debates, such as nation-making warfare, illuminating how the experience of war has affected national, individual, professional, and ideological identities); *Tudor Women* by Alison Plowden (available for the first time in paperback, this classic study of the dominant women of the Tudor era covers domestic and foreign politics, women's status and upbringing, and life for the "average" Tudor housewife in a beautifully written and carefully researched book); *The English Fair* by David Kerr Cameron (old-time fairs were colorful, boisterous, and often bawdy, but they were also a vital part of England's economy. This intriguing new study examines a long-neglected subject and its impact on trade and everyday lives); *HM Submarines in Camera: 1901–1996* by Cdr. J. J. Tall and Paul Kemp (illustrated throughout with archive photographs and accompanied by detailed captions, gives a graphic view of the submarines that have made history); *The Southern Pacifics: Bulleid's Radical Design* by Roger J. Mannion (this third volume in a trilogy of works on the Southern Pacific steam trains covers the design and development of the engine, the Southern Pacific people, construction, design changes, the Light Pacifics, the operation of the locomotives and service during the war years); *Oral History: A Handbook* by Ken Howarth (a wide-ranging, practical introduction for amateurs and professionals that explains oral history recording and its uses); and *Ormskirk: The Making of a Modern Town* by Mona Duggan (in this important contribution to the ongoing debate on the success or failure of market towns during this period, local author Mona Duggan traces changes in every aspect of the town's experience: economy, education, religion, culture, and the leisure scene).

Query letters and SASEs should be directed to:

Peter Clifford, Publishing Director

Jane Crompton, Senior Commissioning Editor, General History

Jaqueline Mitchell, Senior Commissioning Editor, Biography and Heritage

Jonathan Falconer, Senior Commissioning Editor, Military History

Simon Fletcher, Senior Commissioning Editor, Pictorial and Regional History

TAMARIND

P.O. Box 52
Camberley North Wood
Middlesex HA6 IUN
England
(44) 181 866 8808
fax: (44) 181 866 5627
TamarindLTD@aol.com (e-mail)

Tamarind was founded in 1987 by Verna Wilkins to publish books that give a high, positive profile to black children. Black children were being ignored, by not being represented in books aimed specifically at children. From the hundreds of books produced each year, only very few presented black children as the main protagonists. A large percentage of those few were stereotyped and negative.

Tamarind believes that the early years of childhood are important in their own right, as well as being the foundation for later life. Inclusion in high-quality provision in their learning material and education is a right as well as a long-term investment in the futures of all children. Children should be valued, and their full development is possible only if they live in an environment that respects their individual identity, culture, and heritage, and when positive action is taken to support this. Many black children are excluded from high-quality picture books, yet children need successful role models. They need to see people like themselves, unselfconsciously leading successful lives so that they know it is possible for them, too. Thus, every attempt should be made to redress the balance in publishing early-years picture books that influence *all* children, which is why Tamarind is determined to play a significant role in such developments and help children prepare for their adulthood in the new millennium by supplying them with cutting-edge computer-literate tooth fairies and mermaids, female giants, and *loads of fun.*

The houses' success is reflected in the awards that it has received, which include: Young Book Trust—Children's Book of the Year Awards; Nursery and Creche—Gold Award for Best Product, American Bookseller—Pick of the Lists, and the National Curriculum—Key Stage One, 75,000 sold.

Classic Tamarind fare: *Ben Makes a Cake* by Verna Wilkins (Ben would like to be a chef, and dreams of all the cakes he could make; eventually, he enlists Dad's help to produce something nice for tea—Age 4+); *Boots for a Bridesmaid* (Nicky would rather be a whiz cricketer than a bridesmaid; mother is a wheelchair user—an SIA book depicting disability); *Yohance and the Dinosaurs* by Alexis Obi (strikingly illustrated by Lynne Willey); *Jessica* by Christine Leo, illustrated by Kim Harley (Jessica, a beautiful mermaid who lives in the Caribbean Sea, is a traveler, a fighter against pollution, and a real friend of the animals in the ocean); *Kofi and the Butterflies* by Sandra Horn, illustrated by Lynne Willey (a magical, colorful fantasy book with a realistic conservation theme); *Abena and the Rock: A Story from Ghana* (a tidal wave devastates an entire village and deposits a huge rock in the square. How can it be moved? The story demonstrates pushing and pulling, using appropriate technology—from a series of BBC story books originally used on BBC Schools Television Series, Science Challenge); and *Imagination* (from the *Tamarind Posters* series).

Query letters and SASEs should be directed to:

Peggy Goodall

USBORNE PUBLISHING LTD.

Usborne House
83–85 Saffron Hill
London EC1N 8RT
England
(44) 171 430 2800
fax: (44) 171 430 1562 and
fax: (44) 171 242 0974 (illustrations)
www.kingston.net/ikweb/usborne/

For 21 years Usborne has been publishing books that children love. Usborne is now a household name—at least, in houses that have children—with over 800 books in print in the UK, and an equal success abroad, with books now translated into over 50 languages. The essence of Usborne's corporate philosophy and the secret of its success is really quite simple—*make books that children want to read*, since however worthy, a book is nothing unless a child picks it off the shelves and settles down to read.

Thus, Usborne puts tremendous creative effort into the style, design, and content of their products. Every book has pages bursting with color, humor, and information. Text is broken up magazine style with lots of illustrations or photographs. But it is never forgotten that information will keep the child reading, so the books explain a topic thoroughly, making them suitable for both beginners and those who know a little more about a subject. Many devices are employed to encourage children to study the illustrations rather than simply looking—strip cartoons, speech bubbles, surprise, drama, hand lettering, cutaways, and diagrams—and many books use quizzes and puzzles to draw children in and to reward them by showing how much they have learned.

As Usborne has grown, so have its ambitions. The house now publishes books for all ages on all subjects—everything from mechanics for 5-year-olds *(What Makes a Car Go?)* to stargazing for teenagers *(Astronomy)*. The range of titles for the young and the very young is expanding, with titles covering the new, back-to-basics phonics approach to reading, first geography, pre-school activities, and a variety of educational titles linked to Usborne's enormously successful *Farmyard Tales*. And as the world's first publisher of home-computer books in the early eighties, Usborne is now introducing a completely new collection of computer titles on the modern world of the Internet and the World Wide Web. Other books for older readers include an in-depth, if slightly skeptical, look at the paranormal; a mouthwatering beginner's cookery course; and a compellingly readable new series of adventure stories.

In short, Usborne believes that it is only by providing books for children—not teachers, not librarians, not even parents, but *children*—that they have been so successful in the past 21 years. Every Usborne book is planned, written, and designed with this in mind.

A sample of Usborne's latest fare: *Newspapers Histories* (a series of books that take a fresh and lively look at history: cunningly disguised as tabloid newspapers to capture the shocks, horrors, and sensations of the past with colorful artwork, diagrams, and photographs that depict the trials and triumphs of each era); *The Internet for Beginners: An Usborne Computer Guide* (absent of technobabble, these books are clear and easy to understand; logical text and full-color illustrations help show how to get the most out of your computer); *Alien Abduction? The Evidence and the Arguments* an *Usborne Paranormal Guide* (for children aged 10 and upwards, giving a meticulous and open-minded approach to well-documented stories of paranormal activity); *Dragon Quest,* an *Usborne Fantasy Adventure* illustrated by Nick Harris (for 8-year-olds and upwards); *The Usborne Children's Encyclopedia* by Colin King and Jane Elliot (ideal for school projects, answering questions or for simply enjoying a fascinating browse); *Growing Up: Adolescence, Body Changes and Sex* (from the *Usborne Facts of Life* series—winner of Times Educational Supplement Information Book Award); *Eagle Mountain* by Sarah Dixon (an *Usborne Adventure* book for 8-year-olds and upwards); *Land of the Lost Teddies* by Emma Fischel, illustrated by Daniel Howarth (an Usborne Young Puzzle Adventures series book for 4-year-olds and upwards, aimed at encouraging reading through simple and entertaining stories); *The Usborne Children's Songbook: With Music for Piano, Keyboard, Recorder, Flute, Violin and Guitar* (traditional as well as less familiar tunes, specially arranged to suit children's voices).

Usborne books are distributed by **D Services** of Leicester, England.

Query letters and SASEs should be directed to:

Peter Usborne, Managing Director

Jenny Tyler, Editorial Director

VICTORIA AND ALBERT MUSEUM PUBLICATIONS

160 Brompton Road
London SW3 1HW
England
(44) 171 938 9663
fax: (44) 171 938 8370
www.vam.ac.uk/education/publications/index.html

V & A Publications publishes a broad range of titles covering subjects relating to the outstanding and varied collections held by the museum. The aim is to produce books that reach an international audience and for the imprint to be recognized as a hallmark of high-quality design, extending the reach of the museum to the broadest possible public, both specialist and non-specialist and furthering its original mission to inspire and educate.

The V & A publishing policy has several strands to it: to produce attractive, authoritative books in support of the Exhibitions program; to cater for the general public—museum visitors who want books that complement the collections as well as those who cannot necessarily visit the museum but who have a general (non-specialist) interest in the decorative and fine arts; to provide a resource for practitioners and students in the design field who look to the collections as a source of inspiration and instruction; and to publish new research in the field of art and design.

Hottest from V & A Publications: *Ties* by Avril Hart (fascinating account of the development of the necktie from the 1670s to the present that draws on contemporary pictorial as well as written sources and stunning photographs of high-fashion examples of this essential item of male dress); *The Cutting Edge: 50 Years of British Fashion 1947–1997* edited by Amy de la Haye (now available in trade paperback); *The Cutting Edge* (originally published to accompany one of the V & A's most successful fashion exhibitions, spans 50 years of innovation, classic creativity, and exuberant style); *British Watercolours—at the Victoria and Albert Museum* by Ronald Parkinson (this introduction to British Watercolours featuring 100 of the finest examples from the National Collection at the V & A contains examples from the sixteenth century to the present); *Silver* edited by Philippa Glanville (a lively social history of silver from the Middle Ages to the present day, drawing on a wealth of visual sources).

Also from the V & A: *Four Hundred Years of Fashion* edited by Natalie Rothstein (this bestseller, with its clear and authoritative text, tells the story of men's and women's fashionable dress through the ages, right up to the 1990s); *Chinese Furniture* by Craig Clunas (this study of Chinese furniture, based on the V & A's important collection, ranges from lacquered furniture attributed to the workshops of the Imperial Court to hardwood furniture of the Ming dynasty, covering the period from the fifteenth to the early twentieth centuries); *Aubrey Beardsley* by Stephen Calloway (celebrating the centenary of his death at the tragically early age of 25, this lively new life of Beardsley sets his work against the background of the vibrant artistic, literary, and social life fin-de-siecle London, Dieppe, and Paris and alongside that of contemporaries such as Oscar Wilde and James McNeill Whistler); *A Guide to Early Photographic Processes* by Brian Coe and Mark Haworth-Booth (guide to recognizing the major photographic processes from the period 1840 to 1914 that shows the finest examples of each process; also gives guidance on the care and treatment of old photographs); and *European Sculpture at the Victoria and Albert Museum* edited by Paul Williamson (containing over 100 masterpieces from one of the world's great collections, this beautifully illustrated volume traces the history of postclassical European sculpture from the early Christian period through to the beginning of the twentieth century).

Query letters and SASEs should be directed to:

V & A Publications, as on previous page

WHURR PUBLISHERS LIMITED

19B Compton Terrace
London N1 2UN
England
(44) 171 359 5979
fax: (44) 171 226 5290
info@whurr.co.uk (e-mail)
www.whurr.co.uk

Whurr Publishers Ltd. was founded in 1987 by Colin Whurr, who had been for 10 years a director of Butterworth & Co. (Publishers) Ltd., and who had latterly been the Butterworth chief executive for all scientific, technical, and medical publishing, both in the UK and the U.S.

Whurr Publishers publishes books and journals in "niche" markets such as human communication disorders, occupational therapy, physiotherapy, education, psychology, psychiatry and psychotherapy, and European studies, especially European business. A new development in 1996 was the decision to publish in nursing; the first titles appeared in October 1996. The company's philosophy is that authors and customers in such markets can best be served by a small, specialized company where something akin to old-fashioned service is complemented by the use of the latest publishing technology, and where rapid action and reaction can be taken for granted. Whurr Publishers prides itself on the speed with which it can publish both journal issues and books, and on the quality of its design and production.

The company now publishes fifteen academic and professional journals, and some 200 books. Its plan is to continue to expand in its current markets, at a measured rather than at a particularly rapid pace. Whurr Publishers treasures its independence, and remains convinced that specialized markets are best served by relatively small people-oriented companies such as itself.

Representative of Whurr's specialist list: *All in the Mind: The Essence of Psychology* by Adrian Furnham (highly readable book that considers some of the most interesting and controversial questions in the ever-popular discipline of psychology: Is psychology no more than common sense dressed up in jargon? Is it a science? And what did Freud really say?); *Down's Syndrome: Psychological, Psychobiological and Socio-Educational Perspectives* edited by Jean A. Rondal, Juan Perera, Lynn Nadel, and Annick Comblain (this comprehensive and authoritative survey will be of interest to students, university teachers, and professionals in the fields of psychology, psycholinguistics, genetics, neurology, and special education); *From Pain to Violence: The Traumatic Roots of Destructiveness* by Felicity de Zulueta (begins by defining "violence" as distinct from "aggression," then attempts to trace its origins, highlighting the polarization between those who believe mankind to be "innately" violent and those who see violence as the outcome of man's life experiences); *Hypnosis in Europe* edited by Peter Hawkins and Michael Heap (with hypnosis in Europe at a significant and eventful period in its evolution, this book provides a timely state-of-the-art overview that examines what has gone before, what is happening now, and in what direction ideas and practices are heading).

Also from Whurr: *Florence Nightingale and the Nursing Legacy*, 2nd edition, by Monica E. Baly (study based on research into the records of the Nightingale Fund and how it was used to finance various experiments in nursing and midwifery training in the nineteenth century); *Know Yourself! Self-Awareness Activities for Nurses and Other Health Care Professionals* by Philip Burnard (a thought-provoking book that offers nurses and other health-care professionals practical guidance on how to develop self-awareness as a means of enhancing the care they give others; contains some 80 activities as practical guides to the various approaches to self-awareness, which include the physical approach, thinking, feeling, sensing, and intuition); *Dyslexia: Parents in Need* by Pat Heaton (addresses some of the main issues relating to the enormous range and variety of needs that parents and family of dyslexic children experience); *The Code-Muller Protocols: Assessing Perceptions of Psychosocial Adjustment in Aphasia and Related Disorders* by Chris Code and Dave Muller (manual providing a review of contemporary knowledge of emotional and psychosocial reactions to brain damage and aphasia and current approaches to assessment); and *European Handbook of Organisations* by Hans-Albrecht Schraepler (provides a practical and concise source of information on European and international organizations contributing to the future of the continent of Europe).

Whurr titles are distributed by **Turpin Distribution Services** of Hertfordshire, England.

Query letters and SASEs should be directed to:

Colin Whurr, Publisher

THE WOMEN'S PRESS LTD.

34 Great Sutton Street
London EC1V 0DX
England
(44) 171 251 3007
fax: (44) 171 608 1938
jas@interbooks.com (e-mail)
www.the-womens-press.com

The Women's Press—a member of the **Namara Group**—is Britain's leading women's publishing house. Established in 1978, it publishes high-quality fiction and nonfiction from outstanding women writers worldwide. An exciting and diverse list includes literary fiction, detective novels, biography and autobiography, health, women's studies, handbooks, literary criticism, psychology and self-help, and the arts. There is also the popular *Livewire Books* series for young women and the bestselling annual *Women Artists Diary,* featuring beautiful color and black-and-white illustrations from the best contemporary women's art.

A Women's Press selection: *By the Light of My Father's Smile* by Alice Walker (in this magical novel, Alice Walker explores the consequences and reverberations of one act of deceit, and the importance of atonement, healing, and recovery); *Bittersweet: Contemporary Black Women's Poetry* edited by Karen McCarthy (the poets in *Bittersweet* take us from sweet moments in the water at birth, through the challenges of childhood and adolescence, to uncovering where our ancestors walked the earth); *A Second Skin: The Significance of Clothes* edited by Kirsty Dunseath (top contemporary writers explore the significance of clothes, which have marked a particular point in their lives, touching on themes such as identity, memory, family, sexuality, rebellion, and tradition); *The Female Odyssey: Visions for the 21st Century* edited by Helen Windrath and Charlotte Cole (in this wide-ranging and visionary book, key women from around the world assess the current position of women and share their views, hopes, and dreams for the future of womankind as we enter the new millennium); *Leaning Towards Infinity* by Sue Woolfe (a passionate and daring exploration of motherhood, genius, love, and betrayal; tells the story of three women—mother, daughter, and granddaughter—who are bound not only by the inescapable ties of family but also by the mysterious and exotic world of mathematics); *While Other People Sleep: A Sharon McCone Crime Thriller* by Marcia Muller (Sharon McCone is known as one of the best detectives in the business—until her untarnished reputation is threatened by an imposter, a mysterious woman who bears an uncanny physical resemblance to McCone, possesses chilling knowledge of her life, is handing out her business cards, advising clients, and picking up men); *A Message for the Media: Young Women Talk* edited by Jane Waghorn (in this fascinating, funny, angry, and dynamic collection, young women examine all aspects of the media; describe the impact that TV, magazines, and advertisements have on their lives; and send strong messages to the people in charge about the changes they would like to see); and *A Woman's Book of Shadows: Witchcraft—A Celebration* by Elisabeth Brooke (a compendium of the magic lore, psychic skills, rituals, and spells needed to practice witchcraft today, together with a detailed history of European witchcraft).

Query letters and SASEs should be directed to:

Kirsty Dunseath, Acquisitions Editor

Helen Windrath, Acquisitions Editor

Charlotte Cole, Acquisitions Editor

HANS ZELL PUBLISHING CONSULTANTS

11 Richmond Road
P.O. Box 56
Oxford OX1 2SJ
England
(44) 1865 511428
fax: (44) 1865 311534
hzell@dial.pipex.com (e-mail)
www.hanszell.co.uk/

Hans Zell Publishing Consultants provides consultancy services to publishers and academic institutions, in particular providing advisory services and individual project management for publishers, research institutes, and the book community in Africa and in other developing countries.

The house specializes in the following areas: scholarly publishing, especially university press publishing, and publishing by research institutions and NGOs, including editorial and financial management, administration, marketing and promotion, pricing and distribution, general publishing management, and dealing with author and publisher contracts; journals publishing management, including subscription management and fulfillment, financial control, journals promotion, and market assessments; reference book publishing, particularly for reference resources focusing on Africa and the developing world, including research, project evaluations, editorial services, and market assessments; training—in-house or through workshops and seminars—in editorial and production management, financial planning, and all areas of marketing.

Also, Hans Zell handles marketing and distribution of books on African and development studies, and African literature and culture—providing a range of specialist mailing list services in this area. Assignments may be short-term or one-off, or providing continuing help and back-up on an ongoing basis, and finally, clients range from individual publishers, authors, or individual organizations to international donor agencies.

Examples of Hans Zell publishing projects: *Book Marketing & Distribution: A Practical Handbook for Publishers in Developing Countries* edited by Hans M. Zell (this handbook, which provides a compendium of practical advice on all aspects of marketing and distribution for publishers in Africa, and those in other parts of the developing world, aims to assist not only publishers, especially small publishers, but research institutions and NGOs with publishing programs); *A Handbook of Good Practice in Journal Publishing,* 2nd revised edition, by Hans M. Zell, commissioned by the International African Institute (this handbook aims to assist journal editors in Africa to improve their publishing operations; provides guidelines for good practice, and good housekeeping, not only for those coming to journal publishing for the first time, but also for those who already have some experience in academic serials publishing); *The Electronic African Bookworm: A Web Navigator* developed and maintained by Hans Zell Publishing Consultants (as part of the newly created Web site of the house, this directory of over 800 links and Internet resources has been designed especially for use by the book communities in Africa and by African writers and scholars, particularly those who may be new to the Web; however, Africana librarians, Africanists, and the book professions outside Africa, will also find it helpful and informative).

Query letters and SASEs should be directed to:

Hans Zell, Publisher and Publishing Consultant

Hong Kong and China

ADDISON WESLEY LONGMAN

18 F Cornwall House
Taikoo Place
979 King's Road Quarry Bay
Hong Kong
(852) 2811 8168
fax: (852) 2565 7400/ (852) 2565 6613
www.awl.com/corp/

Business
   Query letters and SASEs should be directed to:

Willie Shen, Managing Director

BREAKTHROUGH

Breakthrough Centre
191 Woosung Street, Kowloon
Hong Kong
(852) 26320000
fax: (852) 7307899

Fiction, Poetry, How-To, Literature, Essays, Humor, Human Relations.
   Query letters and SASEs should be directed to:

Ng Sze Yuen, Director of Publications

CHINESE LITERATURE PRESS

24 Baiwanzhuang Road
Beijing 100037
China
(86) 10 68326678 (voice and fax)
chinalit@public.east.cn.net (e-mail)

Fiction, Poetry, Art
  Query letters and SASEs should be directed to:
Shen Jieying

CHUNG HWA BOOK CO.

Second Floor
5B Ma Hang Chung Road
Tokwawan, Kowloon
Hong Kong
(852) 27150176
fax: (852) 27138202
Cable: 5494
info@chunghwabook.com.hk (e-mail)

Art, Asian studies, Business, Careers, Computers, English, History, Management, Marketing, Philosophy, Self-Help
  Query letters and SASEs should be directed to:
Kwok-fai Chan, Managing Director and Editor-in-Chief

HONG KONG UNIVERSITY PRESS

University of Hong Kong
Pokfulam Road
Hong Kong
(852) 25502703
fax: (852) 28750734
hkupress@hkucc.hku.hk (e-mail)
www.hkupress.org/default.asp

Archaeology, Architecture, Art, Asian Studies, Biography, Biology, Child Care, Communications, Criminology, English as a Second Language, Government, Sciences, Law, Library Science, Nursing, Dentistry, Social Sciences, Women's Studies.
   Query letters and SASEs should be directed to:

Barbara Clarke, Publisher, Rights and Permissions

Dennis Cheung, Editor

THE LAW PUBLISHING HOUSE
17 Denglai Hutong
Guangneidajie
Xuanwugu
Beijing 100053
China
(86) 10 63266790

Nonfiction, Antiques, Education, English, History, How-To
   Query letters and SASEs should be directed to:

Lan Ming Liang, Executive Director, Editorial

LING KEE PUBLISHING GROUP
Top Floor, Zung Fu Industrial Bldg.
1067 King's Road
Quarry Bay
Hong Kong
(86) 2 5616151
fax: (86) 2 8111980

Query letters and SASEs should be directed to:

Bak Ling Au, Founder/Owner, Chairman and Chief Executive

Albert Au, Managing Director

PUBLICATIONS

Unit A1, 20/F, Chaiwan Industrial Centre
20 Lee Chung Street
Chaiwan
Hong Kong
(852) 28366180
fax: (852) 28384061/ (852) 28730861

Nonfiction, Psychology, Travel, How-To, Accounting, Animals, Antiques, Business, Career, Child Care, Hobbies, Fiction, Gardening, Health, Mysteries
   Query letters and SASEs should be directed to:

Leung Ka Kei, Publishing Manager

Ms. Tse Yin Fong, Editor

SUN YA PUBLICATIONS

Frm 1306 Eastern Centre
1065 King's Road
North Point
Hong Kong
(852) 25620161
fax: (852) 25659951

Nonfiction and Fiction
   Query letters and SASEs should be directed to:

Irene Yim, Managing Director, Editorial, Rights and Permissions

Yim Ng Seen Ha, Managing Director

UNICORN BOOKS

14/F Zung Fu Ind. Bldg.
1067 King's Road
Hong Kong
(852) 2562-2641
fax: (852) 2811-1980

Self-help, How-To, Antiques, Child Care, Games, Hobbies, Gardening, Chinese Language, Hong Kong History

Query letters and SASEs should be directed to:

Albert K. W. Au, Chief Operating Officer

YAZHOU ZHORKAN

15/F Blk A
Ming Pao Industrial Centre, 18
Da Yip St. Chai Wan
Hong Kong
(852) 2515 5840
fax: (852) 2515 2790
Yzzk@mingpao.com (e-mail)

Asian Studies, Business, Regional
    Query letters and SASEs should be directed to:

Mr. Lop Poon Yau, Chief Editor

Ireland

FOUR COURTS PRESS

Fumbally Court
Fumbally Lane
Dublin 8
Ireland
(353) 1 453 4668
fax: (353) 1 453 4672
info@four-courts-press.ie (e-mail)
www.four-courts-press.ie

Four Courts Press was started in 1970 by Michael Adams as a small press. For many years he ran it in association with Irish Academic Press.

Since 1992 Four Courts Press has expanded rapidly from its theology base, first into Celtic and medieval studies and ecclesiastical history, and most recently into modern history, art, literature, and law. The press welcomes publishing proposals for academic books in all the areas mentioned. Four Courts maintains a sizeable backlist and was recently planning to publish about 60 new books, not counting new impressions.

New from Four Courts: *The Royal Irish Constabulary: A Short History and Genealogical Guide* by Jim Herlihy; *Rebellion in Kildare 1790–1803* by Liam Chambers; *United Irishmen, United States: Immigrant Radicals in the Early Republic* by David A. Wilson; *The Cistercian Abbeys of Tipperary* by Colmcille O Conbhuidhe (edited by Finbarr Donovan); *The Uniforms of 1798–1803* by F. Glenn Thompson (foreword by Patrick F. Nowlan of the Irish Army); *Irish Diplomatic History, 1919–1969* edited by Michael Kennedy and Joseph Morrison Skelly; *Tales of the Elders of Ireland: A Translation of the Irish Acallam na Senorach* by Ann Dooley and Harry Roe; *Irish Poetry Since Kavanagh* edited by Theo Dorgan; *Marriage: Sex, Celebration and Law* by John Carreras.

Query letters should be directed to:

Michael Adams, Publisher

Martin Fanning, Editorial Production

Ronan Gallagher, Marketing and Production

Martin Healy, Director, Production

GILL & MACMILLAN PUBLISHERS

Goldenbridge Industrial Estate
Inchicore
Dublin 8
Ireland
(353) 1 453 1005
fax: (353) 1 454 1688
gillmac@indigo.ie (e-mail)

Gill & Macmillan is an Irish house that publishes books under its **Newleaf** imprint "dedicated to the well-being of your mind, body and soul." The Newleaf list continues to grow in strength, building on its already established reputation for publishing books that help to transform the way people think, widen their horizons, and empower them to grow with a deeper understanding of their whole self.

In its most recent catalog of offerings it is proud to have world-renowned names such as Gabrielle Roth, Patricia Kaminski, and the contemporary mystic Osho. Also featured are new and outstanding authors, including Michael Levin, Stella Resnick, and Leon Nacson, whose books it feels are bound to inspire and challenge many readers.

Typical of Newleaf's list of spiritually uplifting and challenging titles: *Sweat Your Prayers: Movement as Spiritual Practice* by Gabrielle Roth; *The Pleasure Zone: How to Let Go and Be Happy* by Stella Resnick; *Flowers That Heal: How to Use Flower Essences* by Patricia Kaminski; *Meditation for Absolutely Everyone* by Subagh Singh Khalsa (including audiocassette); *Earthlight: New Meditations for Children* by Maureen Garth; *The Cosmic Game: Explorations in the Frontiers of Human Consciousness* by Stanislav Grof; and *Healing with Nutritional Therapy* by Patricia Quinn (from the excellent *Healing With* series of titles).

Query letters and SASEs should be directed to:

Newleaf, as above

IPA INSTITUTE OF PUBLIC ADMINISTRATION

Vergemount Hall
Clonskeagh
Dublin 6
Ireland
(353) 1 269 7011
fax: (353) 1 269 8644
sales@ipa.ie (e-mail)
www.ipa.ie

The Institute of Public Administration exists to provide education, publishing, research, and training services to the Irish public service—the civil service, the local authorities, the health boards, and the state-sponsored bodies. Its books and periodicals provide information on, and analyses of, the policy areas that are of interest to those who work in the public service and to tertiary-level students of public management.

The importance of the public service generally also makes the IPA's publications of special interest to politicians, public affairs commentators, national interest groups, librarians, and others with a special interest in Irish public affairs—whether in Ireland or in libraries and agencies abroad—who need to maintain a focus on the European union and its member states. IPA's publications deal with subject areas that comprise public management, and cover politics, law, economics, social administration, and management.

From the IPA's current listing of books in print: *Emerging Voices: Women in Contemporary Irish Society* by Pat O'Connor; *Health, Medicine and Politics in Ireland 1900–1970* by Ruth Barrington; *Making Evaluation Relevant: A Study of Policy and Programme Evaluation Practice in the Irish Public Sector* by Richard Boyle; *Irish Resources and Land Use* edited by Desmond Gilmore; *Ireland in the Coming Times: Essays to Celebrate T. K. Whitaker's 80 Years* and *Administration Yearbook & Diary 1999* (editor-in-chief Tony McNamara; an IPA Periodical).

Query letters and SASEs should be directed to:

Eileen Kelly, Sales and Marketing

THE O'BRIEN PRESS LTD.

20 Victoria Road
Dublin 6
Ireland
(353) 1 492 3333
fax: (353) 1 492 2777
books@obrien.ie (e-mail)
www.obrien.ie/default.cfm

The O'Brien Press was established in 1974, evolving out of a family-run printing and type house, and in the past 20 years has established a reputation for quality and excellence in publishing for adults and children.

The first book to launch O'Brien proper was *Me Jewel and Darlin' Dublin* by Eamonn MacThomais, brought out while the author was still in jail, in November 1974. It was an immediate success, has been reprinted many times, and has become a minor classic. To celebrate the Press's 20th birthday, a special anniversary edition of this book was published in November 1994, exactly 20 years to the day from its first publication.

Since then O'Brien has published over 600 books, approximately 250 of which are still in print. From the beginning Michael O'Brien was committed to quality in writing, editing, design, illustration, and covers; this commitment has been recognized in the numerous awards won through the years. Recently this success has extended to awards from abroad also, and O'Brien Press is the only Irish publisher to have received the prestigious International Reading Association Award. The Press has a policy of commissioning work from established authors as well as encouraging talented new writers. The House author list includes: William Trevor, Brendan Behan, President Mary Robinson, Paddy Crosbie, Feargal Quinn, Shay Healy, Bob Quinn, Brendan O'Carroll, Michael Scott, Daniel O'Donnell, Morgan Llywelyn, Peadar O'Donnell, George Otto Simms, Marita Conlon-McKenna, Eilis Dillon, Siobhan Parkinson, Orla Melling, Martin Waddell, Dr. Pat Donlon, Liam Cahill, Brendan O'Brien, Brendan O'Heithir, and others.

O'Brien's publishing program always covers fiction, architecture, travel, humor, the environment, history, biography, classic literature, autobiography, guides, and reference books, among other categories.

Highlights and award-winners from O'Brien: *Crowning the Customer* by Feargal Quinn (a first and successful venture by the Press into the field of business books); *The Mammy, The Chisellers,* and *The Granny* (current bestselling comic trilogy by Brendan O'Carroll); *Under the Hawthorn Tree: Children of the Famine* by Marita Conlon-McKenna (winner of two international awards, No. 1 on the bestseller list for two years, in its fifteenth reprint and now a film); *Sisters . . . No Way!* by Siobhan Parkinson (winner of the overall Bisto prize in 1997); *Four Kids, Three Cats, Two Cows, One Witch (maybe)* also by Siobhan Parkinson (winner of a merit award for children's writing); and *The General* by Paul Williams (now a major film by John Boorman).

Query letters and SASEs should be directed to:

Ivan O'Brien, Editorial

New Zealand

JOHN BENTLEY BOOK AGENCIES

Milford P.O. Box 31-328
Auckland 9
New Zealand
(64) 9 4736920 (voice and fax)

Query letters and SASEs should be directed to:

John Bentley

MICHAEL GIFKINS & ASSOCIATES

7 Carrick Pl. Mt. Eden
P.O. Box 6496
Auckland 1
New Zealand
(64) 9 6303562 (voice and fax)
michael.gifkins@xtra.co.nz (e-mail)

LEARNING MEDIA LIMITED

Te Pou Taki Korero
Level 3, State Services Commission Building
100 Molesworth Street
Box 3293
Wellington
New Zealand
(64) 4 472 5522
fax: (64) 4 472 6444
info@learningmedia.co.nz (e-mail)
www.learningmedia.co.nz (New Zealand)
www.learningmedia.com (U.S.)

Learning Media Limited has a rich heritage in educational publishing that dates back to 1907. Today it is recognized internationally as a leading developer of education programs for children and teachers, providing a diverse range of innovative products and services. Its business goal is to produce the best possible resources to inspire learning. It publishes a broad range of materials in many different media, including books, audiotapes, videotapes, multimedia kits, and computer software, and develops programs that challenge and support children and teachers in many countries.

Clients as diverse as the Reserve Bank, Creative New Zealand, and the new Museum of New Zealand also value Learning Media's expertise in project management and commercial publishing. The publisher ensures that all of its published resources reach a high standard by careful crafting and classroom trials. It places a high premium on staff and provides unique opportunities for a strong pool of talented writers, editors, illustrators, and translators; television, video, and audio producers; software developers and computer graphic designers; musicians; and photographers.

The house has five distinct but interrelated areas of operation. The International team publishes educational programs and resources for sale in New Zealand and overseas and developed the successful Learning Media Literacy program for the United States in 1997. The Maori Publishing team has earned for Learning Media a reputation as New Zealand's largest publisher of quality materials in *te reo Maori*. The Business Development team produces sponsored materials that precisely fit the New Zealand Curriculum for businesses and organizations. The Curriculum team is contracted by the Ministry of Education to publish New Zealand's curriculum documents in both book and computer form. This team also publishes materials in a range of media to help teachers implement the curriculum and works with the Ministry on development. The Children's series team publishes books, audiotapes, charts, and picture packs for New Zealand schools, many in up to six Pacific Islands languages. Among the best known of these sources is the *School Journal*.

A sample from Learning Media's considerable educational range: *Education for the 21st Century* (a three-part document setting the future direction of education in New Zealand); *Emergency!* (English-language collection of stories about emergencies and emergency services); *Tracking Time: 100 Years of Film in Aotearoa New Zealand* (a teachers' pack); *A Day in the Life of My Cat* by Maria Hegarty (from *The Journal of Young People's Writing* series); *He Rauemi Awhina: Index of Maori Language Learning Materials, 1991–1996* (a teachers' index resource); *O Faamalu ma Aitu* (a Samoan translation of a story from Mauke about umbrellas and ghosts); *Hikaki* (a Tokelauan nonfiction account of how to make a fishing rod out of bamboo and use it); *Ko e Afa* (a Tongan translation about a little girl who is comforted by her grandmother during a storm); *Maitai Wera* (a Maori version of a story about an escape of radioactive material); *Nonu* (a nonfiction account of the ways in which the Tokelauan community holds on to its culture and language in a New Zealand city); *A History of New Zealand Rock Music*; *Kiwi Kidsongs I* (a collection of ten songs by resident New Zealand composers and representing different musical styles and cultures); and *Mountain Challenge* by Anne Braun-Elwert and Erica Beuzenberg (a recounting of experiences by the first woman to climb New Zealand's Mount Cook).

Query letters and SASEs should be directed to:

Rupert Alchin, Editor, *Connected* (a mathematics, science, and technology journal in English for ages 3–7)

Galumalemana Afeleti Hunkin, Editor, *Folauga* (a journal in Samoan for early childhood to senior secondary students)

Maringi Riddell, Editor, *He Kohikohinga* (a journal in Maori); *He Purapura*, *Nga Kete Korero, and Pukapuka Reo Rua* (book series in Maori for different age ranges); and *Waiata Kohungahunga* (songs in Maori for early childhood)

Kay Hancock, Editor, *Junior Journal* (a journal in English of fluency level material) and *Ready to Read* (books in English at emergent to early reading level)

Margaret Smith, Editor, *Many Voices* (a professional journal in English for teachers of community languages)

Paora Tibble, Editor, *Nga Korero*, *Te Tautoko*, and *Tuhono* (journals in Maori for different age groups)

Tricia Glensor, Editor, *School Journal* (a journal in English for different age groups) and *School Journal Story Library* (a series of books in English for young teenagers)

Diana Noonan, Editor, *School Journal*

Henare Everitt, Editor, *Te Wharekura* (a journal in Maori for senior secondary level)

Tina Wickliffe, Editor, *Toi te Kupu* (a newspaper in Maori for secondary students)

Don Long, Editor, *Tupu* (a series of books in Samoan, Tongan, Cook Islands Maori, Tokelauan, and Niuean for early childhood to senior secondary level)

Janice Marriott, Producer, *Kiwi Kidsongs* (audiocassette series for young students in English, Maori, and Pacific Islands languages)

Jo Paku, Producer, *Nga Pukorero o te Wa* (audiocassettes oratory)

PLAYMARKET

P.O. Box 9767
Wellington
New Zealand
(64) 4 382 8462
fax: (64) 4 382 8461
www.playmarket.org.nz/index.html

Query letters and SASEs should be directed to:

John Mc Davitt, Executive Officer

Susan Wilson, Script Advisor

CRAIG POTTON PUBLISHING

98 Vickerman Street
P.O. Box 555
Nelson
New Zealand
(64) 3 548 9009
fax: (64) 3 546 9192
info@cpp.co.nz (e-mail)

Craig Potton Publishing is an independent publishing company based in Nelson, New Zealand. Potton publishes lavishly illustrated books of fine quality on a range of subjects by New Zealand authors and photographers, with a particular interest in New Zealand's wild places and natural history, and its art and culture.

Among the house's newest releases are: *Moment and Memory: Photography in the New Zealand Landscape* by Craig Potton (a major collection of Craig Potton's photography, representing his best work of the last 15 years; includes many unpublished photographs and short essays that provide insight into what motivates his photography); *National Parks of New Zealand* by Craig Potton and Annie Wheeler (a photographic tribute to New Zealand's renowned protected wilderness heritage); and *The New Zealand Weather Book* by Erick Brenstrum.

Also from Craig Potton Publishing: *New Zealand Landscapes* by Andris Apse with introductory essay by Andy Dennis (an outstanding bestselling collection of over 100 photographs of New Zealand and its sub-Antarctic islands from one of the country's most successful and innovative landscape photographers); *Te Manawa o Tuhoe: The Heart of Tuhoe* (photography by Terry O'Connor; a Pride in Print Gold Medal Winner); *Offerings from Nepal* by Craig Potton (a Montana Book Award Finalist); *Images from a Limestone Landscape* by Craig Potton and Andy Dennis (a Goodman Fielder Wattie Book Award Finalist); *A Brief Guide to New Zealand Art & Culture* by Naomi O'Connor; *Mastering the Craft Business* by Ann and Bob Phillips; *Secret Power: New Zealand's Role in the International Spy Network* by Nicky Hager; and *Pictures of New Zealand* by Karl Johaentges and Jackie Blackwood (an appealing look at New Zealand through the lens of German photographer Karl Johaentges and the words of Australian Jackie Blackwood.

Craig Potton, which distributes its own titles, also provides distribution for **Exisle Publishing, Hedgehog House, Brabyn Publications,** and (in association with Charles Goulding Ltd.) distributes for **Steele Roberts, Duffy and Snellgrove,** and **Wild South Books.**

Query letters and SASEs should be directed to:

Robbie Burton, Managing Editor

RANDOM HOUSE NEW ZEALAND LTD.

18 Poland Road
Glenfield
Auckland
New Zealand
(64) 9 444 7197
fax: (64) 9 444 7524
admin@randomhouse.co.nz (e-mail)

Following its acquisition of **Godwit Publishing,** Random House NZ now has an extremely strong list in both fiction and nonfiction across a wide range of subject areas and a stable of top authors. The house now produces titles under three imprints: **Vintage, Godwit,** and its own **Random House.**

Vintage has rapidly earned a reputation as New Zealand's premier fiction imprint. Newly out are novels by three of Vintage's most popular bestselling writers: Alan Duff, Barbara Else, and Shonagh Koea. Exciting works by two first-time novelists—Anthony McCarten and Emma Neale—and the well-respected Peter Hawes and Stephanie Johnson add to the impressive lineup.

The Godwit imprint continues to publish in its traditional areas of strength. Highlights here include two natural history titles—*A Field Guide to Auckland* and *The Singing Island: The Story of Tiritiri Matangi*; the spectacular and eagerly awaited *The Native Garden: Design Themes from Wild New Zealand* (the first book devoted to landscaping with native plants); Nancy Tichborne's *Cats* (for cat lovers and watercolor enthusiasts); *100 New Zealand Craft Artists* (which completes Godwit's trilogy of art books); and a marvellous illustrated biography of Hone Tuwhare, to be accompanied by a reissue of his first poetry collection, *No Ordinary Sun*.

The Random House imprint will be publishing a major new title by Maggie Barry and Mary Greene, *Shared Visions* (an inspirational exploration of the pleasures of gardens and food). Peta Mathias's *Salut* and Julie Biuso's *The Long Italian Lunch* continue the food theme with two more high-profile authors; and Ronda Bungay offers a sequel to *Dear Murderer* with *Scarecrows*, a chilling investigation into why women kill.

New titles: *A Field Guide to Auckland: Exploring the Region's Natural and Historic Heritage* by Bruce Hayward, Ewen Cameron, and Graeme Murdoch (finalist 1998 Montana Book Awards nonfiction category); *Mind Switch: The Ultimate Self-hypnosis Experience* by Brian Head; *The Lonely Margins of the Sea* by Shonagh Koea (new dramatic novel by a prize-winning author); *The Singing Island: The Story of Tiritiri Matangi* by Lynnette Moon with photographs by Geoff Moon (tells the remarkable story of the transformation—by reforestation and conservation in less than two decades—of this windswept island into a haven for over 76 species of birds).

Off the backlists: (Vintage) *Studmuffin* by Marilyn Duckworth, and *What Becomes of the Broken Hearted?* by Alan Duff; (Godwit) *Landmarks: Notable Historic Buildings of New Zealand* by David McGill and Grant Sheehan, and *New Zealand Songbirds* by Brian Gill, Juliet Hawkins, and Les McPherson; (Random) *Grasp the Nettle: Making Biodynamic Farming and Gardening Work* by Peter Proctor, and *Book of Beasts* by Jon Gadsby and Rita Parkinson (a children's picture book).

Query letters and SASEs should be directed to:

Jane Connor, Publishing Director

TANDEM PRESS

P.O. Box 34-272
Birkenhead
Auckland 10
New Zealand
(64) 9 480 1452
fax: (64) 9 480 1455
bobross@iprolink.co.nz (e-mail)

Tandem is a small (by U.S. standards) publishing house begun in 1990. But, with over 100 titles already in print, they are enjoying considerable early success.

The company's list, which focuses on New Zealand fiction and general nonfiction, includes among its latest offerings: *Stroppy Sheilas* by Sandra Coney; ("Alice Burn, secretary of the Atalanta Cycling Club and a committed dress reformer, was stopped from going to lectures at Canterbury University in her divided pants. They were said to distract her fellow students even though Alice protested that they were hidden by her academic gown. When a photo of Alice in her knicker costume was displayed in a photographer's window in High Street, a Christchurch matron wrote to the paper protesting, saying that the remarks of male onlookers 'were enough to make the ears of all self-respecting, honest women tingle with shame.'" Alice Burn is just one of the 100 wild and wonderful women in this fascinating and often hilarious collection); *A Passion for Travel: New Zealand Writers and Their Journeys Overseas* edited by Tina Shaw (New Zealanders are among the world's greatest travelers, and this anthology of travel essays by well-known New Zealand writers captures a wide range of personal experiences, from the icy extremes of Antarctica to life in a Turkish village); *In the Sixties* by Frank Habicht (compilation of some of the finest work of one of the photographers of the day, back when London took to the streets and started to live it up; captures the well-known figures of the day—pop idols, the models, the film stars and producers—as well as the ordinary young people enjoying London as it was); *The Visual Diary: Releasing the Artist Within* by Juliet Batten (explains how to keep a visual diary, based on the author's six-week course).

Also from Tandem: *Images of Maori Women: Mataahua Wahine* by Michelle Moir (collection of photographs with accompanying autobiographical text resulting from award-winning photographer Michelle Moir's 1992 travels to many parts of the North Island of New Zealand with her large-format camera to spend time with Maori women, young and old; acknowledges and celebrates images of Maori women as they see themselves today); *Write Your Own CV in 10 Easy Steps* by Paula Stenberg (written with the New Zealand job seeker specifically in mind); *I Love You But . . . How to Stop Doing More Than Your Share of Housework* by Christine Beckett (a comical yet long, hard look at the serious domestic inequality that still thrives in most households today); and *Angel in God's Office: My Wartime Diaries* by Neva Clarke McKenna (the story of one "ordinary" New Zealand girl and how the war changed her life forever as she worked close to the New Zealand men in Italy, close to the killing, the wounding and the surviving).

Query letters and SASEs should be directed to:

Bob Ross, Acquisitions Editor

University of Auckland

Auckland University Press
Private Bag 92019
Auckland
New Zealand
(64) 9 373 3528
fax: (64) 9 373 7465
aup@auckland.ac.nz (e-mail)
www.auckland.ac.nz/aup/

AUP publishes academic titles across a wide range of subjects, including archaeology, art history, biography/autobiography and correspondence, community health, fiction, geography and geology, history, language, literary criticism, Maori studies, media studies, natural history, Pacific studies, poetry, politics, women's studies, as well as produces the *Dictionary of New Zealand Biography* and the *New Zealand Fiction* series.

Recent AUP titles: *The Dictionary of New Zealand Biography: Volume 4, 1921–1940* (general editor Claudia Orange; presents "new" developments of Modern Age New Zealand; Maori are widely represented, with iwi leaders, politicians, doctors, and activists); *The Loving Stitch: A History of Knitting and Spinning in New Zealand* by Heather Nicholson (an engaging history of knitting and spinning; main focus is on a chronological picture of antipodean knitting which is also a history of the domestic lives of women, of their resourcefulness, their talent, and their sociability); *A Civilised Community: A History of Social Security in New Zealand 1898–1998* by Margaret McClure (this pioneering history traces the development of social security policy in New Zealand from the passage of the Old Age Pensions Act in 1898 through to the recent benefit cuts, the 1997 superannuation referendum, and the Code of Social Responsibility of 1998); *Nga Kura Maori: The Native Schools System 1867–1969* edited by Judith Simon (illuminates a neglected and often misunderstood area of Maori history—The New Zealand Native Schools system, which affected most Maori families and many Pakeha ones for over 100 years; draws extensively on oral histories, memories and experiences of the pupils and teachers, and letters; *Early Days Yet: New and Collected Poems 1941–1997* by Allen Curnow (new collection from New Zealand's greatest poet, recognized worldwide as a leading poet writing in English); *A Dictionary of New Zealand Sign Language* edited by Graeme Kennedy (first full description of a language used daily by many New Zealanders; contains over 4,000 signs, including some understood by Maori deaf): and *The New Zealand Experiment: A World Model for Structural Adjustment?* (second edition) by Jane Kelsey (this incisive analysis of New Zealand's fast-changing political life has been updated to take account of the 1996 election and subsequent events).

Query letters and SASEs should be directed to:

Christine O'Brien, Senior Editor

UNIVERSITY OF OTAGO PRESS

P.O. Box 56
Dunedin
New Zealand
(64) 3 479 8807
fax: (64) 3 479 8385
university.press@otago.ac.nz (e-mail)

Otago has recently celebrated its 40th birthday—as the oldest university press in New Zealand. Paradoxically, it is also the youngest, in that it has been a full-time operation only since 1993. Since then, the number of books published has increased every year—and of course there are also the five house journals, including *Landfall.*

Since 1958, the University of Otago Press has published a wide range of books in the fields of literary criticism, the classics, medicine, dentistry, education, history and natural history. In recent times, Otago has widened its embrace to include Maori and environmental studies and fiction. The Press is committed to bringing readers the best of both worlds—special interest academic publications, and general books for information and pure pleasure.

A selection of Otago's newest: *Remember Me: Short Stories* by Linda Burgess (a collection of stories in which the author looks at the stages of life and the workings of memory; begins with a small boy in "Night" and ends with an elderly group in "The Nearly Dead Poets Society," offering some short takes on human relationships and foibles); *The Crystal Messenger* by Pham Thi Hoai, translated by Ton-That Quynh-Du (regarded by many as the most exciting novel to be published in Vietnam since the re-unification of North and South, this book—set in Hanoi in the 1980s— tells the surreal tale of a family coming to terms with the rebuilding of Vietnam after the war and the beginning of consumerism and westernization); *Landfall 1947–1997: A New Zealand Half Century* edited by Peter Simpson and Chris Price (New Zealand's most influential literary magazine just celebrated its fiftieth anniversary, marking this milestone by publishing a commemorative book that places the works of their writers and artists side by side, page after page, over 50 years to provide a great many insights into New Zealand culture and the development of its literature and arts); *Traditional Lifeways of the Southern Maori* by James Herries Beattie, edited by Atholl Anderson (an immensely rich storehouse of fascinating information collected from South Island Maori elders in

1920; details how houses were built, how to make raincoats and sandals, religious beliefs and practices, sport, medical lore, tools, flora and fauna, and much more, all described and explained).

Also from Otago: *Psychology and Family Law: A New Zealand Perspective* edited by M. E. Pipe and Fred Seymour (brings together a wide range of research from the social sciences—psychology in particular—to provide a practical source of information for family lawyers, judges, social workers, psychologists, and other professionals who work with children); *Queer Theory* by Annamarie Jagose (a radical and exciting exploration of the notion of "queer," which challenges existing concepts of gender and sexuality; comprehensive yet concise overview of queer theory, including historical background on the homophile movement, gay liberation, lesbian feminism, AIDS activism, and the new concept of queer); *Introductory Statistical Methods for Biological, Health and Social Sciences* by John Harraway (an essential companion to those undertaking research that involves data collection and analysis; presents the essential introductory statistical methodology in a succinct and accessible manner); *Stained Glass Windows of Canterbury, New Zealand* by Fiona Ciaran (analyzes a collection in the Canterbury region of nineteenth and twentieth century windows of international significance; includes works by Arts and Crafts Movements artists); and *The Earth Garden Book of Alternative Energy* by Alan T. Gray (user-friendly guide on home energy; incorporating experiences of people who use solar, wind, water, or steam power for all their energy needs).

Query letters and SASEs should be directed to:

Wendy Harrex, Managing Editor

Scotland

T & T Clark Ltd. Publishers

59 George Street
Edinburgh EH2 2LQ
Scotland
(44) 131 225 4703
fax: (44) 131 220 4260
mailbox@tandtclark.co.uk (e-mail)
www.tandtclark.co.uk

T & T Clark is a wholly independent specialist Scottish company occupying a publishing niche in the two fields of theology and law. One of the older guard in the industry, it has been publishing since 1821 and consequently has developed both a considerable expertise in its areas of interest and a substantial stable of authors and stocklist. Its aim is to serve the best interests of practitioners and students of both law and theology.

New titles from T & T Clark in law: *Criminal Sentences* by Daniel Kelly (this informative book presents an analysis of modern sentencing practice in Scotland, concentrating on the decisions of the criminal appeal court over the last decade); *Employment Law in Scotland,* 2nd edition, by Victor Craig and Kenneth Miller (a major aim of this handbook is to explain the law of employment as it applies in Scotland and to emphasize the differences both in the law itself and in its interpretation as between Scotland and England); *Justice and Crime: Essays in Honour of the Right Honourable The Lord Emslie* edited by Robert F. Hunter (extensive collection of essays that deal with a wide variety of subjects on the general theme of criminal law and practice; of interest to students, lecturers and practitioners alike); and *A Legal History of Scotland* by David M. Walker (Professor Walker's history, which will be published in seven volumes, is the only attempt yet made to write a chronological narrative account of the development of the Scottish legal system from early times on a substantial scale, with extensive reference to original sources).

New theological books: *Reconstructing Nature: The Engagement of Science and Religion* by John Brooke and Geoffrey Cantor (the authors discuss exciting developments in the sciences—whether in Big Bang cosmology, chaos theory, or genetic engineering—in relation to moral and spiritual questions. In their recent Gifford lectures, they argue that not one but several historical approaches are required to achieve critical perspective and balanced understanding); *Christianity for the Twenty-First Century* edited by Philip F. Esler (Professor Esler, together with a team of expert contributors, considers the resources Christianity has to offer, and within a social framework that is both secular and pluralist, identifies various aspects of Christian tradition that will allow it to meet the demands of the next century); *One God, One Lord: Early Christian Devotion and Ancient Jewish Monotheism,* second edition, by Larry W. Hurtado (the reissue of a classic work, with an extensive new introduction, which evaluates the most recent developments in Christology); and *Truth and the Reality of God: An Essay in Natural Theology* by Ian Markham (Professor Markham places this striking argument, which lies at the very heart of Augustinian theology, within the modern debate about truth and defends its underlying claim: "Belief in the possibility of truth demonstrates a belief in God.").

Query letters and SASEs should be directed to:

Geoffrey Green, Acquisitions Editor, Theology

Mary Jane Bennett, Acquisitions Editor, Law

Dorothy Amos, Acquisitions Editor, Law

MAINSTREAM PUBLISHING CO. LTD.

7 Albany Street
Edinburgh EH1 3UG
Scotland
(44) 131 557 2959
fax: (44) 131 556 8720
mainstream.pub@btinternet.com (e-mail)

Mainstream produces a wide-ranging general list encompassing literature, fiction, biography, history, politics, art, photography, sport, health, and current affairs. Recently, Mainstream announced a new B-format paperback imprint, which fits well with one of its specialties—Mainstream has long been a leading publisher of sports books. Frequently featured in the bestseller lists, twice publisher of the William Hill Sports Book of the Year, and with a star-studded list of authors ranging from high-profile writers to high-profile players, the Mainstream Sport imprint is a welcome innovation for all sports fans.

A selection from Mainstream's current listing: *Sexual Politics: The Rise of the Empowered Woman (Secrets of the World's Most Powerful Women)* by Mona Bauwens and Peter Thompson; *Earth Dwellers: Adventures in the Land of Ants* by Erich Hoyt; *Aleister Crowley: The Beast Demystified* by Roger Hutchinson; *Scottish Art in the 20th Century* by Duncan Macmillan; *Hooligan* by Eddy Brimson (a hard-hitting, no-holds-barred novel about football violence); *Inner Harmony: Achieving Physical, Mental and Emotional Well-Being* by Jan De Vries; *Glencoe and the Indians: A Real-Life Family Saga Which Spans Two Continents, Several Centuries and More Than Thirty Generations to Link Scotland's Clans with the Native Peoples of the American West* by James Hunter; and *Winter Colours: Changing Seasons in World Rugby* by Donald McRae (William Hill Sports Book of the Year Winner); and from Mainstream Sport, *The Geezers Guide to Football: A Lifetime of Lads and Lager* by Dougie Brimson.

Their titles are sold in both trade paperback and hardback format with the distribution being handled by **TBS** of Colchester in Essex.

Query letters and SASEs should be directed to:

John Beaton, Editorial

POLYGON

22 George Square
Edinburgh EH8 9LF
Scotland
(44) 131 650 4217 (or 8436)
fax: (44) 131 662 0053
Jackie.Jones@eup.ed.ac.uk (e-mail)
www.eup.ed.ac.uk

Polygon was set up in the late 1960s by the students of Edinburgh University and began by publishing pamphlets and books on Scottish politics and literature. Since 1988 it has operated under the auspices of its parent company, Edinburgh University Press. Its award-winning list now encompasses new fiction and poetry, critical thinking on politics, culture and education, folklore, oral history, drama, and a wide selection of general books, ranging from travel and archaeological guides to theater and traditional medicines.

In common with its parent company, the past year has been an exciting one for Polygon with growth and development going hand in hand with the continued success, and growing reputation of its list. Polygon has appointed a UK sales agent for the first time (Compass Independent Book Sales), is looking to appoint further agents in countries where it believes the list has real potential, and have relocated the distribution to *Scottish Book Source* in Glasgow.

Polygon titles have been featured on six major prize shortlists in the last 12 months, with prizes being awarded to Aonghas MacNeacail (Stakis Writer of the Year), to John Tranter (Poetry Book Society Special Commendation), to Meg Bateman (SAC Autumn Book Award), and nominations to Ruth Thomas for both the Saltire First Book and

Mail on Sunday/John Llewellyn Rhys Fiction Award. The latest list is similarly burst-ing with talent and prize-winning potential with a short-story collection appropriately called *Shorts*, new fiction from Robin Jenkins and Alexander McCall Smith, essays from the internationally renowned poet/thinker Kenneth White, and new books on the Scottish Theatre and Scotland's environment.

Some of Polygon's newest features: *Shorts: The MacAllan Scotland on Sunday Short Story Collection* edited by Robert Alan Jamieson (the best of contemporary Scottish short-story writing in one volume); *Matthew and Sheila* by Robin Jenkins (a dark and gripping family drama set against the haunting beauty of the Western Isles; *Fragile Land: Scotland's Environment* by Auslan Cramb (the only book to cover Scotland's key environmental issues); *House of Rooms* by Siri Reynolds (exploring love, friendship, desire and loss, this first novel provides a modern take on relationships and infidelity in contemporary Britain); *Hoots! An Anthology of Scottish Comic Writing* edited by Susie Maguire and David Jackson Young; *Healing Threads: Traditional Medicines of the Highlands and Islands* by Mary Beith; *Scottish Customs: From the Cradle to the Grave* by Margaret Bennett; *Hebridean Odyssey: Songs, Poems, Prose and Images* edited by Marion Sinclair (with thirty-five evocative black-and-white photographs, a celebration of the unique cultural inheritance of these islands, offering a glimpse of a way of life which has almost disappeared); and *Scottish Island Hopping: A Guide for the Indepen-dent Traveller* (covering all the major island groups, written by experienced travelers and islanders, and full of inside knowledge and quirky observation—the only island guide you'll ever need).

Query letters and SASEs should be directed to:

Alison Bowden, Rights and Permissions Co-ordinator/Assistant Editor

Jackie Jones, Editorial Director

Marion Sinclair, Consultant Fiction Editor

SAINT ANDREW PRESS

Board of Communication
Church of Scotland
121 George Street
Edinburgh EH2 4YN
Scotland
(44) 131 225 5722
fax: (44) 131 220 3113
cofs.standrew@dial.pipex.com (e-mail)
www.cofs.org.uk

The Saint Andrew Press endeavors to maintain its original aim, which is to publish books for the inquiring layperson on all aspects of the Reformed tradition and to provide a special service to the Church of Scotland, as well as publishing general Christian titles, and others on matters specific to Scottish life.

Recent developments for the Press include its becoming the distributor for **Wild Goose Publications** and the commencement of the re-covering of the William Barclay Daily Study Bible New Testament series, a set of titles from a popular Scottish theologian whose sermons, lectures, books, radio and television appearances enhanced a long-standing reputation as a brilliant communicator of the word of God.

A St. Andrew Press sample: *Pray Now: Daily Devotions with the Church of Scotland* (from the Church of Scotland Panel on Worship); *Sacred Stones Sacred Places* by Marianna Lines with photographs by Paul Turner (a lovingly documented exploration of some remarkable monuments to Scotland's heritage); *George MacDonald: A Devotional Guide to His Writings* by Gary W. Deddo and Cathy A. Deddo; *Human Genetics: A Christian Perspective* (from the Church of Scotland Board of Social Responsibility, a balanced account of current scientific/medical developments and a realistic view of possibilities in the foreseeable future); *Church of Scotland Yearbook* edited by A. Gordon McGillivray (Who's who and what's where in the Church of Scotland); *The Edinburgh Graveyard Guide* by Michael T. R. B. Turnbull (this bestselling guide takes the reader on a leisurely stroll around the Capital's most unusual beauty spots—its graveyards—the final resting-places of Edinburgh's finest and most feared); *Talks for Children* by Beatrice Surtees and Ian MacLeod (popular children's address material for use by ministers and teachers, in church and in school, including "things-to-do," prayers, and suggestions for visual aids); and *The Big Questions*? from the Association for Teachers of Religious Education in Scotland (creation and evolution, evil and suffering, life after death—these subjects pose fundamental questions and are the issues explored in this book for a secondary school audience).

Query letters and SASEs should be directed to:

Lesley A. Taylor, Publishing Manager

NEIL WILSON PUBLISHING LTD.

303a Pentagon Centre
36 Washington Street
Glasgow G3 8AZ
Scotland
(44) 141 221 1117
fax: (44) 141 221 5363
nwp@cqm.co.uk (e-mail)
www.nwp.co.uk/

NWP is a Glasgow-based publisher of all things Scottish for both trade and direct selling. Subjects of interest include both fiction and humor as well as a range of nonfiction titles.

The nonfiction books cover travel and leisure, cookery, outdoors, history, biogra-phy, reference, whisky and beer, true crime, fishing, Scottish adventure memoirs, and reference.

New NWP titles: *In Waiting: Travels in the Shadow of Edwin Muir* by Michael Russell (in the spirit of a similar journey made over 60 years ago, the author seeks to discover what ordinary Scots men and women think, expect, and want in the new millennium); *Scottish Murder Stories* by Molly Whittington-Egan; *Three Verdicts* by Donald Findlay QC (a crime thriller by one of Scotland's leading criminal defense counsels); *The Backpackers Cookbook* by Dave Coustick with foreword by Nick Nairn; *'Ye Cannae Shove Yer Granny Aff A Bus!'* by Allan Morrison (a unique collection of sayings that reveals the relationship between Scottish grandchildren and their Grannies); *Scotch and Water: An Illustrated Guide to the Hebridean Malt Whisky Distilleries* by Neil Wilson with foreword by Charles MacLean; *Capital Walks in Edinburgh: The New Town* by David Dick; *Rob Roy MacGregor* by Nigel Tranter (a gripping historical account of one of Scotland's most legendary sons); *Isle of the Displaced* by Joe Pieri (the memoir of a Glasgow Italian-Scot who was interned in Canada during the Second World War); and *Scotland the Facts* by Michael Turnbull (everything you will ever need to know about Scotland, all in handy pocket format).

Query letters and SASEs should be directed to:

Carole Hopkins, Editorial

Singapore

ADDISON WESLEY LONGMAN

25 First Lok Yang Road
Singapore 62973
(65) 268 2666
fax: (65) 264 1740
enquiry@awl.com.sg (e-mail)
www.awl.com

Business, Mathematics, Accounting, Science
    Query letters and SASEs should be directed to:

Wong Wee Woon, President, AWL Singapore Group

ASIAPAC BOOKS PTE LTD.

996 Bendemeer Road #06–08/09
Kallang Basin Industrial Estate
Singapore 339944
(65) 392 8455
fax: (65) 392 6455
apacbks@singnet.com.sg (e-mail)
www.asiapacbooks.com

This house is best known for its active promotion of English-language comics and books on Chinese philosophy, history, art, and literature. Started in 1982, Asiapac Books was the conception of Ms. Lim Li Kok, who cherished the desire to promote literary works from the Asia Pacific region so that its culture and traditions could enjoy a greater worldwide appreciation. Asiapac's logo, inspired by the Chinese character for Asia, carries the central globe. The globe symbolizes the international market for which it now publishes and distributes in its endeavor to help bridge the East and the West, and its green color expresses Asiapac's commitment to go "green for life." In essence, Asiapac seeks to contribute to individual self-realization through the promotion of quality books and aims generally to serve as a link for a global culture by helping to build Singapore into a cosmopolitan service center. Out of its original intent, Asiapac became an agent for *Panda Books,* an imprint containing the best of the classical and contemporary Chinese literature in paperbacks. Ms. Lim Li Kok also distributed books for Foreign Languages Press and New World Press, both based in China; as well as Joint Publishing Company Limited and Hai Feng Publishing Co. Ltd. of Hong Kong. The house's first publication, *Labour Pains,* came out in 1984. Its success led to the speedy launch of the *Asia Pacific Heritage Series,* which aimed to instill in the present generation and preserve for posterity the cultural traditions of the region. The first comic, *The Sayings of Zhuang Zi*, released in December 1988, saw its initial print run swiftly snatched up. This was the first clear indication that many readers were keenly awaiting an easy and accessible medium that transmitted Chinese thinking and Literary classics.

From these early roots Asiapac has blossomed into a publisher with a substantial holding of book and comic titles. For instance Asiapac now possesses the widest collection of English comics on Chinese culture. It has more than 100 titles in comics covering subjects on Chinese philosophy, war classics, heritage and history, literary classics, as well as myths and legends. Additionally, the martial-art series *Return of the Condor Heroes* (18 volumes) and *Adventures of Wisely* (10 volumes) have been widely acclaimed, the former having sold more than 1 million copies for its Chinese edition alone. The book and comics series offered by Asiapac cover the following categories: martial arts, science fiction, Chinese philosophy, Chinese divination, strategy and leadership, Living 21 series, Chinese culture, Chinese history, Chinese classics, myths and legends, *100 Series Art Album, Collectors' Series,* Chinese language courses, children's books. Moreover, through licensing agreements with over 30 publishing partners, Asiapac's products are now translated, reprinted, and marketed in 15 other countries, including France, Germany, Norway, Finland, Greece, and the Netherlands.

A notable recent development are the Chinese Language programs for adults and children conceived by language expert Ms. Lin Shan. Designed for English-speaking learners, *The Total Chinese Learning Kit* is an integrated language kit that employs the latest technology and learning concepts to equip students to handle most Chinese publications, using compact discs, text and revision books, revision cards, and charts.

Comics from Asiapac: *Sayings of Mencius* illustrated by Tsai Chih Chung, translated by Mary Ng En Tzu; *Fantasies of the Six Dynasties*; *Gems of Chinese Wisdom* illustrated by Wang Xuanming, translated by Leong Weng Kam; *Chinese Eunuchs I, II & III: Inside Stories of the Chinese Court* illustrated by Tian Hengyu, translated by Gong Lizeng, Yang Aiwen, and Wang Xingzheng; *I Ching: A Practical Guide to the Ancient Art of Divination* illustrated by Tan Xiachun, translated by Koh Kok Kiang.

Books: *100 Celebrated Chinese Women* illustrated by Lu Yanguang, edited by Cai Zhuozhi, translated by Kate Foster; *Best Chinese Names* written by Doris Liu, translated by Wu Jingyu, illustrated by Poh Yih Chwen; *Jokes, Riddles & Proverbs from Asia and the Pacific* compiled by Asian Culture Centre for UNESCO; *Fascinating Tales of Old Beijing* by Jin Shoushen, translated by Gladys Yang; *Wisdom Stories* compiled by J. Maurus; *Butcher's Wife* by Li Ang, translated by Howard Goldblatt and Ellen Yeung (annual fiction prize-winner); and from the *Healthy Life Series, The Chinese Way to a Long & Healthy Life* compiled by People's Medical Publishing House.

Query letters and SASEs should be directed to:

Lydia S. Y. Lum, Publishing Director

HEMISPHERE PUBLICATION SERVICES

Golden Wheel Building #04–03
41 Kallang Pudding Road
Singapore 349316
(65) 7415166
fax: (65) 7429356
ashgate@asianconnect.com (e-mail)

Hemisphere is a member of the Taylor & Francis Group that boasts a two-century-old tradition in publishing. Hemisphere was founded as a distinct operation in 1981 and was formerly known as Ashgate Publishing Asia Pacific. It is the exclusive book distributor for several British and American academic and professional publishers. While it does not publish in Singapore, it does market and sell to the Asia Pacific region on behalf of client publishers.

Hemisphere's services are not, however, simply confined to selling, marketing, and distribution. It also supports publishers at book fairs, international conferences, and academic meetings. Hemisphere's staff meets on a regular basis with editorial departments of publishers with whom they have particularly close relationships and thus are able to add considerable value to publishers' penetration of markets in the Asia Pacific region.

Major publishers currently represented by Hemisphere Publication Services include: **The Taylor & Francis Group:** Taylor & Francis, Falmer Press, Psychology Press, Bruntner/Mazel, Accelerated Development, Garland, UCL Press, Guilford Press, and the McGill-Queens University, Northwestern University, and University of Minnesota Presses; **Ashgate:** Gower, Dartmouth, Ashgate/Avebury, Scholar Press; Athlone Press, Aslib, Library Association, Cameron May, Pickering & Chatto, Research Studies Press, Westview Press, Libraries Unlimited, Oryx Press, World Bank, Brookings Institution,

American Psychological Association, ISEAS—Singapore, Singapore University Press, OECD—France.

Hemisphere welcomes interest from any academic or professional publisher who may be seeking representation in the Asia Pacific region and including Australia and New Zealand.

Query letters should be directed to:

Barry Clarke, Managing Director

RECREAIDS

City Warehouse
5 Kaki Bukit Road 2
No. 04–16
Singapore 417839
(65) 7413500 / (65) 7413504
fax: (65) 965 07445979

Self-Help, How-To, Recreation, Child Care, Hobbies
Query letters and SASEs should be directed to:

Ra Perumal, Managing Director

REED INTERNATIONAL

Union Industrial Bldg. 37 Jalan Pemimpin
No. 7–04/05 Block B
Singapore 2057
(65) 258 3255
fax: (65) 258 4461

Nonfiction, Fiction, Education
Query letters and SASEs should be directed to:

Charles Cher, Managing Director

SIMON & SCHUSTER

317 Alexandra Road
Ikea Building No. 04-01
Singapore 159965
(65) 476 4688
fax: (65) 378 0370
prenhall@signet.com.sg (e-mail)

Science, Computers, Management, Psychology, Education, Arts, How-To, Religion, Travel, Psychology, Medicine
   Query letters and SASEs should be directed to:
Gunawan Hadi, Managing Director

SINGAPORE UNIVERSITY PRESS (PTE) LTD.

National University of Singapore
Yusof Ishak House
10 Kent Ridge Crescent
Singapore 119260
(65) 776 1148
fax: (65) 774 0652
suptayp@nus.sg (e-mail)
www.nus.edu.sg

Singapore University Press is the publishing house of the National University of Singapore. Established in 1971, the press has become one of the region's leading English language publishers of academic and scholarly titles, and has acquired an international reputation for its high-quality publications on Southeast Asian and Asian studies. Its publications have also earned international and local publishing awards in recognition of their excellence. In addition to its past focus on Asian studies, the press also publishes books and journals in other academic fields, with plans to expand in areas such as the sciences, engineering, law, and management.

   SUP publications are distributed worldwide, and international marketing opportunities are continually being explored and pursued through means such as the licensing of rights, direct marketing, and collaborations with international publishers such as homegrown *World Scientific Publishing Co. Pte Ltd.*, with whom SUP has recently established a standing arrangement for the co-publication and distribution of suitable titles.

SUP/World Scientific Publishing titles include, for example, *Fields Medallists' Lectures* edited by Sir Michael Atiyah and Daniel Iagolnitzer and *A Handbook of Clinical Nephrology* by Woo Keng Thye.

Also on SUP's current list: *Law, Social Sciences and Public Policy* edited by Anthony Chin and Alfred Choi (brings together lawyers and social scientists to discuss pertinent issues from their relevant expertise in a symbiotic relationship in order to help policy and decision-makers be fair and efficient in implementing or advising regulatory and developmental programs); *China's Political Economy* edited by Wang Gungwu and John Wong (contains articles by some of the leading scholars in the field and offers an up-to-date overview of modern China's political economy that China watchers worldwide would welcome); *The Concise Flora of Singapore: Volume II: Monocotyledons* by Hsuan Keng, S. C. Chin, and H. T. W. Tan (covering the flowering plants, this is a companion volume to the first book which covered the gymnosperms and dicotyledons, thus completing the seed plant flora of Singapore); *Construction Technology for Tall Buildings* by Michael Chew (designed as a textbook in construction technology particularly for land-scarce cities and countries of the region, this book describes in detail the latest construction practices and processes for tall buildings from foundation to roof, with over 270 illustrations); *Resolving Disputes by Arbitration: What You Need to Know* by Catherine Tay Swee Kian (a law text intended for the general reader but one which should also be an equally useful reference for the professional); *Survival Guide to Acute Medicine* edited by Lee Kang Hoe, Jonn Wong, and Tan Chorh Chuan (a handbook designed to aid the management of acute medical emergencies as an easy reference source); *Modernization and Chinese Entrepreneurship: No. 3* (paper from the East Asian Institute Occasional Paper Series prepared by the East Asian Institute and intended for policy makers and readers who want to keep abreast of the latest developments in China); and *Journal of Southeast Asian Studies* (published by SUP for the Department of History at the National University of Singapore, this internationally recognized journal is indispensable to scholars and academics as well as those interested in keeping themselves informed of current research work on Southeast Asia).

SUP welcomes good quality, original, and well-written works for the academic community, professionals, and informed general public. Would-be authors should send SUP: a brief synopsis of the work highlighting its objectives, approach, and special or unique features that would recommend it for publication; chapter contents, introduction, and preface (if available); estimated length; intended audience and anticipated size; information on known competing publications; and authors' or contributors' c.v. (publications, academic qualifications, and/or affiliations).

In the first instance, query letters and SASEs should be directed to:

Patricia Tay, Managing Editor

TIMES EDITIONS

Times Centre
One New Industrial Road
Singapore 536196
(65) 380 7384
fax: (65) 285 4871

Political Science, Cooking, Gardening, Literature, Government
  Query letters and SASEs should be directed to:

Shirley Hew, General Manager

Shova Loh, Senior Editor

JOHN WILEY & SONS

2 Clementi Loop 129809
Singapore 0512
(65) 463 2400
fax: (65) 463 4605 or (65) 463 4606
wiley@signet.com.sg (e-mail)

  Query letters and SASEs should be directed to:

Steven Miron, Managing Director, Asia

South Africa

ACORN BOOKS

Box 4845
Randburg 2125
28 Abercorn Avenue
Craighall Park
Johannesburg 2196
South Africa
(27) 11 880 5768
fax: (27) 11 880 5768

Acorn Books was founded in 1984 by Eleanor-Mary Cadell, a former acquisitions editor of MacMillan South Africa. Acorn publishes works on natural history, specializing in high-quality monographs. Current titles include: *Botswana, A Brush with the Wild* by Paul Augustinus; *African Thunder: The Victoria Falls* by Jan and Fiona Teede; *The Slipper Orchids* by Esme F. Hennessy and Tessa Hedge.

   Direct query letters and SASEs to:

Audrey Walker

ANANSI PUBLICATIONS

10 Forest Road
Oranjezicht
Cape 8001
South Africa
(27) 21 968 411
fax: (27) 21 969 698

Anansi specializes in publishing picture books for young children, and sets very high standards of excellence for both writing and illustration. Anansi accepts only those books that, for example, *The Horn Book Guide* would classify as "outstanding" or "superior." Anansi declares in its policy statement: "It is our belief that literary excellence and excellence in graphic art, in the final instance, deal with the universal qualities of man and that all great literature is essentially based on universal moral values. By definition, therefore, literary and graphic excellence excludes propaganda of any kind, didacticism, stereotyping of characters and/or places, any form of racism or discrimination whether pertaining to sex, traditions, cultures, or religion and the promotion of perverse values and practices (such as Satanism)." And thus, Anansi endeavors "to pursue excellence in the technical execution of our books that matches the excellence of the content."

Query letters and SASEs should be directed to **Anansi.**

THE INSTITUTE FOR REFORMATIONAL STUDIES

Potchefstroom University for Christian Higher Education
Private Bag X6001
Potchefstroom 2520
South Africa
(27) 18 299 1623
fax: (27) 18 299 2799
irsajvdw@puknet.puk.ac.za (e-mail)
www.puk.ac.za/indexe.html

The aim of The Institute for Reformational Studies—founded in 1962—is, as its name indicates, to study and promote a Biblical-reformational view of life. It achieves this aim by developing and defining a world view—at philosophical, religious, and scholarly or scientific levels—as an integrated, interpretive set of confessional perspectives on reality that underlie human activity, shape it, motivate it, and give it direction and meaning to enable man to fulfill his calling in the world.

In practical terms, the Institute strives to accomplish its goals in three ways: through research, conferences, and publications. The IRS publishes books in four series of the University's publication program as well as two journals. Their study pamphlets are short studies (about 25 pages per issue) of which 12 numbers are published annually. The IRS brochures are more extensive in volume and reflect more intensively on topical issues that are of vital importance to Christians. The IRS *Collections* series are publications by different authors that run to about 500 pages and concentrate on one central theme. The latest project, *Christian Literature for Africa,* is a project on Christian Literature written by African people.

Orientation, an international circular of the Potchefstroom University for Christian Higher Education, is a journal of about 150 pages. First published in 1976, one number is published annually. It is a truly international journal and is at present distributed to over 1,000 addresses in 60 countries worldwide. *Word and Action* is a quarterly that was started in the 1950s, but since 1992 it has been published jointly by the IRS and the

Reformational Movement of Southern Africa. Since the IRS is a nonprofit organization and is subsidized by the Potchefstroom University for Christian Higher Education, it is able to offer its publications at a very reasonable price.

A sample of IRS products: *A Christian Perspective on Hypnosis* by K. Arabindan; *A Christian Perspective on Work and Labour Relations* by H. Antonides; *An African Response to the Question of Apartheid* by Y. Turaki; *A Christian Perspective on Motivation* by M. Scott; *Visions of Man and Freedom in Africa* edited by M. Waijaki, Y. Turaki, B. J. van der Walt, et al; *The Bible and Islam* by B. M. Madany; *Perspectives on Technology and Culture* by E. Schuurman; *Heartbeat: Taking the Pulse of Our Theological-Philosophical Heritage* by B. J. van der Walt, and *Our Reformational Tradition: A Rich Heritage or Lasting Vocation?* from the Institute's *Collections* series.

Query letters and SASEs should be directed to:

IRS, Editorial, as on previous page

JUTA & COMPANY LTD.

Mercury Crescent
Wetton 7780
P.O. Box 14373, Kenwyn 7790
South Africa
(27) 21 797 5101
fax: (27) 21 762 7424
books@juta.co.za (e-mail)
www.juta.co.za

As southern Africa's largest privately owned publishing house, established in 1853, Juta plays a critical role in meeting the needs of increasingly diverse markets. Through its national marketing, sales and distribution networks, retail outlets, southern African subsidiaries, agents abroad and international distribution rights, Juta delivers a range of uniquely South African works covering adult education, business management, health care, the sciences, arts, and humanities. From the Juta perspective, South African national education policy rightfully demands that its success be gauged against its ability to empower all South Africans educationally. They therefore publish relevant student textbooks of the best quality at the most competitive prices. Internal organizational flexibility allows Juta to continue with its meaningful contribution to national education policy development and, by consulting stakeholders, it is constantly forging new partnerships. As Juta put it: "Our commitment to product excellence and service quality arises from our corporate values and affirmative action programs, driven by individuals dedicated to the continuing intellectual and economic upliftment of all our communities."

A selection from Juta's extensive listings: *A Guide to Learning* by A. P. Craig and J. L. Bradbury; *Practical Accountancy, New VAT edition* by J. J. van Lill, L. G. Hechter, H. A. van Niekerk, and J. Vorster; *Arbitration in South Africa: Law and Practice* by D. Butler and E. Finsen; *Business Computing: An African Perspective* by G. J. Erwin and C. N. Blewett; *Municipal Administration: A Handbook,* fourth edition, by D. L. Craythorne; *Rising to the Challenge of Change: A History of Black Nursing in South Africa* by T. G. Mashaba; *Clinical Ethics: A Christian Approach* by L. R. Uys and J. H. Smit; *Teaching Primary Health Care* by C. Winberg; *Fundani 2: The Zulu Collection* (a level-2 set of titles for adult education courses from the *Fundani* series); and *Nelson Mandela: Inkokeli Ngokuzalwa (Nelson Mandela: Born to Lead)* by the ABE Development Services Trust (telling the story of the life of Nelson Mandela from his childhood to his election as president).

Juta is always interested in proposals for new books. A short synopsis and an indication of the student market for which the book is intended should be submitted to the publishing director or the appropriate commissioning editor in the authors' field of interest.

Thus, query letters and SASEs should be directed to:

Eve Horwitz Gray, Publishing Director

Adele Levitan, Publishing Manager

Brian Wafawarowa, Commissioning Editor, Communications Studies, Literature and Language, Education, Foundation and Access Courses

Lynell Walker, Commissioning Editor, Business Studies and Accounting

Garry Rosenberg, Commissioning Editor, Public Administration, Education, Literature, Foundation and Access Courses

Pranill Ramchander, Commissioning Editor, Health Studies, Tourism, Science and Technology

OCEANOGRAPHIC RESEARCH INSTITUTE

2 West Street
Durban
P.O. Box 10712
Marine Parade 4056
South Africa
(27) 31 373536
fax: (27) 31 372132

The Oceanographic Research Institute (ORI) is the research arm of the South African Association for Marine Biological Research (SAAMBR). SAAMBR is a unique non-governmental center for marine science, conservation, and education. Founded in 1951 after a campfire discussion that took place during a scientific expedition to Tongaland, this independent and not-for-gain institution was established specifically to provide "knowledge and advice about the sea" to people and the government concerning the wise use and conservation of marine resources. SAAMBR's activities are driven by a vision to bring about healthy coastal and marine ecosystems, rich in biodiversity, while providing people throughout Southern Africa with safe and sustainable opportunities for economic development, healthy food, and quality recreation.

One of the objectives of the ORI is to make available expert scientific information and to publish scientific papers of excellence and to produce authoritative scientific documents and statements on marine and coastal conservation.

From the ORI: *Marine Linefish: Status, Stocks and Statistics* (Proceedings of the 2nd National Marine Linefish Symposium, edited by L. E. B. Beckley & R. P. Van Der Elst); *Marine Linefish: Priority Species and Research Objectives in Southern Africa* (a special ORI publication edited by R. P. Van Der Elst and F. Adkin)**;** *Transkei Coastal Fisheries Resources* by P. J. Fielding, W. D. Robertson, A. H. Dye, B. J. Tomalin, R. P. Van Der Elst, L. E. B. Beckley, B. Q. Mann, S. Birnie, M. H. Schleyer, and T. A. Lasiak (report on the survey of fisheries resources on the Transkei coast that was carried out by the ORI and the University of Transkei); and *Transkei Coastal Fisheries Resources: Phase 2—Resource Utilisation, Development and Tourism* (a special ORI publication by W. D. Robertson and P. J. Fielding).

Query letters and SASEs should be directed to:

The Oceanographic Research Institute, as on previous page

UNIVERSITY OF NATAL PRESS

Private Bag X01
Scottsville 3209
South Africa
(27) 331 260 5226
fax: (27) 331 260 5801
books@press.unp.ac.za (e-mail)
www.unpress.co.za

University of Natal Press publications cover history, general literature, African literature, natural science, religion, social studies, gender studies, genealogy, and reference.

Recent UNP titles include: *Alone Among the Zulus* by Catherine Barter; *Black Valour* by Norman Clothier; *Enterprise and Exploitation in a Victorian Colony* by Bill Guest; *Flowers of the Natal Drakensberg* by Olive M. Hilliard; *Hinduism in Natal* by Alleyn Diesel; *Liquor and Labor in Southern Africa* by Jonathan Crush; *Pietermaritzburg 1838–1988* by J. Laband; *The Rand at War 1899–1902* by Diana Cammack; *Recueil de Nouvelles Francaise* by William J.D. Lewis; *Servants and Gentlewomen to the Golden Land* by Cecillie Swaisland; *White Girl in Search of the Party* by Pauline Podbrey; and *Zulu Medicinal Plants* by A. Hutchings.

Query letters and SASEs should be directed to:

Sajida Mia, Marketing Assistant

Wales

GOMER

J. D. Lewis & Sons Ltd.
Gomer Press
Llandysul
Ceredigion SA44 4BQ
Wales
(44) 1559 362371
fax: (44) 1559 363758
gwasg@gomer.co.uk (e-mail)
www.gomer.co.uk

Gomer Press, the largest publishing house in Wales, was established in 1892 by John David Lewis and is still owned by the same family.

Each year Gomer publishes approximately 25 titles for adults and 5 to 10 titles in English for children under the **PONT** imprint. The number of titles published each year in Welsh is about 75. Gomer's range of titles and subjects is wide, from literary works to collections of postcards and studies in railway history, but all of the publications have a Welsh flavor or interest. For example, in 1995 Gomer Press published the first edition of George Borrow's *Wild Wales* ever to be put out by a Welsh press. Among the latest titles is *Between Sea and Sky* (a collection of superb photographs by Peter Hope Jones with accompanying extracts from poetry by R. S. Thomas). The English-language program that bears the PONT imprint publishes novels, short stories, and poetry—again, all with a Welsh flavor or interest, but with a relevance to young people everywhere. Two of its titles, *Sion and the Bargain Bee* (the third in a series devoted to the re-telling of Welsh legends, by Jenny Sullivan with full-color illustrations by Jac Jones) and *Alwena's Garden* by Mary Oldham (a novel for teenagers dealing with the problems of juvenile rheumatoid arthritis), have both been shortlisted for the Tir na n-Og award.

New from Gomer: *The Land and The Sea* by Kyffin Williams (a visual art title); *Diaries from the Welsh Countryside: A Homeland Year* edited by Jon Gower; *A Welsh House and Its Family: The Vaughans of Trawsgoed* by Gerald Morgan (a history title); *A Private Language? A Dip into Welsh Literature* by Marion Eames; and from PONT, *Thoughts Like an Ocean* edited by Nick Nuttall and Andy Hawkins (a children's poetry anthology). In Welsh: *Cofio Tryweryn* by Watcyn L. Jones; *Trwy Ddulliau Chwyldro: Hanes Cymdeithas yr Iaith Gymraeg, 1962–1992* by Dylan Phillips; *Wyneb yn Wyneb/Face to Face* by Jon Dressel and T. James Jones; *Yr Hirdaith* by Elvey MacDonald; and *Bugail Eryri* by Keith Bowen.

Gomer books are distributed in the UK by the **Wales Book Council** and by **Beekman Publishing Inc.** in the U.S.

Query letters and SASEs should be directed to:

Sue Davies

Y LOLFA

Talybont
Ceredigion
Cymru SY24 5AP
Wales
(44) 1970 832304
fax: (44) 1970 832782
ylolfa@ylolfa.com (e-mail)
www.ylolfa.com/

Y Lolfa is a unique Welsh language house. Established in the late sixties in an old warehouse in the village of Talybont, in the middle of the west coast of Wales, it is not far from the university town of Aberystwyth. Many of its ideas and ideals originated in that politically heady period. It was unofficial printer to the activist Cymdeithas yr Iaith (the Welsh Language Society), which was—and still is—campaigning for full status for the Welsh language. In addition, the house has always supported the Plaid Cymru aim of a sovereign Welsh state. However, with a name like Y Lolfa they do not take themselves *too* seriously. It literally means *The Lounge,* with a second meaning of "Lol" — place, (Lol — fun or nonsense), which is the satirical magazine it created. Embracing the then revolutionary and cheap method of small-offset printing, Y Lolfa began producing a range of lively, informal material mainly for the young. They then gradually aimed for a wider market including Welsh language learners and visitors to Wales. The success of books like *Welsh is Fun* (150,000+ sold) enabled the house to publish more substantial books about Welsh culture and politics. Y Lolfa was able to develop a central interest in contemporary Welsh-language literature, and at the same time extend its publications range to include music, art, cookery, and even diaries. The children's books are completely home-grown. Y Lolfa has a policy of not adapting from other languages owing to the house's fundamental belief in supporting Welsh artists, authors, and designers rather than importing books from overseas. All titles are printed in-house and any outwork (such as hardback binding) also is performed in Wales. In spite of its being a commercial operation, Y Lolfa remains committed to changing the political status quo in the hope of helping to achieve full independence for Wales.

Y Lolfa is the proud publisher of the last two works of Professor Leopold Kohr, the brilliantly provocative Austrian economist who originated the "small is beautiful" philosophy. Also of recent note are the stimulating essays of Harri Webb, who in *No Halfway House* states: "Wales is marching backwards into independence, everybody desperately pretending that we are going somewhere else."

Y Lolfa boast a fine quality catalog with a solid list of offerings in both the Welsh and English languages. In the Welsh: *Amdani!* by Bethan Evans (literature); *Blwyddyn a 'Chydig* (20) by Alun Llwyd (poetry); *Cymru'r Cynfas Wales on Canvas* by Hywel Harries (art); *Castell Marwolaeth Boenus ac Erchyll* by Rolant Ellis (children's); *Gwyliau Cochyn Bach* by Hilma Lloyd Edwards (for the very young); and *Ceidwad y Gannwyll* by Robat Arwyn a Robin Llwyd ab Owain (music).

English titles: *Artists in Snowdonia* by James Bogle; *The Legends of King Arthur* by Rhiannon Ifans; *Welsh Is Fun* by Heini Gruffudd and Elwyn Ioan; *Pigs & Ingots: The Lead Silver Mines of Cardiganshire* by Tina Carr and Annemarie Schone; *Fighting for Wales* by Gwynfor Evans.

Trade orders are welcome with worldwide distribution handled by **Drake International.**

Query letters and SASEs should be directed to:

Y Lolfa, as on previous page

PART TWO

Writer's International Directory of Literary Agents

Canada

Author Author Literary Agency Ltd.

12000 37th Street, SW
P.O. Box 34051
Calgary, AB T3C 3W2
Canada
403-242-0226

Agent: Joan Rickard, President
Born: Toronto, Ontario.
Education: Business instructor, Alberta Vocational College; editorial consultant.
Career history: Published author of numerous magazine articles and two books. Agency is now in its fifth year.
What are the subjects and categories you are most interested in agenting? Fiction/nonfiction, adult and juvenile: novels, short-story collections, scholarly, New Age.
What are the subjects and categories you are not interested in agenting? No poetry, screenplays, or magazine short stories/articles.
What is the best way for a prospective client to initiate contact with you? Submit entire manuscript proposal, or sample chapters.
Do you have a reading fee policy? No reading fee.
Client representation in the following categories:
   Nonfiction: 45%
   Fiction: 50%
   Children's: 5%
   Textbooks: 0%
What is your commission structure? 15% domestic (Canadian); 20% foreign (non-Canadian).
Approximate number of titles sold last year: 4.
Approximate percentage of all submissions (from queries through manuscripts) that you reject: 95%.
Representative titles sold:
   Battling the Bulge by Roderick W. Dingwall, MD (Commonwealth)
   Ice Break by Kim Kinrade (Commonwealth), national bestseller
   Why Elephants and Fleas Don't Sweat by Gideon Louw, Ph.D. (Detselig)
   Wild Liard Waters by Ferdi Wenger (Caitlin)

Description of the Client from Hell: Frequent phone calls, is singularly self-focused and dictatorial. If the proposal or book doesn't sell or doesn't sell well, it's the agent's and/or publisher's fault.

Description of Dream Client: Dream clients—most of my people—are talented authors who are mature and professional in performance and attitude. Patience, in what is an excessively tight publishing market, and a sense of humor are helpful allies, too. We share the view that the author-agent union is a partnership with reciprocal trust and respect.

What are the most common mistakes clients make when soliciting you to represent them? Improperly presented proposals. There is an abundance of good reference books on the market or in libraries to teach writers the basic mechanics and techniques: proper formatting, spelling, punctuation, composition, etc. Good writing is the marriage of creative style and professional presentation. The former is an art, the latter is a skill. Both may be significantly improved if writers do their homework and study the craft before placing their proposal on agents' and publishers' desks. And, remember that unlike authors—who have only their own proposals to think about—agents are busy folks trying to cram two hours into every one servicing numerous authors' proposals and published titles.

What can writers do to enhance their chances of getting you as an agent? Be courteous. Don't unnecessarily phone agents. Submit neat professionally presented proposals.

Why did you become an agent? I love the world of writing. With my experience as an editor and author, it was an obvious, and highly satisfying, direction.

What might you be doing if you weren't an agent? Author and editorial consultant.

Pontifications: Study your chosen genre thoroughly to learn style/technique and what publishers are contracting. It is not the agent's or publisher's job to teach creative writing courses, or revamp the mechanics of formatting, punctuation, and composition. Most will not, or will charge extra for this service. Please ensure that manuscripts are properly formatted; double-spaced throughout, about 250 words per page (e.g. Font Times New Roman 13); allow 1" margins on all sides; indent paragraphs five character spaces. No dot matrix of disk submissions. Include a brief high-impact synopsis of your proposal (as seen on the back of book jackets) and bio. Each may be less than but not exceed 100 words (double-spaced). Canadian SASE or IRC's or money orders must be enclosed or manuscript/inquiries will not be returned. If a work is good enough and appeals to a broad enough market that it is worth the publisher's investment of considerable dollars, with patience and perseverance it should, eventually, find its place on the market.

Publishers are looking for material that is, in their opinion very well written—although we all we all sometimes wonder about their choices—especially by authors with impressive portfolios, whose works are not so controversial that they detract rather than attract sales, yet are distinctive enough to separate themselves from what's already out there. Simple. Most writers believe their proposals to be above the crowd; some are even correct. Believe in yourself and your writing. Be willing to learn. Persevere!

For writers who need guidance with the basics, we offer a "Crash Course Kit" in Business Letters, Punctuation/Information Guide, and Manuscript Formatting for $8.95 including shipping and handling.

J. KELLOCK AND ASSOCIATES LTD.

11017 80th Avenue
Edmonton, AB T6G 0R2
Canada
403-433-0274

Agent: Joanne Kellock

Education: BA, Honors English, University of Alberta; graduate studies, University of Alberta and Harvard/Radcliffe.

Career history: Sales rep., while still at university, for Penguin, Pan, Fontana, Van Nostrand Reinhold, Macmillan Canada (university text market). Bantum publicist; author promotion. Marketing manager: Government of Canada, National Museums of Canada, Ottawa, Ontario, Literary Agent full time since 1987.

Hobbies/Personal Interests: Classical music, collecting paintings and sculpture, cooking for guests only.

What are the subjects and categories you are most interested in agenting? Literary fiction, all categories works for children, creative nonfiction, extraordinary well-written commercial genre.

What are the subjects and categories you are not interested in agenting? Poetry, essays, short stories (unless from previously published writer), and esoteric, New Age texts.

What is the best way for a prospective client to initiate contact with you? Query letter—no initial telephone calls please.

Do you have a reading fee policy? Yes, a fee is charged for previously unpublished writers, or published writers of, say, non-fiction, who have now written a novel or a work for children.

Fee Schedule: $140 U.S., for three chapters plus a brief synopsis. If style works with subject, or subject is something that is selling today, balance read free of charge. $110 U.S. for picture book for children.

Client representation in the following categories:
   Non-fiction: 30%
   Fiction: 30%
   Children's/Young Adult: 40%
   Textbooks: 0%

What is your commission structure? 15% North America; 20% foreign and UK unless subject is one I handle myself in UK, i.e., works for children, fiction, and some non-fiction.

Approximate number of titles sold last year: 15.

Approximate percentage of all submissions (from queries through manuscripts) that you reject: 90%.

Representative titles sold:

Children's titles:

Into the Mouth of the Wolf by Martyn Godfrey (Tundra Books, Canada).

Dinosaurs by Martyn Godfrey (McClelland & Stewart, Canada); comic book.

Helping Hands Club by Martyn Godfrey (Scholastic Canada).

Subria, Subria by Tolowa Mollel (Holiday House, NY); picture book.

To Dinner for Dinner by Tolowa Mollel (Holiday House, NY); picture book.

Walking a Thin Line by Sylvia McNicoll (Scholastic Canada).

Dribble, Dribble by Sylvia McNicoll (Scholastic Canada).

I Spy Private Eye by Estelle Salata (ITP Nelson, Canada).

The Ghost Who Would Dance Forever by Gisela Sherman (Scholastic Canada).

This Means War by Bev Spencer (Scholastic Canada).

Trapped in Ice by Eric Walters (Scholastic Canada).

Adult Fiction:

Blame It on the Spruce Budworm by Susan Haley (Gaspereau Press, N.S.).

Description of the Client from Hell: Those who do not read the complete listing in Jeff Herman's Writer's International Guide.

Description of your Dream Client: The client that presents me with a knock-your-socks-off novel or creative work of non-fiction. The client who behaves professionally and does not barrage me with letters, faxes, telephone calls soon after submission. The client who always encloses SASE, plus necessary postage for responses to queries, toing and froing of material, or return of material, and knows, that first, that I do require a fee from all previously unpublished writers—magazines, newspapers, or periodical publications are not books—and also that I cannot mail to the U.S. without U.S. postage.

What are the most common mistakes clients make when soliciting you to represent them? Initial telephone query calls; cover letter carelessly written and mistake-ridden; manuscript carelessly written, filled with typos, spelling errors, grammar errors, and that old saw—errors in logic.

What can writers do to enhance their chances of getting you as an agent? They are not guilty of any of the most common mistakes (see above question).

Why did you become an agent? Evolution—it seems to me that anyone who starts out anywhere in the publishing industry, stays. Most of us seem to move around within the industry. I have a love of literature.

What might you be doing if you weren't an agent? Running an art gallery or doing an honors degree in 17th century history; but I would rather be reading Jane Austen.

Pontifications: Why is it everyone today thinks that they can write a book. So you want to write a novel, are you prepared to spend the next ten years of your life learning how?

England

A & WATT LTD.

20 John Street
London WC1N 2DR
England

Agent: Derek Johns.
   Born: July 5, 1948.
   Career History: Random House, New York; Granta, UK; Bodley Head, UK.
   What are the subjects and categories you are most interested in agenting? Literary fiction and nonfiction; Irish and Indian writing.
   What are the subjects and categories you are not interested in agenting? Poetry, commercial, science fiction.
   What is the best way for a prospective client to initiate contact with you? To send synopsis and 2–3 chapters.
   Do you have a reading fee policy? No.
   Client representation in the following categories:
   Nonfiction: 40%
   Fiction: 60%
   Children's: 0%
   Textbooks: 0%
   What is your commission structure? 10% UK sales; 20% rest of world.
   Approximate number of titles sold last year: 30
   Approximate percentage of all submissions (from queries through manuscripts) that you reject: 99%
   Representative titles sold:
   The American Century by Martin Walker (Knopf U.S.; Chatto UK).
   Biography of Capa by Alex Kershaw (Harcourt Brace U.S.; Macmillan UK).
   Visible Worlds by Marilyn Bowering (Flamingo UK).
   The White Bone by Barbara Fowdy (Flamingo UK).
   The Guilty by Claire Messud (Picador UK).
   The Last Resort by Alison Lurie (Chatto UK).

Description of your Dream Client: Hard-working, open-minded, cooperative, patient, reasonable.

What are the most common mistakes clients make when soliciting you to represent them? Moving too fast (being too pushy, for example); writing silly attention-grabbing gimmicky letters; not enclosing writing sample.

What can writers do to enhance their chances of getting you as an agent? Write a simple letter showing some idea of how the world of books works and the process of submitting work to agencies. Wait patiently for a reply; or if they must chase, do it politely, understanding that the agent may be busy.

DARLEY ANDERSON LITERARY, TV, AND FILM AGENCY

Estelle House
11 Eustace Road
London SW6 1JB
England
(44) 171 385 6652
fax: (44) 171 386 5571
DANDER6652@aol.com (e-mail)

Agent: Darley Anderson.
  Born: July 28, 1942.
  Education: Cambridge University England (Selwyn College).
  Career History: 25 years in book publishing as an editor and publisher.
  Hobbies/Personal Interests: Growing roses/gardening; the stock market; cricket; food.
  What are the subjects and categories you are most interested in agenting? Commercial fiction and nonfiction; all types of thrillers; all types of women's fiction; crime; Irish novels.
  What are the subjects and categories you are not interested in agenting? Poetry, academic books.
  What is the best way for a prospective client to initiate contact with you? Send first three chapters with brief synopsis and return postage.
  Do you have a reading fee policy? No reading fee, but writer must include return postage with submission.
  Client representation in the following categories:
  Nonfiction: 25%
  Fiction: 75%
  Children's: 0%
  Textbooks: 0%

What is your commission structure? 15% UK; 20% foreign language; 20% film/TV; 15–20% U.S.

Approximate number of titles sold last year: 80

Approximate percentage of all submissions (from queries through manuscripts) that you reject: 85%

Representative titles sold:

Thriller: *Killing Floor* by Lee Child (Putnam U.S. and Transworld UK).

Crime Thriller: *Every Dead Thing* by John Connolly (Simon & Schuster U.S.; Hodder & Stoughton UK).

Memoir: *Dublin Made Me* by Peter Sheridan (Penguin U.S.; Macmillan UK).

Description of the Client from Hell: Someone who can't leave me to negotiate their deals without interfering all the time.

Description of your Dream Client: All my writers are dream clients. They trust me; I trust them.

What are the most common mistakes clients make when soliciting you to represent them? Not having given realistic thought to the marketplace for their books.

What can writers do to enhance their chances of getting you as an agent? Being 100% professional.

Why did you become an agent? To work with writers and book people; to make money; to be my own boss.

What might you be doing if you weren't an agent? Nothing useful. Perhaps living a life of leisure.

Pontifications: You won't get a better agent than me if I love what you write and if you are writing for the reading public, not the literary establishment.

CURTIS BROWN GROUP, LTD.

Haymarket House
28/29 Haymarket
London SW1Y 4SP
England
(44) 0171 396 6600
fax: (44) 0171 396 0110/1
cb@curtisbrown.co.uk (e-mail)

Agency History: Established 1899.

What are the subjects and categories you are most interested in agenting? Wide range of fiction—literary and commercial and nonfiction.

What are the subjects and categories you are not interested in agenting? Poetry.

What is the best way for a prospective client to initiate contact with you? Letter, synopsis, three chapters.

Do you have a reading fee policy? No fee.

Client representation in the following categories:

Nonfiction: 47.5%

Fiction: 47.5%

Children's: 5%

Textbooks: 0%

What is your commission structure? Books: 10% UK, 20% non-UK; Media: 10% UK, 15% non-UK.

Approximate number of titles sold last year: 500+

Approximate percentage of all submissions (from queries through manuscripts) that you reject: 90%

Description of the Client from Hell: Not a dream client.

Description of your Dream Client: One whose work we have successfully sold to every market in the world, including film rights, or one that we believe one day will have success.

What are the most common mistakes clients make when soliciting you to represent them? Carelessly written letter with grammatical errors, unfocused synopsis, unrealistic expectations.

What can writers do to enhance their chances of getting you as an agent? Brief focused letters and an ability to summarize their work in a unique and accessible way.

Why did you become an agent? Each of our nine book agents would answer differently!

What might you be doing if you weren't an agent? There is no other life!

Pontifications: The ability of the individual agent is paramount. The strengths of the agency in all aspects of rights exploitation, including film and television, are essential.

FELICITY BRYAN

2A North Parade
Banbury Road
Oxford OX2 6PE UK
England
(44) 1865 513816
fax: (44) 1865 310055

Agent: Felicity Bryan.

Born: United Kingdom.

Education: A degree in History of Art from the Cortauld Institute, London.

Career History: Was a journalist for various newspapers, including *The Economist* and the *Washington Post,* before joining Curtis Brown. Set up her own agency in Oxford in 1988.

What are the subjects and categories you are most interested in agenting? Science, current affairs, literary fiction, history, biography.

What are the subjects and categories you are not interested in agenting? Short stories, poetry, how-to books, horror, science fiction, light romance, technical.

What is the best way for a prospective client to initiate contact with you? Approach by letter including a synopsis, two or three sample chapters, c.v. if nonfiction, return postage.

Do you have a reading fee policy? No.

Client representation in the following categories:

Nonfiction: 60%

Fiction: 40%

Children's: 0%

Textbooks: 0%

What is your commission structure? 10% on sales made within the UK; 20% on U.S. and translation.

Approximate percentage of all submissions (from queries through manuscripts) that you reject: around 90%

Representative titles sold:

The Cornflake House (literary fiction) by Deborah Gregory (UK Pan Macmillan).

An Instance of the Fingerpost (literary historical) by Iain Pears (Random House UK).

Humanity: The Recent Moral History by Jonathan Glover (Jonathan Cape UK).

A History of British Civilisation by Roy Strong (Random House UK).

Genome (science) by Matt Ridley (Fourth Estate UK).

Brain Sculpture (science) by Ian Robertson (Transworld).

The Sixties Satirists (culture) by Humphrey Carpenter (Gollancz).

What are the most common mistakes clients make when soliciting you to represent them? Telling the publisher what the market is for this book.

Why did you become an agent? Because I love the process of finding an exciting writer, matching him or her with the perfect publisher, and seeing the result. It feels creative.

What might you be doing if you weren't an agent? Film production; journalism.

MERRIC DAVIDSON LITERARY AGENCY

12 Priors Heath
Goudhurst
Kent TN17 2RE
England
(44) 1580 212041

Agent: Merric Davidson; Wendy Suffield.

Career History: Ex-publisher.

What are the subjects and categories you are most interested in agenting? Contemporary fiction, literary fiction, children's.

What are the subjects and categories you are not interested in agenting? Sci-fi, fantasy, crime, horror, romance, historical, saga—unless written from a literary, unique angle.

What is the best way for a prospective client to initiate contact with you? Query letter, short synopsis; return postage a must.

Do you have a reading fee policy? No.

Client representation in the following categories:

Nonfiction: 10%

Fiction: 70%

Children's: 20%

Textbooks: 0%

What is your commission structure? UK 10%

Approximate number of titles sold last year: 10

Approximate percentage of all submissions (from queries through manuscripts) that you reject: 95%+

Representative titles sold:

Jelly Roll by Luke Sutherland (Anchor).

Honey-Dew by Louise Doughty (Simon & Schuster).

The Drumbeat of Jimmy Sands by Murray Davies (HarperCollins)

Description of the Client from Hell: Unreasonable.

Description of your Dream Client: Reasonable.

What are the most common mistakes clients make when soliciting you to represent them? Trying to make us laugh in unfunny cover letters.

What can writers do to enhance their chances of getting you as an agent? A professional, neat approach. No padding, just facts.

Why did you become an agent? The challenge!

DORIAN LITERARY AGENCY

Upper Thornehill
27 Church Road
St. Marychurch
Torquay TQ1 4QY
England
(44) 1803 312095 (voice/fax)

Agent: Dorothy Lumley.

Born: Near London, 1949.

Education: Wycombe High School, Leicester University, Psychology B.A.

Career History: Paperback editor/editorial director and some freelance editing/reading 1972–86. One year in London agency. Launched own agency in 1986.

Hobbies/Personal Interests: Ballroom dancing; gardening; wildlife conservation; sculpture; usual: reading, movies (especially old B&W), cooking.

What are the subjects and categories you are most interested in agenting? Popular fiction—romance, historical, crime, science fiction, fantasy, horror.

What are the subjects and categories you are not interested in agenting? Poetry, children's, academic, political.

What is the best way for a prospective client to initiate contact with you? By letter, enclosing outline and 1–3 chapters.

Do you have a reading fee policy? No reading fee.

Client representation in the following categories:

Nonfiction: 20%

Fiction: 80%

Children's: 0%

Textbooks: 0%

What is your commission structure? 10% UK and translation (after foreign agent commission, if applicable); 15% U.S.

Approximate number of titles sold last year: Depends how you want to calculate this: head contract first-time sale = 30 books (excluding all further rights, translation, film, etc), which is more like 200.

Approximate percentage of all submissions (from queries through manuscripts) that you reject: I reject 95–98% of initial queries of the manuscripts I ask to see (about 1 or 2 a month).

Representative titles sold: (In the past month or so)
Brian Lumley's *Labeer to Hudder* (Hudder).

Dee Williams' *Labert to Headling* (Cockney Saga).

Two books by Dennis Elchison (Fanucci, Italy).

Second Word (romance) by C. Vincent (Scarlet).

A hardback romance by Anne Gunig (Seven House).

What are the most common mistakes clients make when soliciting you to represent them? Strangers who use my first name only, and who are very pushy.

What can writers do to enhance their chances of getting you as an agent? Sadly, nothing. I can only represent as many clients as I have time for; no one can "manufacture" the magic ingredients that will make me fall for something and decide to give it space.

Why did you become an agent? I was asked by certain clients to represent them during a period when I was freelancing and I said yes!

What might you be doing if you weren't an agent? Pursuing my hobbies! But to earn a living—writing, consultative editorial work, freelance editing.

Pontifications: Know your market—who you are trying to reach as a reader. Keep it simple. Write from the heart if possible.

JURI GABRIEL

35 Camberwell Grove

London SE5 8JA

England

(44) 171 703 6186 (voice/fax)

Agent: Juri Gabriel.

Born: July 27, 1940; Tallinn, Estonia.

Education: Charterhouse and Jesus College, Oxford.

Career History: Worked briefly in television and for Tharmisand Hudson Publishers. Since 1967 I have been at various firms and in various combinations: writer and translator (20 years); photographer, lecturer (19 years); copywriter, book packager, publishing and marketing consultant, reviewer and feature writer, literary agent (17 years); and chairman of Dedalus, publishers of literary fiction (14 years).

What are the subjects and categories you are most interested in agenting? Literary fiction and quality fiction and nonfiction; wit and intelligence.

What are the subjects and categories you are not interested in agenting? Science fiction; poetry; short stories; children's. Anything lacking wit and/or intelligence.

What is the best way for a prospective client to initiate contact with you? Letter, synopsis, three sample chapters, and return postage.

Do you have a reading fee policy? No reading fees.

Client representation in the following categories:

Nonfiction: 45–50%

Fiction: 45–50%

Children's: 0%

Textbooks: 3–5%

What is your commission structure? 10% home; 20% foreign.

Approximate percentage of all submissions (from queries through manuscripts) that you reject: 99%

Representative titles sold:

Exquisite Corpse by Robert Irwin (Dedalus and eight or so other publishers throughout the world).

Prayer—Cushions of the Flesh by Robert Irwin (Dedalus and six others).

A White Merc with Fins by James Hawes (Cape and thirteen others).

The Royal Society of Medicine Encyclopedia of Family Health by Dr. Robert Youngson (Bloomsbury).

Winners and Losers: The Business Strategy of Football by Stefan Szymanski and Tim Kuypers (Penguin).

The Cold War by David Miller (John Murray).

When We Die by Professor Cedric Mims (Robinson).

Film options on *Exquisite Corpse*, *A White Merc with Fins*, and David Madsen's *Confessions of a Flesh-Eater*.

What are the most common mistakes clients make when soliciting you to represent them? Lack of talent.

What can writers do to enhance their chances of getting you as an agent? And if you can take that . . .

Why did you become an agent? I found myself saying, "Oh, give it to me. I'll sell it." The next stage was to get paid for it.

What might you be doing if you weren't an agent? Publisher, TV producer, photographer, writer, antique dealer.

GREENE & HEATON LTD.

37 Goldhawk Road
London W12 8QQ
England
(44) 181 749 0315
fax: (44) 181 749 0318

Agents: Carol Heaton; Judith Murray; Antony Topping.

Born: Heaton: December 22, 1945; Dublin. Murray: July 31, 1967; Montreal. Topping: July 17, 1972; Manchester.

Education: Heaton: HCJ, Dublin; Sorbonne, Paris. Murray: B.A. Honors Wadham College, Oxford, English Language and Literature First Class. Topping: B.A. Honors St. Anne's College, Oxford, English Language and Literature 2:1.

Career History: Heaton: Literary Agent, Penguin Rights Director, Literary Agent. Murray: Literary Scout for Foreign Publishers and Editor. Topping: Bookseller.

What are the subjects and categories you are most interested in agenting? Heaton: Women's commercial fiction, literary fiction, literary biography, travel, history. Murray: Women's commercial fiction, literary fiction, literary biography, travel. Topping: Literary fiction/thriller, nonfiction, travel.

What are the subjects and categories you are not interested in agenting? Science fiction, fantasy, children's fiction, original scripts or screenplays.

What is the best way for a prospective client to initiate contact with you? Send a letter, synopsis, and 2–3 sample chapters and return postage. No submissions by fax. Sample chapters must be typed, double-spaced, unbound.

Do you have a reading fee policy? No.

Client representation in the following categories:

Nonfiction: 40%

Fiction: 60%

Children's: 0%

Textbooks: 0%

What is your commission structure? Information on application.

Approximate percentage of all submissions (from queries through manuscripts) that you reject: 85%

What are the most common mistakes clients make when soliciting you to represent them? Making the approach by fax, or generally not doing research properly, which results in unsuitable submissions, sloppy presentations, not including return postage.

What can writers do to enhance their chances of getting you as an agent? Doing the opposite of all or the above. Showing that they are professional, realistic, and have researched and know their market and the competition.

Why did you become an agent? Love of reading.

What might you be doing if you weren't an agent? Lotus-eating.

GREGORY & RADICE AUTHORS' AGENTS

3 Barb Mews
London W6 7PA
England
(44) 171 610 4676
fax: (44) 171 610 4686

Agents: Jane Gregory, Lisanne Radice.

What are the subjects and categories you are most interested in agenting? Quality fiction, mystery, commercial, and literary.

What are the subjects and categories you are not interested in agenting? Poetry, fantasy, science fiction, educational/academic, children's books.

What is the best way for a prospective client to initiate contact with you? Write a letter enclosing a complete synopsis of the plot plus the first three chapters.

Do you have a reading fee policy? No.

Client representation in the following categories:

Nonfiction: 15%

Fiction: 84%

Children's: 1%

Textbooks: 0%

What is your commission structure? 15% on sales to UK publishers; 20% on sales of translation rights to U.S.

Approximate number of titles sold last year: 60 titles in UK alone. We then went on to sell these same books abroad.

Approximate percentage of all submissions (from queries through manuscripts) that you reject: We believe that there were approximately 3,000 submissions last year and we took on 4 authors.

Description of the Client from Hell: Authors who ask for editorial advice, and when the typescript is delivered, it is obvious they have not taken in even one point; authors who have no respect for delivery dates; authors who are rude and aggressive for no reason.

Description of your Dream Client: Writes a brilliant bestselling book once a year, is charming and witty, appreciates the advice given, and likes working as part of a team.

What are the most common mistakes clients make when soliciting you to represent them? Not being entirely open and frank about their literary history.

What can writers do to enhance their chances of getting you as an agent? A willingness to listen to suggestions.

Pontifications: We are a unique agency—each author is handled by both partners—Lisanne Radice deals with all editorial matters and so would be an author's first contact; Jane Gregory sells, draws up contracts, and runs the administration.

CHRISTOPHER LITTLE LITERARY AGENCY

10 Eel Brook Studios
125 Moore Park Road
London SW6 4PS
England
(44) 171 736 4455
fax: (44) 171 736 4490
100555.3137@compuserve.com (e-mail)

Agents: Christopher Little and Patrick Walsh.

What are the subjects and categories you are most interested in agenting? Thrillers, popular science, literary fiction, narrative nonfiction.

What are the subjects and categories you are not interested in agenting? Science fiction, poetry, short stories.

What is the best way for a prospective client to initiate contact with you? By letter or fax outlining writing project and history, if any.

Do you have a reading fee policy? No.

Client representation in the following categories:

Nonfiction: 45%

Fiction: 45%

Children's: 10%

Textbooks: 0%

What is your commission structure? 20% for worldwide representation; 15% for domestic.

Approximate number of titles sold last year: 100–150

Approximate percentage of all submissions (from queries through manuscripts) that you reject: 95%

Representative titles sold:

Fermat's Last Theorem by Simon Singer (nonfiction; sold in 31 languages).

The Lazarus Child by Robert Manson (2nd novel—deals totaling U.S. $2.5 million to date worldwide).

The Miracle Strain by Michael Cordy (1st novel sold in 24 languages—deals totaling U.S. $2 million).

Harry Potter and the Philosopher's Stone by J. K. Rowling (1st young adult novel; has won several prizes and made its author close to U.S. $1 million to date).

Description of the Client from Hell: Overly demanding, untalented, and unrealistic.

Description of your Dream Client: As above, reversed.

What are the most common mistakes clients make when soliciting you to represent them? Incessant phone calls chasing for a response.

What can writers do to enhance their chances of getting you as an agent? Nothing.

Why did you become an agent? Love of books.

LIMELIGHT MANAGEMENT

33 Newman Street
London W1P 3PD UK
England
(44) 171 637 2529
fax: (44) 171 637 2538

Agent: Fiona Lindsay.

Born: Glasgow, February 10, 1958.

Education: University of Glasgow, M.A. Degree in Medieval History/Sociology.

Career History: 10 years of book publishing; 3 years in PR, marketing, and sales for Dorchester Hotel.

Hobbies/Personal Interests: Horse riding, yoga, antique collecting.

What are the subjects and categories you are most interested in agenting? Cookery, gardening, antiques, interior design, wine, health, and other lifestyle areas.

What are the subjects and categories you are not interested in agenting? Fiction.

What is the best way for a prospective client to initiate contact with you? By letter with SAE.

Do you have a reading fee policy? No.

Client representation in the following categories:

Nonfiction: 100%

Fiction: 0%

Children's: 0%

Textbooks: 0%

What is your commission structure? 15% home; 20% overseas.

Approximate number of titles sold last year: 60

Approximate percentage of all submissions (from queries through manuscripts) that you reject: 95% of unsolicited submissions.

Representative titles sold:

The Essential Garden Book by Dan Pearson and Sir Terence Corisur (Conran Octopus).
Eating In by James Martin (Mitchell Beasley).
The Royal Horticultural Society's Pests and Diseases by Pippa Greenwood (Darling Kindersley).
Oz Clarke's Wine Atlas by Oz Clarke (Little, Brown).

Description of the Client from Hell: A client who has too much time on his/her hands and chases me constantly while I've explained publishers don't buy instantly.

Description of your Dream Client: Someone who lets me get on with it.

What are the most common mistakes clients make when soliciting you to represent them? Bad mouths my existing clients or is rude to me or my assistant.

What can writers do to enhance their chances of getting you as an agent? Get as much publicity as possible in the media about themselves and their given talent(s).

Why did you become an agent? Public demand—Lifestyle was not such an important area for "literary" agents and also I could cover all areas—TV, radio, personal appearances, product endorsement, journalism, and books.

What might you be doing if you weren't an agent? Running a horse sanctuary in the Cotswolds.

Pontifications: Believe in your idea by all means, but try not to have just one you're obsessed with. Be creative and grow.

ANDREW LOWNIE LITERARY AGENCY

17 Sutherland Street
London SW1V 4JU
England
(44) 171 828 1274
fax: (44) 171 828 7608

Agent: Andrew Lownie.

Born: November 11, 1961, Kenya.

Education: M.A., History, Magdalene College, Cambridge (President of the Union); M.Sc., American History, Edinburgh University.

Career History: Graduate trainee at Hodder & Stoughton after working as a journalist for the *Times* and *Spectator;* joined John Farquharson Literary Agency in 1985, became director in 1986; and started own agency in 1988.

Hobbies/Personal Interests: Music, theatre, and outdoor pursuits.

What are the subjects and categories you are most interested in agenting? History (especially social and military), biography and memoir (especially celebrity memoir), politics and investigative journalism, true crime and espionage, major reference, and UFOs.

What are the subjects and categories you are not interested in agenting? Any fiction, children's and young adults, poetry, screenplays.

What is the best way for a prospective client to initiate contact with you? Query letter with synopsis, sample chapter, and SASE.

Do you have a reading fee policy? No reading fee.

Client representation in the following categories:

Nonfiction: 90%

Fiction: 10%

Children's: 0%

Textbooks: 0%

What is your commission structure? Worldwide commission 15% (including subagents).

Approximate number of titles sold last year: about 50

Approximate percentage of all submissions (from queries through manuscripts) that you reject: 95%

Representative titles sold:

Chequers by Norma Major, wife of the Prime Minister (HarperCollins)—History of Prime Minister's country house.

The Oxford Classical Dictionary (latest version) edited by Simon Hornblower (Oxford University Press).

The Cambridge Guide to Literature in English (latest version) edited by Ian Ousby (Cambridge University Press).

Raj by Lawrence James (Little, Brown)—History of the British in India.

Lost Civilisations of the Stone Age by Richard Rudgley (Random House)—anthropology.

Wordsworth by Juliet Barker (Literary biography).

Alien Base (on UFOs) by Timothy Good (Random House UK and others).

The Uninvited (accounts of alien abductions) by Nick Pope (Simon & Schuster).

The FBI Files (FBI investigations into UFOs) by Nick Redfern (Simon & Schuster).

Blind in One Ear by Patrick Macnee—Showbiz memoir.

Description of the Client from Hell: Demanding, unappreciative, devious, unprepared to take advice, verbose, arrogant.

Description of your Dream Client: Professional, pleasant, self-motivated, well-connected in literary circles, reliable, productive, and with realistic expectations.

What are the most common mistakes clients make when soliciting you to represent them? Ignorance of the market and the agency's specializations, sending an unsolicited manuscript, and not including SASE.

What can writers do to enhance their chances of getting you as an agent? Professional presentation, give thought to the market for their book.

Why did you become an agent? Attracted to the combination of academia and business; the opportunity to deal with a wide variety of people and subjects and to discover and nurture creative talent. Offered a job after a chance meeting with John LeCarre and his agent.

What might you be doing if you weren't an agent? I have written or edited several books, including a literary guide to Edinburgh and biographies of Guy Burgess and John Buchanan so might be combining writing with journalism or broadcasting.

JOHN PAWSEY

60 High Street
Tarring
Worthing BN14 7NR
England
(44) 01903 205 167 (voice and fax)

Agent: John Pawsey.

Career History: Former national journalist and book editor with several leading UK publishers. Literary agent since 1976, running own agency since 1981.

Hobbies/Personal Interests: Music, film, sport, current events.

What are the subjects and categories you are most interested in agenting? Biography, business, sport, popular culture, current affairs, category fiction.

What are the subjects and categories you are not interested in agenting? Children's, science fiction/fantasy, horror, original stage, screen and radio scripts, poetry, short stories, journalism, academic, esoteric/specialist.

What is the best way for a prospective client to initiate contact with you? Letter with brief synopsis/sample, plus return postage.

Do you have a reading fee policy? No reading fee unless previously agreed.

Client representation in the following categories:

Nonfiction: 80%

Fiction: 20%

Children's: 0%

Textbooks: 0%

What is your commission structure? UK (Home), 10–15%; Abroad, 19–25% (shared with associates).

Approximate number of titles sold last year: 25

Approximate percentage of all submissions (from queries through manuscripts) that you reject: 95%

Representative titles sold:
Nonfiction:
Get the Job You Want by Grappo (Kogan Page).
The Money Maze by Cohen (Orion).
The Story of Chess Records by Collins (Bloomsbury).
The World of Golf by Davies (HarperCollins).
All Our Todays by Donovan (Cape).
Life and Times of Ronnie Scott by Green (Simon & Schuster).
Information Overload by Lewis (Penguin).
Jack Nicholson (biography) by Schiach (Batsford).
Fiction:
Apron Strings by Wright (Little, Brown).
The Italian Girl by Hall (Constable).

Description of the Client from Hell: No such animal. Anyone willing to devote their time and energy to putting at least 50,000 words on paper has always had my respect.

Description of your Dream Client: No such animal. I get as much satisfaction opening doors for a new client as I do in banking money for my most successful clients.

What are the most common mistakes clients make when soliciting you to represent them? Failing to indicate where the work on offer has already been submitted. Failing to check whether their idea isn't already on the market. Picking a genre/setting/period to write about that is not currently being published.

What can writers do to enhance their chances of getting you as an agent? Observe the above, and be succinct.

Why did you become an agent? To work with people more creative than I.

What might you be doing if you weren't an agent? Writing.

Pontifications: Keep writing—without your efforts, agents and publishers wouldn't exist.

EDDISON PEARSON LITERARY AGENCY

44 Inverness Terrace
London W2 3JA
England
(44) 0171 727 9113
fax: (44) 0171 7279143
box1@eddisonpearson.com (e-mail)

Agent: Clare Pearson.
  Born: England, 1969.
  Education: Cambridge University, MA in History, Scholarship.

Career History: Editor/Agent.

What are the subjects and categories you are most interested in agenting? Contemporary/literary fiction; literary nonfiction; children's books; film.

What are the subjects and categories you are not interested in agenting? Mass-market fiction, formula romance, and horror.

What is the best way for a prospective client to initiate contact with you? Letter and some samples of writing.

Do you have a reading fee policy? No.

Client representation in the following categories:

Nonfiction: 25%

Fiction: 50%

Children's: 25%

Textbooks: 0%

What is your commission structure? 10% for UK sales; 15% for other sales; 20% of sub-agent used for sale of foreign rights.

Approximate number of titles sold last year: 12 (first year trading)

Approximate percentage of all submissions (from queries through manuscripts) that you reject: 95%

Representative titles sold:

Millais by G. H. Fleming (Constable, London).

Émigré Journeys by Abdullah Hussein (Serpent's Tail, London).

The Caged Birds by Frederick Lipp (Holiday House).

How to Clone a Sheep by Hazel Richardson (Oxford).

Description of the Client from Hell: One who fails to appreciate the amount of work that an agent has to put in, and the risk inherent is that work—we only get paid if the book sells.

Description of your Dream Client: As long as clients appreciate what we do and are reasonably polite and friendly, we're happy to accommodate lots of different personalities and temperaments—variety is the spice of life!

What are the most common mistakes clients make when soliciting you to represent them? Assuming that we have nothing better to do than read their work.

What can writers do to enhance their chances of getting you as an agent? Accompanying their work with an apt, well-written letter.

Why did you become an agent? I enjoy the autonomy that comes with running my own business. Nothing beats the excitement of finding wonderful new writers and helping them achieve their potential. The work is wonderfully varied and one has to draw on a diverse range of skills. The professional relationships with authors are rewarding.

What might you be doing if you weren't an agent? I'd probably be an editor— as I was before.

Pontifications: Don't forget that there are more publishable writers in the world than there is space on literary agents' books—even if you don't immediately find an agent, you may succeed on your own.

LAURENCE POLLINGER LTD.

18 Maddox Street, Mayfair
London W1R OEU
England
(44) 171 629 9761
fax: (44) 171 629 9765
LaurencePolliger@compuserve.com (e-mail)

Agents: Directors: Gerald J. Pollinger (Managing Director), Juliet Burton, Heather Chalcroft, Lesley Hadcroft.

Born: Pollinger: July 1, 1925; New Malden, Surrey, England.

Education: Pollinger: Private Schools, University.

Career History: Pollinger: Royal Air Force, Royal Air Force Regiment, Author's Agent.

Hobbies/Personal Interests: Aircraft identification, model railroads, philately, gardening.

What are the subjects and categories you are most interested in agenting? We are always on the lookout for new authors who have potential.

What are the subjects and categories you are not interested in agenting? Textbooks, reference books, nonfiction articles, poetry, plays.

What is the best way for a prospective client to initiate contact with you? Write a letter telling us what they have available and ask us whether we would be interested. A long bit of unpublished material can be very off-putting; a synopsis and a couple of chapters is the best approach. Tell us about one or two projects at first.

Do you have a reading fee policy? No, reading fees attract value-added tax. We do request return postage, and a contribution of £20 towards our editorial expenses, which is refunded if we place the book.

Client representation in the following categories:

Nonfiction: 20%

Fiction: 45%

Children's: 35%

Textbooks: 0%

What is your commission structure? On sales in the English language we deduct on the price obtained a commission of:

15% on British Commonwealth book rights

15% on Motion Picture, Drama, Television, and Sound Broadcasting rights

15% on United States rights

15% on original magazine, newspaper, and serial rights

And on sales in translation:

20% on all translation rights

A higher commission is charged on the sale of rights in translation form to cover both the higher administration expenses and the commission payable to our associate representatives. The only disbursements charges made for:

Special mailing costs occasioned by emergencies or at an author's request.

Legal charges incurred on behalf of the author.

Copies of books and/or magazines purchased on behalf of the authors where necessary for the offer of additional (including translation) rights of their published material.

Photocopying at the author's request.

Approximate number of titles sold last year: About 100 novels, 300 children's books, options on a dozen films at least, two major television series.

Approximate percentage of all submissions (from queries through manuscripts) that you reject: About 90%

Representative titles sold:

Crime: Barbara Paknadal trilogy (Headline Books).

TV: Eight series of *Heartbeat* by Nicholas Rhea (Yorkshire TV).

Women's fiction: *Annie* trilogy by Maureen Lee (Orion Books).

Sport: *He Always Puts It to the Right* by Clark Miller (Gollanz).

American: *He Moved Like the Wind (Geronimo)* by David Roberts (Random House).

Film: *The Magic Sword/A Quest for Camelot* by Vera Chapman (Warner Bros.).

Children: *Hatched* by Gary Paulsen (to 20 countries).

Biography: *D. H. Lawrence (Vol. III)* by David Ellis (Cambridge University Press).

Description of the Client from Hell: We don't have any. Agent-Author is a marriage; they can also divorce!

Description of your Dream Client: Any grateful author who acknowledges our assistance—and many do.

What are the most common mistakes clients make when soliciting you to represent them? Illiteracy. Poor presentation. Overly long letters telling us that their friends and relations loved the book.

What can writers do to enhance their chances of getting you as an agent? Nothing. Bribery does not work.

Why did you become an agent? Hereditary.

What might you be doing if you weren't an agent? On the staff of the Royal Air Force.

SHEIL LAND ASSOCIATES LTD.

43 Doughty Street
London WC1N 2LF
England
(44) 171 4059351
fax: (44) 171 8312127

Agents: Sonia Land (Chief Executive and Agent), Anthony Sheil, Luigi Bonomi, Simon Trewin, Vivian Green, and John Rush (Film Agent).

What are the subjects and categories you are most interested in agenting? All forms of fiction and nonfiction from commercial to literary. Particularly commercial women's fiction, "male" thrillers, autobiographies/biographies of celebrities, politics, general nonfiction, cookery-lifestyles books.

Approximate number of titles sold last year: 500

Approximate percentage of all submissions (from queries through manuscripts) that you reject: 90%

Representative titles sold:

The Wizard (literary fiction) by Seamus Deane (Vintage/Cape).

Letter to Lorenzo (fiction) by Amanda Prantera (Bloomsbury).

Flora Brittanica (encyclopedia) by Richard Mabey (Reed/Random).

The First World War Intelligence and Warfare (nonfiction) by John Keegan (Cape/Vintage).

Riven Rock (literary fiction) by T. Correghan Boyle (Bloomsbury).

Ingenious Pain (literary fiction) by Andrew Miler (Sceptre).

The Little Book of Calm by Paul Wilson (Penguin UK).

Hair Power by Nicky Clarke (Transworld)—nonfiction by hairdresser to the rich and famous (Princess Di, Spice Girls, and others).

The Complete Illustrated Guide to Feng Shui (nonfiction) by Lillian Too (Element).

The Solace of Sin (commercial women's fiction) by Catherine Cookson (Transworld).

Endurance (literary fiction) by Caroline Alexander (Knopf).

Mrs. Chippy's Diary by Caroline Alexander (HarperCollins).

The Biography of Isaiah Berlin by Michael Ignatieff.

Description of the Client from Hell: The client that is "full of hot air"—the arch procrastinator who talks more than he/she writes, lags behind schedule, commits libel through plagiarizing work. The client who fails to recognize that commission is well earned.

Clients who cannot take criticism and constructive help with their work and generally failure to work as a team with their agent.

Client who never leaves you alone to get on with selling his rights, who does not wish to hear the sad truth of his work, and rejects all advice from his agent.

Description of your Dream Client: A writer who produces quality work within the agreed dateline. A writer who trusts their agent sufficiently to believe that their agent is trying to get the best deal possible that will provide lasting income and which will both enhance as well as protect their interests.

A writer whose work is *bestselling!*

What are the most common mistakes clients make when soliciting you to represent them? Potential clients saying that they're writing only because they're out of a job and need a big advance to finance their writing. Potential clients not prepared to improve their manuscript unless a publisher makes an offer. Telling you that they have already submitted their manuscript to a number of publishers, all of whom have rejected their work and so now are approaching an agent, one of many approaches. Those who state their writing is a work of genius that must be published.

What can writers do to enhance their chances of getting you as an agent? First, writers who can *write* in their chosen genre; who are focused, determined, and committed to their writing. Writers who can put together a strong covering letter, synopsis, and sample chapters. Writers with a strong c.v. which, at minimum, demonstrates that they are promotable if they are not already published authors.

SINCLAIR-STEVENSON

3 South Terrace
London SW7 2TB UK
England
(44) 0171 581 2550 (voice and fax)

Agent: Christopher Sinclair-Stevenson.

Born: London, June 27, 1939.

Education: Eton, Cambridge University.

Career History: Publisher (Hamish Hamilton, Sinclair-Stevenson) 1961–1995; Agent 1995–present.

Hobbies/Personal Interests: Music, food, travel—particularly France.

What are the subjects and categories you are most interested in agenting? Fiction, biography, history, politics.

What are the subjects and categories you are not interested in agenting? Science fiction, romantic fiction, science, children's books.

What is the best way for a prospective client to initiate contact with you? Letter with short proposal.

Do you have a reading fee policy? No, but I also have an advisory capacity for non-clients, charging £25–£75 depending on the length.

Client representation in the following categories:
Nonfiction: 70%
Fiction: 30%
Children's: 0%
Textbooks: 0%
What is your commission structure? 10%
Approximate number of titles sold last year: 30
Approximate percentage of all submissions (from queries through manuscripts) that you reject: 90%
Representative titles sold:
My Name Escapes Me by Alec Guinness (Penguin).
The City of Light by David Selbourne (Little, Brown).
Biography of Laurens Van Der Post by J.D.F. Jones (John Murray).
Biography of Empress Elizabeth of Austria by Andrew Sinclair (Constable).
Falling in Love by Sheila Sullivan (Macmillan).
Novel by Teresa Waugh (Gollancz).
Autobiography by H. C. Robbins Landon (Thames & Hudson).
Cookbook by Jennifer Paterson (Headline).
History of 20th Century by Christopher Lee (BBC).
Novel by Jennifer Johnston (Hodder).
Rex Harrison by Patrick Garland (Macmillan).
The Myth of the Goddess by Jules Cashford (Orion).
Description of the Client from Hell: The client who sends a handwritten note with a closely typed script and no return envelope (or one with inadequate postage). But I don't have any!
Description of your Dream Client: The one who delivers on time, never telephones me on weekends, occasionally takes me out to lunch, writes wonderful books.
What are the most common mistakes clients make when soliciting you to represent them? See above. And those who write supporting letters that try to be funny and end up either facetious or arrogant.
What can writers do to enhance their chances of getting you as an agent? Send intriguing letter.
Why did you become an agent? Because I stopped being a publisher.
What might you be doing if you weren't an agent? Writing. I do anyway.
Pontifications: A well-presented script goes a long way to prejudice me in the author's favor. A writer should become a friend. If you don't like the writer you shouldn't take him/her on. Publishers are often slow, lazy, incompetent—but there are still, even in a corporate world, a remarkably large number of good ones, even publishers who read books and like books (and authors).

SOLO LITERARY AGENCY LTD.

49–53 Kensington High Street
London W8 5ED UK
England
(44) 171 376 2166
fax: (44) 171 938 3165

Agent: Don Short.
  Born: October 23, 1932.
  Education: Chiswick Polytechnic, London.
  Career History: Journalist/Newspaper columnist; Literary agent, 1980–present.
  Hobbies/Personal Interests: Tennis, gardens.
  What are the subjects and categories you are most interested in agenting? Autobiographies.
  What are the subjects and categories you are not interested in agenting? Academic works, reference/textbooks.
  What is the best way for a prospective client to initiate contact with you? By mail.
  Do you have a reading fee policy? No.
  Client representation in the following categories:
  Nonfiction: 95%
  Fiction: 5%
  Children's: 0%
  Textbooks: 0%
  What is your commission structure? 15% UK and Commonwealth; 20% overseas.
  Approximate number of titles sold last year: 20
  Approximate percentage of all submissions (from queries through manuscripts) that you reject: 80%
  Representative titles sold:
  Dudley Moore Authorized Biography by Barbra Paskin (Macmillan).
  Jimmy White: Behind the White Ball by Jimmy White (Hutchison).
  By Camel Across Australia by Alexandra Bannister Hughes (HarperCollins).
  Savage Seas by Rosemary Kingsland (Boxtree).
  Description of the Client from Hell: Authors who call through the night with amendments to their manuscripts. Authors who call from bookshops complaining that their title is not on the shelf. Authors who persistently query account statements and express surprise when overseas territories reject their precious work.
  Description of your Dream Client: An author who sends a thank-you note.

What are the most common mistakes clients make when soliciting you to represent them? That they've already been turned down by other agents or even publishers but would like to leave you to pick up the crumbs.

What can writers do to enhance their chances of getting you as an agent? To be inspirational and realistic about the potential and limitations of their subject matter.

Why did you become an agent? After life on a daily UK newspaper—there was only one route to go. Being a masochist helps.

What might you be doing if you weren't an agent? Tending my garden.

Pontifications: If fame is the motive for writing a book, then forget it. You've got more chance with a lottery ticket.

J. M. Thurley Management

30 Cambridge Road
Teddington
Middlesex TW11 8DR
England
(44) 181 977 3176
fax: (44) 181 943 2678
JMTHurley@aol.com (e-mail)

Agent: J. M. Thurley.
Born: Pakistan.
Education: Taunton School (private) M.A.; Honors English, Dip. Ed. St. Catharine's College, Cambridge.
Career History: Articled to Arthur Anderson. Joined 20th Century Fox as Executive Assistant to UK CEO (son-in-law of Darryl Zanuck). Left to join Dina Lom Associates (Literary Agents). In 1976 set up J. M. Thurley Management.
Hobbies/Personal Interests: Writing (five published novels); painting (several exhibitions); foreign travel; cooking; walking.

What are the subjects and categories you are most interested in agenting? Fiction (BIG thrillers); Nonfiction: eclectic list that covers star biographies, royal biographies, historical books, scientific/medical/psychiatric/self-help. Some television and film.

What are the subjects and categories you are not interested in agenting? First-person biographies by unknowns. Trend following writing attempting to emulate Turow, Grisham, etc. First-person stream-of-consciousness flowery would-be literary outpourings.

What is the best way for a prospective client to initiate contact with you? Prospective clients should write with a brief description of what they wish to send.

Do you have a reading fee policy? No reading fees.

Client representation in the following categories:

Nonfiction: 40%

Fiction: 50%

Children's: 0%

Textbooks: 10%

What is your commission structure? 15% UK; 20% other territories.

Approximate number of titles sold last year: around 50

Approximate percentage of all submissions (from queries through manuscripts) that you reject: Reject 98% of submitted material.

Representative titles sold:

The Boaties: A History of the SBS by John Parker (Headline).

The Song of the Greys by Nigel Kerner (Hodder).

The Truth by Peter James (Orion).

Denial by Peter James (Orion).

Hot Toddy by Frank Palmer (Constable).

The Ghost Maker by Victor Davis (Gollancz).

The History of the Foreign Legion by John Parker (Piatkus).

Description of the Client from Hell: The Client from Hell (and I've had a few) are clients who get a decent deal and then moan that Stephen King/Jeffrey Archer/John Grisham don't write half as well and why are they getting more money.

Description of your Dream Client: The Dream Client is the professional who listens to advice, acts on it, produces a salable manuscript, and actually thanks you when you successfully conclude a deal.

What are the most common mistakes clients make when soliciting you to represent them? Turnoffs: clients who demand instant reactions, clients who tell me how good they are, clients whose families have told them the sun shines from every orifice and who cannot believe that I don't agree, would-be clients who write individual letters while touting to every agent in town.

What can writers do to enhance their chances of getting you as an agent? The bottom line is they must be good. I like realistic people who are adult in their responses and accept that not everyone will like them, that not getting accepted is rarely the fault of the agent and far more often a failure in the material, and that I give loyalty and value its reciprocation.

Why did you become an agent? I became an agent because my background is in world literature, which I love passionately.

What might you be doing if you weren't an agent? If I weren't an agent, I'd be a lawyer. They get (marginally) worse press, but better paid.

Pontifications: Some idiot said everybody had one book in them. This is manifestly not true. Writing a brilliant novel is not a function of intelligence. It is rather best tackled by those who have understood that writing is a devious and manipulative activity, and that a writer's aim must be to keep somebody turning over the pages of a book on his or her lap rather than going out to do one of a hundred other things that might seem, on the face of it, far more enjoyable. It is *never* a flat, chronological, expository recital of events, and can only work when the craft of creating hints, hooks, allusions that aren't immediately explained is thoroughly absorbed by the would-be author.

IRELAND

Jonathan Williams Literary Agency

2 Mews, 10 Sandycove Avenue West
Sandycove
County Dublin
Ireland
(44) 353-1-2803482
fax: (44) 353-1-2803482

Agent: Jonathan Williams.

Born: Briton Ferry, Glamorgan, Wales; December 9, 1943.

Education: University of Hull (B.A. Honours); University College, Dublin (M.A.).

Career History: Worked for publishers in Canada and Ireland before setting up as a literary agent.

Hobbies/Personal Interests: Music (classical and jazz), travel, walking.

What are the subjects and categories you are most interested in agenting? Fiction (especially literary); memoirs; current affairs (social and political); anthologies.

What are the subjects and categories you are not interested in agenting? Science fiction; fantasy; business and banking books; play scripts; film scripts; religious books.

What is the best way for a prospective client to initiate contact with you? Send a letter of inquiry (with a stamped, addressed reply envelope or return postage) or a preliminary phone inquiry.

Do you have a reading fee policy? I charge a reading fee only if an author wants to have a very quick verdict (within 10 days).

Client representation in the following categories:

Nonfiction: 65%

Fiction: 30%

Children's: 5%

Textbooks: 0%

What is your commission structure? 10% for home sales; 15% for foreign sales.

Approximate number of titles sold last year: 35

Approximate percentage of all submissions (from queries through manuscripts) that you reject: 97%

Representative titles sold:

The Life and Death of a Crime Reporter by Emily O'Reilly and Veronica Guerin (Vintage, Random House).

The Burning of Bridget Cleary by Angela Bourke (Random House).

The Ireland Anthology edited by Sean Dunne (St. Martin's Press).

Blue Guide Ireland by Brian Labov (A&C Black and Norton).

The Hellbox by Greg Delanty (Oxford University Press).

Wilde the Irishman by Jerusha McCormack (Yale University Press).

An Intelligent Person's Guide to Ireland by John Waters (Duckworth).

Mortally Wounded by Michael Kearney (Simon & Schuster).

The Angel Tapes by David Kiely (St. Martin's Press).

Seaspray and Whisky: Reminiscences of a Tramp Ship Voyage by Norman Freeman (The Alcadine Press).

What are the most common mistakes clients make when soliciting you to represent them? Assuring you, before you have read of word of their typescript, that they have written a bestseller.

What might you be doing if you weren't an agent? Working in book publishing.

NEW ZEALAND

PLAYMARKET

P.O. Box 9767
Te Avo Te Whanganvi-a-Tara
Wellington
New Zealand
(64) 4 382 8462
fax: (64) 4 382 8461
plymkt@clearnet.nz (e-mail)
www.playmarket.org.nz

Agent: Ciuy Boyce.
   Education: New Zealand Drama School graduate, 1983.
   Career History: Program Manager of Fortune Theatre (Dunedin), Bets Theatre (Wellington), and Downstage Theatre (Wellington).
   What is the best way for a prospective client to initiate contact with you? Phone, fax, e-mail, Web site, come in.
   Do you have a reading fee policy? Yes, $60NZ

RICHARDS LITERARY AGENCY

P.O. Box 31240
Milford
Auckland
New Zealand
(64) 9 410-5681
fax: (64) 9 410-6989

Agent: Ray Richards.
   Born: Dannevirke, New Zealand; February 1, 1921.
   Education: Hamilton High School; Wellington College.

Career History: Book Publisher, Managing Director and Vice Chairman Reed New Zealand; Chairman Reed Australia 1946–76; Executive Director Book Publishers Association of New Zealand 1977–78; Literary Agent 1977–present date.

Hobbies/Personal Interests: Making books.

What are the subjects and categories you are most interested in agenting? Top-quality fiction and nonfiction; illustrated reference books for children from preschool to young adult.

What are the subjects and categories you are not interested in agenting? Run-of-the-mill fiction and nonfiction; pseudo-anything; short stories; articles; poetry; children's books that are not irresistible.

What is the best way for a prospective client to initiate contact with you? Inquiry letter with synopsis, bio, sample chapter(s), SAE.

Do you have a reading fee policy? No reading fees.

Client representation in the following categories:

Nonfiction: 20%

Fiction: 40%

Children's: 30%

Textbooks: 10%

What is your commission structure? 10% commission is based on payments received.

Approximate number of titles sold last year: 100

Approximate percentage of all submissions (from queries through manuscripts) that you reject: 95%

Representative titles sold:

Maori Art by Dr. Terence Barrow (Reed Publishing).

The Long Italian Lunch (travel cookbook) by Julie Biuso (Random House).

Dare Truth or Promise (YA novel) by Paula Boock (contracted by Longacre for New Zealand, Hyland House for Australia, The Women's Press for Europe, Houghton Mifflin for North America).

Starbright and the Dream Eater by Joy Cowley (Penguin British rights, Harper Collins North America).

Starring Polly (fiction trilogy) by Tessa Duder (Penguin).

Grandma Garvey Goes to School (picture book) by Jenny Hessell and Trevor Pye (Scholastic).

Live Bodies (novel) by Maurice Gee (Penguin for Australia and New Zealand, Faber for British rights).

Exotic Trees of New Zealand (two volumes, 2,000 color plates) by Professor J. T. Salmon (Reed Publishing New Zealand).

Children's trade and educational books by Joy Cowley, Diana Noonan, Pauline Cartwright, Alan Trussell-Cullen, and others; contracted with Boyds Mills Press, U.S.; HarperCollins, U.S.; Dominie Press, U.S.; Philomel, U.S.; Scholastic, U.S.; The Wright Group, U.S.

Description of the Client from Hell: An ego without expertise or experience.

Description of your Dream Client: A market-attuned person of high endeavor, who has revised and revised—and who listens.

What are the most common mistakes clients make when soliciting you to represent them? Talking too much, over-sure of the merit of their work, paying no attention to the realities of the marketplace.

What can writers do to enhance their chances of getting you as an agent? Gaining our interest and involvement as their first priority and maintaining that attitude with good communications and willing cooperation.

Why did you become an agent? Because I am addicted to the making of essential books and the welfare of their authors.

SOUTH AFRICA

FRANCES BOND LITERARY SERVICES

P.O. Box 223
Westville 3630
KwaZulu Natal
Republic of South Africa
(27) 31 824532
fax: (27) 31 822620

Agents: Frances Bond, Managing Editor; Eileen Molver, Chief Editor.
   Born: Bond: London; Molver: Durban, R.S.A.
   Education: Bond: C.C.E, M.R.I.M.; Molver: Matriculation.
   Career History: Bond: Longman Rhod. Sales Manager; Macmillan S.A. Ed. Manager, Natal; Trade Winds Sales Manager and Owner; Co-Principal of School of Creative Writing; Publishing Consultant to the Alan Paton Trust.
   Molver: Tutor School of Writing; Full-time writer (16 books published); Chief tutor and Co-Principal of School of Creative Writing.
   What are the subjects and categories you are most interested in agenting? In South Africa, we cover a broad spectrum of fiction, nonfiction, and children's writing.
   What are the subjects and categories you are not interested in agenting? We do not handle poetry, films, or dramatic presentation unless they are an offshoot of one of our own publications.
   What is the best way for a prospective client to initiate contact with you? We like an initial letter introducing the prospective writer and a short memo about the work on offer. We insist on a SAE.
   Do you have a reading fee policy? We do have a reading fee policy due to the number of emerging new writers we are compelled to handle in a young country like South Africa. So much untapped writing ability requires help in getting their work to publishing stage.
   Client representation in the following categories:
Nonfiction: 30%
Fiction: 30%
Children's: 40%
Textbooks: 0%

What is your commission structure? 15% within Central and South Africa; 20% worldwide.

Approximate number of titles sold last year: Confidential.

Approximate percentage of all submissions (from queries through manuscripts) that you reject: 70%

Representative titles sold:

Bethel and the Bad Thing by Eileen Molver (Tafelborg Publishers).

Guide to Creative Writing by Bond/Molver (Forest Publishers).

Cry the Beloved Country by Alan Paton (Edicione, Barcelona, Spanish).

Cry the Beloved Country by Alan Paton (Shuter & Shooter, Zulu).

The Principal by Alan Paton (Film adaptation).

The Principal by Roy Sargeant (Film/book tie-up).

Songs of Africa (poetry) by Alan Paton (Gecko Books).

Kenny's Secret by Ruth Jacobson (Forest Publishers).

The Quantum Theory by Dr. I. Weinberg (Forest Publishers).

My Nine Lives (autobiography) by Ruth Jardine (Forest Publishers).

Description of the Client from Hell: 1) A new writer whose book gets published and "bombs." 2) A new writer who submits a 1,600-page work "unnumbered." 3) A writer who writes on computer paper, continuous, unnumbered, unstripped, and not separated.

Description of your Dream Client: "A dead one" whose work is out of copyright.

What are the most common mistakes clients make when soliciting you to represent them? 1) New writer who submits a 1,600-page book without first submitting a concept. 2) New writer who submits a 3-volume book with no introductory letter, no synopsis, and no track record in publishing. 3) Rings me on my private line after 7 P.M. 4) Takes us to task when the book "bombs." 5) Uses two agents at the same time.

What can writers do to enhance their chances of getting you as an agent? 1) Remember that, as writers, they are businesspeople and conduct themselves and their affairs in a business-like manner. 2) Remember they are writing for readers 'out there,' not for their own self-glorification. 3) Have the courtesy of sending a SAE when making first-time inquiries, especially when writing from abroad. 4) Always make appointments for consultation. 5) Take advice from us and act on it—after all, we have been in publishing for some 30 years.

Why did you become an agent? Because after many years of working in publishing houses I wanted closer association with my writers and to be part of a great book possibly emerging. I have had a lifetime love affair with words and this would bring me closer to them.

What might you be doing if you weren't an agent? Sitting with my feet up with a box of Belgium chocolates having time to read at long last my copy of *A Suitable Boy.*

Pontifications: "The statistical chances of becoming a bestselling writer are approximately the same as being struck by lightning while being attacked by a Great White Shark" (by Dan Simmonds).

Never forget that besides being endowed with a computer, typewriter, or pad and pencil, a writer has the use of the "third eye." This is the equipment that is provided in all writers that enables them to bring the imagery into their writing, so vital if the book is to be brought to life.

LITERARY DYNAMICS

Postnet Suite 222
P.O. Box 51037
Musgrave 4062
South Africa
(27) 31 21 6919
literary@saol.com (e-mail)

Agent: Isabel Cooke.

Born: May 20, 1947, Johannesburg.

Education: B.A. (Rand) 1968—Sociology; Diploma, Short Story and Novel Writing (University of Natal).

Career History: Literary Agent since 1992—took over deceased agency. Prior to that, librarian/editor.

Hobbies/Personal Interests: Theatre, yoga, music, New Age philosophy, women's interests, foreign languages.

What are the subjects and categories you are most interested in agenting? Fiction (thrillers), nonfiction (biographies), metaphysical genre, motivational works, business books.

What are the subjects and categories you are not interested in agenting? Children's literature, erotica, religious works.

What is the best way for a prospective client to initiate contact with you? Telephone, fax, e-mail. No unsolicited submissions.

Do you have a reading fee policy? As I am a literary consultant and not only an agent, I charge a fee for an in-depth evaluation and writing tuition and guidance.

Client representation in the following categories:
Nonfiction: 40%
Fiction: 60%
Children's: 0%
Textbooks: 0%

What is your commission structure? 15% local; 20% overseas

Approximate number of titles sold last year: 6

Approximate percentage of all submissions (from queries through manuscripts) that you reject: 80% But then I work together with a potential author until the manuscript is marketable.

Representative titles sold:

Proverbial Stress Busters by L. Schlebusch (Human & Rousseau).

Practical Tendering Skills by K. Fagan (Maskew Miller).

Understanding Taxation by K. Fagan (Maskew Miller).

Best of Mbingeni Ngema (anthology of plays) by Mbingeni Ngema (Via Afrika).

Improve Your Self Image by W. Schramm (Van Shaik).

Corporate Communication by Cooke & Fowler (Maskew Miller).

Glading Greg by '64 Intruder (Aegina).

Old Warrior by D. Smargiassi (Heinemann).

Thand Goes to Town by M. Braithwaite (Heinemann).

City Kids by M. Braitwaite (Via Afrika).

Three Against the Big Boys by M. Braitwaite (Via Afrika).

On His Own Terms by M. Ndawonde (Via Afrika).

Lion's Choice by R. Harris (Via Afrika).

Oliver, Daphne by Ebony Elephant (Via Afrika).

Little Sorrow by P. Owen (Tafelberg).

The Lost Princess by P. Owen (Kwela).

Man of Two Worlds by W. Cibane (Kwela)

Golden Rain by G. Hilliar (Robert Hale).

Description of the Client from Hell: Someone who doesn't listen to my informed opinion and rewrites without taking cognizance of my recommendations. Tells me that their cousin, aunt, professor loved the work, and that 200,000 copies will be sold.

Description of your Dream Client: Someone who listens, learns, and produces a much better product that will have a publisher panting.

What are the most common mistakes clients make when soliciting you to represent them? Bad presentation. Taking it for granted that they're accomplished enough for me to handle. Expecting everything for nothing. Phoning me after hours.

What can writers do to enhance their chances of getting you as an agent? By being dedicated and committed to learning the craft. Appreciating that my evaluations are given to ensure that their writing impresses. Treating me like the professional that I am.

Why did you become an agent? I am an author who was contracted to my predecessor. When she died, I assume control because I saw handling my own work and that of others as a challenge. I am also in the unique position of living in a country undergoing social change and a completely new direction in literature.

What might you be doing if you weren't an agent? I am not only an agent but am attached to four businesses. 1) Literary Dynamics—Executive Editor; 2) Odoli Manufacturing—Managing Member of a company propagating Zulu royalty and traditions in book form; 3) Hello Durban—Editor; 4) Nippon Industries—Consultant to a Singapore businessman with interests in South Africa.

Pontifications: Seeking a competent agent is an asset to any aspiring writer because with such an individual advising and backing them, writers have an incredible support system. In the choppy waters of publishing, a dedicated agent goes that extra mile for her clients. However, writers shouldn't expect an agent to be omnipotent. My contract states that I cannot guarantee publication.

PART THREE

Insider Road Maps to Your International Success

The Book Market
in the United Kingdom

JULIE DEVILLERS

Writers who are interested in submitting work in the United Kingdom can benefit from learning the basics about its book-publishing industry. The UK ranks fourth in the world for book sales, following the United States, Germany, and Japan, and just ahead of France and Spain.

According to Literary Agent Gerald Pollinger of the Laurence Pollinger Agency, the publishing industry in the UK is now comprised of half a dozen conglomerates, each of which encompass a number of imprints they have acquired. There are a few independent medium-sized houses, and a lot of small publishers. More books are now sold in paperback form than before; library sales are lower, and, Pollinger notes, children's books are increasingly important.

Literary Agent Darley Anderson at the Darley Anderson Literary Agency observes that ownership of the major publishers is now international and crosses borders. He states:

> But of course people in the companies who make the day-to-day decisions and make the companies tick are predominately nationals of the individual countries. Particular strengths of the UK industry are 1) The UK publishers have been and continue to be very good book exporters, selling outside of the UK market. There are two reasons for this. We have historically been an empire and know our way around other countries. Our domestic market is much smaller than the American market, and therefore we are more historically dependent on the export markets.

2) The UK has a huge pool of writing talent. We are quite good at channeling talented writers. We may be a relatively small country but we have such writing talent, which is why bestsellers are often from the UK.

Judy Piatkus, publisher and managing director of Piatkus Books, points out that more than 100,000 new titles come out every year in the UK, and the market is only 66 million people, a fifth the size of the United States market.
Piatkus states:

> This is wonderful for the consumer as there is a lot of choice, but it is very hard for publishers and authors because new books are taking up the space on the shelves all the time. Booksellers cannot possibly stock all the new titles that are offered and they can't foresee which ones are necessary, making it difficult sometimes to find the books that were widely reviewed in the last week. In addition, all the media is national so that is difficult to target specific towns for publicity.
>
> The British excel at beautifully illustrated titles, which are frequently excellent value for the money. There are a large number of bookshops, both chains and independents, and they are currently seen as 'hot' places to go. More and more people are reading bestsellers and talking about them. Publishing in England is exciting and vibrant and looks set to stay that way for some time to come.

Other events have been changing the industry in the UK The arrival of Borders Bookstore brought the first of the American superstores to British soil. The retail world of publishing has been changing rapidly with the arrival of the superstore, discounted books, and the merging of major book chains.
According to Piatkus, the market is changing all the time and the books that are hot topics in one season may not be selling well in the next. She goes on to say,

> The UK used to follow American trends, but now that the media is so instantaneous and the Internet is so influential, it is hard to see so easily what trends will be coming next. The market for fiction seems to be moving upwards and more people are reading literary novels. However, this is partly because many of the chain bookshops don't stock the more down-market books in any quantity and, until recently, the bestseller lists were based on sales through chain bookshops and independents. This did not include WH Smiths and other popular outlets, which meant that the sales were weighted towards more up-market fiction. This is now being addressed, but it does seem as if the attractively designed and intriguing trendy B-format novels will continue to feature heavily as a growing trend.
>
> On the nonfiction side, the collapse of the Net Book Agreement, which is still relatively recent in the UK, has meant that publishers and booksellers have had the opportunity to look at new ways of marketing and promoting books using price and other activities in a sophisticated way. Many opportunities are now open to the UK book trade to market and promote the books that were not there 3 years ago. There is

an explosion of creativity in the marketing of books, which is obviously having an effect in the amount of media coverage of books and their influence—both conscious and unconscious—on the general public.

Trends in the publishing industry include a proliferation of media-related titles. We are also continuing to see the joining together of more and more smaller companies to make fewer larger companies. Partnerships between companies, such as wholesalers and publishers or wholesalers and booksellers (which would have been unheard of a couple of years ago), are becoming more common. The big companies are certainly getting bigger in every way. However, because publishing is such a creative business, there will always be new start-ups. New techniques under development in the printing industry may mean that short-run publication becomes much less expensive and it will be possible to keep books in print for longer periods. The Internet will also play its part in helping consumers access single titles that they cannot find in their local shops.

Another opportunity for publishers in the UK has risen as a result of the abolition of Net Book Agreement; books are available in many more outlets. Non-book outlets such as supermarkets and other stores are devoting more space to books and frequently price-promoting them so that the consumer has become much more aware of them. Books are now widely available to a lot of consumers who might never have gone into a bookshop and the sophisticated marketing and attractive packages are appealing to many who would not previously have considered themselves book buyers. While publishing is obviously subject to fluctuations in the general economy, it seems very buoyant in the UK at present.

For a few years, a focus of publishing in the UK was on the new multimedia.

"After an initial flurry, multimedia publishing has suffered a recession in the UK with the leading publishing houses closing their lists," Pollinger says. "Although CD-ROM and DVD will never replace the written word in book form, it is possible that well after the millennium, when all the new computers are 'compliant,' there might well be a revival of multimedia publishing. The Internet is busy at present, but everything else seems to be on 'hold.'"

The mass production of expensive CD-ROMs and their disappointing sales have led to the initial, although possibly temporary, downfall of the hyped multimedia market. While children's, reference, and educational multimedia survived (and in some cases flourished), general titles failed. In the UK, while a significant percentage of homes have computers, only a small number had CD-ROMs. It appears that the American market will dominate the multimedia market in the near future.

"The publishers who are doing well in the UK seem to be concentrating on what they do best and looking after their core business," Piatkus says. "There are currently huge opportunities to sell books successfully in the UK and other world markets, and those people who are focusing on simply doing that seem to be achieving the best results."

Insight from a British Publisher

STUART PROFFITT
Publishing Director of Penguin Press

What is your background?

I started working in publishing in 1983—straight from the university—as editorial assistant at HarperCollins. I held a number of posts there, and in 1991 was appointed publisher of the trade division for fiction and nonfiction. I joined Penguin on July 1, 1997, and am now the publishing director of the Penguin Press division.

What are your responsibilities?

Penguin is one of the leading serious nonfiction publishers in the UK. My division publishes books on economics, science, and similar topics, as well as Penguin classics—thousands of volumes—and reference books.

How can a writer improve?

The most important thing for a writer to do is to write a good book. I believe quality comes through in the end. For any kind of writing, if the book is good enough and original enough, it will eventually be recognized as long as the author is persistent.

What makes your day?

I'm pleased when a book that we published and into which we invested time is recognized—in a way we'd want it to be recognized. It's exciting when our books sell.

Should a writer submit to a literary agent or editor?

It depends on the kind of book. It often makes sense to submit to a literary agent.

How can a writer make contacts in the book publishing industry?

Be published. Write a good book, get it published, and then you will make more contacts.

What are unique aspects of book publishing in the UK?

Book sales are strengthening in many quarters. Britain is a very creative nation at the moment, especially in nonfiction. Publishers come around the world to exchange ideas with us. It's an exciting time.

What are hot topics in the UK?

There are perennial topics, and then there are passing fads such as the *Titanic*. We're interested here in subjects of more lasting value.

How has the market changed?

The mid-list has disappeared. Exposure is much more immediate, if it's going to happen at all. Since the abolition of the Net Book Agreement, books are discounted, which has brought all kinds of changes in its wake.

What are trends in the publishing industry?

The arrival of on-line bookselling challenges traditional bookselling, though what changes this will bring about remain to be seen. Professional marketing conglomerization (takeovers of houses by large corporations) has resulted with both positive and negative effects.

What is the general attitude in your country toward book publishing?

Most people are cautious because there are questions concerning the economy, and books are perceived as luxury items. I am optimistic toward book publishing, though, especially since Penguin just won Publisher of the Year in the book awards.

Do you have any other tips for writers?

Yes. Don't write unless you've got something to say. Too much is written, and too much is published that is of little value.

What impact has the Internet had on you?

The Internet saves a great deal of time. We can now communicate by e-mail internally and with authors and agents externally. But it has not changed the way writers send submissions. I would not accept a submission over the Internet. Penguin does have a number of Web sites, which we use primarily to promote our many diverse activities. Not many people use multimedia publishing in the UK. It is a specialized activity.

View of a UK Publisher

JUDY PIATKUS
Publisher and Managing Director, Piatkus Books

About the publishing house . . .

Piatkus Books is an independent publishing company in the UK It has been in business successfully for 20 years and publishes a wide range of nonfiction and fiction, including health, new age, cookery, biography, popular psychology, business, self-help, and fiction. The company is highly regarded throughout the UK book trade as it has high profile with several bestselling backlist titles and was one of the first publishing companies to be established by a woman.

About her responsibilities . . .

There are two kinds of managing directors: one who works with facts and figures and one who works more intuitively. I am more inclined to be intuitive. I experience a constant conflict between my role as managing director, which is to make a profit and look to the future financially, and my role as publisher, which is about publishing and selling books we believe in and taking frequent chances. My role also includes ensuring that the company has a clear focus and program so that every one of the twenty people we employ inside the office (as well as all those we work with outside the office) knows exactly what we're doing and why we're doing it. I also believe that publishing books—especially in the general area—should be fun; therefore, I try to ensure that my colleagues and I create an enjoyable atmosphere so our employees look forward to coming to work every day.

On improving your chances of becoming published . . .

The answer to this question varies for nonfiction and fiction. For nonfiction, if you write practical books, you need to know as much as possible about your own field and where to find answers and information about the areas you are not so familiar with. If you write nonfiction for entertainment or popular fiction, you need to persevere. Writing is a craft, and the more you write, the more proficient you will become. For some people, writing is a gift they have, and developing that gift is what it's all about. For other people, it's about talent, and sometimes you'll reach a point where you have to recognize that you've gone as far as you can go. When it comes to presenting your work to publishers, there are professional and unprofessional ways of doing it. I would recommend people to join writers' groups, read writers' magazines, and study several of the large number of books on the market that tell you in detail how to get published as these will answer all your questions.

Another way writers can improve their chances of becoming published is to take advice from people whose opinions they respect. I have seen many would-be authors with a lot of talent who don't succeed because they feel they know better than their publishers so won't listen to guidance or gentle criticism.

On what "makes her day . . ."

It makes my day when we acquire an exciting book that we will be able to publish, and when exciting things happen to the books we are publishing. I get excited when we get big orders for books with big expectations but even more excited when we get big orders for small books that we worked hard on and for which we see our publicity and marketing efforts paying off. I get excited when we get good orders from book clubs and when we get repeat orders from all outlets over the years so we can keep books in print. I get excited when I read a new piece of work, or come across a new idea, and I can see how we can manifest it in book form and how we can go about selling it. That is certainly the creative part of the job.

What would a writer be surprised to know . . .

Writers are often surprised to know how often book titles are changed, how often early projects turn into different projects later on, how much rewriting and revising many bestselling authors have to do, how much rewriting and revising many publishers have to do for their bestselling authors, how hard some publishers work on their behalf, and how sales of so many books are even less than their own.

Agent or no agent?

It is always exciting to find a promising new novel in the slush pile, but most fiction is handled by agents. Novels that come in from a reputable literary agent are always looked at more carefully than are those that come in direct from the public.

On the nonfiction side, books for entertainment are best sold through agents. However, books that have a practical or niche area can be sent direct to the editor in a publishing company who is responsible for that particular list. Not all literary agents have knowledge of the different areas of the market, and some do not always know the best publishing house to approach. The writer of a book in a particular area will probably have a number of books from publishers who publish in their niche area, and there might be a particular company by whom the author would like to be published so there's no reason authors should not submit the book direct.

On making contacts in the book publishing industry . . .

There is nothing that an editor in book publishing likes more than finding a new author in his or her area. A well-targeted and well-written cover letter about the book you want to write–particularly in nonfiction—will usually get you a response from an efficient editor, and he or she will be intrigued to read your work. It is also helpful to get to know people in the media who might be prepared to give your book a plug and to make friends with your local bookseller, all the while being careful not to be too pushy. Many authors antagonize their local outlets by demanding to know why their books aren't being stocked. The sales department in your publishing company will give you advice about how to network with the trade.

On the hot topics in her country . . .

Hot topics in the UK are biography (especially by leading authors), media tie-ins, cookery by Delia Smith and others, children's books, and literary fiction and nonfiction. Areas that often do particularly well in the States (such as self-help, spirituality, and politics) are way down the list of popular areas in the UK.

On the trends in the publishing industry . . .

Trends in the publishing industry include a proliferation of media-related titles. We are also continuing to see the joining together of more and more smaller companies to make fewer larger companies. Partnerships between companies, such as wholesalers and publishers or wholesalers and booksellers (which would have been unheard of a couple of years ago) are becoming more common. The big companies are certainly getting bigger in every way. However, because publishing is such a creative business, there will always be new start-ups. New techniques under development in the printing industry may mean that short-run publications become much less expensive and it will be possible to keep books in print for longer periods. The Internet will also play its part in helping consumers access single titles that they cannot find in their local shops.

On inside tips for writers . . .

Becoming successful as a writer is principally about discipline and perseverance. It's lovely to read about writing and to talk about it. But those who succeed are the ones who sit down at their desk every day and put in the hours. It is helpful to talk to other people and to read about how to market and sell your work. It is also important not to be too distressed by setbacks. Everyone who works in any field will have difficult days and disappointments. For writers this is particularly hard, as they often have no one with whom to share their distress, and they may have spent so long working on a particular project. The important thing is to get back in there and keep going—maybe to write something different or to target a different audience. Take advice from those people who know what they are talking about, and follow it to the best of your ability. And always be generous to other writers because there is room for everyone. Never feel that you can't make it because there are too many people at the top. If you have what it takes, your time will come.

On the Internet . . .

We use the Internet for research, but not much more at this point. Sometimes nonfiction writers back up a paper approach to us with a Web site address to give us some idea of what their area of expertise is. However, we don't accept electronic submissions. We want them to arrive in the post so that they can be dealt with in the normal way. We don't want to have to go to the trouble of printing them out or reading them on screen. Some of the larger UK publishers have Web sites. Those who haven't are probably developing them and will have them shortly.

A UK Agent Talks About the Publishing Industry

DARLEY ANDERSON
Owner, The Darley Anderson Literary Agency

His background . . .

I was educated at Cambridge in theology and worked in book publishing for a while as a religious book editor. But I learned that most people who work in publishing in this country don't make a high salary. I decided to make some money, and started an agency specializing in women's popular fiction.

What he does . . .

I believe literary agents should offer three things to a new writer.

Editorial input. Most manuscripts need work before they are offered to publishers.
Emotional support. Agents need to be part encouraging and part taskmaster.
Market choices. We've got to take the book and sell it in a major market—the UK and the U.S.—and then in English-speaking markets elsewhere and foreign language markets.

The good literary agent holds the author's hand and tries to police that author's career, thus limiting mistakes by the author and the publisher. I place great store by the legendary agent Swifty Lazar's words: "There are some authors who I wouldn't represent for 50% because I don't like them and we wouldn't get on." While I understand the first-time author just wants to be taken on, it works best if the agent and author are well matched. Writers should remember that editors move around and publishing houses are reorganized so the independent agent is likely to be the most stable contact in an author's world where there are few long-term relationships.

In the UK, having an agent is *essential* for selling fiction; for nonfiction it's preferable. A fiction writer definitely should try to get an agent. First, a good agent will have something to offer editorially, and second, publishers will take more notice. The slush pile is so big in many larger publishing houses that they won't consider unagented fiction. An agent with a good track record has a better chance of being taken more seriously and getting a good deal. In nonfiction, at least in the negotiating stage, you'll get a better deal with an agent. In 99.9% of the cases, you'll be better off with an agent representing you.

A writer should contact an agent by . . .

Using the old method of mailing a brief synopsis for fiction, including sample chapters and return postage. For nonfiction, a detailed proposal and preferably a sample of the writing is preferred.

The biggest mistakes writers make . . .

Not being professional is a writer's biggest mistake. I notice that, very much so in this country, writers consistently do not pay enough attention to business matters. They should have a professional attitude toward their careers, more than most of them do. Writers must come to terms that their creative work will become a product, and they should be frank with themselves about what they really want in a career. For example, Frederick Forsyth, the writer's journalist, decided what he wanted—the folding stuff, money. He was likely to be focused and businesslike, I imagine. A writer who wants money should look at the marketplace. Forsyth might have recognized that the fiction writer who is most likely to make money is the author of thrillers. It is the big genre in the worldwide market.

I wish writers would clearly define what they want. Ninety-nine percent of the time you can't have it all; you won't write a bestseller. Now, writing for critical acclaim is different. Writing for personal satisfaction is different. Define your aim and study the marketplace. Make your plan accordingly.

Not enough writers do their market research first. In the UK, historical romantic fiction is now out of fashion. If you sit down and write a historical romance, chances are you are not likely to get it published. Thinks in terms of another market in which that might work, such as the States.

On what authors can do to be professional . . .

1) Focus on what you want to achieve with your writing.
2) Assess the marketplace.
3) Make decisions based on 1 and 2.

And, in the end, don't be too enamored with every word you've written. Remember that the editor is trying to make your work more salable. Do not resent their suggestions. Many writers don't take sufficient account of the fact that what they've written becomes a product. The product has to compete for shelf space with a huge number of other books, and it has to compete with all of the other aspects of entertainment industry. A book must increasingly be well written to sell. The unique selling point of the book versus other multimedia is the quality of writing and storytelling.

On representing new writers . . .

Not all agents are willing to represent new writers. The top, really rich UK agents, for example, aren't hungry enough. But, new good writers are in demand. New writers have never had so many opportunities. Agents and publishers are actively looking for new writers of outstanding commercial books.

On finding an agent . . .

Read through a writer's guide carefully. These books give information that can help you find the agent who's right for you. Pick up recent books in your area and look at the acknowledgments page. In many instances the author will thanks the agent and editor by name. If you want to be really professional, pick up the publishing journal in your country, for example in UK you might read *The Bookseller.* Think of the information that is there for the writer!

I recommend drawing up a list of six agents that seem right for you. Send your material to the top agent on your list. Let the agent know that he or she is the only one to whom you are submitting. Don't phone after 10 minutes or 10 days and say, "Have you got it?" But don't let this agent sit on your work for more than 2 months either. If you can't get an answer by then, move down the list. Some people say that sending to one agent at a time is rather time-consuming, and shouldn't a writer send to all six agents on the list? If you do, make it clear that you're sending it elsewhere and will give priority to whomever comes first.

I don't mind representing authors outside my country. In fact, one of my bestselling authors lives in the States and another in Ireland. As long as I have reasonable access to them—the middle of the Sahara might be a problem—I don't mind where they are. The world is shrinking; communication is easier.

Once the book is sold . . .

Too many writers think they just have to write a book and hit lucky and continue writing. The writer's role has increased in the marketing of the book to the consumer. The classic example of this was Jacqueline Susann, who wrote *Valley of the Dolls.* She toured the United States at her own expense after the publisher's official tour ended.

That is why her books went to the top of the bestseller list and stayed. More recently, Shirley Conran did this successfully with *Lace and Crimson*.

On the "hot" topics now . . .

In the UK, the literary novel, the horror novel, the thriller are, of course, pretty common genres. Specific to the UK, discovery books are big because of the success, particularly in longitude. Something I've noticed is that one book captures the public's imagination and takes off, causing publishers, who seem to have a herd instinct, to look for similar books. One popular genre is the Nick Hornsby-type book, which are young male type—"lit lads" we call them. SAS (Special Forces) fiction, which is a subcategory of military, true-life adventure, was recently in vogue, but that perhaps has peaked. Also, football (American soccer), including fiction or nonfiction about personalities, was popular due to the World Cup. And, cookery books have long been a staple but are hotter than ever, particularly the celebrity chef genre. In the UK we also are obsessed with gardening so that subject is a continual seller. And, the New Age, Eastern philosophy books are up and coming.

His insider tip for writers . . .

Hm. If you want a good agent . . . hire me!

Discussion with a UK Agent

GERALD POLLINGER
Laurence Pollinger Literary Agency

On his background . . .

After University and wartime service in the Royal Air Force in 1947, I joined the agency founded by my father in 1930.

On the agent's primary tasks . . .

An author's agent acts as a business manager for authors. He tries to be an editor, a psychiatrist, an accountant, a lawyer, and an Indian chief.

His primary task is to access the author's material, find the best outlet for it, negotiate and conclude a contract with a purchaser (subject to the author's approval), and administer matters thereafter arising out of the contract.

Agent or no agent?

It is always better to have an agent at the outset. An agent is on the side of the author. A publisher is on his own side.

On how to approach him . . .

We like to receive a letter, fax, or e-mail briefly describing what the writer has to offer. We can then suggest a course of action, such as (to take just one example) asking the author to send us a synopsis and a couple of chapters of a novel he or she is writing.

On the biggest mistake writers make . . .

I think that approaching more than one agent at the same time is probably the biggest mistake a potential client might make.

On submitting to agents outside your own country . . .

Yes, but most indigenous agents have their own associates in other countries. However, if you live in France, for example, and have written a book about Canada, by all means approach a Canadian agent rather than a French one.

On hot topics in the UK . . .

"Hot topics" change weekly. By the time I say *Titanic* or *the euro*, the world will have moved on.

On the publishing industry . . .

There are half-a-dozen conglomerates, each of which encompass a number of imprints they have acquired. Then there are a few independent medium-sized houses, and a lot of small publishers.

On the unique aspects of UK publishing . . .

In many respects there are parts of UK publishing that are regarded as occupations for gentlemen for whom auctions and multiple submissions and hype are anathema.

On the profitability of book publishing . . .

Publishing is profitable, but not for everyone; figures are published regularly in trade magazines.

On trends in book sales . . .

More books are now sold in paperback form than before; library sales are lower. Children's books are more important than previously.

On new challenges facing writers . . .

Electronic publishing, information technology, sales on the Internet, new devices (like digital video disks), and knowing how to cope with them as well as with a computer are all challenges! Territorial and subsidiary rights are being eroded.

On representing new authors . . .

Of course agents will work with new authors. Where else would the new talent come from?

On making contacts in the industry . . .

Use a directory like the *Literary Market Place* (U.S.) or *The Writer's and Artist's Yearbook* (UK).

On agents charging fees . . .

Some agents request a contribution towards their editorial expenses; they should not charge reading fees (which are subject to tax).

On the Internet . . .

We took the Internet in our stride. Writers still need to send hard copy, but it is useful to know whether they have their work on disk. Bear in mind that not all machines are compatible.

Talking with a UK Agent

JON THURLEY
J. M. Thurley Management

On his background . . .

I graduated with Honours from Cambridge, receiving a diploma with an Education qualification, and am the author of five published novels. I began my career with 20th Century Fox UK as executive assistant to the CEO. I then moved to an agency, and have operated my own company for 23 years. My clients range through the media from film and TV writers to novelists, biographers, and academics.

Agent or editor?

A writer should secure an agent first.

On first contacting him . . .

I prefer an introductory letter giving the author's general curriculum vitae and an overview of the project to be considered before I ask for or decline further material.

On the biggest mistakes writers make . . .

Not studying the market—or even recognizing that there is a market. I wish prospective clients would understand that agenting in all its aspects is a business, and there must be a relationship between the time an agent spends on a project and the contribution that project will make to his overheads. Too many prospective clients see themselves as artists whom the world owes a living, and whose work should immediately be read.

On submitting to agents outside your own country . . .

I tend to be suspicious of writers from other countries approaching me. It suggests they have been unsuccessful in their own territory.

On unique aspects of book publishing in the UK . . .

Unique to UK publishing is the length of time it takes to get a response. UK publishers in general are extremely slow, with a few honorable exceptions.

On hot topics in his country . . .

This is a huge area that is best addressed by considering the weekly list of bestsellers (fact and fiction) published in *The Sunday Times.*

On the profitability of book publishing . . .

I suspect publishing is moving towards an American model. The old days of a midlist supported by bestselling authors is past. Most projects must have lead title potential (particularly first books) to be taken seriously.

One or two of the big publishers in the UK demonstrate that publishing can be very profitable. Fiction is the big gamble, but can pay off extremely well, as is evidenced by books such as *The Horse Whisperer, Bridges of Madison County*, and others; but nonfiction also pays well, as we've seen with Stephen Hawking's *A Brief History of Time* and Dava Sobel's *Longitude.*

On trends in book sales . . .

Book sales tend to polarize around bestsellers that are well hyped. The number of books bought per capita in the UK is pathetically low in comparison to France and Italy.

On the new challenges facing writers . . .

The perennial challenge is writing the books they *want* to write whilst satisfying the demands of the market.

On representing unknown writers . . .

I do—provided those writers have talent, ability, and a capacity for hard work.

One making contacts in the industry . . .

Numerous writers groups of varying excellence can be found listed in the various trade publications. These provide a forum not only for discussions, but for contacts. And, of course, a successful project has contacts approaching the writer rather than the other way round.

On agents charging fees to review work . . .

Some agents do charge fees. It is an individual choice that very much depends on the time required to make the necessary difference between success and failure. Taking on clients then working with them and taking the gamble with them takes time. And where we think a writer shows promise that might be fulfilled with professional help, we suggest they use the services of an editor, since we do not have the resources to cope with the heavy submission list.

On other inside tips . . .

The prime tip for a writer is to study the market and write for his or her chosen market. Too many feel that a stream-of-conscious novel, or a detached account of the life of an obscure Victorian painter, must fascinate editors and publishers as much as it does them.

Yes—you can be van Gogh and sell one painting during your life time—but agenting/publishing/television/film are all concerned with making a profit rather than fostering great and obscure art. Sad, but true. A facetious tip—but one containing a grain of truth—is to remember that publishers in general don't much like authors in general, particularly those who have a reputation for whining that they haven't been able to find a copy of their latest book in the kiosk in Timbuktu.

How has the Internet influenced your agency?

The Internet hasn't directly influenced us—except in terms of the material we receive. We don't accept electronic submissions. Some publishers and agents do have Web sites; we don't. Multimedia publishing in the UK is very much in its infancy.

What Sells Overseas

JEFF HERMAN

There is a primary question overseas publishers will ask when they consider acquiring a book: Has it been published in the United States? Getting your book published in the U.S. gives it a certain amount of credibility. An author who has been published in the U.S. and is now trying to get a new U.S. agent or publisher has a leg up, so to speak. She or he has already been in effect prequalified by being previously published.

A similar advantage would apply to a writer who has an agent versus one who does not have an agent. A publisher would perceive the writer with an agent as prequalified, since the agent is making a contingency bet that the book he or she has written is publishable. The fact that the writer has an agent says something to the publisher, who is in turn willing to give much higher-quality access, if not acquisition. Whether or not the book you are offering has been published in the U.S., you have been published before in the U.S., or you have an agent—all have an impact on whether you're likely to become published overseas.

Only a fraction of what gets published in the U.S. is going to get published overseas. And when we are talking about being published overseas, we are actually talking about only a handful of markets that can have any real impact on your pocketbook. Japan is a huge consumer economy. Its population is over 200 million and it is a middle-class, educated, industrialized country. Germany also is a major market with a huge population that is middle-class, educated, and industrialized. And the same could be said of the United Kingdom, France, and (to a lesser extent with respect to its tastes) Italy. Spain and South America also are markets with some impact. I also throw into the mix Taiwan, which is a voracious consumer of U.S. books. Although Taiwan is not a big consumer market, it is a vibrant one that is educated and middle class. And, what's happening more and more (in spite of everything that you read!), Taiwan is the market through which you can get books into the People's Republic of China without a experiencing a bootlegging situation.

When you negotiate foreign publishing rights, it's also important that you know to what market you're actually selling. For instance, when you sell the rights to Germany, you are basically confined to the country of Germany. However, if you sell to Brazil, you also gain a cross-market in Portugal. A Brazilian publisher who wants to acquire a book will likely ask for the world Portuguese rights as well, thus will market to both countries. You might negotiate so the rights are separate for each country, unless the publisher is willing to pay a premium for rights to offer your book in more than one country.

With respect to "Spanish-language rights," this term encompasses numerous Spanish-speaking countries. Very often, when Spanish publishers want to acquire Spanish-speaking rights, they can in turn license the book or export the book into Latin America. Again, you do not need to automatically give the publisher the world rights or rights outside the publisher's immediate country when you sell your book. These rights are negotiable. You might be able to negotiate additional payment for books sold outside the publisher's country, or you can seek other publishers for other territories. These are details that you can discuss when you negotiate with the publisher, especially if you have representation by an agent who is handling your foreign rights.

When acquiring the rights to a book, a UK publisher will probably want what is known as Commonwealth rights, which allow the publisher to publish the book in all of the UK's former colonies. This is usually not of major consequence because you would find it hard to regulate the sales of books in these countries (many of which are Third World countries) in any legal way. The best way to get any accountability for what is being sold in, for example, Nigeria or Sri Lanka (which would be in English) is to have a UK publisher who has a vested interest in knowing that your book is being legitimately distributed and accounted for. For that reason, my opinion is that it is usually desirable to go ahead and give the UK publisher the entire Commonwealth. On paper, it looks like you're yielding rights to a huge number of territories, but the Commonwealth actually does not encompass a very large English-speaking middle class.

Remember, only a fraction of what is sold in the U.S. is exportable. Being exportable means that other countries would want to acquire the rights to publish it. What books are these different countries likely to acquire? It is not uniform since each country tends to have its own tastes. The German market will want to acquire some types of books that the Japanese or British would not be interested in. Therefore, you can't assume that because one country is willing to pay a large amount of money for a book, all countries will want it.

Certain books, however, are "slam dunks" everywhere. A Grisham book, because of the author's massive success and the popularity his books have generated here in the U.S., can now pretty much just turn around and get published in any market in the world. This status had to be earned first. In my view, the author's tremendous success in the U.S. is what gave his books the international credibility that enable them to travel. In addition, Grisham books are not strictly novels that only a U.S. reader would appreciate.

Subject is another factor. Some countries have certain proclivities as to what they are looking for in the U.S. market. For instance, the Japanese and Chinese tend to be very interested in U.S. business titles. The Germans are attracted to our technical materials and scientific books, and (for whatever reason) they are fascinated with the American folklore of the Wild West and Native American cultures. Other markets are much more discriminating. The French, for instance, tend to feel that their culture is the one that counts; therefore, they are not usually seeking to acquire books from other cultures.

I use the term "reverse engineering" in the context of getting published overseas. If you have written a book that you know is a darn good one, but haven't been able to publish it in the U.S., nothing can keep you from trying to get it published overseas first. If you succeed in selling it overseas, you might then try to sell the translation or North American rights in the U.S. once it hits publication in its territory. An example might be a book about England in the fourteenth century. The U.S. market for that book may be limited, but you might find a bigger market in the UK for a book about its own history during this time period. So it might be more feasible to get it published in England first and then to try later to get it published as an export or translation product in the U.S.

Your agent or publisher, if you have one, will maneuver you through the foreign rights process. They will offer a clear picture of the feasibility of selling your book overseas. many authors recognize that selling books outside their own country does not automatically result in enormous financial gain. However, there is a certain amount of prestige when a book has crossed the borders of its own country. And, the author can take pride in knowing his or her book has the opportunity to find an audience in another land.

The Query Letter and Nonfiction Book Proposal

JEFF AND DEBORAH HERMAN

Your first contact with an agent or publisher is through a query, which is a short letter that serves as an introduction to encourage the recipient to request to see more of your work. The query letter asks prospective agents and publishers if they would like to see more about your proposed idea. If your work is fiction, you should indicate that a manuscript or sample chapters are available on request. If your work is nonfiction, you should offer to send a proposal, and if you have them, sample chapters.

The letter should be only one page long, if possible. Your goal is to pique the interest of a person who has very little time and probably very little patience. You want to entice him or her to keep reading and ask for more.

Your query letter should be as polished as possible so the editor will be impressed with you as well as your idea. Invest in state-of-the-art letterhead with a logo, on white, cream, or ivory paper with black ink.

The query letter can be sent with a package, which includes a short resume, media clippings, or other favorable documents. Include a self-addressed stamped envelope (SASE) with enough postage to return your entire package. For fiction writers, a short (one- to five-page) double-spaced synopsis of the manuscript will be helpful and appropriate.

The query generally follows a simple format: 1) the lead, 2) the supporting material/persuasion, 3) the biography, and 4) the conclusion/pitch.

The lead. The goal of the lead is to catch the catch the agent's or editor's attention. Determine what is most important about the book you're trying to sell, and write your letter accordingly. You can begin with a lead similar to what you'd use to grab the reader in a book article or a book chapter. You can use an anecdote, a statement of facts, a question, a comparison, or whatever you believe will be the most powerful. Remember, your letter may never be read beyond the lead, so make that first paragraph your hook.

Supporting material/persuasion. If your project is fiction you can include an excerpt or summary, much in the form as a movie preview. If you are selling a nonfiction book, you may want to include a brief summary of hard evidence, gleaned from research, that will support the merit of the idea. Focus on selling your topic and credentials. Include a few lines about what the publishing house will gain from the project. If you have brilliant marketing ideas or know of a well-defined market for your book where sales will be guaranteed, include these.

The biographical section. In the query, all you want to include are the most important and relevant credentials that will support the sale of the book. You can include, as a separate part of the package, a resume or biography that will elaborate further. Include all relevant experiences that support your ability to write the book, hobbies or non-job-related activities if they are related to your book, impressive press clippings about you, a list of speaking appearances, and copies of reviews about any books you have written.

The conclusion/pitch. Ask for the sale. Use phrases such as "I look forward to a speedy response." Thank the reader for his or her attention in the final sentence.

After you've sent the letter, it's time to wait a bit. Don't call the editor or agent. You have sent the query to invite a response, so be patient.

Suppose you receive a positive response to your query letter. An agent or editor calls you and requests your entire fiction manuscript or nonfiction book proposal. Congratulations, you have passed hurdle one! If your work is fiction, you should promptly send a professional-quality manuscript, packaged neatly.

If your work is nonfiction, you will send a nonfiction book proposal. A nonfiction book proposal is a sales brochure. The proposal's structure, contents, and size can vary substantially, and it's up to you to decide the best format for your purpose. The average length is usually between 15 and 30 double-spaced pages, and the typical sample chapter an additional 10 to 20 double-spaced pages. But sometimes proposals reach 100 pages, and sometimes they're only 5 pages total. There are, however, standard guidelines you might choose to follow.

Title page. The title page can be considered very important since it's what is seen first. The title page should be neatly and attractively spaced. Try to think of a title that's attractive and effectively communicates your book's purpose. The title page should contain only the title, your name, address, and telephone number, and the name, address, and telephone number of your agent (if you have one).

Overview.   The overview is a terse statement, one to three pages, of your overall concept and mission.

Biographical section.   This section tells who you are and why you're the ideal person to write this book. Highlight all your relevant experience, including media and public-speaking appearances, and list previous books and/or articles published by and/or about you. Many writers use the third-person here.

Marketing section.   This is where you justify your book from a commercial perspective. Who will buy it? Be demographically sophisticated.

Competition section.   The competition section is where you describe major published titles with concepts comparable to yours. Describe the leading half-dozen titles or so (backlist classics as well as recent books) and explain why yours will be different.

Promotion section.   Here you suggest possible ways to promote and market the book. Sometimes this section is unnecessary; it depends on your subject and on what, if any, realistic promotional prospects exist. This would include most major electronic broadcast and print media outlets, advertising, and maybe even some weird contests. You want to guide the publisher toward seeing realistic ways to publicize the book.

Chapter outline.   This is the meat of the proposal. Here's where you finally tell what is going to be in the book. Each chapter should be tentatively titled and abstracted. At their best, chapter abstracts read like mini-chapters, as opposed to telling the publisher or agent, "I will do . . . and I will show . . . " It's also a good idea to preface the outline with a table of contents.

Sample chapters.   Sample chapters are recommended. A strong, well-developed proposal might be enough. However, especially if you're a first-time writer, one or more sample chapters will give an opportunity to show your stuff. It will help dissolve an editor's concerns about your ability to actually write the book, thereby increasing the odds that you'll receive an offer. Sample chapters also can increase the size of the advance.

Other materials.   There are a variety of materials you may wish to attach to the proposal:

- Endorsement letters from known authors if available
- Any recent publicity you have received to show you are promotable
- A headshot photo of yourself

For further examples of book proposals that sold and why, see *Write the Perfect Book Proposal* by Jeff and Deborah Herman (Wiley).

How a Writer Can Sell Rights Overseas

JEFF HERMAN AND JULIE DEVILLERS

One way for writers to expand their sales is to look overseas. Overseas sales can mean selling the American edition "as is" to an English-speaking country, or it can mean selling the rights to publish in another language.

If the writer has a literary agent, the agent will handle the foreign rights sales on the writer's behalf. If the book has been published, the publishing company might control foreign rights and be responsible for selling the book overseas. If a writer doesn't have an agent or publisher, or the rights have reverted back, she might pursue foreign sales on her own.

The writer first needs to determine the kind of sale he wants: Is it a primary sale or is it a secondary sale? A primary sale is the sale of a book that has not been published in North America. A secondary sale is a book that has been previously published in North America. Secondary sales cover books currently in print, as well as those that have gone out of print.

Suppose you are interested in obtaining secondary rights for your book. First, consider to whom you will send it. A first step might be to get an agent in the relevant country to represent you. This agent will perform the same function that a domestic agent would. Or, you might try to directly contact a person at a publishing house in the country in which you are trying to get published.

Before sending copies of your book around the world, consider that shipping materials by airmail can be $20 to $30 per package. To avoid this cost, you can first initiate contact with publishers by query. Follow the protocol for query letters used in the

United States. You should include supporting materials, such as a color copy of the book cover and any reviews or publicity your book has received. Send your bio and any information about your career background that is relevant to the book. Encourage the publisher's interest before you go to the expense of shipping your book.

If possible, include an e-mail address or fax number for the publisher to reach you. Having access to the Internet will save substantial time and money. You can communicate through e-mail at a nominal cost overseas. The second best way to communicate is via fax. In the past, obtaining foreign rights was an enormous expense. For quick transfer of mere correspondence, a cable would average $30 a pop. The common use of the fax machine, and now the Internet, has allowed the "rest of us" to do business virtually everywhere.

Now suppose you are interested in obtaining *primary rights* for a work. Let's assume you wrote the work in English. As an unpublished manuscript, your work would be difficult to take straight to translation. An example of when a writer might seek primary rights in a foreign country is when he or she has written a manuscript specific to a country, such as "The History of Poland," which he tries to pitch to a Polish publisher. It is unlikely that a country would want to translate a mystery novel, for example, if the U.S. market rejected it first.

Recognize that the United States is the cultural powerhouse, the current "Hellenizer" of the world. When something is made in the U.S., as far as mass-market products go, it has been prequalified. Any intellectual property that has been published in the U.S. has much more leverage worldwide. One example that people are surprised to hear is that the Japanese love to read business books by U.S. authors. People forget that Japan is predominantly a culture of enhancers, not creators. So, bear in mind that having something published in the U.S. is a real foot in the door for an author.

There are obstacles if your work has not sold in the United States, but it is not impossible to publish it elsewhere. To consider whether or not you should seek a primary sale, think about whether the work has universal significance. If you determine that it is so clearly focused on the U.S. market, or your own country's market, that it wouldn't be relevant in another country, a primary sale is highly unlikely. For example, a nonfiction manuscript on lowering property taxes in the U.S. wouldn't be relevant outside the States.

Next, determine whether the subject of the work is something relevant to a particular country. If so, exploit that angle when you pitch the book to that country.

Then, follow the same route described above for secondary markets. Recognize that sending raw manuscripts overseas can amount to a small fortune, so a query letter can be used to gauge initial interest. And while you should be up front that your work is unpublished, don't make a big deal of the fact.

Hopefully, agents and publishers will respond favorably to your work and from there you'll get an offer, sell the foreign rights, and truly become an international writer.

The Foreign Rights Agreement

JEFF HERMAN

Foreign rights are the subsidiary rights to publish a work outside its originating country or territory. Your contract with your agent or domestic publisher will indicate who has the authority to contract with foreign publishers. Foreign rights are negotiated by your literary agent if you have one, or by your publisher if don't have an agent, or possibly by you. Foreign rights include translation, which are rights to publish in a particular country or worldwide rights in that particular language. Your contract with your domestic publisher will specify which rights they own and which rights, if any, you retain.

If your domestic publisher is responsible for foreign rights, the royalties are generally split anywhere from 50/50 to 80/20 in your favor. If your agent is responsible for the sale, she or he might work with foreign agents based in each home country since they have the requisite contacts and speak the native tongue. Your agent and the sub-agent would each then receive 10 to 15 percent commission.

Foreign rights often are sold at international book fairs, such as the Frankfurt Book Fair held in October. More than 8,500 exhibitors from almost 100 countries attend Frankfurt, and publishers meet with agents and packagers to negotiate foreign rights.

A sample foreign rights contract begins on the following page.

This Agreement, entered into on_____between (Proprietor) and c/o The Jeff Herman Agency, LLC. and_____(Licensee), will put the following terms and conditions into effect, upon signing:

- The Licensee shall pay the Proprietor the following advance, upon the signing of this agreement:

- The royalty rate for the title shall be_____of the selling price.

- The Licensee shall report to the Proprietor at least every six (6) months about all sales results and pay any royalties due. The first such report to be provided within nine (9) months of the title's publication.

- The Licensee will have eighteen (18) months upon the signing of this Agreement to publish the respective title(s), or all rights shall immediately revert to the Proprietor. Advance monies would not be subject to return.

- If the Licensee keeps any of the titles out of print in any six (6) month period after the first twenty-four (24) months that the title is in print, the rights to that title granted to the Licensee herein will be revertible to the Proprietor upon written request by the Proprietor.

- Six (6) complimentary copies of each title shall be provided to the Proprietor by the Licensee,

- The title's cover and all catalogue copy and advertisements will state the respective authors' names.

- The Licensee shall make or cause to be made at his expense the translation into the aforementioned language(s) and will promptly secure whatever copyright protection may be available in the said territory with respect to the work and the said translation. The title of the work shall appear beneath the title of and on the back of the title page of every copy issued. Copyright notice shall be printed exactly as it appears in the Proprietor's edition of the work.

- This agreement shall be valid for an initial period of three (3) years after the date of first publication of the work in the said language. It shall remain in force thereafter as long as the Licensee shall annually sell and account for 200 copies minimum of the said work(s) per title. Otherwise this agreement shall be deemed canceled and all rights conveyed herein shall automatically revert to the Proprietor.

- All rights now existing or which may hereafter come into existence and which are not specifically granted herein are reserved exclusively by the Proprietor.

page 1 of 2

- If at any time after the date of the first publication in the said language the work goes out of print and the Licensees do not within thirty (30) days after receipt of written notice from the Proprietor commit themselves to bring out a new edition of the said work within six (6) months, then all rights granted to the Licensee under this agreement shall terminate and revert to the Proprietor without further notice of procedure. The work shall be considered out of print in the aforesaid language if no royalty statement has been received within three (3) months after the due date or if there are no less than 200 copies available for sale to the general public, in good condition.

- In the event of sales of copies as a remainder, the royalty to be paid to the Proprietor shall be 10% of the sum received by the Licensee on the condition, however, that the sale is not effected below cost, but the Licensee shall not remainder any copies of the said work before two (2) years of their first publication, and shall give written notice of it to the Proprietor.

- The Licensee shall not assign this license nor issue the work under any imprint other than his own without written permission of the Proprietor.

- In the event of the Licensee becoming insolvent or being declared bankrupt, or otherwise unable to meet their obligation whether by voluntary act or order or decree of any court, or violate any clause of this agreement (except clauses 2, 5, 6, 10, 11, which provide for the automatic termination of this agreement in case of violation), and fail to rectify such violation within one month of having received written notice from the Proprietor to do so, this agreement shall become automatically null and void, and the license granted herein shall revert at once to the Proprietor without prejudice to the Proprietor's right of recovery of any sums due under the terms of this agreement and/or damages.

- All monies and statement due the Proprietor shall be payable to The Jeff Herman Agency, LLC., 332 Bleecker Street, Suite G-31, New York, NY 10014, USA, whose receipt and clearance thereof shall be a valid discharge of the Licensee's obligations herein.

For Proprietor   For Licensee

_____   _____

The Jeff Herman Literary Agency, LLC.

Date: Date:

page 2 of 2

The International Writer and the Internet

Julie DeVillers

The Internet is making the world smaller. Communication between continents can take place in a matter of seconds. E-mail, chat groups, and Web sites are making borders seem obsolete. The international writer who doesn't take advantage of the new technology can miss out on the limitless opportunities that are becoming available at breathtaking speed. Using the Internet is even more important to the international writer than the domestic one.

Think back to the "olden days"—pre-Internet, that is. A writer would write up a query, post it by mail, and anxiously wait for a response from the agent or publishing company. Well, the Internet has not exactly changed that protocol—yet. Most publishing companies and agents still emphatically prefer to receive their initial contact from a writer in the "traditional" arrangement—through hard copy and regular post, otherwise known as "snail mail." However, once initial contact has been made, editors and agents often enthusiastically take advantage of the Internet as a form of communication for two major reasons: It's quicker. It's cheaper.

Reason #1: It's quicker. The Internet provides speed and convenience never known before. No longer does an editor have to wait 7 to 10 days for the post arrival of an overseas author's chapter. No longer does the writer have to endure the already agonizing suspense plus the additional 7- to 10-day period to receive edits or comments in return. A file attached to an e-mail is faster than even a fax, with the added bonus that the document can be altered by the receiver as needed. A writer who can e-mail doesn't have to worry about making it to the post office before closing time or dropping a package off for express delivery. A few clicks of the button and a manuscript can be sent thousands of miles, day or night, and the writer doesn't even have to leave home.

Reason #2: The Internet saves money. And, for most writers, whose publishing successes don't quite equal Tom Clancy's, saving money is a large bonus. Sending a file over the Internet for free versus Fed-Exing documents for 30 to 50 American dollars or even airmailing can add up to big savings. E-mailing is also cheaper than leaving messages long-distance on an editor's voice mail. Real-time conversations over the Internet often can be more cost-effective than phone conversations.

The Internet is a useful tool for your publishing endeavors in other ways. If you are Internet savvy, you can research your market on the World Wide Web. The ways are endless. Need to identify a publisher who publishes books in your genre? Hit the book store Web sites, run a search for your topic, and check which publishers come up.

Then, check out the publishers' online catalogs. Why wait for weeks for a catalog request when you have the Web? Increasingly, publishing companies are offering Web sites where information about their lists can be gleaned, including submission guidelines.

Writers who keep up with the publishing industry stay ahead of other writers. A few strokes on your keyboard, and you can learn about forthcoming books, trends, and who's who at the publishing houses on the Internet. Such sites as www.the book seller.com, England's premier publishing industry periodical's online version, and the *Jeff Herman Report* at www.JeffHerman.com, published by the author of this book, provide valuable "insider' information for writers.

The writer should not underestimate the power of the Internet as a networking tool. Join one of the myriad of writers' forums, listservs, and communities. They offer endless opportunities for writers to meet and communicate with fellow writers, editors, and other publishing aficionados worldwide. Speaking of the communication benefits, recognize that an e-mail is less obtrusive than a phone call. The writer who wishes to check on the status of her manuscript need not fear interrupting her busy editor by phone—she can e-mail the request. Polite, less bothersome, yet effective.

Are you ready to promote yourself as a writer, your manuscript, or your published book? (The answer to that question should be unequivocally yes.) Besides becoming involved in the Internet community of writers and getting your name known, the 'Net offers other opportunities for self-promotion. Develop your own Web site or post your promotional information on somebody else's. Send a press release around the world to your targeted audience. Note that there is an Internet protocol you need to know before entering uninvited into other people's e-mails, lists, and writers' groups. Otherwise, you run the risk of becoming known for your "spam," or uninvited information that has a reputation similar to telemarketing calls during dinnertime or a mailbox stuffed with junk mail. Gain more information about this topic by reading a book on promoting yourself on the Internet, or hire an Internet publicist to do the work for you.

The following is a primer of definitions for terms used in this essay, as well as other terms an Internet-savvy writer should know. It certainly is not exhaustive, but toss a few of these words into your conversations at your next writers' conference and impress your fellow writers with your know-how.

The Internet: The general name for the global collection of computer networks linked worldwide. Nickname: The Net.

E-mail (Electronic mail) Messages that are sent from a person at one computer to people at other computers, as in: "E-mail the manuscript to our publishing house, because we are very interested in publishing it."

Flame: A nasty e-mail you might receive if you breach Internet protocol, for example by posting an inappropriate message on a bulletin board. You might receive a flame if you send a sales message for your new meat-and-potatoes cookbook to the vegetarian newsgroup.

Bulletin board (BBS): Message areas where people post messages others can read. Think of it as a hallway bulletin board, without the thumbtacks.

Listserv: The most common mailing lists, as in "I've subscribed to a listserv for soon-to-be-published mystery writers."

Modem: The piece of computer equipment needed to go online, allowing a computer to "talk" to other computers. Your modem can be internal (inside your computer) or external (hanging on the outside).

Newsgroups: Discussion groups on the Internet, as in "Check out misc.writing, a newsgroup for new writers and seasoned professionals."

Online: Any action taken while a computer is connected to another one. The generic term for being hooked up, usually to the Internet.

Post: To send a message to a newsgroup, mailing list, or bulletin board. Remember that different newsgroups, mailing lists, and bulletin boards have different protocol for posting.

Spam: To send multiple irrelevant messages. The response to spamming can range from a flame from an annoyed person to a virus sent to your computer.

URL: The address of a Web site on the Internet. For example, the URL of the publisher of this book's Web site is www.primapublishing.com.

The World Wide Web: The most organized part of the Internet that has interconnected pages which include text, graphics, video, and audio. The "Web" has become the "in" place to be.

PART FOUR

International and Domestic Resources

International
Web Sites for Writers

A writer in Hong Kong finds information about a publisher in England instantaneously. A writer in Canada participates in an Irish writers' circle. The writer in Australia reads breaking news about the book-publishing industry in England the day it happens. A writer in South Africa finds an audience for her work in Scotland. On the World Wide Web, this is not only possible but it's easy.

Writers and members of the International book publishing community are increasingly adding sites to the Internet. Many of these Web sites are listed below, categorized by the country of origin with a special category of general International Sites at the end of the listings. We look forward to receiving your suggestions for additional international Web Sites.

AUSTRALIA AND NEW ZEALAND

ALLIANCE
www.alliance.aust.com/1-1.htm

The Alliance is the union that covers everyone in the media, entertainment, sports, and arts industries. Alliance members can expect:

- that wages and working conditions are improved and protected
- free legal advice on employment matters from in-house lawyers
- free contract advice
- recommended minimum freelance rates for journalists, photographers, artists, and professionals in PR and book publishing

AURORA AUSTRALIS

www.australis.org/

Aurora Australis is a "gateway to the very best in contemporary Australian writing, created by some of the country's most admired authors." It includes a searchable index and Internet links.

AUSTRALIAN BOOK WEB

www.books.aus.net/html/news.html

The Australian Book Web offers a WebRing that works by joining together booksellers, publishers, literary and writing sites, and any other key sites of relevance to book lovers or people in the industry. They also offer *BookMall,* featuring secure online ordering so that booksellers can offer their inventory online.

THE AUSTRALIAN BOOKSELLERS ASSOCIATION INCORPORATED

www.aba.org.au/association.html

The Australian Booksellers Association Incorporated protects and promotes the interests of booksellers throughout Australia. The objectives of the Association are:

- to provide a variety of training and educational facilities for its members
- to establish bonds between booksellers all over Australia
- to enhance the unique role of books in our society
- to foster and encourage the selling of books
- to provide a national forum for member booksellers
- to provide technical advice and information to booksellers
- to represent booksellers' interests in contacts with organizations within the book trade

AUSTRALIAN FILM COMMISSION

www.afc.gov.au/about/whowe/index.html

The Australian Film Commission provides screen cultural and industry support through a range of measures, which include:

- project development through script and other pre-production assistance
- post-production grants and low-budget production funding
- grants in support of a vigorous and diverse screen culture

- international promotion of Australian productions and marketing advice
- creative interactive media development, production, and exhibition

AUSTRALIAN PUBLISHERS ASSOCIATION

www.publishers.asn.au/

The Australian Publishers Association is the peak industry body representing the diversity and commonality of its members' interests. The APA aims to:

- initiate programs that contribute to the developments of publishing in Australia.
- vigorously protect and further the interests of copyright holders, agents, and licensees.
- actively represent members' interests to government and other organizations as appropriate.
- encourage excellence in writing, editing, design, production, marketing, and distribution of published works in Australia.
- protect freedom of expression.
- promote members' published works to consumers via the Australian Book Fair and other major marketing events.
- promote Australian publishing overseas.
- offer training and industry development programs to its members and to the industry at large.
- manage members' funds to the further interests of the industry.

AUSTRALIAN SOCIETY OF AUTHORS

www.asauthors.org/about_the_asa.html

The Australian Society of Authors promotes and protects the professional interests of Australian literary creators. The pivotal position in the industry allows them to represent members in negotiations and disputes, and to provide advice on industry standards and practices.

COPYRIGHT AGENCY LIMITED

www.copyright.com.au/

Copyright Unlimited Agency is a copyright management company that centrally manages the copyright interests of thousands of publishers and authors. The aim is to promote awareness of and respect for copyright. Visitors may become members at no charge. The site includes other pertinent Internet links.

FELLOWSHIP OF AUSTRALIAN WRITERS

www.writers.asn.au/faw/

The Fellowship of Australian Writers aims to bring together all those interested in writing for their professional, cultural, and social benefit, and to provide advice and information to them. Its more than 2,000 members are writers from diverse fields.

THE INTERNATIONAL LIBRARY OF POETRY—AUSTRALIA

www.poetry.com/ilp/australia.html

The International Library of Poetry—Australia was founded to promote the artistic accomplishments of contemporary poets. They seek new poetic talent to submit new or unpublished poetry for possible publication. They award $12,000 in prizes.

NATIONAL BOOK COUNCIL

home.vicnet.net.au/~abr/NBC/welcome.htm

The National Book Council strives to advance the promotion of books and reading in Australia. They aim to:

- bring individuals who privately or professionally have an interest in books together with organizations
- encourage the free flow of books
- publish and circulate information about books and encourage the ownership and use of books
- assist in the development of a strong book industry in all aspects, including authorship, publishing, bookselling, and library use
- persuade Federal, State, and Local governments to give every support to the book and encourage the freedom from undesirable restrictions
- promote the writing and reading of books and of Australian books in particular
- support library funding as a right for all Australians

NEW ZEALAND WRITERS GUILD

www.wga.org/iawg/nz.html

The Guild is a professional association for writers in film, television, theatre, radio, video, and multimedia. Its objectives are to promote and protect the interests of its members and provide a link for writers to their peers and the entertainment industry in general. Members receive newsletters and an info-sheet regularly. They also offer contract advice, credit arbitration, craft evenings, and workshops.

THE SOCIETY OF WOMEN WRITERS AUSTRALIA
home.vicnet.net.au/~swwvic/sww.html

The first object of The Society of Women Writers Australia was to organize local women writers into a group that would welcome to Sydney the women delegates, and wives of delegates, to the Imperial Press Conference in 1925. Today it aims to draw together women engaged in the writing profession.

WHO WHERE WHAT
www.adelaide.net.au/~dyoz/www.html

Who Where What provides members with an informative newsletter and backup information. Their annual contest provides writers with assessment of their work through judge comments and score sheets. Smaller contests are run throughout the year. Workshops are available when possible and tip sheets are available to members through snail mail.

CANADA

THE ASSOCIATION OF CANADIAN PUBLISHERS
www.digitalbookworld.com/ACP/welcomeinfo.html

The Association of Canadian Publishers represents over 135 Canadian-owned book publishers and members of the literary, general trade, education, and scholarly sectors. Through all its activities, the ACP encourages the writing, publishing, distribution, and promotion of Canadian books. The mission is to support the development of a strong, independent, and vibrant Canadian-owned publishing industry.

CANADIAN AUTHORS ASSOCIATION
www.canauthors.org/homepage.html

The Canadian Authors Association is Canada's national writing organization. The Canadian Authors Association Homepage includes a series of pages describing the activities of the association at the national level. *Canadian Author—On-Line Edition* is the electronic version of Canada's national writing magazine. The CAA Victoria & Islands Branch Home Page lists the activities of fifteen CAA branches in cities across Canada. The CAA Writing Links Index Page offers a very well-organized list of Internet links sorted by genre.

CANADIAN BOOK REVIEW ANNUAL

www.interlog.com/~cbra/

The Canadian Book Review Annual is "the most comprehensive collection of authoritative reviews of English-language trade, scholarly, and reference books published in Canada each year." Since 1975 it has reviewed more than 23,000 Canadian books.

CANADIAN CHILDREN'S BOOKS CENTRE

www3.sympatico.ca/ccbc/mainpage.htm

The Canadian children's Book Centre "helps the creative talent of Canada—the writers, the illustrators—reach the people who count: the readers. An investment in The Canadian Children's Book Centre is an investment in your child's future as a Canadian." The site includes biographies and bibliographies of touring authors and illustrators.

CANADIAN CHILDREN'S LITERATURE REVIEW

www.interlog.com/~cbra/CCLR/home.html

The Canadian Children's Literature Review is a wonderful resource for parents, students, librarians, teachers, and booksellers. It includes a useful consumer guide and is helpful in identifying resources for students.

CANADIAN POETRY ASSOCIATION

www.mirror.org/groups/cpa/

The aims of the Canadian Poetry Association are:

• to promote the reading, writing, publishing, and preservation of poetry in Canada through the individual efforts of members

- to promote communication among poets, publishers, and the general public
- to encourage leadership and participation from members and to encourage the formation and development of autonomous local chapters

CANADIAN SOCIETY OF CHILDREN'S AUTHORS, ILLUSTRATORS AND PERFORMERS

La société canadienne des auteurs, illustrateurs, et artistes pour enfants
www.interlog.com/~canscaip/
Canadian Society of Children's Authors, Illustrators and Performers (CANSCAIP) is a group of professionals in the field of children's culture. CANSCAIP is instrumental in the support and promotion of children's literature through newsletters, workshops, meetings, and other programs for authors, parents, teachers, librarians, and publishers. It includes Internet links.

CITATION

www.harbour.sfu.ca/ccsp/citation/
Citation is a source of information for Canadians and Canadian publishers looking for information about publishing on the Internet, doing business on the Internet, or publishing for the Internet. Included are lists of publishers, booksellers, libraries, literary magazines, and other related international Web sites.

THE CRIME WRITERS OF CANADA

www.swifty.com/cwc/cwchome.htm
The Crime Writers of Canada pages are intended to offer news and information about members and their books. It includes award lists, directories of members' works, mystery links, and the Crime Writers of Canada cookbook.

FEDERATION OF BRITISH COLUMBIA WRITERS

www.swifty.com/bcwa/index.htm
The federation of British Columbia Writers seeks to serve the needs of established and emerging writers. The Federation helps to improve working conditions and expand

support programs for writers. They provide members with up-to-date information that helps locate larger audiences.

Forthcoming Books

www.nlc-bnc.ca/forthbks/efbintro.htm

Forthcoming Books lists titles processed by the National Library of Canada's Canadian Cataloguing in Publication (CIP) program. Approximately 1,600 publishers participate in the Canadian CIP program. The entries are listed alphabetically.

Manitoba Writers' Guild Inc.

www.mbwriter.mb.ca/

The Manitoba Writers' Guild aims to promote the art in all its forms in Manitoba. They offer a manuscript reading service, bulletin boards, and literary awards.

Shiba Hill

http://members.tripod.com/~ShibaHill

Shiba Hill is an "authors cooperative," a place where authors can showcase their works for potential agents and/or publishers. Shiba Hill is not an agent or publisher, rather it strives to help other writers. The site includes the H.E.L.P. Fund Bookstore, which consists of signed books by authors including Raymond E. Feist, Stephen G. Esrati and Irene Hofstein, William Quick, and Jack Mingo. It has a comprehensive list of Internet links to writing organizations, literary agent information, research links, and other writing links.

Wordwrights Canada

home.ican.net~susioan/

Wordwrights Canada is an editing and author service for those who strive for a high professional standard in their fiction, nonfiction, and poetry. Founded on a belief in the power and integrity of language, Wordwrights Canada has made its aim: "The right words in the best places." They offer handbooks for writers, writing contests, editing services, educational services, and Internet links.

WRITER'S BLOCK

www.niva.com/writblok/

Writer's Block is a "creative reference for today's writers." It is a connection to professional writers and editors, and the secrets that have made them among the best in their field. Some issues that it deals with are electronic publishing and intellectual property law, a hypothesis about the replacement of words with video images, and a musing about the little words that pervade language.

WRITERS' FEDERATION OF NEW BRUNSWICK

www.sjfn.nb.ca/Community_Hall/w/Writers_Federation_NB/index.htm

The Writers' Federation of New Brunswick is a community of writers, both emerging and established, who strive to develop the craft of writing and who work to promote and encourage the literary arts in New Brunswick. It includes events, a literary competition, and Internet links.

WRITERS' FEDERATION OF NOVA SCOTIA

www.chebucto.ns.ca/Culture/WFNS/index.html

The Writers' Federation of Nova Scotia aims to foster creative writing and the profession of writing in Nova Scotia; to provide advice and assistance to writers at all stages of their careers; to encourage greater public recognition of Nova Scotian writers and their achievements; and to enhance the literary arts in our regional and national culture. It includes online markets and resources, information about Nova Scotian writers, and competitions, newsletters, and workshops.

THE WRITERS GUILD OF ALBERTA

www.writersguild.ab.ca/

The Writers Guild of Alberta is a community of writers that exists to support, encourage, and promote writers and writing; to safeguard the freedom to write and read; and to advocate for the well-being of writers. They list Canadian author readings and writers-in-residence programs, and plan to establish an e-mail database for timely announcements.

WRITERS GUILD OF CANADA

http://home.ican.net/~wgc/One_Sheet.html

The Writers Guild of Canada is an organization of freelance writers working in film, television, and radio production in Canada. It administers, negotiates, and enforces collective agreements that set out minimum rates, terms, and conditions of work in the Guild's jurisdiction (all English-language production in Canada). The Guild helps resolve disputes regarding work conditions, writing credits, contracts, and collections.

THE WRITERS' UNION OF CANADA

www.swifty.com/twuc/

The Writers' Union of Canada is a national organization of professional writers of books for the general public. The Union works to advance conditions for all writers, to unite writers for the advancement of their common interest, and to foster writing in Canada. The site includes a resource guide for writers called *Dear Writer,* competitions and awards, technical publications, manuscript evaluation services, and guidelines for hosting a successful signing.

HONG KONG

HONG KONG ARTS CENTRE

www.hkac.org.hk/intro.htm

The Hong Kong Arts Centre aims to make drama, dance, music, film, video, visual, literary, and applied arts comprehensible, accessible, and fulfilling to as many people as possible. The Education Department has organized an array of literature workshops on novel, poetry, and editing, and research programs. Quality student works were selected to be published by the Hong Kong Arts Centre in a bid to encourage students to write and read literature.

THE HONG KONG WRITERS' CIRCLE

http://home.netvigator.com/~lwgray/

The Hong Kong Writers' Circle offers a new literary magazine called *Dim Sum,* which is devoted to fiction from and about South East Asia. Submissions can be made through this site. They also offer a short-story workshop, forums and chat rooms for discussion, an "Ask the expert" page for answers to literary questions, and a guest book. The program schedule lists at least one literary event per month.

IRELAND

DUBLIN WRITERS' WORKSHOP
www.dublinwriters.org/about.html

The Dublin Writers' Workshop began in 1982 and has been housed in a number of Dublin pubs. Many of its members have published novels and collections and have won prizes like the Hennessy Award and the Kavanagh Prize. In 1997 the workshop moved online and launched an online version of their quarterly, *Acorn,* called *Electric Acorn* in its online presence. The workshop hopes to provide an online forum for its members and guests as well as hosting other Irish arts organizations. Visitors are encouraged to join the mailing list.

IRISH WRITERS' CENTRE

Áras na Scríbhneoirí
www.atlanticisland.ie/atlanticisland/writers/

Housed in three stories of a building in Dublin, the Irish Writers' Centre was established to promote and assist in the development of contemporary Irish writing. It acts as an umbrella body for four constituent organizations: *The Irish Children's Book Trust, The Irish Translators' Association, The Irish Writers' Union,* and the *Society of Irish Playwrights.* Some of the basic aims of the Irish Writers' Centre are:

- to assist writers to pursue their work
- to promote cultural exchange of a literary nature between Ireland and other countries
- to organize and promote a program of literary activities, including seminars, readings, lectures, and workshops
- to cultivate an interest both at home and abroad in the work of contemporary Irish writers.

THE IRISH WRITERS' UNION

Comhar na Scríbheoirí
www.homepages.iol.ie/~carrollm/iwu.htm

The Irish Writers' Union strives to organize writers in Ireland; advance the cause of writing as a profession and as a form of work; achieve better remuneration and more favorable conditions for writers; provide advice, assistance, and support to individual writers in their relations with publishers and other uses of their work; provide a means for the expression of the collective opinion of writers on matters affecting their profession; contribute to educational policy insofar as it relates to the art of writing and the use of literature in the educational system; and influence the way in which the literary estates of former generations of writers are managed.

READ IRELAND BOOKSTORE

www.readireland.ie

The Read Ireland Bookstore is a place where consumers may browse or search for books on Ireland. It features a book of the month in both fiction and nonfiction, Read Ireland features (which includes the "best of" lists and author features), and a monthly best sellers list.

UNITED KINGDOM

ACHUKA—CHILDREN'S BOOKS UK

www.achuka.co.uk/index2.html

Achuka is the "chock-full, eyes-peeled, independent children's books site." The emphasis is on original content and its aim is to be an informative, reliable, and thought-provoking site covering the children's books market in the U.K. It offers author interviews, chat rooms, news, and author-illustrator links.

THE ASSOCIATION OF BRITISH SCIENCE WRITERS

http://dspace.dial.pipex.com/town/square/ac073/absw.htm

The Association of British Science Writers exists to help those who write about science and technology and to improve the standard of science journalism in the U.K. The Association publishes a regular newsletter, *The Science Reporter,* and co-sponsors awards for outstanding science journalism.

BOOK WEB

www.bookweb.co.uk/

Book Web is a miscellany of Book trade information with hypertext links and e-mail forms for book publishers and others. It offers service to those involved in the sale and distribution of books who are seeking a Web presence.

THE BOOKSELLER

www.thebookseller.co.uk/

The Bookseller offers many resources for writers who are interested in publishing in Britain and in Europe in general. It offers directories, an analysis of the Euro book trade, a buyer's guide, a searchable guide to the industry, and information on book publishing in Britain. There is a debate forum and job listings as well.

THE ELECTRIC EDITORS

www.ikingston.demon.co.uk/ee/abt_02.htm

The Electric Editors aims to become the primary source on the Internet for everyone looking to satisfy a professional need related to the publication of the written word, and the primary medium of communication between in-house and freelance staff. Electric Editors includes e-mail discussion lists and Internet links for publishing professionals, including editors, proofreaders, indexers, translators, authors, and publishers.

EUROPEAN FEDERATION OF FREELANCE WRITERS

www.eurofed.org/main.html

The Federation provides a range of services specifically designed to give the maximum support and value to its members, as well as providing a forum for opinions and an opportunity for networking both within a local and international environment. Full-time or part-time writers are eligible for membership.

THE INTERNATIONAL LIBRARY OF POETRY—UNITED KINGDOM

www.poetry.com/ilp/uk.html

The International Library of Poetry—United Kingdom was founded to promote the artistic accomplishments of contemporary poets. They seek new poetic talent to submit new or unpublished poetry for possible publication. They award £12,000 in prizes.

INTERNATIONAL WRITER

www.ndirect.co.uk/~int.writer/Webpage%20proper%201.0%20regular/Home page/main.html

The International Writer is dedicated to helping writers by providing lists of services available to writers, explanations of various aspects of writing and publishing, and directories of writers' groups.

THE PUBLISHING TRAINING CENTRE AT BOOK HOUSE
www.train4publishing.co.uk/bookhouse/about/index.htm

The Publishing Training Centre has moved from being a provider of core editorial skills training for book and journal publishers to offering nearly 60 different courses in the complete range of publishing and management skills. It includes outplacement and career counseling, using its intimate knowledge of the U.K. publishing industry.

THE PUBLISHERS ASSOCIATION
www.publishers.org.uk/welcome.htm

The Publishers Association is the focal point for all book, journal, and electronic publishers in the U.K.; it is where publishers come together to identify and discuss the main issues facing their industry and where the policies are developed that drive the PA's campaigns to ensure a secure trading environment for our industry.

REAL WRITERS
http://turtledesign.com/RealWriters/different.htm

Real Writers is a "support and appraisal service" for writers to receive individual attention and assessment of their work. The tutors are working writers, making their living by the pen or word processor, who spare a few hours each week to work with the clients. They set individually designed tasks and activities for writers without the use of standardized exercises or dated course material. Tuition is set on an individual basis.

SOCIETIES FOR WRITERS & AUTHORS
www.wwwebguides.com/authors/society/authors/auth.html

The Societies for Writers & Authors is an independent trade union with great scope to assist authors. Members may ask for general and legal advice in connection with their work—marketing, contracts, publishers, broadcasting, and so on. The Society is also working on the issue of electronic rights. The Society publishes a quarterly magazine, *The Author*, and a supplement, *Electronic Author*. It also offers quick guides to such matters as income tax, VAT, libel, and publishing contracts.

STRATFORD-UPON-AVON WRITERS WORLD-WIDE
www.clafarge.com/writers/

The "Stratford-upon-Avon Writers' Circle" is a group of fifteen members that meet every month to read and discuss their work. They have developed "Stratford-upon-Avon Writers World-Wide," a group unlimited by numbers or location, in which the Writers Circle will list their latest works as well as those selected from their online audience by their Inner Circle.

THE WRITERS GUILD OF GREAT BRITAIN
www.writers.org.uk/guild/Home/HomeBody.html

The Writers' Guild of Great Britain aims to ensure that writers of all media are properly represented. Here, writers form the strong organization needed to get a fair deal in today's increasingly competitive and ruthless market.

GENERAL INTERNATIONAL WEB SITES

THE INTERNATIONAL AFFILIATION OF WRITERS GUILDS
www.iawg.org/

The International Affiliation of Writers Guilds is a confederation of the primary writers guilds for audio-visual writers, mainly covering film and television. The member guilds work together to further the cause of audio-visual writers worldwide through collective action, coordinated agendas, mutual support, and common representation in international venues.

INTERNATIONAL LITERARY MARKET PLACE
http://ilmp.bookwire.com/advertise.asp

Literary Market Place has "long been recognized as the single most comprehensive source of information about all aspects of the American book publishing industry." It is used to find shipping agents, literary agents, book manufacturers, and publishers. It is a searchable index.

PUBLISHERS CATALOGUES HOME PAGE
www.lights.com/publisher/

The Publishers' Catalogue Home Page is a searchable index of publishers that is organized by geographic location. It also includes other Internet links to publisher-related sites.

PUBLISHERS ONLINE WEEKLY: INTERNATIONAL
www.bookwire.com/PW/global.articles

Publishers Online Weekly is an indispensable resource for information about the publishing world from all around the globe. Primarily a news site, it keeps those thirsty for the industry of publishing satiated. It lists articles by title and also includes individual country reports.

SCREENWRITERS & PLAYWRIGHTS HOME PAGE
www.teleport.com/~cdeemer/scrwriter.html

This page is designed to meet the special needs of screenwriters and playwrights. It includes resources for screenwriters, playwrights, and general writing. *Screenwright, an electronic tutor* is a "remarkable, ground-breaking screenwriting tutorial" that "promises to become the bible of screenwriting."

THE WORLD WIDE WEB VIRTUAL LIBRARY—PUBLISHERS
www.comlab.ox.ac.uk/archive/publishers.html

Publishers is a collection of selected publishers, publishing companies, bookstores, broadcasters, electronic journals, and other online publishing sites. It is a browsing index that can be searched as well.

Domestic Web Sites for Writers

One of the most valuable aspects of the World Wide Web for international writers is that it provides the opportunity to explore the world of publishing in the United States. This annotated list of Web sites offers descriptions of some of the most useful sites for writers. For your convenience, sites are grouped according to the following categories:

- Publishing Resources
- Mystery Resources
- Science Fiction Resources
- Romance Resources
- Poetry Resources
- Screenwriting Resources
- Horror Resources
- General
- How Tos
- Megasites

PUBLISHING RESOURCES

1001 WAYS TO MARKET YOUR BOOKS
www.bookmarket.com/1001bio.html

1001 Ways to Market Your Book is a site that offers a book-marketing newsletter, consulting services, and book-marketing updates. Other topics include success letters, author biographies, sample chapters, and tables of contents.

THE AUTHOR'S GUILD

www.authorsguild.org/

For more than 80 years the Guild has been the authoritative voice of American writers . . . its strength is the foundation of the U.S. literary community. This site features contract advice, a legal search, information on electronic rights, details on how to join the organization, a bulletin index, publishers row, a listing of board members, and current articles regarding the publishing field. There is also a link for **Back-in-print.com,** an on-line bookstore featuring out-of-print editions made available by their authors.

ASSOCIATION OF AMERICAN PUBLISHERS, INC.

www.publishers.org/home/index.htm

The Association of American Publishers, Inc. "is the principal trade association of the book publishing industry." The site includes information and registration for annual meetings and conferences, industry news, information about book publishing, industry statistics and issues, and copyright data.

ASSOCIATION OF AUTHOR'S REPRESENTATIVES, INC.

www.bookwire.com/aar

The Association of Author's Representatives, Inc. is "an organization of independent literary and dramatic agents." It is a member-only site that offers information about finding an agent, Internet links, a newsletter, and a canon of ethics.

BOOKLIST

www.ala.org/booklist/index.html

Booklist is a "digital counterpart of the American Library Association's *Booklist* magazine." In the site is a current selection of reviews, feature articles, and a searchable cumulative index. Review topics include books for youth, adult books, media, and reference materials. The site also includes press releases, the best books list, and subscription information.

BOOKNOTES

www.booknotes.org/right.htm

Based on the book and television program "Booknotes" on C-SPAN, this site allows one to learn about the authors who have appeared on the program, read transcripts from the program, watch RealVideo clips from authors who were featured in this book, preview the upcoming "Booknotes" schedule, listen to recent "Booknotes" programs in their entirety in RealAudio, and learn about the publishing industry in general. The site also features message boards, a link to the C-SPAN bookstore, and message boards.

BOOKREPORTER

www.bookreporter.com/brc/index.asp

Bookreporter is a site that offers book reviews, and a perspectives section that deals with topics such as when a book becomes a movie. It features a daily quote by a famous author.

BOOKTALK

www.booktalk.com/

This site is a publishing insider's page where you'll find out who's hot and what's up. It features links to get in touch with authors, agents, and publishers, as well as a slush pile and bookstores.

BOOKWIRE

www.bookwire.com/

Partners with *Publishers Weekly, Literary Market Place,* and the *Library Journal* among others, BookWire is a site that offers book industry news, reviews, original fiction, author interviews, and guides to literary events. The site includes publicity and marketing opportunities for publishers, authors, booksellers, and publicists, and it includes a list of the latest BookWire press releases.

BOOKZONE, INC.

www.bookzone.com/profile/

"BookZone, Inc. was founded in 1994 to increase book sales and profits for publishers." The site features a Super Catalog of books, thousands of book-related links, industry insights and resources, publishing news, and site hosting, development, and on-line marketing.

THE BOOK REPORT

www.bookwire.com/tbr/

The Book Report is "where readers meet readers and readers meet writers." It is a conversational site where visitors may talk about books they have recently read or get tips on great new books from other visitors. The site also includes book reviews and transcriptions of an exclusive chat with authors.

R. R. BOWKER

www.bowker.com/

R. R. Bowker is a site that offers a listing of books in print on the Web, books out of print, an on-line directory of the book publishing industry, a data collection center for R. R. Bowker publications, and a directory of vendors to the publishing community.

THE CHILDREN'S BOOK COUNCIL

www.cbcbooks.org/

"CBC Online is the Web site of the Children's Book Council—encouraging reading since 1945." It provides a listing of articles geared toward publishers, teachers, librarians, booksellers, parents, authors, and illustrator—all those interested in the children's book field.

HUNGRY MIND REVIEW

www.bookwire.com/hmr

The Hungry Mind Review is a national magazine that presents essays, author interviews, children's book reviews, nonfiction reviews, and a section on poetics and poetry reviews. Hungry Mind Review is also offered in print version with each issue built around a particular theme.

INDISPENSABLE WRITING RESOURCES

www.stetson.edu/~rhansen/writweb.html

The Indispensable Writing Resources site offers a categorized listing of Internet writing resources. Categories include on-line writing labs and centers, general writing/ grammar, subject-specific writing, and a miscellaneous collection of writers' resources. It is a searchable site that offers a writing and style library as well as reference material.

LIBRARY JOURNAL DIGITAL

www.bookwire.com/ljdigital/

Library Journal Digital is a site that offers articles about news in the publishing industry, editorials, a calendar of events, video reviews, audiobook reviews, bestseller news, and a job search section.

LITERARY MARKET PLACE

http://lmp.bookwire.com/

The Literary Market Place Web site offers information about publishers, which are categorized by U.S. book publishers, Canadian book publishers, and small presses, as well as literary agents (including illustration and lecture agents). The site also offers trade services and resources.

PARA PUBLISHING

www.parapublishing.com/cgi-bin/WebObjects?welcome=publisher-visitor

The Para Publishing Book Publishing Resources page offers "the industry's largest resources/publications guide," a customized book writing/publishing/promoting information kit, as well as current and back issues of their newsletter. The site also includes research links, a listing of suppliers, and mailing lists.

PUBLISHERS WEEKLY ONLINE

www.bookwire.com/pw/pw.html

Publishers Weekly Online offers news about the writing industry in general as well as special features about reading and writing in general and genre writing. The site also includes news on children's books, bookselling, interviews, international book industry news, and industry updates.

PURE FICTION

www.purefiction.com/start.htm

Based in London and New York, Pure Fiction is a Web site "for anyone who loves to read—or aspires to write—bestselling fiction." The site includes reviews, previews, writing advice, an on-line bookshop, a writers' showcase, Internet links, and more. Pure Fiction also offers a mailing list.

READERSNDEX

www.ReadersNdex.com/

ReadersNdex is a searchable site designed to give "access to the most up-to-date information about your favorite authors and titles, regardless of publisher affiliation." Books on ReadersNdex are cross-referenced by author, title, subject, and publisher, and may be purchased through the bookstore, the Tattered Cover, or from the publisher. The Bookshelf section is designed for browsing the available books. The site also includes a Reading Room where users can read magazines and reviews; access links to the Web sites of participating publishers; and utilize the searchable index of books.

SENSIBLE SOLUTIONS FOR GETTING HAPPILY PUBLISHED

www.happilypublished.com/

The Sensible Solutions for Getting Happily Published site is "designed to help writers, publishers, self-publishers and everyone else who cares about reaching readers, including editors, agents, booksellers, reviewers, industry observers and talk-show hosts . . . and aims to help books get into the hands of the people they were written for." It includes information about finding a publisher, ways for publishers to raise revenues, the self-publishing option, how to boost a book's sales, and sensible solutions for reaching readers.

SHAW GUIDES, INC., WRITER'S CONFERENCES

www.shawguides.com/writing/

Shaw Guides: Writers Conferences is a subscription-based listing of sponsors and the following month's writers conferences calendar.

SMALL PUBLISHERS OF NORTH AMERICA

www.spannet.org/home.htm

Small Publishers of North America is a site for "independent presses, self publishers, and savvy authors who realize if their books are to be successful, they must make them so." The site offers pages for "fun, facts, and financial gain." They offer a newsletter.

THE WRITE PAGE

www.writepage.com/index.html

The Write Page is "an on-line newsletter with over 300 pages of author and book information for readers and how-to information for writers of genre fiction." Genres that the site deals with include science fiction, romance, historical novels, murder mysteries, techno-thrillers and also children's, young adult, nonfiction, poetry, and small press publications. Articles grapple with issues such as how to write and get published, research, tools of the trade, and listings of conferences and contests.

THE WRITER'S RETREAT

www.angelfire.com/va/dmsforever/

The objectives of The Writer's Retreat are "to provide a meeting place for writers everywhere, to provide market information, to list relevant Internet links, to list inspirational and motivational information and quotations for writers of all races, creeds, and backgrounds, and to have and provide fun while doing it!"

THE WRITERS' BBS

www.writers-bbs.com/home/shtml

The Writers' BBS is intended for "authors, poets, journalists, and readers" and highlights writers' chat rooms, discussion forums, and an e-zine for beginning writers called

"Fish Eggs for the Soul." It also includes games, personal ads, copyright information, mailing lists, Internet links, an adults-only section, and the on-line King James Bible.

WRITERS CLUB

www.writersclub.com/

Writers Club is a site that aims to provide "services and information to support, educate, and encourage writers in both their professional and personal lives." The site offers publishing and agent information, industry newsletters, articles on writing, and a mentor program. It also offers author interviews and message boards.

WRITERS NET

www.writers.net/

Writers Net is a site that "helps build relationships between writers, publishers, editors and literary agents." It consists of two main sections: The Internet Directory of Published Writers, which includes a list of published works and a biographical statement, and The Internet Directory of Literary Agents, which lists areas of specialization and a description of the agency. Both are searchable and include contact information. Writers Net is a free service that hopes to "become an important, comprehensive matchmaking resource for writers, editors, publishers and literary agents on the Internet."

THE ZUZU'S PETALS LITERARY RESOURCE

www.zuzu.com

The Zuzu's Petals Literary Resource site focuses on a comprehensive list of writers' resource links and information. It includes a bookstore, discussion forums, its literary magazine (*Zuzu's Petals Quarterly Online*), art news that reports on news in the literary world, and contests.

MYSTERY RESOURCES

AMERICAN CRIME WRITERS LEAGUE

www.klew.com/acwl.html

The American Crime Writers League was established "by a group of writers who wanted a private forum for exchanging ideas, complaining about almost anything, and trying to understand this decidedly wacky business." The site includes information about interviews, conference information, agents' home telephone numbers, reviews, interviews, and more.

CLOCKTOWER FICTION

www.clocktowerfiction.com/

Clocktower Fiction aims to "provide free quality original fiction for avid readers." Clocktower Fiction publishes *Outside: Speculative and Dark Fiction,* which is a freelance, paying on-line publication that is published three times a year. The site provides links to resources on grammar, writing, and other relevant topics, and covers a variety of genres including mystery, science fiction, macabre, suspense thrillers, and noir fiction.

CLUELASS HOME PAGE

www.cluelass.com/TOC.html

The ClueLass Home Page offers awards for mystery fiction and nonfiction, information about conferences and conventions, and mystery groups for writers and fans. It includes information about markets, other contests, reference material, and on-line support, as well as listings of mystery magazines and newsletters, an international directory of mystery booksellers and publishers, and factual links about crime, forensics, and investigation.

CRIMEWRITING.COM

www.hollywoodnetwork.com:80/Crime/

Crimewriting.com offers advice from experts, a homicide desk with two detectives and homicide investigators, a forum to post a description of manuscripts, books and book proposals, and a crime writer's consultants center. Individual rooms hosted by crime-related professionals offer an insider's view of the crime world, including information on narcotics, crime labs, criminology, cults, gangs, terrorism, and robbery. The site also offers a glossary of crime terms and slang related to street gangs, drugs, and other topics.

A GUIDE TO CLASSIC MYSTERY AND DETECTION

http://members.aol.com/wg4273/classics.htm

A Guide to Classic Mystery and Detection is "an educational site containing reading lists and essays on great mysteries, mainly of the pre-1960 era." Topics of the Web site include a brief history of classic mystery fiction and long-term trends in mystery fiction. It also includes information about such authors as Edgar Allen Poe, Nathaniel Hawthorne, Herman Melville, Agatha Christie, and S. S. Van Dine. The site is divided into important time periods in mystery fiction: the nineteenth century, the turn of the century, the Golden Age, and the Van Dine school.

MYSTERYNET.COM

http://discuss.MysteryNet.com

MysteryNet.com is "a place for aspiring and published writers to discuss the ins and outs of writing a mystery . . . exchange advice, get helpful hints and post any information that you have on how to write a whodunit." The site includes discussions categorized by topics such as elements of a mystery, general information on getting published, and research. It offers a contest and includes Internet links.

MYSTERY AND DETECTIVE FICTION SITES

http://umbc7.umbc.edu/~lharris/mystsite.htm

The Mystery and Detective Fiction Sites page offers listing of resources from Animals in Mysteries to True Crime. Others focus areas of the site include authors' interviews and articles, characters, chat lines, conventions, discussion groups, newsletters, e-zines, mailing lists, on-line mysteries, publishers, reviews, and bookstores.

MYSTERY ON-LINE

www.webinspect.com/mystery.htm

Mystery On-Line is a work-in-progress site of a mystery novel on the Web. Amateur and published writers may submit chapters for the Mystery On-Line continuing story. Each month a new chapter is selected and published on the site from the submissions. The site also includes mystery writing links, book reviews, and a link to on-line bookstore.

MYSTERY WRITERS OF AMERICA

www.mysterynet.com/mwa/

Mystery Writers of America "helps to negotiate contracts, watches developments in legislation and tax law, sponsors symposia and mystery conferences, and publishes books." The site includes mystery links, awards, a calendar of events, writers discussions, and a new on-line mystery every day. It was established to promote and protect "the interests and welfare of mystery writers and to increase the esteem and the literary recognition given to the genre."

THE MYSTERY WRITERS' FORUM

www.zott.com/mysforum/default.html

The Mystery Writers' Forum consists of "mystery writers and aspiring mystery authors who are sharing our trials, tribulations, and research problems and triumphs on a supportive, threaded bulletin board system." The site includes a bookstore, Internet links, and cyber-crime references.

THE MYSTERIOUS HOME PAGE

www.webfic.com/mysthome/mysthome.html

The Mysterious Home Page is "a guide to mysteries and crime fiction on the Internet." The site offers newsgroups, mailing lists, information on conferences and conventions, publishers, book dealers, interactive fiction, reviews, and electronic mysteries.

SISTERS IN CRIME

www.books.com/sinc/home.htm

Sisters in Crime is a Web site devoted to "combat discrimination against women in the mystery field, educate publishers and the general public as to inequities in the treatment of female authors, raise awareness of their contribution to the field, and promote the professional advancement of women who write mysteries." The site includes information about local chapters of Sisters in Crime, offers mystery links and on-line bookstores.

SHORT MYSTERY FICTION SOCIETY

www.thewordjammer.com/smfs/

The Short Mystery Fiction Society "seeks to actively recognize writers and readers who promote and support the creative art form of short mysteries in the press, in other mystery organizations, and through awards." The site offers a newsletter and other resources.

SCIENCE FICTION RESOURCES

SFNOVELIST

www.sfnovelist.com/index.html

SFNovelist is "an on-line writing group dedicated to novelists who write 'hard science' SF." It is a highly structured and organized system of the exchange of science fiction manuscripts for consideration by other writers. Its goals are to:

- "become in the marketplace a premier source of novelists who write 'believable/hard science' SF"
- garner the attention of SF publishers, SFWA, and other writers' organizations for SF novelists
- develop a cadre of strong novelists, most of whom become published. (Behind every great writer is usually a group of fellow writers who are equally serious about their writing.)
- establish a presence at major SF writer conferences and conventions
- provide services and information to members that will help them in their search for self-improvement and in getting published, including contacts with other known writers and publishers and sources of distribution and marketing.

SCIENCE FICTION AND FANTASY WORKSHOP

www.sff.net/people/dalton~woodbury/sffw.htp

The Science Fiction and Fantasy Workshop was established "to provide workshop experience through the mail, and to put writers in contact with others in the same situation." The site offers a newsletter that includes articles on topics such as worldbuilding, laws of magic, alien creation, working with editors, and a market column.

SPECULATIVE VISION

http://speculativevision.com

Speculative Vision is a site that offers selections of original science fiction, a music conservatory with TV and movie MIDI files, a discussion board, and Internet links. The Resource Network section contains information about publishers, Web-zines, general science fiction resources, and TV and film news.

ROMANCE RESOURCES

BOOKPAGE

www.bookpage.com

This site provides reviews for current books as well as links to bookstores, libraries, and publishers. The site includes interviews with authors and a special link to Club Oprah's latest pick.

BYRON ROMANCE PORT

www.geocities.com/Athens/8774/index.htm

The Byron Romance Port is a site that is "designed to be a friendly port on the romance reader's voyage around the Internet." It includes a section that discusses what a romance novel is, romance industry fast facts, and thoughts on romance reading. It also includes new romance releases and bestsellers, as well as links to discussion boards, chat rooms, listservs, and newsgroups. Every day the site offers a new romantic idea and love quote.

FROM THE HEART

www.avonbooks.com/avon/romance.html

Sponsored by Avon Books, From the Heart is a site that offers tips for getting a romance idea published as well as a "today in romantic history" section. The site also offers a newsletter and contests.

HEARTREALM ROMANTIC FICTION WEB SITE

http://heartrealm.com/

HeartRealm was created "for the purpose of creating a romance community on the Web, a place where readers, writers, authors, editors, agents, publishers, booksellers, and all enthusiasts and professionals of the romance fiction industry could convene in comfort." The site includes information on publishers and agents, writing critiques, industry data, and resources for research. It also offers e-mail lists and discussion boards.

ROMANCE COMMUNICATIONS

www.romcom.com/

Romance Communications is "devoted to everyone who reads or whose business is the romance genre." The site includes book reviews, articles, author interviews, original stories, contests, advice from experts, interactive games, Internet links, and more.

ROMANCE WRITERS OF AMERICA

www.rwanational.com/OrganizationInfo.htm

The Romance Writers of America's mission statement is to:

- promote excellence in romance fiction
- help writers become published and establish careers in their writing field
- provide continuing support for writers within the romance publishing industry
- promote mutual support among members
- promote and advocate an "author friendly" environment in the publishing industry
- be a strong voice within the romance publishing, wholesaling, and retailing industries
- strive to maintain and increase the market share of romance fiction.

They provide members with a forum to interact with publishing representatives, author advocacy and arbitration, and monthly newsletters. Links on the site include articles about industry news, lists of upcoming releases, and a searchable Romance Novel database.

ROMANTIC TIMES

www.romantictimes.com/g_writer/body.html

The Romantic Times Web site offers expert advice, research topics and Q&A, and how-to resources for romance writing. The site also offers agent listings, publishers, manuscript evaluation services, and promotional opportunities.

ST. ROSE PRESS

http://members.aol.com/silkwisper/Page1.htm

The St. Rose Press Web site was founded to "break in unpublished writers into the publishing industry and give encouragement, faith, and insight to fellow writers." It accomplishes this through "communication, recommendation and referral with major literary editors and publishers who are familiar with the romance genre."

WORD MUSEUM ROMANCE

www.wordmuseum.com/romance.htm

The romance area of Word Museum offers contests, interviews, conferences, reviews, and articles. The spotlight area features a new romance author periodically. The site also offers information on writing markets, manuals, and is searchable.

POETRY RESOURCES

ATLANTIC UNBOUND POETRY PAGES

www.theatlantic.com/atlantic/atlweb/poetry/poetpage.htm

The Atlantic Unbound Poetry Pages are brought by the *Atlantic Monthly*, a literary magazine. The Web site offers reviews of new poetry, a discussion forum, and the

Audible Anthology, which is a collection of poetry sound files, poetry articles, links, and poetry from the *Atlantic Monthly* e-zine. It is a searchable site and offers poetry and literature links.

INKSPOT RESOURCES FOR POETS

www.inkspot.com/genres/poetry.html

Inkspot Resources for Poets offers many Internet poetry links; a poets' chat forum; contests; general resources such as a glossary of poetic terms, mailing lists, courses available, critique groups, and workshops for poets; and articles and essays on writing poetry.

THE INTERNATIONAL LIBRARY OF POETRY

www.poetry.com/nlp/nlp.stm

The International Library of Poetry Web site offers information about its writing competitions, which focus on "awarding large prizes to poets who have never before won any type of writing competition." The site also includes Internet links, a list of past winners, anthologies of winning poems, and chat rooms.

NATIONAL POETRY ASSOCIATION

www.nationalpoetry.org/

The National Poetry Association Web site, supported in part by Grants for the Arts and Maya Angelou, offers an on-line poetry journal called *Poetry USA*, and aims to "promote poets and poetry to wider audiences by all possible means, serving both the literary community and the general public." The site is dedicated to the memory of William Burroughs, Allen Ginsberg, Denise Levertov, and Jack Micheline. It includes information about the National Poetry Association's current projects and offers contests for poets.

PERIHELION ROUND TABLE DISCUSSIONS

www.webdelsol.com/Perihelion/p-discussion3.htm

The Perihelion Round Table Discussions site brings the thoughts of established poets and editors on issues of the Internet and its effect on poetry and the writing of poetry. The site includes a discussion area where readers and visitors may add their insight to the discussions.

POETRY FROM THE MINING CO.

http://poetry.miningco.com/

Poetry from the Mining Co. offers links to such poetry resources as on-line contests and workshops, zines and anthologies, poets from the classical period to the twentieth century, multilingual and poetry translations, festivals and live poetry events, audio poetry archives, publishers, and on-line catalogs. The site offers a poetry newsletter, bulletin board, chat, bookstore, and "gossip on the poetry word circuit." It also includes "an alphabetical listing and links to lit e-zines, anthologies, and the on-line sites of print poetry magazines."

POETRY SOCIETY OF AMERICA

www.poetrysociety.org/

The Poetry Society of America Web site includes information about the newest developments in the Poetry in Motion project, which posts poetry to seven million subway and bus riders in New York City, Chicago, Baltimore, Portland, and Boston. It also includes news about poetry awards, seminars, the tributes in libraries program, poetry in public program, and poetry festivals.

POETRY WORLD: INTERNET CENTER FOR POETS

www.poetryworld.com

Poetry World "is a combination of things: a museum; a library; a book and software store; and a poetry magazine" devoted to "poetry and related information, including software tools for poetry writing and for an enriched enjoyment of poetry for novices, poets of moderate experience, and poetry experts." The site offers a "corrective for people who think they don't like poetry." The site includes contests, sites for kids, a multimedia poetry section, and software information.

POETS & WRITERS

www.pw.org/

Poets & Writers is an on-line resource for creative writers that includes publishing advice, message forums, contests, a directory of writers, literary links, information on grants and awards, news from the writing world, trivia, and workshops.

SCREENWRITING RESOURCES

HOLLYWOOD SCRIPTWRITER

www.hollywoodscriptwriter.com/about/tr.html

Hollywood Scriptwriter is an international newsletter that offers articles on craft and business "to give screenwriters the information they need to work at their careers." The site includes low-budget and indie (independent) markets available for finished screenplays as well as a listing of agencies who are currently accepting submissions from readers of Hollywood Scriptwriter. According to Hollywood Scriptwriter, "people like Harold Ramis, Francis Ford Coppola and Larry Gelbart have generously given of their time, knowledge and experiences to share with HS's readers."

SCREAMING IN THE CELLULOID JUNGLE

http://38.201.147.161/index.html

Screaming in the Celluloid Jungle is a screenwriting site that offers message boards, script sales archives, industry news, box-office statistics, and a writer's forum. Other topics include agents, production companies, a glossary of screenwriting and production terms, articles, producing and directing.

THE SCREENWRITER'S HOME PAGE

http://home.earthlink.net/~scribbler/

The Screenwriter's Home Page offers "articles and interviews by people who work, day in and day out, in the movie business." Its aim is to help "not only with writing, but with the reality of the entertainment world." It includes agent listings, best ways to have your script rejected, professionals' thoughts on screenwriting, and industry news.

SCREENWRITER'S RESOURCE CENTER

www.screenwriting.com

The Screenwriter's Resource Center aims to "provide links to products and services for screenwriters, compiled by the staff at the National Creative Registry™." It includes links to many screenwriting sites, and offers advice and copyright words of warning for writers posting original work on the Internet.

Screenwriter's Utopia

www.screenwritersutopia.com/

Screenwriter's Utopia includes "helpful hints for getting screenplays produced, script development services and contest information." The site includes a screenwriters' work-station, toolkit, agent listings, and creative screenwriting magazines. Interviews with the screenwriters of *Sleepless in Seattle, Blade,* and *The Crow: City of Angels* are featured, and other interviews are archived. The site also includes chat rooms, message boards, a writer's directory, and a free newsletter.

Screenwriters & Playwrights Home Page

www.teleport.com/~cdeemer/scrwriter.html

The Screenwriters & Playwrights Home Page "is designed to meet the special needs of screenwriters and playwrights." Features of the site include screenwriting basics, marketing tips, screenplay formats, agent listings, pitches and query letters, producer listings, writing for actors, and tips from pros. It also offers a free newsletter and Internet resources.

Horror Resources

Classic Horror and Fantasy Page

http://home6.swipnet.se/~w-60478/

The Classic Horror and Fantasy Page aims to "collect links to every work of classic horror and fantasy fiction available on the Internet. The main purpose of this page is not to display the works themselves, but rather to direct the reader to other sites where the works are housed." Some of the authors and works that the site includes are Sir Richard Burton, *The Arabian Nights*, 1850 (translation); Johann Wolfgang von Goethe, *Faust*, 1808; and Edgar Allan Poe, *Collected Works*.

Dark Echo Horror

www.darkecho.com/darkecho/index.html

Dark Echo Horror features interviews, reviews, a writers workshop, dark links, and a newsletter. Articles relate to topics such as the perception and psychology of the horror writer, the "best" horror, and reviews of dark erotica. The site also offers information and links to fantasy writing.

Horror Writers Association

www.horror.org/

The HORROR WRITERS ASSOCIATION (HWA) was formed to "bring writers and others with a professional interest in horror together, and to foster a greater appreciation of dark fiction in general." Bestower of the Bram Stoker Awards, HWA offers a newsletter, late-breaking market news, informational e-mail bulletins, writers' groups, agents FAQ, and links.

HorrorNet

www.horrornet.com/

HorrorNet was created "purely as a way of giving horror fiction a well-needed boost of exposure. My goal here is to provide the most comprehensive Web site for lovers of horror and suspense fiction." The site includes new book releases, events, message boards, chats, links, articles, interviews, book reviews, and original fiction.

Masters of Terror

http://members.aol.com/andyfair/mot.html

Masters of Terror offers information about horror fiction, book reviews, new authors, horror movies author message boards, HorrorNet chat room, and a reference guide and critique of horror fiction that features some 500 authors and 2,500 novels. The site also includes exclusive author interviews, book and chapbook reviews, and horror news.

GENERAL

CHILDREN'S WRITING RESOURCE CENTER

www.write4kids.com/

"Whether you're published, a beginner, or just someone who's always dreamt of writing for kids," here you'll find a free library of how-to information, opportunities to chat with other children's writers and illustrators, links to research databases, articles, tips for beginners, secrets for success as a children's writer, message boards, a children's writing survey, and the opportunity to ask questions of known authors and to register in the site's guestbook to receive free e-mail updates filled with news and tips. The site also features a listing of favorite books, Newbery Medal Winners, Caldecott Award Winners, current bestsellers, and a link to their own children's bookshop.

THE ECLECTIC WRITER

www.eclectics.com/writing/writing.html

This site is an information source for those interested in crime, romance, horror, children's, technical, screen, science fiction, fantasy, mystery, and poetry writing. It features articles, a fiction writers' character chart, resources by genre, reference materials, research, general writing resources, on-line magazines and journals, writing scams, awards, and a writing-related fun page.

THE INKWELL WRITERS CONNECTION

http://home.earthlink.net/~natura/

"The Inkwell is a place for writers to connect. This site has private writers workshops, a survey form, guestbook, on-line magazine, on-line newsletter, and a link to the Inkwell Message Boards." The site also features links for Inkwell "NewEra Novels," games, a message forum, a workshop inquiry form, writers' private critique groups, a workshop hostess page, and background music.

MIDWEST BOOK REVIEW

www.execpc.com/~mbr/bookwatch/mbr/pubinfo.html

Responsible for "Bookwatch," which offers a weekly television program that reviews books, videos, music, CD-ROMS, and computer software, as well as five monthly newsletters for community and academic library systems, and much more. This site features reviews from the Midwest Book Review, which was founded in 1980.

PAINTED ROCK

www.paintedrock.com/memvis/memvis1.htm

"Painted Rock provides services to non-published writers, published writers, and readers." Free features on the site include information on a free 12-week Artist's Way program, message boards, goal writing groups, writing topics, a book discussion group, a research listserv, and *The Rock,* an on-line magazine. In addition to their free services, the site offers paid on-line writing classes, a subscription-based newsletter, and two bookstores, as well as advertising, promotion for authors, and Web-site hosting and design.

THE PURPLE CRAYON

www.users.interport.net/~hdu/

At this site, you'll find articles, mostly for writers and illustrators, and selected links to resources for writers, editors, teachers, librarians, parents, and others.

THE SLUSH PILE

www.theslushpile.com/

Featured as a "Yahoo Pick of the Week," this site "is the place for authors of children's books who don't have agents, who don't have connections, who aren't celebrities and who basically have to claw their way to fame and fortune through the slush pile. That means most everybody." The site features submissions, articles, interviews, Web site links for writers, offline resources, and on-line resources.

THE SOCIETY OF CHILDREN'S BOOK WRITERS AND ILLUSTRATORS

www.scbwi.org/

This Web site "has a dual purpose: It exists as a service to our members as well as offering information about the children's publishing industry and our organization to non-members." It features a listing of events, awards and grants, publications, information for members, information on how to become a member, and a site map.

VICTORY PAGE

www.crayne.com/victory/

For fiction writers, this site has articles on writing resources and how to help you write better, a list of links for and about writing, publishers, agents, and science fiction, a science fiction writing workshop, and an opportunity to subscribe to *Victory's Motivational Newsletter.*

WESTERN WRITERS OF AMERICA, INC.

www.imt.net/~gedison/wwahome.html

"WWA was founded in 1953 to promote the literature of the American West and bestow Spur Awards for distinguished writing in the western field." The site offers information about Old West topics, a listing past of Spur Award winners, and opportunities to learn about WWA and the Spur Award, to apply for membership in WWA, to subscribe to *Roundup Magazine,* or contact western authors whose work interests you.

WRITE PAGE AUTHOR LISTING INFORMATION

www.writepage.com/pageinfo.htm

This site offers authors a chance to create their own Web sites with the help of Callie Goble. It answers many questions Web-site creators might have, such as "How long CAN my page be?" "How long does it take to get listed?" "What sort of exposure will my books get?" "What does the competition charge?"

WRITERS' EXCHANGE

http://writerexchange.miningco.com

Writers' Exchange offers links on various topics from agents to humor, to writers' resources, as well as interviews, information about upcoming writing conferences, writing classes, information about markets, bulletin boards, chat rooms, newsletters, and opportunities to shop in their bookstore, video store, and marketplace.

WRITERSPACE

www.writerspace.com/

"Writerspace specializes in the design and hosting of Web sites for authors. We also provide Web services for those who may already have Web sites but wish to include more interactivity in the way of bulletin boards, chat rooms, contests, and e-mail newsletters." The site also features an author spotlight, contests, workshops, mailing lists, bulletin boards, chat rooms, romance links, a guestbook, and information on topics such as adding your link, Web design, Web hosting, the site's clientele, and rates.

THE WRITERS' PEN

http://members.xoom.com/WritersPen/index.html

The Writers' Pen began with a weekly chat meeting and has evolved into its own chat room. The site features a roster of its members, chat rooms, links to other Web sites, and opportunities to read its newsletter or shop its bookstore.

HOW TOS

THE EDITORIAL EYE

www.eei-alex.com

The Editorial Eye Web site consists of a sampler of articles originally printed in the newsletter by the same name. The articles discuss techniques for writing, editing, design, and typography, as well as information on industry trends and employment. The Eye has been providing information to publications professionals for 18 years.

INKSPOT

www.inkspot.com

Inkspot provides articles, how-to tips, market information, and networking opportunities. Special features include a FAQ for beginners, classifieds, and a section for young writers. Information is sorted by genre.

MISC. WRITING

www.scalar.com/mw

"Misc.writing is a Use Net newsgroup that provides a forum for discussion of writing in all its forms—scholarly, technical, journalistic, and mere day-to-day communication." Web site resources include a writer's bookstore and market information.

SHARPWRITER.COM

www.sharpwriter.com/

SharpWriter.Com is a practical resources page for writers of all types—a "writer's handy virtual desktop." Reference materials include style sheets, dictionaries, quotations, and job information. The "Office Peacemaker" offers to resolve grammar disputes in the workplace.

WRITERS' CLUB

www.writersclub.com

The Writer's Club is a membership-based, electronic service featuring agent and publisher information, discussion forums, and general information for writers of a variety of genres. They strive to provide "services and information to support, educate, and encourage writers in both their professional and personal lives."

MEGASITES

ACQWEB

www.library.vanderbilt.edu/law/acqs.acqs.html

The site is the "gathering place for librarians and other professionals interested in acquisitions and collection development." The site provides a directory of publishers and vendors and "Web News for Acquiring Minds."

@WRITERS: FOR WRITERS ON THE INTERNET

www.geocities.com/Athens/Acropolis/6608

The @writers site includes information about markets, links to a myriad of Internet resources, and reviews of writing-related books. It also provides a technical Q&A section to answer questions about hardware, software, and the Internet. Also available is a chat room and monthly newsletter subscription.

AMERICAN BOOKSELLERS ASSOCIATION

www.bookweb.org

The American Booksellers Association is a trade association representing independent bookstores nationwide. The site links members to recent articles about the industry and features Idea Exchange discussion forums.

AUTHORLINK

www.authorlink.com

This information service for editors, literary agents, and writers boasts more than 165,000 loyal readers per year. Features include a "Manuscript Showcase" that contains 500+ ready-to-publish, evaluated manuscripts.

THE AUTHORS REGISTRY

www.webcom.com/registry/authordir.html

The Authors Registry is an extensive directory of authors with contact addresses, phone numbers, fax numbers, and e-mail addresses. Authors are free to list the contact information of their choice in this searchable database. This site contains instructions for accessing the registry.

AYLAD'S CREATIVE WRITING GROUP

www.publication.com/aylad

This site provides a forum for "people to get their work read and critiqued by fellow writers on a friendly atmosphere." The service is free and all writing forms are welcome. The site includes links to other resources for writers.

CRITIQUE PARTNER CONNECTIONS
http://members.tripod.com/%7EPetalsofLife/cpc.html

Users of Critique Partner Connections pay a one-time fee of $15.00 to be matched with a fellow writer for the purpose of critiquing one another's work. Maintainers of this site strive to match people with similar interests and critique styles.

THE EDITOR'S PEN
www.pathway.net/dwlcey/

The Editor's Pen site exists to connect "sites for and about writers, editors, and indexers." It includes links to lists of freelancers and on-line dictionaries. Other interesting links include an "Edit challenge" and "Quotable words of editorial wisdom."

ENCYCLOPEDIA BRITANNICA
www.eb.com/

This service is subscription based and allows the user to search the *Encyclopedia Britannica.* New users can try a "sample search."

FORWRITERS.COM
www.forwriters.com/

This "megasite" provides numerous links to writing resources of all kinds. It lists conferences, markets, agents, commercial services, and more. The "What's New" feature allows the user to peruse what links have recently been added under the various categories.

INNER CIRCLE
www.geocities.com/SoHo/Lofts/1498

The Fictech Inner Circle was started in April 1997 as "a means for writers—especially new and unpublished writers—to correspond through e-mail with others of similar interest." Membership is free and provides the opportunity to communicate with over 1,500 writers from around the globe.

INTERNATIONAL ONLINE WRITERS ASSOCIATION

www.best.com/~kali/iowa/iowa/section-a1.html

IOWA's purpose is to "offer help and services to writers around the world through shared ideas, workshops, critiques, and professional advice." Services include real-time monthly workshops, real-time weekly critiques, and periodic round robins. The site also includes a library of essays, poems, short stories, and novel chapters.

INTERNET WRITING WORKSHOP

www.geocities.com/~lkaus/workshop/index.html

The Internet Writing Workshop exists to "create an environment where works in progress can be passed around and critiqued, to help us improve these works and to improve as writers," as well as to provide support for writers. The service is membership-based and includes a variety of genres.

LOCAL WRITERS WORKSHOP

http://members.tripod.com~lww_2/introduction.htm –

The Local Writers Workshop is an Internet forum for works in progress, especially those "in the early stages of revision." The creators of this membership-based site pride themselves on its community ethic.

THE NATIONAL WRITERS UNION

www.nwu.org/nwuinf1/htm

The National Writers Union is the trade union for freelance writers of all genres. The Web site provides links to various service of the Union, including grievance resolution, insurance, job information, and databases.

THE NOVEL WORKSHOP

www.ameritech.net/users/novelshop/index.html

The Novel Workshop is an "on-line writer's colony; a place where writers—from novice to professional—gather to critique, advise, and encourage each other." The site provides links to other resources for writers and a list of suggested books.

PEN AMERICAN CENTER

www.pen.org/

PEN is an international "membership organization of prominent literary writers and editors. As a major voice of the literary community, the organization seeks to defend the freedom of expression wherever it may be threatened, and to promote and encourage the recognition and reading of contemporary literature." The site links to information about several PEN-sponsored initiatives, including literary awards.

POETS AND WRITERS

www.pw.org/about.htm

Poets and Writers is a nonprofit organization focusing on the "source of literature, providing support and exposure to writers at all stages in their development." *Poets and Writers On-Line* provides a "user-friendly vehicle for the exchange of ideas." The site also includes "Literary Horizons" promoting the professional development of writers.

REFERENCE SHELF

http://Alabanza.com/kabacoff/Inter-Links/reference.html

The Reference Shelf site provides quick access to words, facts, and figures useful when writing and fact-checking. A special "words" section features dictionaries, acronym finders, and links to computer-jargon

SHAWGUIDES: WRITER'S CONFERENCES

www.shawguides.com/writing

The Shaw Site for Writers Conferences allows the user to search for information about 400 conference and workshops worldwide. An e-mail service can be used to get updates about conferences that meet user criteria for dates, topics, and locations. Other resources include "Quick Tips," links to organizations, and information about residencies and retreats.

A WEB OF ON-LINE DICTIONARIES

www.facstaf.bucknell.edu/rbeard/diction.html

This index of on-line dictionaries includes 165 different languages and gives preference to free resources. A new feature allows the user to translate words from any European language to any other.

WEBSTER DICTIONARY

www.m-w.com/netdict.htm

Like its paper counterpart, this Web-based dictionary provides definition to words and phrases sought by users. For word lovers, features like "Word of the Day" and "Word Game of the Day" are included as well.

WOMEN WHO WRITE

http://memers.aol.com/jfavetti/womenww/www.html

Women Who Write is a "collage of women based all over the United States with a passion for writing." The site provides useful links and a large dose of encouragement to women writers of all experience levels.

THE WELL

www.well.com/

The WELL (Whole Earth Lectronic Link) is an on-line gathering place that its creators call a "literate watering hole for thinkers from all walks of life."

THE WRITE PAGE

www.writepage.com

The Write Page is dedicated to information about genre fiction with an emphasis on authors and new book releases. Writers can find how-to information for genres ranging from romance to techno-thrillers. The on-line newsletter includes publishing tips and information about conferences.

WRITER'S TOOLBOX

www.geocities.com/Athens/6346/body.html

The site contains a "diverse and ever-growing collection of Internet resources for writers." The resources are categorized for many types of writers from technical writers and PR professionals to fiction and drama writers. The site also includes links to software for writers and business resources.

THE WRITERS CENTER

www.writer.org/aboutwc.htm —the writers center

The Writers Center is a Maryland-based nonprofit that "encourages the creation and distribution of contemporary literature." On the Web site, they provide information on their 200+ yearly workshops and links to their publication *Poet Lore* and *Writer's Carousel.*

WRITERS GUILD OF AMERICA WEST

www.wga.org/manual/index.hml

The WGA West site provides information about the Guild and its services such as script registration. Other links to writing resources are provides as well.

WRITERS ON THE NET

www.writers.com

"Writers on the Net is a group of published writers and experienced writing teachers building an on-line community and resource for writers and aspiring writers." A subscription to the mail list provides a description and schedule of classes provided by the site and a monthly newsletter.

WRITERS WRITE[REG]

www.writerswrite.com

This "mega-site" provides a myriad of resources including a searchable database of on-line and print publications in need of submissions. The Writers Write[reg] chat room is open 24 hours for live discussion.

WRITELINKS

www.writelink.com/

The site provides an array of services including workshops, personalized tutoring, and critique groups. "WriteLinks is designed to be of value to all writers, regardless of their experience, genre or focus."

WRITERSNET

www.writers.net/about_body.html

This Web site "helps build relationships between writers, publishers, editors, and literary agents." Currently includes two searchable directories associated with the free service: *The Internet Directory of Published Writers* and *The Internet Directory of Literary Agents.*

UNITED STATES COPYRIGHT OFFICE

http://lcweb.loc.gov/copyright/

The United States Copyright Office site allows the user to find valuable information about copyright procedures and other basics. In addition the user can download publications and forms and link to information about international copyright.

Other Resources

Book Trade Reference Books and Journals

Australia

Books

APA Directory of Members
Australian Publishers Association Ltd.
89 Jones Street, Suite 60
Ultimo
New South Wales 2007
Australia
(61) 2 92819788
fax: (61) 2 92811073
apa@magna.com.au (e-mail)

AUSTRALIAN BOOK REVIEW

National Book Council
Suite 3, 21 Drummond Place
Carlton
Victoria 3053
(61) 3 6638657
fax: (61) 3 6638658

Publishers reviews and articles on Australian books and writing.

AUSTRALIAN BOOKS IN PRINT

D. W. Thorpe
18 Salmon Street
Port Melbourne
Victoria 3207
Australia

Mailing Address:
P.O. Box 146
Port Melbourne
Victoria 3207
Australia
(61) 3 9245 7370
fax: (61) 3 9245 7395

WRITERS AND PHOTOGRAPHERS MARKETING GUIDE

Directory of Australian and New Zealand Literary and Photo Markets
Australian Writers and Professional Service
Scott House
140 Flinders Street
Melbourne
Victoria 3000
Australia
(61) 3 6546211
fax: (61) 3 6509648

Journals

AUSTRALIAN BOOKSELLER AND PUBLISHER

D. W. Thorpe
18 Salmon Street
Port Melbourne
Victoria 3207
Australia

Mailing Address:
P.O. Box 146
Port Melbourne
Victoria 3207
Australia
(61) 3 9245 7370
fax: (61) 3 9245 7395

AUSTRALIAN GOVERNMENT PUBLICATIONS

National Library of Australia
Parkes Place
Publications Section, Culture and Education Services Division
Canberra
Australian Capital Territory 2600
Australia
(61) 6 2621365
fax: (61) 6 2734493

AUSTRALIAN NATIONAL BIBLIOGRAPHY

National Library of Australia
Parkes Place
Canberra
Australian Capital Territory 2600
Australia
(61) 6 2621646
fax: (61) 6 27344933

Published monthly, cumulative triennually, with annual cumulations, microfiche.

AUSTRALIAN SOCIETY OF INDEXERS NEWSLETTERS

Australian Society of Indexers
P.O. Box R598
Royal Exchange
New South Wales 1225
Australia
(61) 3 9571 6341 (voice and fax)
mindexer@interconnect.com.au (e-mail)

Monthly (excluding January and December). Also available by e-mail. Some discounts available.

BIBLIONEWS AND AUSTRALIAN NOTES AND QUERIES

Book Collectors Society of Australia
16 Edwin Street (South)
Croydon
New South Wales 2132
Australia
(61) 2 7988984 (voice and fax)
jeff@bespl.com.au (e-mail)

Issued quarterly to members.

GUIDE TO NEW AUSTRALIAN BOOKS

D. W. Thorpe
18 Salmon Street
Port Melbourne
Victoria 3207
Australia

Mailing Address:
P.O. Box 146
Port Melbourne
Victoria 3207
Australia
(61) 3 9245 7370
fax: (61) 3 92457395

THE PRINT PRODUCTION DIRECTORY
Reed Business Publishing
Level 12, North Tower
Chatswood Plaza
New South Wales 2057
Australia
(61) 2 9372 5222
fax: (61) 2 9412 3572

Production specifications for newspapers and magazines.

VICTORIAN GOVERNMENT PUBLICATIONS (VGP)
State Library of Victoria
328 Swanston Street
Melbourne
Victoria 3000
Australia
(61) 3 9669 9920
fax: (61) 3 96691480
dianneb@slv.vic.gov.au (e-mail)

Published monthly.

WEEKLY BOOK NEWSLETTER
D. W. Thorpe
18 Salmon Street
Port Melbourne
Victoria 3207
Australia

Mailing Address:
P.O. Box 235
Port Melbourne
Victoria 3207
Australia
(61) 3 9245 7370
fax: (61) 3 9245 7395

AUSTRALIAN BOOK REVIEW

www.vicnet.net.au/~abr/Welcome.html

Published by the National Book Council, the Australian Book Review Web site; includes an index, recent issues, and subscription information. Issues include cultural studies, essays, a music section, biography, history, Chinese studies, politics, fiction, poetry, and young fiction.

CHILDREN'S BOOK COUNCIL

www.slsa.sa.gov.au/cbca/index.html

According to the Children's Book Council, its main objective is the encouragement of children's reading, which they attempt to achieve through several methods: sponsoring The Children's Book of the Year Awards; providing information on and encouragement to authors and illustrators; organizing exhibitions and activities during Children's Book Week; supporting children's library services; and promoting high standards in book reviewing. The Council distributes a quarterly journal, *Reading Time*, to review all books for children and young people published in Australia, as well as overseas books of quality, particularly New Zealand titles.

VICTORIAN GOVERNMENT PUBLICATIONS

www.slv.vic.gov.au/slv/govpub/

The State Library of Victoria publishes Victorian Government Publications (VGP), a database listing Victorian government publications held by the State Library. The site is organized by jurisdiction—Victoria, Australia, Australian Capital Territory, New South Wales, Northern Territory, Queensland, South Australia, Western Australia, Tasmania, Canada, and Great Britain. It offers a glossary of government terms.

Canada

BOOKS FOR EVERYDAY

70 The Esplanade, Suite 210
Toronto
Ontario M5E 1R2
Canada
(416) 360-0044
fax: (416) 941-9038

CANADIAN BOOK INDUSTRY STANDARDS ADVISORY COMMITTEE

c/o Ten Wynford Heights Crescent, Suite 165
Son Mills
Ontario M3C 1K8
Canada
(416) 447-4005
fax: (416) 447-1591

CANADIAN BOOK MANUFACTURERS' ASSOCIATION

75 Albert Street, Suite 906
Ottawa
Ontario K1P 5E7
Canada
(613) 236-7208
fax: (613) 236-8169

Mailing Address:
5805 Whittle Road, Suite 210
Mississauga
Ontario L4Z 2J1
Canada

CANADIAN BOOKSELLERS ASSOCIATION

301 Donlands Avenue
Toronto
Ontario M4J 3R8
Canada
(416) 467-7883
fax: (416) 467-7886

THE CANADIAN CATALOGUING IN PUBLICATION PROGRAM—ACQUISITION AND BIBLIOGRAPHIC SERVICES BRANCH

National Library of Canada
395 Wellingtonn Street
Ottawa
Ontario K1A 0N4
Canada
(819) 994-6881
fax: (819) 997-7571
cip@nlc_bnc.ca (e-mail)

CANADIAN CENTRE FOR STUDIES IN PUBLISHING

Simon Fraser University at Harbour Centre
515 W. Hastings Street
Vancouver
British Columbia V6B 5K3
(604) 291-5074
fax: (604) 291-5098
ann.cowan@sfu.ca (e-mail)

THE CANADIAN CHILDREN'S BOOK CENTRE

35 Spadina Road
Toronto
Ontario M5R 2S9
Canada
(416) 975-0010
fax: (416) 975-1839
ccbc@1global.com (e-mail)

CANADIAN COPYRIGHT INSTITUTE

35 Spadina Road
Toronto
Ontario M5R 2S9
Canada
(416) 975-1756
fax: (416) 975-1839

CANADIAN ISBN AGENCY

Acquisition and Bibliographic Services Branch, National Library of Canada
395 Wellingtonn Street
Ottawa
Ontario K1A 0N4
Canada
(819) 994-6872
fax: (819) 997-7517
telex: 0534311

CANADIAN MAGAZINE PUBLISHERS ASSOCIATION

130 Spadna Avenue, Suite 202
Toronto
Ontario M5V 2L4
Canada
(416) 504-0274
fax: (416) 504-0437
cindyg@cmpa.ca (e-mail)

CANADIAN POETRY ASSOCIATION

P.O. Box 340, Sta B
London
Ontario N5A 4W1
Canada
(519) 433-8994
fax: (519) 432-6299
resource.center@onlinesys.com (e-mail)

CANADIAN PRINTING INDUSTRIES ASSOCIATION

75 Albert Street, Suite 906
Ottawa
Ontario K1P 5E7
Canada
(613) 236-4208
fax: (613) 236-8169

CANADIAN PUBLISHERS' COUNCIL

250 Merton Street, Suite 203
Toronto
Ontario M4S 1B1
Canada
(416) 322-7011
fax: (416) 322-6999

CCAB INC.

188 Eglinton Avenue E, Suite 304
Toronto
Ontario M4P 2X7
Canada
(416) 487-2418
fax: (416) 487-6405

CHRISTIAN BOOKSELLERS ASSOCIATION, CANADA

679 Southgate Drive
Guelph
Ontario NIG 4S2
Canada
(519) 766-1683
fax: (519) 763-8184

CRIME WRITERS OF CANADA

Box 113, 3007 Kingston Road
Scarborough
Ontario M1M 1P1
Canada
(416) 782-3116
ujan@cenvme.cencol.on.ca (e-mail)

EDITORS ASSOCIATION OF CANADA

35 Spadina Road
Toronto
Ontario M5R 2S9
Canada
(416) 975-1379
fax: (416) 975-1839

THE FEDERATION OF BRITISH COLUMBIAN WRITERS

Box 2206, Main P.O.
Vancouver
British Columbia V6B 3W2
Canada
(604) 683-2057
fax: (604) 683-8269
fedbcwrt@pinc.com (e-mail)

THE LITERARY PRESS GROUP OF CANADA

2 Goucester Street, Suite 301
Toronto
Ontario M4Y 1L5
Canada
(416) 413-4929
fax: (416) 413-4920
craig&udslaudrum@canbook.org (e-mail)

NATIONAL PRESS CLUB OF CANADA

150 Wellington Street
Ottawa
Ontario K1P 5A4
Canada
(613) 233-5641
fax: (613) 233-3511

ONTARIO TRADE SHOWS LTD.

1606 Sedlescomb Drive, Unit 8
Mississauga
Ontario L4X 1M6
Canada
(905) 625-7070
fax: (905) 625-4856
Print Ontario, Automotive Bldg., CNE Grounds
Toronto
Ontario
Canada

ORGANIZATION OF BOOK PUBLISHERS OF ONTARIO

720 Bathurst Street, Suite 301
Toronto
Ontario M5S 2R4
Canada
(416) 536-7584
fax: (416) 536-7692

England

Books

BOOKDEALERS IN INDIA AND THE ORIENT

Richard Joseph Publishers Ltd.
Unit 2 Monks Walk
Farnham
Surrey GU98HT
England
(44) 1252 734347
fax: (44) 1252 734307
rgoe01@aol.com (e-mail)

A directory of antiquarian booksellers in India and Oriental countries.

BPIF LIST OF MEMBERS

British Printing Industries Federation
11 Bedford Row
London WCIR 4DX
England
(44) 171 2426904
fax: (44) 171 4057784

Directory of information on the BPIF and the printing industry.

THE BRITISH LIBRARY GENERAL CATALOGUE OF PRINTED BOOKS

Bowker-Saur Ltd.
Maypole House, Maypole Road
East Grinstead
West Sussex RH19 1HU
England
(44) 1342 330100
fax: (44) 01342 330198/330192
custserv@bowker-saur.co.uk (e-mail)

BRITISH WORDS ON CASSETTE

Bowker-Saur Ltd.
Maypole House, Maypole Road
East Grinstead
West Sussex RH19 1HU
England
(44) 1342 330100
fax: (44) 1342 330198/330192
custserv@bowker-saur.co.uk (e-mail)

A directory of spoken word cassettes available in the UK.

CAROUSEL—THE GUIDE TO CHILDREN'S BOOKS

Jenny Blanch
7 Carrs Lane
Birmingham B4 7TG
England
(44) 121 643 6411
fax: (44) 121 643 3152

Published triennially.

Cassel and The Publishers Association Directory of Publishing in Great Britain, the Commonwealth, Ireland, Pakistan and South Africa

Cassel PLC

See entry under International Bibliography, Books.

China: A Survey of the Book Market

British Council, Publishing Promotion Unit
Medlock Street
Manchester M15 4AA
England
(44) 161 9577182
fax: (44) 161 9577168
100702.32@compuserve.com (e-mail)

A guide to the directories published in the UK and Ireland.

Directory of Members

Booksellers Association of Great Britain and Ireland
Minister House, 272 Vauxhall Bridge Road
London SW1V 1BA
England
(44) 171 834-5477/834-8812 (voice and fax)
100437.2261@compuserve.com (e-mail)

Available: 1996–97 edition. New edition due in August 1999.

Directory of UK and Irish Book Publishers

Includes distributors, sales agents, and wholesalers.

Booksellers Association of Great Britain and Ireland
Minister House, 272 Vauxhall Bridge Road
London SW1V 1BA
England
(44) 171 834-5477
fax: (44) 171 834-8812
100437.2261@compuserve.com (e-mail)

Full details on over 2,500 UK and Irish publishers and their distributors. Includes over 8,000 imprint references. Available: 1997 edition, L45 plus L5 overseas delivery.

DIRECTORY OF WRITERS' CIRCLES, 8TH EDITION

Jill Dick
Oldacre, Horderns Park Road
Chapel-en-le Frith
High Peak SK23 9SY
England
(44) 1298 812305

jillie@cix.compulink.co.uk (e-mail)

GUIDE TO LITERARY PRIZES

Book Trust
Book House, 45 East Hill
Wandsworth
London SW18 2QZ
England
(44) 181 8709055
fax: (44) 181 8744790

Looking for an Author? A Directory of Authors, Illustrators and Poets Who Participate in Book Events

Young Book Trust
Book House, 45 East Hill
Wandsworth
London SW18 2QZ
England
(44) 181 8709055
fax: (44) 181 8744790

A guide to authors and illustrators who are willing to visit schools or participate in book events; compiled by Young Book Trust.

100 Best Books

Young Book Trust
Book House, 45 East Hill
Wandsworth
London SW18 2QZ
England
(44) 181 8709055
fax: (44) 181 8744790

Young Book Trust's selection of paperbacks for children 12 and under.

OP Title Listing—On Microfiche

J. Whitaker and Sons Ltd.
12 Dyoff Street
London WC1A IDF
England
(44) 171 4206000
fax: (44) 171 8362909

Listing of 900,000 out-of-print titles.

OUTLETS FOR SPECIALISTS NEW BOOKS IN THE UK: A SUBJECT-CLASSIFIED, DESCRIPTIVE DIRECTORY

Peter Marcan Publications
P.O. Box 3158
London SE1 4RA
England
(44) 171 3570368

Entries on some 800 businesses of many kinds (including museums/art gallery shops, periodicals, and associations, as well as related directories).

PRINTING TRADES DIRECTORY

Benn Business Information Services Ltd.
Riverbank House, Angel Lane
Tonbridge
Kent TN9 1SE
England
(44) 1732 362666
fax: (44) 1732 767301

RELIGIOUS BOOKS IN PRINT

J. Whitaker and Sons Ltd.
12 Dyott Street
London WC1A 1DF
England
(44) 171 4206000
fax: (44) 171 8362909

Lists over 28,000 titles plus a directory of 1,400 publishers and distributors.

SHEPPARD'S BOOK DEALERS IN THE BRITISH ISLES

Richard Joseph Publishers Ltd.
Unit 2, Monks Walk
Farnham
Surrey GU9 8HT
England
(44) 1252 734347
fax: (44) 1252 734307
rjoe01@aol.com (e-mail)

Directory of antiquarian and secondhand book dealers.

UK BOOK PRINTERS 1995

Book Production Section BPIF
British Printing Industries Federation
11 Bedford Row
London WC1R 4DX
England
(44) 171 2426904
fax: (44) 171 4057784

Published biannually.

UK BOOK PRINTERS 1997

Book Production Section BPIF
British Printing Industries Federation
11 Bedford Row
London WC1R 4DX
England
(44) 171 2426904
fax: (44) 171 4057784

Yearbook.

WALFORD'S GUIDE TO REFERENCE MATERIAL

Library Association Publishing
7 Ridgmount Street
London WC1E 7AE
England
(44) 171 6367543
fax: (44) 171 6363627
lapublishing@la-hq.org.uk (e-mail)

Available: 7th edition in 3 volumes; published yearly.

WHITAKER'S ALMANAC

J. Whitaker and Sons Ltd.
12 Dyott Street
London WC1A 1 DF
England
(44) 171 4206000
fax: (44) 171 8362909

General reference book, including information on British government.

WHITAKER'S DIRECTORY OF PUBLISHERS

J. Whitaker and Sons Ltd.
12 Dyott Street
London WC1A 1 DF
England
(44) 171 4206000
fax: (44) 171 8362909

Lists over 8,000 of the most active publishers in the UK.

Journals

THE AUTHOR

Society of Authors
84 Drayton Gardens
London SW10 9SB
England
(44) 171 3736642
fax: (44) 171 3735768

BOOK AND MAGAZINE COLLECTOR

Diamond Publishing Group Ltd.
43–45 Street
Mary's Road, Ealing
London W5 5RQ
England
(44) 181 5791082
fax: (44) 181 5662024

BOOKBANK

J. Whitaker and Sons Ltd.
12 Dyott Street
London WC1A 1 DF
England
(44) 171 4206000
fax: (44) 171 8362909

CD-ROM listing (in ISBN sequence) of over 700,000 books in print form, as well as over 26,000 publishers/distributors in the UK and Western Europe. Covers in-print, recently out-of–print, and forthcoming titles.

BOOKBANK OP

J. Whitaker and Sons Ltd.
12 Dyott Street
London WC1A 1 DF
England
(44) 171 4206000
fax: (44) 171 8362909

CD-ROM containing details of over 800,000 out-of-print titles; updated annually.

BOOKBANK WITH SABIP

J. Whitaker and Sons Ltd.
12 Dyott Street
London WC1A 1 DF
England
(44) 171 4206000
fax: (44) 171 8362909

A monthly service combining the *BookBank* database with the Southern African Books in Print listing of over 30,000 titles from 800 publishers.

BOOKBANK WITH THORPE-ROM

J. Whitaker and Sons Ltd.
12 Dyott Street
London WC1A 1 DF
England
(44) 171 4206000
fax: (44) 171 8362909

CD-ROM containing all the information listed on *BookBank* with the addition of full bibliographic details for English-language books published in Australia, New Zealand, and the Pacific Islands.

BOOKS FOR KEEPS

School Bookshop Association
6 Brightfield Road
London SE12 8QF
England
(44) 181 8524953
fax: (44) 181 3187580

Reviews of children's books.

BOOKS IN THE MEDIA

Bookwatch Ltd.
15–Up, East Street, Lewin's Yard
Chesham
Bucks HP5 1AQ
England
(44) 1494 792269
fax: (44) 1494 784850
100675.1643@compuserve.com (e-mail)

Founded in 1979, Books in the Media contains weekly listings of all National Daily and Sunday Press Reviews, TV and radio program tie-ins, serializations, best seller lists, and some trade news and comment, Inc. sales index; published Saturdays.

THE BOOKSELLER

J. Whitaker and Sons Ltd.
12 Dyott Street
London WC1A 1 DF
England
(44) 171 4206000
fax: (44) 171 4206102 (advertising)/4206103 (editorial)/8362909 (subscriptions)
information@bookseller.co.uk (e-mail)

Weekly book trade newspaper.

BOOKSELLING

Booksellers Association of Great Britain and Ireland
Minister House, 272 Vauxhall Bridge Road
London SW1V 1BA
England
(44) 171 8345477
fax: (44) 171 834 8812
100437.2261@compuserve.com (e-mail)

BRITISH HUMANITIES INDEX

Bwoker-Saur Ltd.
Maypole House, Maypole Road
East Grinstead
West Sussex RH19 IHU
England
(44) 1342 330100
fax: (44) 1342 330198/330192
custserv@bowker-saur.co.uk (e-mail)

Quarterly index of humanities-related articles published by British newspapers and journals.

BRITISH NATIONAL BIBLIOGRAPHY

British Library National Bibliographic Service
Boston Spa
Wetherby
West Yorks LS23 7BQ
England
(44) 1937 546613
fax: (44) 1937 546586
nbs-info@bl.uk (e-mail)

Weekly publication with two interim cumulations for January–April and May–August and an annual volume.

BRITISH PRINTER

Miller Freeman
Sovereign Way
Tonbridge
Kent TN9 1RW
England
(44) 1732 364422
fax: (44) 1732 361534

CHAPTER ONE

Alliance of Literary Societies
Clatterwick Hall, Little Leigh
Northwich
Cheshire CW8 4RJ
England
(44) 1606 891303

Published annually each April.

GLOBAL BOOKBANK

J. Whitaker and Sons Ltd.
12 Dyott Street
London WC1A 1DF
England
(44) 171 4206000
fax: (44) 171 8362909

CD-ROM containing the combined Whitaker, Bowker, and D. W. Thorpe in-print and forthcoming databases from the most comprehensive listing available of English language books, maps, and associated products. There are two services: premium-2 disks for comprehensive searching and Finder-1 disk for fast searching and ordering.

The Good Book Guide

The Good Book Guide
24 Seward Street
London EC1V 3PB
England
(44) 171 490990
fax: (44) 171 4909909
enquiries@good-book-guide.co.uk (e-mail)

Monthly book review magazine, subscription only.

ISBN Listing—On Microfiche

J. Whitaker and Sons Ltd.
12 Dyott Street
London WC1A 1DF
England
(44) 171 4206000
fax: (44) 171 8362909

Listing in ISBN sequence of over 1,500,000 titles on the Whitaker database; includes 850,000 out-of-print titles.

Learned Publishing

Association of Learned and Professional Society Publishers
17 Orchard Close
Shillingford OX10 7HQ
England
(44) 181 6580459
fax: (44) 181 6633583

Quarterly publication.

PR Planner UK

PR Planner Ltd.
Hale House, 290–296 Green Lanes
London N13 5TP
England
(44) 181 8820155
fax: (44) 181 8860703

Press directory.

Publishing News

Publishing News Ltd.
43 Museum Street
London WC1A ILY
England
(44) 171 4040304
fax: (44) 171 2420762

Published weekly.

The School Librarian

School Library Association
Liden Library
Barrington Close, Liden
Swindon
Wilts SN3 6HF
England
(44) 1793 617838

TIMES LITERARY SUPPLEMENT

Times Newspapers Ltd.

See entry under Literary Periodicals.

WHITAKER ROM

J. Whitaker and Sons Ltd.
12 Dyott Street
London WC1A 1DF
England
(44) 171 4206000
fax: (44) 171 8362909

TFPL International CD-ROM Directory containing information on over 10,000 CD-ROMs and multimedia titles. Updated semi-annually.

Web Sites

BRITISH PRINTING INDUSTRIES FEDERATION

www.bpif.org.uk/index.html

The British Printing Industries Federation is "the business support organization for employers in the printing, packaging and graphic communications industry." Visitors to the Web site may search for appropriate suppliers for printed communications, read about the 1999 National Negotiations, and view the weekly *UPdate.online* business bulletin. It also includes press releases and news, industry profiles, a Y2K discussion forum, and employment opportunities.

THE BOOKSELLERS ASSOCIATION OF GREAT BRITAIN AND IRELAND

www.booksellers.org.uk/

The Booksellers Association of Great Britain and Ireland Web site offers discussion groups, a document library, a press release library, searchable press release indexes, book industry links, and professional development information. According to the Web site, "The Booksellers Association of Great Britain and Ireland, representing over 95% of booksellers in the UK and Ireland, is committed to providing the widest possible range of services to its membership, the value of which far outweigh the cost of being a member."

BRITISH OFFICIAL PUBLICATIONS CURRENT AWARENESS SERVICE

www.bopcas.com/

Visitors of The British Official Publications Current Awareness Service may:

- Browse lists of UK Parliamentary or Departmental publications indexed by date, publication type, and policy area. These lists can be displayed or returned to their computer over the Internet.
- Search the database for details of specific UK Parliamentary or Departmental publications matching their queries. The search results be displayed or returned to their computer over the Internet.

The following Electronic Mail Policy Awareness Lists are available at present to fee-paying subscribers: defense, Northern-Ireland, economy, sci-tech, education, Scotland, environment, statistics, Europe, transport, health, Wales, law, and welfare-reform.

Topics covered/papers included: Acts of Parliament (Local and Personal), Acts of Parliament (Public and General), Command Papers, Departmental Publications, Green Papers, House of Commons Bills, House of Commons Papers, House of Commons Library Research Papers, House of Lords Bills, House of Lords Papers, Standing Committee Reports.

LONDON REVIEW OF BOOKS

www.lrb.co.uk/

The London Review of Books Online offers selections from the current issue, archives, subscription information, newly discovered letters, as well as selections from recent issues and archives. It is a searchable site.

Ireland

Journals

BOOKS IRELAND

Jeremy Addis
11 Newgrove Avenue
Dublin 4
Ireland
(353) 1 2696185 (voice and fax)

The trade journal and review medium of the Irish publishing industry, published nine times each year.

IRISH PUBLISHING RECORD

National Library of Ireland
Kildare Street
Dublin 2
Ireland
(353) 1 6030200
fax: (353) 1 6766690

Lists books, pamphlets, new periodical titles, yearbooks, and musical scores published in both Ireland and Northern Ireland within the preceding year. Government publications of general interest are also listed.

JOURNAL OF THE IRISH COLLEGES OF PHYSICIANS AND SURGEONS

Irish Colleges of Physicians and Surgeons
The Mercer Library, Mercer Street Lower
Dublin 2
Ireland
(353) 1 4780674
fax: (353) 1 4022457
jicps@rcsi.ie (e-mail)

Published quarterly.

Israel

Books

ISRAEL BOOK TRADE DIRECTORY

Israel Export Institute—Book and Printing Center
29 Hamerad Street
Jerusalem 91076
Israel

Mailing Address:
P.O. Box 4405
Tel Aviv 68125
Israel
(972) 2 432147
fax: (972) 2 338626

Published biennially.

Journals

BIBLIOGRAPHY OF MODERN HEBREW LITERATURE IN TRANSLATION

The Institute for the Translation of Hebrew Literature

See entry under Library Reference, Journals.

KIYAT SEFER

Jewish National and University and Library
P.O. Box 34165
Jerusalem 91341
Israel
(972) 2 6585019
fax: (972) 2 6511771
jnl@rami.huji.ac.il (e-mail)

National Bibliography (published quarterly).

New Zealand

Books

NEW ZEALAND BOOKS IN PRINT

D. W. Thorpe
18 Salmon Street
Port Melbourne
Victoria 3207
New Zealand

Mailing Address:
P.O. Box 146
Port Melbourne
Victoria 3207
(64) 3 9245 7370
fax: (64) 3 9245 7395

Journals

NEW ZEALAND NATIONAL BIBLIOGRAPHY

National Library of New Zealand
P.O. Box 1467
Wellington
New Zealand
(64) 4 743000
fax: (64) 4 7473161
karen.rollitt@natlib.govt.nz (e-mail)

Published monthly.

SPOTLIGHT

City Communications Ltd.
P.O. Box 37567
Parnell
New Zealand
(64) 9 357-6319
fax: (64) 9 357-6318

Published monthly.

Singapore

Books

BOOKS ABOUT SINGAPORE

National Library
Stamford Frd
Singapore 0617
(65) 3323660
fax: (65) 3323611
cfwrefdv@technet.sg (e-mail)

The memoranda of books registered in the *Catalogue of Books Printed or Published in Singapore* under the provisions of the Printers and Publishers Act. Published biannually.

BOOKS IN SINGAPORE
Chopmen Publishers
865 Mountbatten Road 05–28/29
Katong Shopping Centre
Singapore 1543
(65) 3441495
fax: (65) 3440180

A survey of publishing, printing, bookselling, and library activity.

SINGAPORE PERIODICALS INDEX
National Library
Stamford Road
Singapore 0617
(65) 3323606
fax: (65) 33714770

Published annually.

Journals

NBDCS NEWS
National Book Development Council of Singapore (NBDCS)
Bukit Merah Branch Library
Bukit Merah Central
Singapore 0315
(65) 2732730
fax: (65) 2706139

Published quarterly; distributed free.

SINGAPORE BOOK WORLD

National Book Development Council of Singapore
Bukit Merah Branch Library
Bukit Merah Central
Singapore 0315
(65) 273732730
fax: (65) 2706139

Reviews of Singapore-published books and articles on the book trade and reading trends.

SINGAPORE NATIONAL BIBLIOGRAPHY (SNB)

National Library
Stamford Road
Singapore 6117
(65) 3323606
fax: (65) 3371470

Published quarterly with annual cumulation.

Scotland

Books

DIRECTORY OF PUBLISHING IN SCOTLAND

Booksellers Association of Great Britain and Ireland
Minster House 272, Vauxhall Bridge Road
London SW1V 1BA
England
(44) 131 2286866
fax: (44) 131 2283220

An annual handbook for the Scottish book world, listing Scottish publishers, details of related organizations, the addresses of major Scottish bookshops, and information on support services.

NEW BOOKS FROM SCOTTISH PUBLISHERS

Scottish Publishers Association
Scottish Book Centre, 137 Dundee Street
Edinburgh EH11 1BG
Scotland
(44) 131 2286866
fax: (44) 131 2283220

Published biannually.

Journals

BOOKS IN SCOTLAND

Ramsay Head Press
15 Goucester Place
Edinburgh EH3 6EE
Scotland
(44) 131 2255646 (voice and fax)

Quarterly magazine.

South Africa

Books

CATALOG OF BOOKS (ENGLISH) PUBLISHED IN SOUTHERN AFRICA, STILL IN PRINT (1970)

Struik Publishers
P.O. Box 1144
8000 Cape Town
(27) 21 6740/517128
fax: (27) 21 6744

Wales

Books

LLAIS LLYFAU/BOOKS IN WALES

Cyngor Llyfrau Cymraeg/Welsh Books Council
Castell Brychan
Aberystwyth
Ceredigion SY23 2JB
Wales
(44) 1970 624151
fax: (44) 1970 625385

Articles on the Welsh book scene. Lists and reviews of Welsh-language books and English-language books of Welsh interest. Published quarterly.

Literary Associations and Societies

Australia

Association for the Study of Australian Literature Ltd.

School of Humanities, Griffith University
Nathan
Brisbane OLD 4111
Australia
(61) 7 38757165
fax: (61) 7 38757730
p.buckridge@hum.gu.edu.au (e-mail)

President: Professor Robert Dixon; Secretary: Dr. Patrick Buckridge;
Publications: *Notes and Furphies.*

Australiasian Association for Lexicography

Linguistics Department, Macquarie University
Sydney
New South Wales 2109
Australia
(61) 2 8508 736
fax: (61) 2 8508240
dblair@pip.engl.mq.edu.au (e-mail)

President: Colin Young; Vice President: Mary Laughren; Secretary: David Blair.
Publications: *Australex* newsletter.

AUSTRALIAN LIBRARY PUBLISHERS' SOCIETY

Barr Smith Library
University of Adelaide
Adelaide
South Australia 5005
(61) 8 303-5370
fax: (61) 8 3034369
rchoate@library.adelaide.edu.au (e-mail)

Represents 33 library publishers and markets; approximately 300 publications. Convener: Ray Choate.

THE AUSTRALIAN SOCIETY OF AUTHORS LTD.

P.O. Box 1566
Strawberry Hills
New South Wales 2012
Australia
(61) 2 93180877
fax: (61) 2 93180530
asauthors@peg.pegasus.oz.au (e-mail)

Executive Director: Lynne Spender. Publications: *The Australian Author* (quarterly); *Australian Book Contracts*; *The Good, The Bad and The Greedy*.

AUSTRALIAN WRITERS' GUILD LTD.

60 Kellett Street
Kings Cross
New South Wales 2011
Australia
(61) 2 3577888
fax: (61) 2 3577776

Executive Officer: Chris Sharp; President: Geoffrey Atherden.
Publications: *The Writers' Directory: Writers for Screen, Stage, Radio and Television in Australia; A Matter of Cultural Sovereignty* (a symposium).

BIBLIOGRAPHICAL SOCIETY OF AUSTRALIA AND NEW ZEALAND (BSANZ)

Monash University Library
Wellington Road
Clayton
Victoria 3168
Australia
(61) 3 9052689
fax: (61) 3 9052610

Secretary: Richard Overell. Publications: *Bulletin* (quarterly); *Broadsheet* (triennially).

BOOK COLLECTORS' SOCIETY OF AUSTRALIA

c/o The Treasurer
64 Young Street
Cremorne
New South Wales 2090
Australia
(61) 2 7988984 (voice and fax)

President: Jeff Bidgood. Publications: *Biblionews and Australian Notes and Queries* (quarterly), plus *Index 1947–1979* and *Index 1979–1983*.

CHILDREN'S BOOK COUNCIL OF AUSTRALIA

P.O. Box 387
Croydon
Victoria 3136
Australia

FELLOWSHIP OF AUSTRALIAN WRITERS

GPO Box 3448
Sydney
New South Wales
Australia

President: Hilarie Lindsay; Secretary: Betty Bennel. Miscellaneous: Twenty-one regional branches in suburbs of Sydney and country towns; 1,000 members. *Publications Bulletin* (bimonthly).

FELLOWSHIP OF AUSTRALIAN WRITERS FEDERAL COUNCIL

The Council is re-formed in a different state branch every two years.

FELLOWSHIP OF AUSTRALIAN WRITERS (VIC) INC.

P.O. Box 528
Camberwell
Victoria 3124
Australia
(61) 903 9349 3722 (voice and fax)

President: Adrian Peniston-Bird. Membership: 2,500. All awards open the second week of September and close the third week of November each year. Publications: monthly bulletins; occasional publications.

INTERNATIONAL PEN (MELBOURNE CENTRE)

P.O. Box 1056, Clifton Hill
Melbourne
Victoria 3068
Australia
(61) 3 898-7889
fax: (61) 3 663-8658

President: Judith Buckrich; Secretary: Thomas Shapcott.

INTERNATIONAL PEN (SYDNEY CENTRE)

P.O.B. 153
Woolahra
New South Wales 2025
Australia
fax: (61) 2 9731453
President: Deirdre Hill. Publications: *Newsletter* (quarterly).

KEESING PRESS, IMPRINT OF THE AUSTRALIAN SOCIETY OF AUTHORS LTD.

NSW Writers' Centre
P.O. Box 1056
Rozelle
New South Wales 2039
Australia
(61) 2 9 555-9757
fax: (61) 2 9 818-1327
nswwc@ozemail.com.au (e-mail)

Executive Director: Irina Dunn. Publications: *Newswrite* (journals directory).

POETRY SOCIETY OF AUSTRALIA

Grosvenor Street
P.O. Box N110
Sydney
New South Wales 2000
Australia
(61) 2 423861

Joint Secretaries: Robert Adamson, Debra Adamson.
Publications: *New Poetry* (quarterly); also poems, articles, reviews, notes and comments, interviews.

SOCIETY OF WOMEN WRITERS (AUSTRALIA)

C1–Post Office
Coromandel Valley 5051
Australia
(61) 908 2701371 (voice and fax)

Federal President: Pamela McKee. The Society is served by a changing State Federal committee, which is nominated by a State branch every two years. Publications: *The Woman Writer.*

Web Sites

BIBLIOGRAPHICAL SOCIETY OF AUSTRALIA AND NEW ZEALAND (BSANZ)

www.uq.edu.au/~enctiffi/bsanz.htm

The Bibliographical Society of Australian and New Zealand produces a "flourishing quarterly scholarly journal," the *Bulletin,* and has an active publishing program. It holds regular conferences, sponsors an annual prize for an essay by a young scholar, includes conference information, and offers an essay prize. Members also receive a newsletter, the *Broadsheet.*

THE FELLOWSHIP OF AUSTRALIAN WRITERS

www.fawwa.org.au/index.html

The Fellowship of Australian Writers is "the largest literary organization in Western Australia, and owner of the newly-restored, historic Tom Collins House Writers Centre in Cottesloe." The site offers discussion areas for general chat and creative writing.

THE FELLOWSHIP OF AUSTRALIAN WRITERS (VIC) INC.

http://home.vicnet.net.au/~richard/faw.htm

According to The Fellowship of Australian Writers Web site, its aims are to:

- encourage and provide advice to aspiring and established writers and to assist them in every way possible;
- disseminate information on writing opportunities and awards and conduct its own National Literary Awards;

• cooperate with other organizations to improve conditions for Australian writers.

The Fellowship of Australian Writers publishes six issues of their newsletter, *The Bulletin* each year. Through this publication, members are regularly informed on forthcoming national competitions and awards as well as information on publishing opportunities. The site offers information about the fellowship's many literary awards.

THE AUSTRALIAN SOCIETY OF INDEXERS

www.zeta.org.au/~aussi/

According to the site, the objectives of the Australian Society of Indexers are:

- to improve the quality of indexing in Australia
- to promote the training, continuing professional development, status and interest of indexers in Australia
- to act as an advisory body on indexing to which authors, editors, publishers, and others may apply for guidance
- to provide opportunities for those interested in and connected with indexing to meet and exchange information, ideas, and experience relating to all aspects of indexing to establish and maintain relationships between the Society and other bodies with related interests
- to publish information in accord with the foregoing objectives.

Areas of interest on the site are events and courses, indexing-related resources, indexing software, a newsletter, and prizes and awards.

AUSTRALASIAN UNIVERSITIES LANGUAGE AND LITERATURE ASSOCIATION

www.arts.su.edu.au/Arts/departs/conf2/home.html

AULLA aims to "advance study and research in all fields of language and literature in universities and other tertiary institutions of Australia and New Zealand. It also seeks to give help and support to colleagues working in the Asia-Pacific region. While the major emphasis is on the promotion of pure research, it is recognized that the health of the various disciplines represented by AULLA requires a vigorous program of applied research in all areas related to language and literature teaching." The Web site offers information about a call for papers, proposed papers, and the University of Sydney Language Centre.

Canada

ANTIQUARIAN BOOKSELLERS ASSOCIATION

Box 75035, Cambrain Post Office
Calgary
Alberta T2K 6J8
Canada
(403) 282-5832
fax: (403) 289-0814

CANADIAN EDUCATION ASSOCIATION

252 Bloor Street W, Suite 8–200
Toronto
Ontario M5S 1V5
Canada
(416) 924-7721
fax: (416) 924-3188

ASSOCIATION FOR THE EXPORT OF CANADIAN BOOKS

504–1 Nicholas
Ottawa
Ontario K1N 7B7
Canada
(613) 562-2324
fax: (613) 562-2329
aecb@magi.com (e-mail)

ASSOCIATION OF BOOK PUBLISHERS OF BRITISH COLUMBIA

100 W Pender, Suite 107
Vancouver
British Columbia V6B 1R8
Canada
(604) 684-0228
fax: (604) 684-5788

ASSOCIATION OF CANADIAN PUBLISHERS

2 Gloucester Street, Suite 301
Toronto
Ontario M4Y 1L5
Canada
(416) 413-4929
fax: (416) 413-4920

ASSOCIATION OF CANADIAN UNIVERSITY PRESSES

c/o University of Manitoba Press
10 St. Mary, Suite 700
Toronto
Ontario M4Y 2W8
Canada
(416) 977-85850
fax: (416) 978-4738

AUDIT BUREAU OF CIRCULATIONS, CANADIAN OFFICE

151 Bloor Street W, Suite 850
Toronto
Ontario M5S 1S4
Canada
(416) 962-5840
fax: (416) 962-5844

BOOK AND PERIODICAL COUNCIL
35 Spadina Road, 3rd Floor
Toronto
Ontario M5R 2S9
Canada
(416) 975-9366
fax: (416) 975-1839

THE BOOK PUBLISHERS ASSOCIATION OF ALBERTA
10523–100 Avenue
Edmonton
Alberta T5J 0A8
Canada
(403) 424-5060
fax: (403) 424-7943

THE CANADA COUNCIL
350 Albert Street
Ottawa
Ontario K1P 5V8
Canada
(613) 237-3400; (800) 263-5588
fax: (613) 566-4390

Mailing Address:
Box 1047
Ottawa
Ontario K1P 5V8
Canada

CANADIAN AUTHORS ASSOCIATION

Box 419
Campbellford
Ontario K0L 1L0
Canada
(705) 653-0323
fax: (705) 653-0593
aq476@freenet.carleton.ca (e-mail)

CANADIAN BOOKSELLERS ASSOCIATION

301 Donlands Avenue
Toronto
Ontario M4J 3R8
Canada
(416) 467-7883
fax: (416) 467-7886

Annual Convention and Trade Fair:
Toronto, Ontario, Canada
June 26–30, 1997

CANADIAN LIBRARY ASSOCIATION

200 Elgin Street, Suite 602
Ottawa
Ontario K2P 1L5
Canada
(613) 232-9625
fax: (613) 563-9895
ai077@reenet.carleton.ca (e-mail)

Annual Conferences:
Ottawa, Ontario, Canada: June 19–22, 1997
Victoria, British Columbia, Canada: June 18–21, 1998

Canadian Printing Industries Association

75 Albert Street, Suite 906
Ottawa
Ontario K1P 5E7
Canada
(613) 236-7208
fax: (613) 236-8169

National Convention Queenslanding
Niagara on the Lake, Ontario, Canada: October 1996
National Convention, Saskatoon
Saskatchewan, Canada: October 1997

Writers' Union of Canada

24 Ryerson Avenue
Toronto
Ontario M5T 2P3
Canada
(416) 703-8982
fax: (416) 703-0826

Calendar of book trade and promotional events

The Champlain Society

Box 592, Sta R
Toronto
Ontario M4G 4E1
Canada
(416) 482-9635
fax: (416) 482-19341

LEAGUE OF CANADIAN POETS

54 Wolseley Street, 3rd Floor
Toronto
Ontario M5T 1A5
Canada
(416) 504-1657
fax: (416) 703-0059
league@io.org (e-mail)

PEN CANADA

The Writers Centre
24 Ryerson Avenue, Suite 309
Toronto
Ontario M5T 2P3
Canada
(416) 703-8448
fax: (416) 703-3870

PERIODICAL WRITER'S ASSOCIATION OF CANADA

54 Wolseley Street
Toronto
Ontario M5T 1A5
Canada
(416) 504-1645
fax: (416) 703-0059
pwac@sources.com (e-mail)

PLAYWRIGHTS UNION OF CANADA
54 Wolseley Street
Toronto
Ontario M5T 1A5
Canada
(416) 703-0201; (800) 561-3318
fax: (416) 703-0059

TNG CANADA
Affiliate of TNG Newspaper Guild
30 Concourse Gate, Unit 103
Nepean
Ontario K2E 7V7
Canada
(613) 727-0990
fax: (613) 836-5894

Web Sites

CANADIAN AUTHORS ASSOCIATION
www.canauthors.org/
The Canadian Authors Association is Canada's national writing organization. According to the Web site, the "CAA has played a key role in the support and development of the Canadian writing community. It has charitable status as a registered National Arts Service Organization." The site includes branch information, writing links, publications, writing awards, copyright and conference information.

PEN CANADA
www.pencanada.ca/profile/profile.htm
PEN Canada "works on behalf of writers, at home and abroad, who have been forced into silence for writing the truth as they see it. PEN Canada is for debate and against silence. We lobby governments in Canada and internationally, organize petitions, send

letters, faxes, and postcards to lobby for the release of persecuted writers, and conduct public awareness campaigns about freedom of expression." The PEN Canada Web site offers membership information, a writers-in-prison committee, information about upcoming events, as well as information about censorship in Canada.

England

AGATHA CHRISTIE SOCIETY

P.O. Box 985
London SW1X 9XA
England
agathachristie@dial.pipex.com (e-mail)

ALLIANCE OF LITERARY SOCIETIES

71 Stepping Stones Road
Coventry CV5 8JT
England
(44) 1203 592231

ASLIB: THE ASSOCIATION FOR INFORMATION MANAGEMENT

Information House 20–24 Old Street
London EC1V9AP
England
(44) 171 2534488
fax: (44) 171 4300514

ASSOCIATION FOR ART HISTORIANS
Cowcross Court, 77 Cowcross Street
London ECIM 6BP
England
(44) 171 4903211
fax: (44) 171 4903277
telex: 35343 MOHNPRO 9

ASSOCIATION OF BRITISH SCIENCE WRITERS
23 Savile Row
London W1X 2NB
England
(44) 171 43912105
fax: (44) 171 9733051

AUTHOR-PUBLISHER ENTERPRISE
See New Meridian Ltd.

AUTHORS' CLUB
40 Dover Street
London W1X 3RB
England
(44) 171 4998581
fax: (44) 171 4090913

FRANCIS BACON SOCIETY INC.
Canonbury Tower, Islington
London N1
England

THE BEATRIX POTTER SOCIETY

32 Etchingham Park Road
Finchley
London N3 2DT
England
(44) 181 3468031

E. F. BENSON SOCIETY

The Old Coach House, High Street
Rye
Sussex TN31 7JF
England
(44) 1797 223114

BOOKS ACROSS THE SEA

The English-Speaking Union
37 Charles Street
London W1X 8AB
England
(44) 171 493328
fax: (44) 171 4956108
esu@mailbox.ulcc.ac.uk (e-mail)

BRITISH AMERICAN ARTS' ASSOCIATION (UK)

116 Commercial Street
London E1 6NF
England
(44) 171 2475385
fax: (44) 171 2475256

BRITISH FANTASY SOCIETY

2 Harwood Street
Heaton Norris
Stockport SK4 1JJ
England
(44) 161 4765368

THE BRITISH SCIENCE FICTION ASSOCIATION LTD.

60 Bournemouth Road
Folkestone
Kent CT19 5AZ
England
(44) 1303 252939 (voice & fax)
mks_pk@cix.compulink.co.uk (e-mail)

THE BRONTE SOCIETY

The Bronte Parsonage Museum
Hawworth, Keighley
W. Yorks BD22 8DR
England
(44) 1535 642323
fax: (44) 1535 657131

THE BROWNING SOCIETY

Cherry Tree Cottage, Fyning Lane
Rogate
Petersfield GU31 5DQ
England
(44) 1730 821666
fax: (44) 1730 821620

BYRON SOCIETY (INTERNATIONAL)

Byron House
6 Gertrude Street
London SW10 0JN
England
(44) 1 3525112

RANDOLPH CALDECOTT SOCIETY

See Randolph Caldecott Society.

CAMBRIDGE BIBLIOGRAPHICAL SOCIETY

University Library, West Road
Cambridge CB3 9DR
England

DARESBURY LEWIS CARROLL SOCIETY

See Daresbury Lewis Carroll Society.

THE CHESTERTON SOCIETY

(44) 1295 720869
fax: (44) 1865 248403

CHILDREN'S BOOKS HISTORY SOCIETY

25 Field Way
Hoddesdon
Herts EN11 0QN
England
(44) 1992 464885 (voice & fax)

THE JOHN CLARE SOCIETY

The Stables, la West Street
Helpston
Peterborough PE6 7DU
England
(44) 171 401818
fax: (44) 171 4031418

DARESBURY LEWIS CARROLL SOCIETY

Clatterwick Hall, Little Leigh
Northwich
Cheshire CW8 4RJ
England
(44) 1606 891303

THE DICKENS FELLOWSHIP

Dickens House, 48 Doughty Street
London WC1N 2LF
England
(44) 171 4052127
fax: (44) 171 8315175

EARLY ENGLISH TEXT SOCIETY

Christ Church
Oxford OX1 1DP
England

EDUCATIONAL LOW-PRICED BOOKS SCHEME

6 Swan Centre, Fishers Lane
Chiswick
London W4 1RX
England
(44) 181 7428232
fax: (44) 181 7478715

THE EIGHTEEN NINETIES SOCIETY

97d Brixton Road
London SW9 6EE
England
(44) 171 5824690

ENGLISH ASSOCIATION

University Leicester, University Road
Leicester LE1 7RH
England
(44) 116 252-3982
fax: (44) 116 252-2301

THE ENGLISH-SPEAKING UNION OF THE COMMONWEALTH

37 Charles Street
London W1X 8AB
England
esu@mialbox.ulcc.ac.uk (e-mail)

GAY AUTHORS WORKSHOP

BM Box 5700
London WC1N 3XX
England
(44) 171 5205223

THE GEORGE ELIOT FELLOWSHIP

71 Stepping Stones Road
Coventry CV5 8JT
England
(44) 1203 592231

GREEN ROUND PRESS

Imprint of The Author Machen Society

THOMAS HARDY SOCIETY

P.O. Box 1438
Dorchester
Dorset DT1 1YH
England
(44) 1350 251501

IVY BOOKS

c/o Ivy Books
351 Woodstock Road
Oxford OX2 7NX
England
(44) 1865 310987/515962

JANE AUSTEN MEMORIAL TRUST

Jane Austen's House
Chawton Alton
Hants GU34 1SD
England
(44) 1420 83262

THE RICHARD JEFFERIES SOCIETY

45 Kemerton Walk
Swindon
Wilts SN3 2EA
England
(44) 1793 521512

THE JOSEPH CONRAD SOCIETY (UK)

c/o POSK, 238–46 King Street
London W6 ORF
England

KEATS-SHELLEY MEMORIAL ASSOCIATION

Honorary Secretary, Ilewis Road
Radford Semele
Leamington CV31 1UB
England
(44) 1892 533452
fax: (44) 1892 51412

KIPLING SOCIETY

2 Brownleaf Road
Brighton BN2 6LB
England
(44) 1273 303719 (voice and fax)

CHARLES LAMB SOCIETY

1A Royston Road
Richmond
Surrey TW 10 6LT
England
(44) 181 9403837

LANCASHIRE AUTHOR'S ASSOCIATION

Heatherslade, 5 Quakerfields
Westhoughton, Bolton
Lances BL5 2BJ
England
(44) 1942 791390

LONDON WRITER CIRCLE

37 Manor Farm Road
Bittome Park SO9 3FQ
England

THE ARTHUR MACHEN SOCIETY

19 Cross Street
Caerleon Gwent NP6 1AF
England
(44) 1633 422520
fax: (44) 1633 421055

MEDICAL WRITERS GROUP

Society of Authors
84 Drayton Gardens
London SW10 9SB
England
(44) 171 3736642
fax: (44) 171 3735768
authorsoc@writers.org.uk (e-mail)

THE MERVYN PEAKE SOCIETY

2 Mount Park Road
Ealing
London W5 2RP
England
(44) 181 5669307
fax: (44) 181 9910559

WILLIAM MORRIS SOCIETY

Kelmscott House, 26 Upper Mall
London W6 9TA
England
(44) 181 7413735

THE NATIONAL POETRY FOUNDATION (1981)

Reg Charity no: 283032
27 Mill Road
Fareham
Hants PO 16 0TH
(44) 1329 822218 (voice and fax)

The National Poetry Foundation is the only body in the poetry world (outside of normal grant agencies) to give financial support to poets. The foundation publishes books at no cost to individual subscribers when their work is deemed to be of high enough standard.

NEW MERIDIAN LTD.

7 Kingsland Road
West Mersea
Colchester CO5 8RB
England
(44) 1206 382558
100412.603@compuserve.com (e-mail)

OXFORD BIBLIOGRAPHICAL SOCIETY

c/o Bodlein Library
Oxford OS1 3BG
England
(44) 1865 277102
fax: (44) 1865 277182
telex: 83656

ENGLISH CENTRE OF INTERNATIONAL PEN

7 Dilke Street
Chelsea
London SW3 4JE
(44) 171 3526303
fax: (44) 171 3510220

THE POETRY SOCIETY COMMUNICATIONS
22 Betterton Street
London WC2H 0BU
England
(44) 171 2404810
fax: (44) 171 240818
poetrysoc@dial.pipex.com (e-mail)

RANDOLPH CALDECOTT SOCIETY
Chatterwick Hall, Little Leigh
Northwich
Cheshire CW8 4RJ
England
(44) 1606 891303

THE ARTHUR RANSOME SOCIETY
Romantic Novelists' Association
17 Queens
Tintinhull
Somerset AB22 8PG
(44) 1935 822808

ROYAL LITERARY FUND
144 Temple Chambers Temple Avenue
London EC4Y 0DA
England
(44) 171 3531750 (voice and fax)

THE ROYAL SOCIETY FOR THE ENCOURAGEMENT OF ARTS, MANUFACTURERS AND COMMERCE-RSA

8 John Adam Street
London
England
(44) 171 9305115
fax: (44) 171 8395805
rsa@rsa.ftech.co.uk (e-mail)

ROYAL SOCIETY OF LITERATURE OF THE UNITED KINGDOM

1 Hyde Park Gardens
London W2 2LT
England
(44) 171 7235104
fax: (44) 171 4020199

THE DORTHY L. SAYERS SOCIETY

Rose Cottage, Malthouse Lane
Hurstpierpoint
West Sussex BN6 9JY
England
(44) 1273 833444
fax: (44) 1273 835988

SHAKESPEAREAN AUTHORSHIP TRUST

11 Old Square
Lincoln's Inn
London WC2A 3TS
England
(44) 171 2426995 (voice and fax)

THE SHAW SOCIETY

51 Farmfield Road
Bromley
Kent BR1 4NF
England
(44) 181 6973619 (voice and fax)

SOCIETY FOR THE STUDY OF MEDIEVAL LANGUAGES AND LITERATURE

Department of English, De Montfort University
The Gateway
Leicester LF1 9BH
England
(44) 1865 57775 (voice and fax)
cal@vax.ox.ac.uk (e-mail)

SOCIETY OF FREELANCE EDITORS AND PROOFREADERS

Mermaid House, 1 Mermaid Court
London SE1 1HR
England
(44) 171 4035141

THE SOCIETY OF WOMEN WRITERS AND JOURNALISTS

110 Whitehall Road
Chingford
London E4 6DW
England
(44) 181 5290886

The Tilling Society

5 Friars Bank, Pett Road
Guestling
East Sussex TN35 4ET
England

The Tolkien Society

Flat 6, 8 Staverton Road
Oxford
Oxom OX2 6XJ
England
(44) 0865 278874
fax: (44) 1865 278855
anniehaward@spc.ox.ac.uk (e-mail)

Translators Association

84 Drayton Gardens
London SW10 9SB
England
(44) 171 3736642
fax: (44) 171 3735768
authorsoc@writers.org.uk (e-mail)

The Association is a specialist group representing published literary translators within the Society of Authors.

H. G. Wells Society

49 Beckingthorpe Drive
Bottesford
Nottingham NG13 0DN
England

West Country Writers' Association

Malvern View, Garway Hill
Orcop
Hereford HR2 8EZ
England
(44) 1981 580435 (voice and fax)

Web Sites

The Alliance of Literary Societies

www.sndc.demon.co.uk/als.htm

The Alliance of Literary Societies is a collection of various literary organizations. Each affiliated society receives a number of free copies of the annual fanzine "Chapter One" for distribution amongst its members. According to the Web site, the society is in the process of drawing up a panel of speakers on literary subjects for the benefit of Alliance members.

Association of Art Historians

http://scorpio.gold.ac.uk/aah/

The Association of Art Historians was formed "to promote the study of art history. It represents the interests of art and design historians in all aspects of the discipline, including art, design, architecture, photography, film and other media, cultural studies, conservation and museum studies." The site includes news and issues, information about conferences and calls for papers, publications, jobs and services, and resources—research queries, on-line discussion lists, and links to other sites

Lewis Carroll Society of North America

www.lewiscarroll.org/

The LCSNA is a nonprofit organization "dedicated to furthering Carroll studies, increasing accessibility of research material, and maintaining public awareness of Carroll's contributions to society." The site includes upcoming meetings and announcements, and Carroll-related information. The society is looking for Lewis Carroll letters related to mathematics.

THE JOSEPH CONRAD SOCIETY (UNITED KINGDOM)

www.pmpc.napier.ac.uk/scob/conrad/conrad.HTML

The Joseph Conrad Society Web site offers information about the Annual International Conference and other Conrad conferences worldwide, a call for papers, prizes awarded by the Joseph Conrad Society (UK), Conrad texts available online, Conrad Publications available from the Society, and links to related Web sites.

THE GEORGE ELIOT FELLOWSHIP

http://lang.nagoya-u.ac.jp/~matsuoka/Eliot.html

According to the Web site, "the George Eliot Fellowship exists to honour George Eliot and to promote interest in her life and works. Its objects are to gather together admirers of the novelist and to encourage the collection of books, manuscripts, letters, portraits and other articles associated with her for public display as well as to observe her birth day each year."

THE ENGLISH-SPEAKING UNION

www.esu.org/

The English-Speaking Union's purpose is to "promote international understanding and human achievement through the widening use of English as the language of our global village." According to their Web site, the English-Speaking Union:

- promotes English in international public speaking and debate for the support of worldwide communication and dialogue;
- encourages the enjoyment and constructive use of English through educational programs;
- provides a forum for international friendship through our network of branches worldwide and our headquarters at Dartmouth House;
- initiates and administers international youth exchange and work experience schemes;
- focuses on key current affairs issues through regular international conferences, seminars, and meetings;
- provides and create cultural activities;
- facilitates and authorizes the establishment of ESUs worldwide;
- ensures the coordination and coherence of our activities through the skill and dedication of our staff and voluntary helpers;

- relies upon the enthusiasm and support of all our members; and
- works in close and innovative partnership with our corporate members and sponsors.

THOMAS HARDY ONLINE SOCIETY

www.prestigeweb.com/hardy/hardy.html

At The Thomas Hardy Online Society, visitors may download *Tess of the D'Urbervilles, Jude the Obscure, The Mayor of Casterbridge, A Pair of Blue Eyes, Far from the Madding Crowd,* and *The Return of the Native* for free. The site also includes critiques, a short introduction to Thomas Hardy, and an opportunity to post messages related to Hardy works.

THE KIPLING SOCIETY

www.kipling.org.uk/

The Kipling Society issues a quarterly journal and holds regular meetings in London and Sussex. At these, invited speakers address a wide range of interesting topics related to Kipling's life and work. A well-attended annual lunch-time meeting is held each summer in London, with a distinguished guest speaker. The Society also maintains a comprehensive research library housed at City University, London, which may be consulted by members.

The editor of the journal is glad to receive, from members and non-members alike, articles and letters bearing on the life and works of Kipling.

THE BEATRIX POTTER SOCIETY

www.charitynet.org/~beatrixpottersociety/index.html

According to the Web site, "The Beatrix Potter Society is registered as a charity in the United Kingdom and exists to promote the study and appreciation of the life and works of Beatrix Potter (1866–1943) who was not only the author of *The Tale of Peter Rabbit* and other classics of children's literature, but also a landscape and natural history artist, diarist, farmer and conservationist—in the latter capacity she was responsible for the preservation of large areas of the Lake District through her gifts to the National Trust. The Society upholds and protects the integrity of the inimitable and unique work of Beatrix Potter, her aims and bequests."

Ireland

IRISH ACADEMY OF LETTERS

School of Irish Studies, Thomas Prior House
Merrion Road
Dublin 4

Secretary: Sean J. White.

IRISH PEN

Rosslyn, Killarney Road
Bray
Co Wicklow
Ireland

President: Mr. O. Z. Whitehead; Secretary: Arthur Flynn.

Israel

ACUM LTD. (SOCIETY OF AUTHORS, COMPOSERS AND MUSIC PUBLISHERS IN ISRAEL)

ACUM House, 118 Rothschild Blvd.
Tel Aviv 61140
Israel
(972) 3 6841414
fax: (972) 03 6850119

Director General: Ran Kedar; Secretary: Nilli Werker.

ENGLISH LANGUAGE EDITORS' ASSOCIATION (ELEAS)

P.O. Box 1570
Jerusalem 91013
Israel
(972) 2 6433816
fax: (972) 2 6438232
davidg@mofet.macam98.ac.il (e-mail)

Contact: David Grossman.

MEKISE NIRDAMIN SOCIETY

P.O. Box 4344
Jerusalem
Israel
(972) 2 636072

President: Professor Abramson; Secretary: Prof. I. Tashma.
Publishes Hebrew works of the older classical Jewish literature.

PALESTINE PEN CENTER

Al Khaldi St 4, Wadi Al Juz
Jerusalem
Israel
(972) 2 6262970
fax: (972) 2 6264620

President: Hanoch Awwad. Formerly: PEN Centre for Palestine Writers.

PEN CENTRE FOR PALESTINIAN WRITERS

See Palestine PEN Centre.

ISRAELI PEN CENTRE

Israeli PEN Centre
c/o Hanoch Bartov
6 Kaplan Street
P.O. Box 7203
Tel Aviv
Israel
fax: (972) 3 6964937

President: Hanoch Bartov; Secretary: Rubin Riva.

New Zealand

COPYRIGHT LICENSING LTD.

P.O. Box 386
Auckland 1
New Zealand
Chairman: Rosemary Stagg.

DICKENS FELLOWSHIP

65 Mitchell Street
Brooklyn
Wellington 2
New Zealand

Secretary: Maybelle Ryan.

NEW ZEALAND BOOK COUNCIL

P.O. Box 11377
Wellington
New Zealand
President: Fiona Kidman; Executive Director: Philippa Christmas.
Publications: *Writers in Schools; Book Buyers in New Zealand; Books You Couldn't Buy* (censorship in New Zealand); *Landmarks of New Zealand Writing to 1945.*

NEW ZEALAND COUNCIL FOR EDUCATIONAL RESEARCH

Education House, 178–182 Willis Street
Wellington 1
New Zealand

Mail Address:
P.O. Box 3237
Wellington 1
New Zealand
(64) 4 384-7939
fax: (64) 4 384-7933
anne.meade@buw.ac.nz (e-mail)

Director: Dr. A. Meade.
Publications: Annual report; biannual newsletter; research reports.

NEW ZEALAND SOCIETY OF AUTHORS

P.O. Box 34
631 Birkenhead
Auckland 10
New Zealand

Publications: *New Zealand Author* (bimonthly).

NEW ZEALAND WRITERS GUILD
Private Bag 5, Newton
Auckland
New Zealand
(64) 9 3601527 (voice and fax)

President: Judy Callingham; Administrator: Evelyn Scott.

NGA PUNA WAIHANGA
P.O. Box 1512
Rotorua
New Zealand
(64) 7 3628070
fax: (64) 7 3462768

President: Para Matchitt. Formerly New Zealand Maori Artists and Writers Society Inc. Publications: *Pingao: The Golden Sand Sedge 1991; Te Moano: Twenty years of Maori Artists 1993.*

PEN INC.
See New Zealand Society of Authors.

Web Sites

NEW ZEALAND SOCIETY OF AUTHORS
http://arachna.co.nz/nzsa/index.html

The New Zealand Society of Authors is "an association of writers working together to improve conditions for New Zealand writers—raising their profile and encouraging fair treatment by others." Publications include leaflets and research studies produced by NZSA, and The New Zealand Author. The site includes a model standard contract, legal advice, awards and fellowships, and a legal advice service.

NEW ZEALAND WRITERS GUILD

http://writersguild.org/iawg/nz.html

The New Zealand Writers Guild is "a professional, nonprofit association for writers in film, television, theatre, radio, video and multimedia." According to the Web site, its objectives are to promote and protect the interests of its members and provide a link for writers to their peers and the entertainment industry generally. The site offers a bimonthly newsletter, *WriteUp*, and our regular new infosheet *The Write Stuff*. Other services include contractual advice, credit arbitration, craft evenings, workshops, and registration service.

Scotland

ASSOCIATION FOR SCOTTISH LITERARY STUDIES

c/o Depth of Scottish History
9 University Gardens
University of Glasgow
Glasgow G12 8QH
Scotland
(44) 141 3305309
cmc@arts.glaac.uk (e-mail)

EDINBURGH BIBLIOGRAPHIC SOCIETY

Department of Special Collections
Edinburgh University Library, George Square
Edinburgh EH8 9LJ
Scotland
(44) 131 6503412
fax: (44) 131 6506863
telex: 7272442

PEN Scottish Centre

33 Drumsheugh Gardens
Edinburgh EH3 7RN
Scotland
(44) 131 2251038 (voice and fax)

Wales

Arts Council of Wales

9 Museum Place
Cardiff CF1 3NX
Wales
(44) 1222 394711
fax: (44) 1222 221447

Thomas Ellis Memorial Fund

University Registry
University of Wales, Cathays Park
Cardiff CF1 3NS
Wales
(44) 1222 382656
fax: (44) 1222 396040
jasmine@bredon.demon.co.uk (e-mail)

Yr Academi Gymreig (The Welsh Academy)

3rd Floor, Mount Stuart House
Mount Stuart Square, The Docks
Cardiff CF1 6DQ
Wales
(44) 1222 492025
fax: (44) 1222 492930
dafr@celtic.co.uk (e-mail)

LITERARY PERIODICALS

Australia

THE AUSTRALIAN AUTHOR

The Australian Society of Authors Ltd.
P.O. Box 1566
Strawberry Hills
New South Wales 2010
Australia
(61) 2 93180877
fax: (61) 2 93180530
asatuhors@peg.pegasus.o.2.au (e-mail)

Published quarterly.

AUSTRALIAN BOOK REVIEW

National Book Council
Suite 3, 21 Drummond Place
Carlton
Victoria 3053
Australia
(61) 3 96638657
fax: (61) 3 9663865
abr@vicnet.net.au (e-mail)

Published ten times a year.

AUSTRALIAN LITERARY STUDIES

University of Queensland Press
P.O. Box 42
Saint Lucia
Queensland 4067
Australia
(61) 7 33652452/33652453
fax: (61) 7 33651988
uqpbris@peg.apc.org.au (e-mail)

Academic/scholarly publication; published biannually.

BIBLIONEWS AND AUSTRALIAN NOTES AND QUERIES

Book Collectors' Society of Australia
c/o The Treasurer
64 Young Street
Cremorne
New South Wales 2090
Australia
(61) 2 7988984 (voice and fax)

Published quarterly.

BROUHAHA

Poetry Society of Australia
P.O. Box N110, Grosvenor Street
Sydney
New South Wales 2000
Australia
(61) 2 423861

Published quarterly.

ISLAND

Island Magazine Inc.
P.O. Box 210
Sandy Bay
Tasmania 7005
Australia
(61) 3 62262325
fax: (61) 3 62262765
island@english-utas-edu-au (e-mail)

Published quarterly.

NEW CEYLON WRITING

Nacquarie University
School of English and Linguistics
North Ryde
New South Wales 2109
Australia
(61) 2 805-8776
fax: (61) 2 805-7849

Creative and critical writing.

OVERLAND

The O L Society Ltd.
P.O. Box 14146 MCMC
Melbourne
Victoria 8001
Australia
(61) 3 96879875
fax: (61) 3 96875918
lansyson@vut.edu.au (e-mail)

Published quarterly.

QUADRANT

Quadrant Magazine Co. Inc.
46 George Street
Fitzroy
Victoria 3065
Australia
(61) 3 417 6855
fax: (61) 3 416 2980
quadrnt@ozemail.com.au (e-mail)

Published ten times per year.

READING TIME

Children's Book Council of Australia
Box 62
Ashmont
New South Wales 2650
Australia
(61) 69 254907 (voice and fax)
jchohen@csu.edu.au (e-mail)

Published quarterly; yearly index of reviews and articles.

SOUTHERLY

English Association, Sydney Branch
4 Belgrave Street
Cremorne
New South Wales 2090
Australia
(61) 2 8182591
fax: (61) 2 8185332

Southerly issues a quarterly publication of short stories, poetry, and literary criticism about Australian writers. First published in 1939.

WESTERLY

The Center for Studies in Australian Literature
English Department, University of Western Australia
Nedlands
West Australia 6009
(61) 8 9380 2101
fax: (61) 8 9380 1030
westerly@uniwa.uwa.edu.au (e-mail)

Published quarterly.

Web Sites

WRITERS' CENTRES ON THE WEB

www.ozemail.com.au/~awol/wcentres.htm

Writers' Centres on the Web is a listing of writing centers for Australia. Included are The Central West Writers' Centre, The Northern Rivers Writers' Centre, and Varuna Writers' Centre Katoomba Varuna. The site includes detailed information about the origins and current practices of each of these centers and is currently working on including other writing centers on their Web site.

Canada

CANADIAN AUTHOR

Canadian Authors Association
Box 419
Campbellford
Ontario L0L 1L0
Canada
(705) 653-0323
fax: (705) 653-2593
canuth@redden.on.ca (e-mail)

CANADIAN PRINTER

Maclean Hunter Ltd.
777 Bay Street
Toronto
Ontario M5W 1A7
Canada
(416) 596-2639
fax: (416) 596-5965

CHILDREN'S BOOK NEWS

Children's Book Centre
35 Spadina Road
Toronto
Ontario M5R 2S9
Canada
fax: (416) 975-1839
ccbc@1global.com (e-mail)

CURRENT CANADIAN BOOK

John Coutts Library Services Ltd.
6900 Kinsmen Court
Niagara Falls
Ontario L2E 7E7
Canada
(905) 356-6382; (800) 263-1686
fax: (416) 356-5064
telex: 0615299
coutts@wizbang.coutts.om.ca (e-mail)

THE GRAPHIC MONTHLY

North Island Sound
1606 Sedlescomb Drive, Suite 8
Mississauga
Ontario L4X 1M6
Canada
(905) 625-7070
fax: (905) 625-4856

JOURNAL OF SCHOLARLY PUBLISHING

5201 Dufferin Street
North York
Ontario M3H 5T8
Canada
(416) 667-7781
fax: (416) 667-7881

QUILL AND QUIRE
70 The Esplanade, Suite 210
Toronto
Ontario M5E 1R2
Canada
(416) 360-0044
fax: (416) 955-0794
quill@hookup.net (e-mail)

England

AGENDA
The Agenda and Editions Charitable Trust
5 Cranbourne Court
Albert Bridge Road
London SW 11 4PE
England
(44) 171 2280700 (voice and fax)

AMBIT
Dr. Martin Bax
17 Priory Gardens
London N6 5QY
England
(44) 181 3403566

Poetry, prose, short fiction and illustrations, and reviews.

THE BOOK COLLECTOR

The Collector Ltd.
P.O. Box 12426
London W11 3FW
England
(44) 171 7923492 (voice and fax)
fax: (44) 171 3880854

BOOKS MAGAZINE

Publishing News Ltd.
43 Museum Street
London WC1A 1LY
England
(44) 171 4040304
fax: (44) 171 2420762

CRITICAL QUARTERLY

Blackwell Publishers Ltd.
108 Cowley Road
Oxford OX4 1JF
England
(44) 1865 791100
fax: (44) 1865 791347
jnlinfo@blackwellpublishers.co.uk (e-mail)

ENVOI

Envoi
44 Rudyard Road
Biddulph Moor
Staffs ST8 7JN
England
(44) 1782 517892

GRANTA

Granta Publications Ltd.
2–3 Hanover Yard, Noel Road
London N1 8BE
England
(44) 171 704996
fax: (44) 171 7040474

LITERARY REVIEW

Namara Group
44 Lexington Street
London W1R 3LH
England
(44) 171 4379392
fax: (44) 171 7341844
litrev@dircon.co.uk (e-mail)

LITMUS

Stukeley Press
Stukeley Street, Drury Lane
London WC2B 5LJ
England

LONDON REVIEW OF BOOKS

Nicholas Spice
28 Little Russell Street
London WC1A 2HN
England
(44) 171 4043336
fax: (44) 171 4043337

ORBIS

Orbis
199 The Long Shoot
Nuneaton
Warwicks CV11 6IQ
England
(44) 1203 327440 (voice and fax)

Independent British literary quarterly with international connections. Publishes mainly poetry, but uses some prose and letters; also features news, educational, and review columns.

OUTPOSTS POETRY QUARTERLY

Hippopotamus Press
22 Whitewell Road
Frome
Sommerset BA11 4EL
(44) 1373 466653 (voice and fax)

New Poetry, translations, essays, and reviews.

PAUSE

The National Poetry Foundation
27 Mill Road
Fareham
Hants PO16 0TH
England
(44) 1329 822218 (voice and fax)

PN REVIEW

Carcanet Press Ltd.
Fourth Floor, Conavon Court, Blackfriars Street
Manchester M3 5BQ
England
(44) 161 8348730
fax: (44) 161 83200814
pnr@carcanet.u-net.com (e-mail)

Features poetry and literary criticism.

POETRY NOW

Poetry Now
33 Belgrade Road
Stoke, Newington
London N16

POETRY REVIEW

Poetry Society, Inc.
22 Betterton Street
London WC2H 9BU
England
(44) 171 2404810
fax: (44) 171 2404818
poetrysoc@dial.pipex.com (e-mail)

THE RIALTO

P.O. Box 309, Aylsham
Norwich
Norfolk NR2 6LN
England

SIGNAL

Thimble Press
Lockwood, Station Road
Woodchester
Stroud Glos GL5 5EQ
England
(44) 1453 873716
fax: (44) 1453 878599

Approaches to children's books.

STAND MAGAZINE

Stand Magazine
179 Wingrove Road
Newcastle-upon-Tyne NW4 9DA
England
(44) 191 2733280 (voice and fax)

THE TIMES LITERARY SUPPLEMENT

The Times Supplement Ltd.
Admiral House, 66–68 East Smithfield
London E1 9XY
England
(44) 171 7823000
fax: (44) 171 7823100

VIGIL

Vigil Publications
12 Priory Mead
Bruton
Sommerset BA10 0DZ
England
(44) 1749 813349
miked@argonet.co.uk (e-mail)

Publishes poetry and prose with the accent on developments in form and structure applied to contemporary themes.

WRITERS NEWS

Writers News
P.O. Box 4
Nairn IV 12 4HU
England
(44) 1667 454441
fax: (44) 1667 454401

Information on markets, competitors, short story competitions, and how-to articles—for both the established and aspiring writer.

Ireland

COMHAR

Comhar
5 Rae Mhuirfean
Ath Cliath
Ireland

Text in Irish.

Israel

AREIL: THE ISRAEL REVIEW OF ARTS AND LETTERS

Weill Publishers
214 Jaffa Road
Jerusalem 94383
Israel
(972) 2 5381515/5380281
fax: (972) 2 5380626

JERUSALEM REPORT

Jerusalem Report
22 Yosef Rivlin Street
P.O. Box 1805
Jerusalem 91017
Israel
(972) 2 6291011
fax: (972) 2 6291037
jrep@attmail.com (e-mail)

MODERN HEBREW LITERATURE

The Institute for the Transition of Hebrew Literature
P.O. Box 10051
Ramat Gran 52001
Israel
(972) 3 5796830
fax: (972) 3 5796832
hamachon@inter.net.it (e-mail)

TEL AVIV REVIEW

Ah'shav Publishers
3 Smolenskin Street
Tel Aviv 63415
Israel

Mailing Address:
P.O. Box 3421
Tel Aviv 63415
Israel
(972) 3 5245120/226583

New Zealand

AUMLA

Australasian Universities Language and Literature Association
Department of French, University of Canterbury
Private Bag 4800
Christchurch 1
New Zealand
(64) 3 3667-001, ext. 8544
fax: (64) 3 3642-999
m.burrell@fren.canterbury.ac.nz (e-mail)

Journal of literary criticism, philology and linguistics; published in English with occasional articles in French, German, or Spanish.

ISLANDS

Robin Dudding
4 Sealy Rd, Torbay
Auckland 10
Australia

A New Zealand quarterly of arts and letters.

QUOTE UNQUOTE

Quote Unquote
53 Princes Street, Northcote Point
Auckland 1309
New Zealand
(64) 94801452
fax: (64) 9 4802637
quotes@iconz.co.nz (e-mail)

Monthly magazine on New Zealand books and arts with reviews, interview, profiles and general articles, plus full list of all new titles published.

TAKANHE MAGAZINE

The Takanhe Publishing Collective
P.O. Cox 13–335
Christchurch 8001
New Zealand

Scotland

CENCRASTUS

Cencrastus
1, Abbeymount Techbase
Edinburgh EH8 8EJ
Scotland
(44) 131 661587
106536.755@compuserve.com (e-mail)

Scottish and international literature, arts, and affairs.

CHAPMAN

Chapman
4 Broughton Place
Edinburgh EH1 3RX
Scotland
(44) 131 5572207
fax: (44) 131 5569565

South Africa

Acta Classica

Classical Association of South Africa
c/o Dept of Classics
University of South Africa
Pretoria 0003
South Africa

Mailing Address:
P.O. Box 392
Pretoria 0003
South Africa
(27) 12 4296501
fax: (27) 12 4293355
bothmh@alpha.unisa.ac.za (e-mail)

Akroterion

University of Stellenbosch
Department of Classics, Private Bag X1
Matieland
Stellenbosch 7602
South Africa
(27) 21 8083136
fax: (27) 21 8084336
classics@maties.sun.ac.zq (e-mail)

English in Africa

Institute for the Study of English in Africa
Rhodes University, Box 94
Grahamstown 6140
South Africa
(27) 461 26093
fax: (27) 461 25642
jenny@aardvark.ru.ac.za (e-mail)

Critical articles and book reviews on all aspects of African literature written in English.

JOURNAL OF LITERARY STUDIES

Journal of Literary Studies, Unisa Printers
Theory of Literature, UNISA
P.O.B. 392
Pretoria 0001
South Africa
(27) 12 4296614/4296700
fax: (27) 12 4293221
graberc@alpha.unisa.ac.za (e-mail)

Journal to provide a forum for the discussion of literary theory, methodology, research and related matters, features articles, commentary, book reviews, and general announcements.

NEW COIN

Institute for the Study of English in Africa
Rhodes University, Box 94
Grahamstown 6140
South Africa
(27) 461 26093
fax: (27) 461 25642
jenny@aardvark.ru.ac.za (e-mail)

New South African poetry, interviews with poets, and poetry reviews.

NEW CONTRAST

South African Literary Journal Ltd.
P.O. Box 3841
Cape Town 8000
South Africa

Publishes South African poetry, short fiction, essays, criticism, book reviews, graphic art, and general cultural commentary.

SCRUTINYZ: ISSUES IN ENGLISH STUDIES IN SOUTHERN AFRICA

University of South Africa
P.O. Box 392
Pretoria 0001
South Africa
(27) 12 4296602/4296342
fax: (27) 12 4293221

Literary articles and reviews.

SHAKESPEARE IN SOUTHERN AFRICA

Shakespeare Society of Southern Africa
c/o ISEA, Rhodes University
P.O. Box 94
Grahamstown 6140
South Africa
(27) 461 26093
fax: (27) 461 25642
jenny@aardvark.ru.ac.za (e-mail)

African commentary and reviews on all aspects of Shakespeare studies and performance, with a particular emphasis on the response to Shakespeare in southern Africa.

SOUTH AFRICAN JOURNAL OF AFRICAN LANGUAGES

African Language Association of Southern Africa
Department of African Languages
University of Port Elizabeth
P.O. Box 1600
Port Elizabeth 6000
South Africa
(27) 41 5042225
fax: (27) 41 5042574
ngahmt@upe.ac.za (e-mail)

STAFFRIDER

Staffrider
P.O. Box 421007
Fordsburg 2033
South Africa

TYDSKRIF VIR LETTERKUNDE

Tydskrif Vir Letterkunde
Posbus 1758
Pretoria 0001
(27) 12 3226404
pietechj@alpha.unisa.ac.za (e-mail)

Web Sites

ACTA CLASSICA

www.unisa.ac.za/dept/class/casa/actacl.html

Acta Classica is "the official journal of the Classical Association of South Africa [and] is distributed from Unisa." The journal is published annually and the Web site offers details about the most recent issue as well as the archived editions. Some topics included in the most recent edition include "Why conscience makes cowards of us all: a classical perspective" and "The character of Deianeira in Sophocles' Trachiniae."

DIRECTORY OF WRITERS' CIRCLES

www.cix.co.uk/~oldacre/

The Directory of Writers' Circles offers names and contact information for over 600 groups and circles. Visitors to the site may explore a sample directory page in order to gauge its usefulness to their particular needs.

LEARNED PUBLISHING

www.alpsp.org.uk/lp95.htm

Learned Publishing is the journal of the Association of Learned and Professional Society Publishers, and is published quarterly. The Web site includes articles on such topics as Journal Production Course, progress through collaboration, rethinking the library's role in publishing, and The Institute of Publishing, and copyright issues. The site invites news and articles concerning all aspects of learned journal and academic publishing.

THE TIMES LITERARY SUPPLEMENT

www.the-tls.co.uk/

The Times Literary Supplement "carries comprehensive reviews, not only of the latest books, but also recent film productions, theatre, opera, broadcasting, the sciences and the arts. In each issue there are usually half a dozen essays, some two dozen detailed book reviews, several newly published poems, and a detailed listing of the 200 or so books of note published recently."

GRANTA

www.granta.com/

The Granta Web site offers information about the most current topic explored by this highly regarded literary journal. The introduction provides an explanation and background information about the topic around which the issue is based. The contents of the issue are listed and visitors to the site may read a sample as well as obtain subscription and ordering information. The site also offers similar information about back issues and a readers' survey.

LITERARY REVIEW

www.users.dircon.co.uk/~litrev/

The Literary Review Web site offers reviews of such works as "We Wish to Inform You That Tomorrow We Will Be Killed with Our Families" (an account of the struggles in Rwanda), "Pushkin's Button," "Blood and Vengeance: One Family's Story of the War in Bosnia," "Facing the Extreme: Morality and Heroism in Auschwitz and the Gulag," and "Voltaire's Coconuts: or Anglomania in Europe" among others. The site includes a poetry report, a Crime Report by Philip Oakes, and poetry prizes, and offers a mailing list.

Wales

PLANET—THE WELSH INTERNATIONALIST

Berw Cyf
P.O. Box 44
Aberystwyth
Ceredigion
Wales
(44) 1970 611225
fax: (44) 1970 611197

International Trade Shows

Of course, because dates and locations are always changing, information on the following conferences and events should be verified well ahead of time.

January

THE LITERARY CONGRESS TRADESHOW
Phoenix, AZ, USA

Eileen Dengler
2667 Hyacinth Street
Westbury, NY 11590
(516) 338 6312
fax: (516) 333 0689
readingent@aol.com (e-mail)
www.literarycongress.com

The Literary Congress focuses on marketing, promotion, sales, and operations issues for bookstores and publishers. The workshops are interactive, with facilitators and delegates sharing success stories. Workshops are scheduled at different hours from the trade exhibit so publishers and booksellers can interact in an educational setting as well as conduct business during separate trade show hours.

January/February

CALCUTTA INTERNATIONAL BOOK FAIR
Calcutta, India

Publishers and Booksellers Guild
Mr. Dwijendranath Basu, Director
5A Bhanwani Dutta Lane
Calcutta 700073 INDIA
(91) 33 241 3680
fax: (91) 33 245-0027 or (91) 33 241 8248
www.westbengal.com/misc/bookfair

Tragically interrupted by fire in 1997, this event has risen phoenix-like to be bigger than ever and the most important literary event in the country. The Delhi Fair, held alternate years, is more for textbooks and library titles. Calcutta is always something worth experiencing and it always begins the last Wednesday of January and runs 12 days.

February

PUBTECH CONFERENCE
Chicago, IL, USA

Jackie Phaney
Chicago Book Clinic
825 Green Bay Rd, Suite 270
Wilmette, IL 60091
(847) 256 8448
fax: (847) 256 8954
kgboyer@ix.netcom.com (e-mail)
www.chicagobookclinic.org

Presented by The Chicago Book Clinic, PubTech features exhibits, seminars, presentations, special luncheon speakers, and the addition of the all new Vendor Village with open forum discussions by industry experts. At PubTech you can gather with industry leaders from major publishers and suppliers for two days of information, education, innovation, and celebration. You will have the opportunity to learn more about: Content delivery options, web publishing, digital printing solutions, electronic production issues, workflow systems, digital asset management, and managing change.

TAIPEI INTERNATIONAL BOOK EXHIBITION (TIBE)
Taipei, Taiwan

Haifa Lu, Exhibitors' Services
Association of Taipei Publishers, Senseio Business Group
B2, 465 Chung-Shiao E. Rd, Section 6
Taipei, Taiwan, R.O.C.
(886) 2 2786 6556
fax: (886) 2 2653 4145
info@tibe.com (e-mail)
www.tibe.com

The Taipei International Book Exhibition is an excellent venue for the already strong Chinese language rights market in Taiwan, with 9000 titles in translation and good possibilities for expansion to the growing Chinese market in the PRC. This fair is a real trade event for the first two days; it attracted 500,000 people in 1998, with over 600 publishers and 1400 booths. The Exhibition is the fourth largest in the world and the largest in Asia.

BOOKTECH
New York, NY, USA

Bill Norton
(215) 238-5287
bnorton@napco.com (e-mail)
www.booktechexpo.com

This annual trade show features technologies and techniques for today's book production professionals, whether you're looking to enhance your knowledge of the latest digital book production technology or want to investigate new vendors.

March

SEYBOLD SEMINARS NEW YORK/PUBLISHING
New York, NY, USA

(888) 800 8922 or (650) 372 7072
www.seyboldseminars.com

The constant innovation of new and advanced technologies—many of them focused on the Web—are fueling the growth of both online and traditional publishing markets today. Recognizing the importance of these new technologies and their fundamental impact on publishers everywhere, sessions explore the most innovative tools, techniques, and business models of publishing online, as well as spotlight the hottest issues in traditional publishing.

LONDON INTERNATIONAL BOOKFAIR
London, England

Olympia
Reed Exhibitions
Oriel House
26 The Quadrant
Richmond, Surrey TW9 1D1 UK
(44) 181 910 7914
fax: (44) 181 910 7930
www.libf.co.uk

This fair is a good follow-up to the Frankfurt Bookfair and is considered the most important spring event in publishing. It attracts many independent publishing houses from the UK and its territories, as well as international houses. Exhibits address all areas of publishing, including small press, academic, and children's publishing concerns.

ASSOCIATED WRITING PROGRAMS ANNUAL CONFERENCE
Fairfax, VA, USA

Tallwood House, Mail Stop 1E3
George Mason University
Fairfax, VA 22030
(703) 993 4301
fax: (703) 993 4302
awp@gmu.edu (e-mail)

The AWP Annual Conference has become the essential gathering for the field of literature. Over 1,000 writers, teachers, publishers, and literary arts administrators attend the conference, which is held in a different part of the country each year. Members of AWP enjoy discounted rates for conference registration. Every conference features a tribute in honor of a major author, readings by other outstanding writers, panel discussions of current issues in contemporary letters, forums on the teaching of creative writing, workshops, open-mike readings, caucus meetings, a bookfair, dances, and talk and speculation about writers, writing, teaching, and publishing.

NORTHERN ARIZONA BOOK FESTIVAL
Flagstaff, AZ, USA

Jeff Biggers, Artistic Director
Northern Arizona Book Festival
c/o Literacy Volunteers of Coconino County
PO Box 2432
Flagstaff, AZ 86003
(520) 556-0313
nabookfest@altavista.net (e-mail)
www.weeklywire.com/nabookfest/

The Northern Arizona Book Festival brings together internationally acclaimed authors at one of the largest author gatherings in the West.

VIRGINIA FESTIVAL OF THE BOOK
Charlottesville, VA, USA

(804) 924 3296
vabook@virginia.edu (e-mail)
www.vabook.org

This festival is held to organize public programming about books, writing, and related technologies. It also provides a forum for discussion about professional writing, publishing, and printing.

April

TOKYO INTERNATIONAL BOOK FAIR
Big Sight, Tokyo, Japan

Executive committee of TIBF
Managed by Reed Exhibitions Japan Ltd.
18F Shinjuku Nomura Bldg.
1-26-2 Nishishinjuku, Shinjuku-ku, Tokyo 163-05 Japan
(81) 3 3349 8501
fax: (81) 3 3345 7929
chan@reed.co.jp (email)

The second largest publishing industry in the world, Japan's international book fair is a unique opportunity to meet the Japanese book market and some of the players in the rest of Asia. Small, compared to others in Asia, but growing, this book fair aims first to be a trade event, attracting international exhibitors for the benefit of Japanese librarians and booksellers. Seven specialized book fairs held concurrently with TIBF, offering focused access to business opportunities, international rights negotiations, joint publishing projects and direct exports. The seven fairs are the Natural Sciences Book Fair, the Humanities and Social Sciences Book Fair, the Children's Book Fair, the Text and Reference Book Fair, the Multi-Media and Electronic Book Fair, the Editorial Production Fair, and the Book Printing and Manufacturing Fair.

BOLOGNA CHILDREN'S BOOK FAIR
Bologna, Italy

Piazza Costituzione 6
40128 Bologna, Italy
(39) 051-282111
fax: (39) 051 282333
dir.com@bolognafiere.it (email)
www.bolognafiere.it

The Bologna Children's Book Fair is an important event in the children's book world. The fair hosts exhibits from 80 countries and specializes in the copyright business and international co-production in the field of book and software publishing for children and young adults. Visiting professionals are limited to those involved in children's publishing, including publishers, authors and illustrators, literary agents, packagers, distributors, printers, booksellers, and librarians.

BUENOS AIRES FERIA INTERNACIONAL DEL LIBRO
Buenos Aires, Argentina

Avda Cordoba 744, PB 1
1054 Buenos Aires, Argentina
(54) 1 322 2165
fax: (54) 1 325 5681
fund@libro.satlink.net (e-mail)
www.el-libro.com.ar

The Fair, carrying the motto "The Book—From Author to Reader," is a unique and vigorous event in the book culture, industry and business. It is organized by Fundación El Libro, an entity that brings together book publishers, writers, booksellers and distributors, printers, importers and exporters. Since 1975, when the first Book Fair was held in Buenos Aires, it has consistently grown to become the most important book exhibition in Latin America and an outstanding worldwide reference point, with over 1,000,000 visitors.

THE BI-ANNUAL BIG APPLE
WRITING WORKSHOP & OPEN HOUSE
Presented by The International Women's Writing Guild
New York, NY, USA

The New York Genealogical Society
124 East 58th Street
New York, NY
(212) 737 7536
fax: (212) 737 9469
iwwg@iwwg.com (e-mail)

The Bi-Annual Big Apple includes a "Meet the Agents" Open House, a popular, tried and true event which the Guild has sponsored in the Spring and Fall for many years. It has yielded many wonderful matches between authors and agents. Agents introduce themselves at the podium and speak about their "shop," trends in the marketplace, hits and misses. Then, over refreshments, members of the audience seek out those agents with whom they wish to meet. After you introduce yourself and speak briefly about your work, the agent will let you know if he or she is interested in hearing from and possibly working with you. Agents, representing fiction, nonfiction, children's books, T.V., and film attend the workshop.

Bogota Feria Internacional del Libro
Santafe de Bogota, D.C. Colombia

CORFERIAS
Carrera 40, No. 22C-67
PO Box 6843
Santafe de Bogota, D.C. Colombia
(57) 1 337 7676
fax: (57) 1 337 7272 or 7271

The first three days of the fair are reserved for the professionals. It might be worth attending to check out the book printing possibilities. In 1997 they combined a conference of English teachers from all over the continent which further stimulated book sales. A variety of countries attend but the dominant presence is the central American countries, from Venezuela to Cuba to Costa Rica. As you would expect of such a territory, the number of exhibitors and visitors is growing every year.

Sao Paulo International Book Fair
Sao Paulo, SP, Brazil

Expocenter Norte, Sao Paul
Camara Brasileira Do Livro
Av. Ipiranga, 1267–10th andar
Sao Paulo, SP, Brazil
(55) 11 225 8277
fax: (55) 11 229 7426
cbl@virtual-net.com.br (e-mail)
www.cbl-net.com.br

This is the biggest book market in Latin America, particularly important to the Portuguese language market. Professionals from all areas of the industry attend the fair, including editors, booksellers, authors, professors, and librarians. The first three days of the fair are reserved for professionals in the book industry. The last nine days are open to the general public as well.

May

SEOUL INTERNATIONAL BOOK FAIR
Korean Exhibition Center (KOEX)
Seoul, South Korea

Choon-Ho Na, President
Korean Book Publishers Association
105-2 Sagan-dong, Chongno.-ku
Seoul 110-190 South Korea
(82) 2 735 2702
fax: (82) 2 738-5414
kpasibf@soback.kornet.nm.kr (e-mail)

Because South Korea is a new member of Berne and a big book market (5000 titles published in translation in 1996), this fair helps encourage international copyright agreements and offers a huge book buying market, though the current economic crisis has slowed things down for the moment. The first day of the fair is for professionals only.

BOOKEXPO AMERICA
USA

(800) 840-5614
fax: (203) 840 9614
inquiry@bookezpo.reedexpo.com (e-mail)
http://bookexpo.reedexpo.com

BEA is the premier book industry exhibition in North America. It combines the traditions of annual book conventions as well as adds new initiatives and programs for all industry constituents. The fair brings booksellers, publishers, media, international representatives, agents, and foreign publishers together to exchange information pertinent to all members of the book community. The fair includes educational seminars, an international rights center, and entertaining author programs.

SINGAPORE WORLD BOOK FAIR
World Trade Center, Singapore

Ms. Ng Siew Wai or Michael Liew
Times Conferences and Exhibitions, Pte Ltd
Times Centre, 1 New Industrial Road, Singapore 536196
(65) 286 4092
fax: (65) 286 5754 or 284-4733
tpl@corp.tpl.com.sg (e-mail)
www.tpl.com.sg

This event has superseded the Festival of Books in September as the place for major English language book publishers to do business in Singapore. It is still primarily a book sale, but there is a special day and a half trade-only space at the beginning of this fair.

HONG KONG BOOK FAIR
Asian Publishing Conference and International Copyright Exchange
Hong Kong Convention & Exhibition Centre, Hong Kong

Michael Kan, Hong Kong Trade Development Council
38F, Office Tower, Convention Plaza
1 Harbour Road, Wanchai, Hong Kong
(852) 2584 4333
fax: (852) 2824 0249
exhibitions@tdc.org.hk (e-mail)

They launched Hong Kong's first ICE, International Copyright Exchange in 1997 as part of the "trade only" days of the event, in an attempt to make Hong Kong the center for Chinese language rights deals, including those between Taiwan and the PRC, both of whom traditionally have large numbers of publishers present at this book fair.

June

THE JERUSALEM INTERNATIONAL BOOK FAIR

PO Box 775
Jerusalem 91007
(972) 2 6240663
fax: (972) 2 6243144
jer_fair@netvision.net.il (e-mail)
www.jerusalembookfair.com

The fair was begun in 1963 and initiates commercial and cultural contact in publishing. The fair, which involves more than 1,000 publishers from more than 60 countries each year, focuses on editors, agents, and foreign rights. Registered trade visitors include publishers, editors, writers, literary media personalities, booksellers, librarians, and journalists. The general public is welcome as well, particularly to appreciate the special cultural focus of the fair, which changes each year.

August

ZIMBABWE INTERNATIONAL BOOK FAIR

Harare, Zimbabwe

Margaret Ling
ZIBF(UK)
25 Endymion Road
London N4 1EE, UK
(44) 181 348 8463
fax: (44) 181 348 4403
margaret.ling@geo2.poptel.org.uk (e-mail)
www.zibf.org

The Zimbabwe Fair is the largest and most diverse exhibition of books, magazines, journals, CD-ROMs, and publishing and printing technology and services in Sub-Sahara Africa. The fair operates as an annual meeting place for northern and southern interests. Each year, a special theme is emphasized in order to highlight particular issues and interests.

ANNUAL SELLING TO HOLLYWOOD SCRIPTWRITING CONFERENCE
Red Lion Hotel
Glendale, CA, USA

Writers Connection
PO Box 24770
San Jose, CA 95154-4770
(408) 445 3600
fax: (408) 445 3609
info@sellingtohollywood (e-mail)
www.selling to hollywood.com

This conference features access to over 50 Hollywood producers, agents, successful writers, TV/studio executives, entertainment attorneys, and industry pros. The format includes panels, seminars, ask-a-pro sessions, individual consultations, and several networking sessions. A complete conference brochure and schedule is available.

September/October

LIBER—SALON INTERNACIONAL DEL LIBRO
Madrid, Spain

Fed. de Editores de Espana
Apdo de Correos 67067, 28042 Madrid, Spain
(34) 1 722 5000
fax: (34) 1 722 578
liber@ifema.es (e-mail)

October

FRANKFURT INTERNATIONAL BOOK FAIR
Frankfurt, Germany

PO Box 100116
Reineckstrasse 3, 60313 Frankfurt am Main 1, Germany
(49) 69 210 2000
fax: (49) 69 210 2227
marketing@book-fair.com (e-mail)
www.franfurt-book-fair.com

This is the largest international bookfair in the world. The fair markets ideas and books and is a meeting point of the electronic media world. Frankfurt is the most important trading event for the international rights and licenses business within the publishing world. Established immediately following World War II, the fair encourages international contact and promotes the economic and cultural interests of Germany's publishers and booksellers.

Index